BRILLIANT MOON

Brilliant Moon

THE AUTOBIOGRAPHY OF DILGO KHYENTSE

Translated and compiled by
Ani Jinba Palmo

Edited by Michael Tweed

Forewords by
His Holiness the Dalai Lama, Dzongsar Khyentse Rinpoche,
Sogyal Rinpoche, and Shechen Rabjam Rinpoche

SHAMBHALA
BOSTON & LONDON
2008

Shambhala Publications, Inc.
Horticultural Hall
300 Massachusetts Avenue
Boston, Massachusetts 02115
www.shambhala.com

9 8 7 6 5 4 3 2 1
First Edition
Printed in the United States of America

⊗ This edition is printed on acid-free paper that meets the American National
Standards Institute Z39.48 Standard.

Distributed in the United States by Random House, Inc.,
and in Canada by Random House of Canada Ltd

Designed by Gopa & Ted2, Inc.

Library of Congress Cataloging-in-Publication Data
Rab-gsal-zla-ba, Dis-mgo Mkhyen-brtse, 1910–1991.
Brilliant moon: the autobiography of Dilgo Khyentse / forewords by the Dalai Lama,
Dzongsar Khyentse, Shechen Rabjam, and Sogyal Rinpoche; translated and
compiled by Ani Jinba Palmo; edited by Michael Tweed.—1st ed.
p.   cm.
Includes bibliographical references.
ISBN 978-1-59030-284-2 (hardcover: alk. paper)
1. Rab-gsal-zla-ba, Dis-mgo Mkhyen-brtse, 1910–1991. 2. Lamas—China—
Tibet—Biography. I. Palmo, Ani Jinba. II. Tweed, Michael. III. Title.
BQ982.A25A3 2008
294.3'923092—dc22
[B]
2008017295

Contents

THE DALAI LAMA

Since the time of the Buddha Shakyamuni himself, there has been a strong Buddhist tradition of recollecting the lives of great teachers and practitioners both as a mark of gratitude and appreciation and as a source of inspiration from which we may still learn. It gives me immense pleasure to know, therefore, that this authentic account of the life and activities of Kyabje Khyentse Rinpoche, who I am fortunate to revere among my own precious teachers, has been prepared to remind those who knew him and inform those who did not of his great qualities.

We first met, propitiously as it turned out, in the Jokhang in Lhasa, when I was just returning from my first pilgrimage to India. However, I did not really get to know him well until much later when we were both living in exile. Characteristically for this great and warmhearted man, he showed tremendous kindness to me in opening up his treasury of experience and knowledge in granting me empowerments, teachings, and transmissions.

Of course, one of the great qualities of the biographies of great beings such as Khyentse Rinpoche is to remind us of what it took for them to become the way they were. Most of us alive today will remember him for the great warmth of his presence, his ever-alert and attentive concern for others, imagining he was always like that. But even great lamas have to work to transform themselves and Khyentse Rinpoche was no exception. From his youth he applied himself unceasingly to study, practice, and teaching, he spent nearly a quarter of his life in retreat, and he kept up that pattern to the end of his life. He was so used to it, he made it look easy. The story of what it took is recorded here.

Traditionally we say that one of the Lama's principal kindnesses is simply his edifying presence here among us. I have no doubt that Kyabje Dilgo Khyentse Rinpoche was among the most accomplished Buddhist masters I have met, yet at the same time he radiated all the warm, uplifting qualities of a genuinely and thoroughly good human being, and as such achievements lie at the heart of Tibet's rich and ancient culture, I think I can say that he was naturally an exemplary Tibetan too. It was a great privilege to have known him; I am sure readers will derive great benefit from becoming acquainted with him to some extent through this book.

Tenzin Gyatso, the Fourteenth Dalai Lama
April 20, 2007
Dharamsala, India

Foreword by Dzongsar Khyentse Rinpoche

HOWEVER SIMPLY I try to tell the story of Dilgo Khyentse Rinpoche's life, however understated my presentation of his vast legacy, I already know that the current generation of students will find it very hard to believe that just one person could accomplish so much in a single lifetime. Yet fantastic tales are an intrinsic part of the Buddhist tradition, and the Mahayana sutras and tantric texts are full of astonishing accounts of the hardship and difficulties that great bodhisattvas of the past had to overcome in order to receive teachings and to practice, as well as descriptions of the vast number of activities great masters engaged in during their lifetimes. Some of the more recent examples are the great Ri-me masters Jamyang Khyentse Wangpo and Jamgon Kongtrül Lodro Thaye, who transformed and revitalized Tibetan Buddhism in the nineteenth century. We can only marvel at the immensity of their output. The amount of texts they wrote alone is so numerous that it's hard to believe that they did anything else in their lives but write; similarly, the list of teachings they received is so long, one wonders how they could have done anything else; and yet they also gave an incredible number of teachings—more, one would have thought, than it's possible to give in one lifetime.

For many of us today such accounts seem dubious at best. However, for someone like me, who has had the opportunity of meeting a great being like Dilgo Khyentse Rinpoche whose activity was just as varied and as vast, it's almost possible to accept the idea that such prolific, selfless beings could have existed in this world. Of course, we read about the remarkable qualities of great masters all the time; there are many books that describe the qualities of highly realized masters, setting out in detail the "right" way for them to live and to behave. For me, though, it would have been impossible to believe that anyone could truly embody so many virtuous qualities and do so much for others if I hadn't met Khyentse Rinpoche. He was the living proof. Without his example, the life stories of the great masters of the past would seem far less credible and much more like ancient legends, like that of Hercules accomplishing his twelve great labors in Greek mythology. (Nevertheless, I do feel sympathy for skeptics and those who didn't have the good fortune to have met and spent time with Khyentse Rinpoche, because even though I witnessed his activities with my own eyes, when I think back, I too find many things hard to believe, so it's no wonder that those who weren't present have their doubts!)

I have to confess that I didn't realize just how remarkable Rinpoche was while he was alive, but only much later when some of his other students and I started trying to emulate his activities. It was then that we began to realize just how hardworking, tireless, and determined he had been, always looking for ways to benefit others and hardly ever doing anything for himself. It seems improbable, I know, but frankly I don't remember Rinpoche ever taking a day off. Of course there were quieter days, but rather than catch up on his sleep or watch a movie, he would gather some of his older students or students of his own masters around him, and they would spend the time talking about their teachers, recounting the important events of their lives and sharing personal memories of them. This was Rinpoche's idea of fun, and for those who were fortunate and wise enough to participate, even this recreational activity of his was tremendously beneficial.

In these degenerate times, when skepticism is valued far more highly than pure perception, many people reading this will probably imagine that, because I'm one of Rinpoche's students and want to promote him, I am exaggerating his extraordinary qualities and accomplishments. My fear is quite the opposite: I'm worried that I'm understating them, as there are neither enough words, nor is there enough time adequately to be able to describe the full scope of his achievements. I hope that eventually some of the more visible handprints of this great man will become known more widely, so that the world will have an opportunity to appreciate him more fully in the future—perhaps in the same way it rediscovered Leonardo da Vinci centuries after he died.

When Bhikshuni Jinba Palmo asked me to write an introduction to the autobiography of Khyentse Rinpoche, on the one hand I was overjoyed to have been considered worthy of the task, while on the other hand I began to worry, well aware that whatever I write, I will only be able to offer a partial glimpse of this extraordinary being. It reminded me of all those times I begged Jamyang Khyentse Chökyi Lodro's old attendant, Tashi Namgyal, to tell me about the life of my predecessor. It was always very frustrating because Tashi Namgyal would respond to my eager questioning with virtual silence since he felt whatever he said could only be misleading. I have much more sympathy for him today as I find myself facing exactly the same problem.

In writing this piece I am offering an introduction to an introduction to Khyentse Rinpoche, and from what I've learned of Vajrayana Buddhism, the act of introduction, particularly of a guru, is of the utmost importance. While followers of the Vajrayana tradition are taught to see their guru as the Buddha—and it is believed that thousands of buddhas will and have come to this world—for individual practitioners it is our own personal guru who is of paramount importance in our spiritual lives: he is the one who interacts with us directly, creates chaos in our organized samsaric life, and, even if he doesn't manage to destroy it completely, will make at least a dent in our bloated egos. Strictly speaking, introducing the guru is the equivalent of introducing the Buddha, and no act is considered to be of greater significance to someone on the spiritual path. Therefore, contributing an introduction to this autobiography of one of the most celebrated and beloved masters of his generation is, I believe, my chance to accumulate a great deal of merit.

If any of you are hoping to read worldly stories full of drama, triumph, climax, suspense, romance, and so on, please let go of that expectation because you won't find such things within these pages. Having said that, from a different perspective it's all here: the heartrending drama of renunciation, the heroic triumph over pride and anger, the climactic conquest of selfishness by planting the seed of *bodhichitta* and the moving romance of the compassion of this unique man whose only wish was to gather to his heart all suffering beings and for whom the notion of ever releasing, abandoning, or rejecting a single one of us simply didn't exist. I doubt there's a novel that will offer a more satisfying and inspiring account of the profound inner journey of a truly extraordinary being than can be found in Rinpoche's autobiography.

In general, the purpose of a story is to introduce a character and to describe his or her ups and downs in a way that readers can identify with, draw inspiration from, or be cautioned by. Rinpoche's autobiography is no exception. On the path of the Dharma we are urged time and again to remember and recount the life stories of the masters of the past; Buddha himself encouraged us to do this because, for example, for some, to hear about Siddhartha's courage at leaving his father's palace and renouncing the world is both encouraging and motivating. Hearing about such things is one thing, but whether or not someone is able to benefit from them depends on his or her own capacity. A student endowed with supreme faculties may achieve what is called liberation upon hearing, but not many of us are that gifted. And while the outer story of Rinpoche's life will certainly inspire us, inner and secret biographies of the great masters are virtually inaccessible because they are inexpressible and unthinkable. I don't say this to be religious or poetic, it's just that there are no words or language capable of fully expressing their true meaning, and very few of us have the potential to comprehend such things.

Tibetans say that everything in life is imitation and it's the one who can imitate the best who is deemed to be the most able. When we look around us, we can see that everyone is trying to imitate everyone else, that we all have role models who we aspire to emulate. Sadly, most of us want to imitate worldly people who are materially successful. We lack the drive or enthusiasm to look for a perfect spiritual role model, and even if we have that drive, from my impure point of view, there aren't that many true spiritual role models left who are worthy of imitation! I feel partially responsible for this situation because I think that deep down in people like myself, something's gone wrong with our motivation, particularly in terms of how we see our gurus.

For example, I remember clearly one occasion when Rinpoche had to leave Kathmandu to go to Bhutan and I was being left behind. I was devastated. I had always felt as though Rinpoche was my father, and on this particular day it was as if my father, the most important person in my life, was abandoning me. Looking back, I think I felt that way because my feeling for Rinpoche was based on my own insecurity rather than a genuine wish for enlightenment. And although it was his job to correct his students, it wasn't his style to humiliate any of us by publicly pointing out when our motivation was wrong. In fact, I found that he reinforced my own feelings because he always behaved as if he really were my father. I can still feel his huge hand tenderly caressing my head, letting me know that he would be back soon and I didn't need to worry, while I gritted my teeth, determined to keep up the illusion that I could handle anything, all the while desperately fighting back the tears.

The point here is that my capacity to appreciate him fully was distorted by my narrow view of him as the father figure I longed for. Even today, as I replay what memories I have of him and of the little things he did, it breaks my heart to realize that at the time I considered most of his activities to be quite ordinary, never even suspecting their true purpose. I feel sad and a little ashamed about it now and try to console myself with the knowledge that although it's a bit late, these days I have a much better idea of how to interpret his activities and realize more fully the extent of his greatness.

I must confess that to this day I don't know if the feeling I have for Rinpoche is real devotion or some sort of attachment, because genuine devotion, as explained in the tantras, is said to go way beyond ordinary concepts. I think the best I can do is aspire to true devotion, and even this ability of mine to aspire I attribute wholly to Rinpoche's influence, whose admiration and devotion for his masters was such an affecting example.

Whenever I look at Khyentse Rinpoche's writings about one of his masters, whether he's describing him in poetry or prose, I feel that I'm not reading a description of a person at all, but instead am receiving a full and complete introduction to the Buddha and Dharma on every level. It's as if he's sweeping us, his readers, away on an extraordinary journey into an entirely new dimension or sphere of existence. I remember so vividly that every time Khyentse Rinpoche even casually mentioned the name of one of his masters, regardless of the circumstances, it was a cause for celebration—the memory of each one was so moving for him.

There was one occasion in particular, when Khyentse Rinpoche traveled into Eastern Tibet with a whole group of us. After quite an arduous journey we reached Derge Gonchen Monastery where thousands of people flocked to catch a glimpse of Khyentse Rinpoche. At one point, a rowdy-looking young man approached him, holding what looked like a bundle of filthy rags. So much was happening at the time that I wasn't paying attention as the young man fumbled to remove the rags and reveal a statue of Manjushri while mumbling something I didn't quite catch. Tulku Pema Wangyal heard him, though, and bent down to whisper into Khyentse Rinpoche's ear. Almost immediately I found myself gazing intently at Khyentse Rinpoche, who, to my astonishment was sobbing uncontrollably like a baby, as if his heart would break. We were all amazed—we'd only rarely seen him cry before—and each one of us experienced the same sense that time itself stood still. Later, I found out what it was that had moved Khyentse Rinpoche so deeply: the statue the young man offered and that had survived the ravages of the Cultural Revolution, had once belonged to Mipham Rinpoche, one of his most beloved teachers.[1]

Everything Khyentse Rinpoche did was always directed by the wishes of his masters or dedicated to the complete fulfillment of their aspirations. In this day and age when everyone strives to be an innovator and to produce something that's completely original, never even thinking of acknowledging those from whom they have plagiarized their ideas, Khyentse Rinpoche was unique: if anyone could have created something completely new in this world, it was Khyentse Rinpoche, and yet his entire life was dedicated to the service of his masters.

If we put the spiritual path aside for a moment and look at Khyentse Rinpoche from a very ordinary point of view, it is still impossible not to admire him, because he had the most easygoing nature of anyone I have ever met. Many lamas, particularly the high lamas, tend to be rather stern and otherworldly; you can't imagine talking to them as you would a close friend, let alone cracking the mildest of jokes in their presence. Khyentse Rinpoche wasn't like that at all; he was very much of this world and never hesitated to offer the warmest and most intimate friendship to everyone he met, never allowing any unnecessary distance to come between them.

He was also a great leader, and just like a majestic American Indian chief or a distinguished samurai general, Khyentse Rinpoche was never affected by chaotic or difficult circumstances, however tumultuous they might be. Instead, he always remained quite still, like a mountain, effortlessly exuding an all-pervasive confidence that itself evoked confidence in those around him, and an absolute, unshakeable equanimity. Not once did we see the slightest indication of him ever getting irritated, even when he was repeatedly confronted with irate tattletales who never tired of complaining about the behavior of one or another of the monks and tulkus in the monastery. No matter what the provocation, instead of scolding, Khyentse Rinpoche would soothe and appease the situation with humor and the gentle power of his presence. So much so that, although he wouldn't budge an inch to act on the complaints made to him, the complainer would nevertheless leave him feeling happy and satisfied.

One of the greatest challenges for any leader is that of finding a way of making all his protégés feel that they are his favorite. To this day I've only met one person who managed to do this really successfully, without being painfully obvious about it. It's a problem I face on a daily basis because I, too, have this label of being a "teacher," but in my experience, however hard I try, most of my students complain that I neglect them or ignore them and that basically I'm not giving them enough attention. With Khyentse Rinpoche it was quite different. From the highest ranked tulkus, to government ministers, to the man who swept the road outside the monastery, each one truly believed that they had a special place in his heart. I can't even begin to fathom how he did it! Perhaps this kind of ability develops when a master truly is what the Tibetans describe as a "wish-fulfilling jewel."

There's a very big difference between living for the Dharma and using the Dharma in order to make a living, and although my judgment is somewhat biased, it looks to me as though most of the so-called spiritual guides operating in the world today are doing the latter. From his earliest childhood until he passed away Khyentse Rinpoche really lived for the Dharma and never once used it to support or enrich his own life, although it would have been quite easy for him to do so. After all, he was a spiritual giant with all the authentic qualities of a great master, and in the course of his life he had built up relationships with all kinds of powerful spiritual and worldly people over whom he could, if he chose, exercise a great deal of influence. He could easily have sold himself very successfully in the spiritual marketplace, and yet I can't remember noticing the slightest trace of that kind of thought ever occurring to him. On the contrary, when ambitious students like myself would suggest that Khyentse Rinpoche should teach a particular person because I felt, for example, that he could be of great help to a monastery, Khyentse Rinpoche wouldn't be remotely interested. Instead, he would start teaching someone completely unknown, like an old nun from somewhere without a name who had turned up on the doorstep that morning, putting all his time and energy into her.

Many people pressed Khyentse Rinpoche strongly to accept the position of Head of the Nyingma Lineage after Dudjom Rinpoche passed away, and eventually he agreed. Looking back, I've come to realize that his style of leadership mirrors almost exactly the descriptions of distinguished generals that can be found in many ancient Asian writings about strategy and war. He didn't, for example, feel the need to snoop around in every single little detail about what was going on—in fact, there were times I wondered if he cared at all! He wasn't like a blade of grass growing on a mountain's peak, bending in whichever direction the wind was blowing. When you are so easily swayed, it may be temporarily satisfying for one person, but at the same time, as we say in Tibetan, you're burning someone else's nose. Neither was he like a block of wood, not taking on responsibility when necessary or being unaware of all that was happening. He was much more like a fine, long silk scarf tied to an enormous rock that's deeply embedded in the mountainside: whenever it was necessary, he would always act, while remaining firmly rooted at all times.

It is quite rare to find a person who can honestly be said to have a complete overview of a situation, be it political, economic, or martial; the same is true of the spiritual world, where it is extremely unusual to find someone who is genuinely concerned with the authentic presentation of Shakyamuni and the Buddhadharma. In Tibet there are four major schools of Buddhism, and each school fiercely preserves and promotes its own traditions. Within each school there are many individual lineages and, particularly in more recent times, these lineages have been far more committed to their own interests than to the interests of Buddhism as a whole. Of course, students who protect their lineage do it with the very best of intentions, immediately seizing upon any potential threat and doing their level best to tackle it. But, in the meantime, they often forget about the bigger picture, so that gradually an interest in Buddhadharma drifts out of their minds altogether. Unfortunately, members of all lineages seem to fall into the same trap, and this is how sectarian attitudes grow and become strong. On top of that, an interest in worldly life inevitably starts to creep in, and when this happens, the welfare of each individual monastery or institution will almost always take precedence over the good of the lineage. As a result, I don't think it's an exaggeration to say that Tibetans have virtually forgotten about Shakyamuni and his teachings.

The great Jamyang Khyentse Wangpo and Jamgon Kongtrül Lodro Thaye, who were the visionaries of nonsectarianism, saw this weakness and realized how important and how necessary it is to uphold all schools and lineages within Buddhism—the evidence of this can be found in their writings. I think it's safe to say that these two exceptional masters made a contribution, either directly or indirectly, to every one of the lineages that have survived to the present day. Khyentse Rinpoche was, in my opinion, the sole authentic holder of the Ri-me tradition that was Jamyang Khyentse Wangpo and Jamgon Kongtrül Lodro Thaye's great legacy, and so far in my life, I've not seen or heard of any other master who genuinely upholds the Ri-me spirit as completely as he did.

Khyentse Rinpoche would never settle for a halfhearted respect for the Ri-me tradition, like those lamas who merely decorated their walls with pictures of Ri-me masters; nor did he use it as a politically correct posture to take in order to promote himself. He genuinely cared about and cherished every single Buddhist lineage, and it was far from uncommon for his attendants unwittingly to upset Khyentse Rinpoche with unfortunate news that would have an impact on the Ri-me movement, like the loss of masters of various lineages or disputes within a lineage.

One way to experience the full flavor of the genius of the Ri-me masters is to read their *Collected Works*. If you then compare them with Khyentse Rinpoche's collected works, you will see that they are all imbued with exactly the same sense of veneration for the teachings of all lineages. This kind of reverence is extremely rare, perhaps even nonexistent, amongst the works of the vast majority of lamas of the past and of the present. Far more often such works include statements by lamas declaring that *their* lineage and *their* work are the greatest of all.

If there are so many bogus Ri-me masters around these days, how can we tell whether or not a master is truly nonsectarian? Is there solid proof that will confirm categorically that someone is a genuine Ri-me master? Of course, it's very difficult to judge whether or not someone has the inner quality of Ri-me. The best we can do is look for outer signs, which is itself a rather limited approach. However I believe that there is one thing that says quite a lot about a person, and that is the number of masters from different lineages he or she has received teachings from. Living, as we do, in a time when lamas and students feel the need to protect each other as if they were jealous spouses, masters who have received teachings from more than a hundred gurus, like Khyentse Rinpoche's predecessor Jamyang Khyentse Wangpo had, are scarce. There are so many students today who think that it's a virtue to have the same kind of loyalty for their guru as ordinary people have for the leader of a political party. This kind of loyalty is really stupid, and their version of one-pointed devotion is, in fact, one-pointed prejudice! Khyentse Rinpoche himself had more than fifty gurus, all from different lineages, with whom he studied for a considerable time to receive the most important teachings, and he felt this experience had been so beneficial that he would insist on sending his own students to receive teachings from a variety of other masters, whether we wanted to go or not.

Looking back at the times I spent with Khyentse Rinpoche, I can still vividly see in my mind's eye something that I doubt I'll ever see again in this life: the steady stream of people from many different lineages and of all ranks, from the highest to the lowest, who daily filed through his room. Of course, I've known many masters who are often visited by followers of their own lineage, but never a master who was visited so consistently by representatives from all lineages. And what else would they come to see him about apart from the Dharma? This proves to me that followers of different lineages completely trusted Khyentse Rinpoche, and in fact many of the great masters that we revere today were his disciples, for example, His Holiness the Dalai Lama, and the late Jamyang Khyentse Chökyi Lodro who was both his guru and his disciple.

The way Tibetan Buddhism is manifesting at the moment, one of my fears is that what these great masters have done for all lineages will be forgotten, because the memory of their achievements is being threatened by the sheer force of sectarianism. It's not just the more materialistic younger generation that harbors sectarian attitudes, even the older, apparently more "wholesome" generation is riddled with such attitudes. Sectarianism is one of the faults that this world has never been able to rectify; even Tibetan lamas don't seem to have the ability to do anything about it. It's not a new problem, either. The history of Tibetan Buddhism is packed with stories about its glorious past, along with a great deal about the lack of interest each lineage has had in its rival's welfare.

These days sectarianism is so strong that it's not unusual to hear even the most accomplished masters making a mockery of the concept of Ri-me, as if it were some kind of mealymouthed goodwill gesture that's not at all achievable. It's as if Jamyang Khyentse Wangpo, Jamgon Kongtrül Lodro Thaye, and their work had already slipped out of this world and into the realm of legend—until, for me at least, this great master Dilgo Khyentse Rinpoche came into existence, whom I witnessed with my own eyes as being the very embodiment of both these great masters.

Khyentse Rinpoche's interest in and concern for all lineages of Tibetan Buddhism could almost be described as fanatical. It was very rare to see him letting time ebb away in any kind of pointless chattering. Most days, from early morning until past midnight, he would be giving teachings, editing teachings, or clarifying teachings, and commissioning sacred books, paintings, and sculptures. He was such an accomplished master that it would hardly seem necessary for him to need to receive teachings himself, and yet whenever he encountered someone who held a lineage that was in danger of being lost—which was quite often because he went out of his way to find them—he would immediately arrange to receive the transmission and teaching from the lineage holder, however unlikely a character that monk or yogi might be. Once, when I was attending Khyentse Rinpoche on a pilgrimage to Tibet, we stopped in Chengdu for a day. According to his schedule, this was to be one of a very few free days during which he would be able to rest. Nevertheless word got around that Khyentse Rinpoche was in town, and a host of visitors arrived at the hotel requesting an audience, including a simple monk who held a very rare teaching that Khyentse Rinpoche had never received. He immediately requested the monk to give it to him, and so, inevitably perhaps, his free day became one of his busiest.

Whenever I traveled with him, I noticed time and again that even on planes or trains, if he wasn't practicing, Khyentse Rinpoche would be writing. He didn't write in order to satisfy a creative urge or to gain fame and glory by coming up with a best-seller, though, and if he wasn't writing an important commentary on a practice, he would be writing to encourage various individuals struggling to serve the Dharma. One such composition is a letter to Chogyam Trungpa Rinpoche that he wrote in a plane:

Brilliant Moon in the Sky, Ocean of Dharma on the Ground*

As old man Brilliant Moon travels in the sky,
Prince Ocean of Dharma remains on the ground;
Though in the illusion of circumstance, there seems to be great
    distance between,
In the mind's heart-realm of one flavor, separations do not exist.

Brilliant Moon's light-garland streams from heaven's height,
From the moment it touches Ocean of Dharma on the ground
It becomes activity for the welfare of others, dispelling the torment
    of the dark age;
Since in the absolute meaning there is no separation, this self-
    expression of auspicious coincidence occurs.

* "Ocean of Dharma" is a translation of the name Chögyam.

The only father Padma Drime's shoot of wisdom
Blossoms by design in Ocean of Dharma's pond,
Brilliant Moon pours on the amrita of truth—
There is no other way for us to meet again and again.

From cool Ocean of Dharma, rivers in the four directions,
East, west, south, north, temporarily flow
But since they are one in the great ocean of buddha-activity for
    the welfare of the teachings and beings,
The prince enters the one realm of Brilliant Moon.

Little teardrops trickle from the corners of the eyes of the
    only son,
And a vivid sadness arises in the old father's mind-moon—
This is the fruition of our mutual prayer not to be separated
    throughout our lives;
Having confidence in this, we rest in uncontrived innate space.

Our sublime guides are like the sun, moon and garlands of
    constellations,
And we are supreme among the fortunate ones who have taken
    over their action.
The benefit to beings of the Rime teachings is inexhaustible;
This is the offering from the feast of meeting the only father guru.

The dark clouds of these degenerate times are blacker than the
    cosmic darkness.
Yet the force of the aspiration to buddha-activity is a powerful
    wind to disperse them.
When it is aroused, it is the time when Brilliant Moon's true
    meaning dawns,
And when Ocean of Dharma spreads, unfolding the treasure of
    true joy and delight.

In the space where thoughts of sadness are groundless and rootless,
One meets one's own mind as the sparkling smile of primordial
    buddha.

The laughing dance of the little boy with cheerfulness and insight,
Liberates happiness and sorrow in the dharmakaya space of equal
  flavor.

It is not far, being self-abiding innate wisdom,
It is not near, being beyond seer and seen;
Being beyond speech, thought, expression, it pervades all,
In the carefree state beyond reference point, there is nothing
  whatever to be done.

If one decides to act, for as long as there is sky,
In time and space, the teachings' benefit to beings cannot be
  exhausted;
It is the buddha-activity of Manjushri, Samantabhadra and the
  Lotus-Born One—
Taking up this burden brings us great satisfaction.

For us yogins, actions and projections without reference-point
  have dissolved;
In the state of relaxation, whatever we do arises as an ornament.
Though born in the dank womb of a grim and horrific dark age,
We cannot help but sing of the thunderous song of delight.

Since the singer's throat is not well, this might irritate your ear
But the true words without deception depict in molten gold.
They give joy to the mind surpassing a hundred thousand songs
  of one's lovers
Pleasing you, they make you smile broadly.

This is the disjointed song of a madman, inimical to the learned.
Being no doha of a siddha, who will pay attention?
Though I know the way things are, I am driven by the strong wind
  ˙of thoughts.
This is written on an airplane, created by fingers moving with the gait
  of an insect.

When I look at the sky, it symbolizes the completely perfect view
On the path of the limitless dharmadhatu

Through this realm of space beyond cares, containing all without
    partiality
Through this vast all-pervading space, the meteor flies.

When I look at space it reminds me of the experience of uncontrived
    meditation
The rainbow clouds, the sun and the moon wander regardless of day
    and night
It is the symbol of vast space, without increase or decrease—
One enjoys the carefree meditation state of one's own innate mind.

The boundless arrangement of earth's mountains, plains and oceans
Symbolizes the action of *bodhichitta* for the welfare of others
It is buddha-activity that puts whatever arises uninhibitedly to the
    benefit of all
Existing spontaneously as long as there is sky.

Sky, ocean, earth and sun and moon
All are of the nature of the four elements and their configurations.
Thus ground, path and fruition are inseparable in the dharmadhatu
    ocean;
Relaxed and refreshed, may I sit, sleep and act.

This song of the journey is a haphazard little one,
In the sky the clouds haphazardly move about,
The gadgetry of the white metal wing acts haphazardly;
I offer this as an old man's haphazard footprint.

With a happy face and white hair, smiling,
The old man totters along supported;
One-pointedly wishing that we meet again soon,
This is respectfully presented by Mangalam who travels on the
    rays of the sun.*

* First published in *Garuda V* by Vajradhatu Publications and Shambhala Publications.
Translation by the Nalanda Translation Committee under the direction of Chögyam Trungpa
Rinpoche. Reproduced with the kind permission of Diana Mukpo and Larry Mermelstein.

During the times when Khyentse Rinpoche stayed in one place for a longer period, there would almost always be some kind of a teaching going on, and if not a teaching, then an intensive practice like a drupchen. Some of those attending, especially the younger rinpoches who were not mature enough to care much whether or not they missed instructions on a page or two of a vast text, would, from time to time, arrive late or leave early. Khyentse Rinpoche always noticed and after the session would quietly call for the young rinpoches, point out to each one of them the page numbers of the texts they'd missed and make sure that someone who had already received the transmission would pass it on to them. In this way, Khyentse Rinpoche would make what should have been the young rinpoches concern his own.

I feel a little anxious that one of Khyentse Rinpoche's most remarkable contributions to the Dharma may not be recognized or acknowledged. While many of us derive tremendous inspiration from his visible and obvious activities, such as the teachings he gave and practices he engaged in, there's an altogether different dimension of his work that's not visible, but is, in fact, one of the greatest of all buddha activities: Khyentse Rinpoche was a tertön, a treasure revealer, and during his life he revealed many new treasure teachings specifically for the benefit of beings like us. I cannot even begin to express how important these teachings are, and contrary to popular belief, they are not easy texts to produce.

Another aspect of his activity as a tertön was that he reinterpreted and clarified many of the treasure teachings that had already been revealed by tertöns of the past, but that were difficult to understand or work with in the form they were in. Khyentse Rinpoche simplified and thoroughly explained these revelations so that they would be accessible to today's students—it's as if he has prepared a delicious meal and the only effort we now have to make is to eat.

Even though making any kind of comparison is extremely unwise, and from the spiritual point of view bordering on the criminal, after having met Khyentse Rinpoche, I couldn't help but compare other lamas I knew with him—such is my deluded habit—and most of the time, unfortunately, I would find many faults. Spiritual masters are said to have a great many different qualities, but three are considered indispensable: to be learned, disciplined, and kind. The *outer* quality, being learned, is the first and most obvious of the three. Not only was Khyentse Rinpoche adorned with an overwhelming abundance of knowledge about the sutras and tantras, philosophy, general medicine and astrology, and poetry—all as a result of decades of hard and diligent study—but as described in the Mahasandhi texts over and over again, the majority of Khyentse Rinpoche's knowledge—the most significant part—wasn't the product of study, but the consequence of the bursting out of his wisdom mind. In this he was just like the great master Rigzin Jigmey Lingpa.

The *inner* quality of a spiritual master is discipline, and it is venerated by the sublime beings as being even more important than being learned. One of the main purposes of discipline in Buddhism is as a skillful means for assisting the discovery of inner truth, rather than yet another code of conduct to be imposed. One of the big problems with codes of conduct is that they tend to breed all kinds of hypocrisy, as well as an unhealthy interest in imposing discipline on others rather than oneself. Khyentse Rinpoche was never one to make people who are not disciplined feel bad about it, unlike many of the so-called pure monks whose version of being disciplined makes everyone else feel guilty. Khyentse Rinpoche wasn't like that at all, and on innumerable occasions I saw him pacify a potentially explosive situation by telling one of his often outrageous jokes.

Although he was a great tantric vidyadhara and extremely disciplined about keeping all his Bodhisattvayana and Vajrayana vows, not only would Khyentse Rinpoche never disregard the *pratimoksha* discipline himself, he always impressed upon his students just how crucial it is to respect the vows of the Shravakayana vehicle. He had the utmost respect for the *pratimoksha* tradition, and countless times I saw him raise his hands in the prostration mudra when he caught sight of saffron-robed Theravadin monks, saying things like, "How fortunate we are to still have the banner of Shakyamuni Buddha, the Lion of the Shakya, Shakya Senge." Again and again he would emphasize that the *Vinaya* is the very root of the Buddhadharma.

Khyentse Rinpoche was extremely disciplined, and this quality was perhaps most apparent during his private moments when almost no one would be there to witness it. Whenever he would practice, be it his daily prayers, a puja, or during one of his many retreats, he would always groom himself immaculately and wear his finest clothes. During drupchens he wouldn't hesitate to adorn himself in the most exquisite brocades and a large variety of sacred hats that were appropriate to the practice. It was quite a different story, though, when VIPs came to visit him; he appeared to make no effort whatsoever with his personal appearance, often receiving kings and queens bare-chested, wearing nothing more than a lower robe that looked very much like a Victorian petticoat! Dressing up for Khyentse Rinpoche had nothing at all to do with putting on a show for others; it was how he would create for himself the perfect atmosphere in which to practice and receive blessings. To me, this is one of many examples of Khyentse Rinpoche's discipline without hypocrisy, where the sole purpose of discipline was not to impress people, but to create an atmosphere of inspiration.

Even in stressful circumstances, like trying to organize a particular ritual in an out-of-the-way part of Tibet where certain offering substances weren't available, or when ten thousand people turned up out of the blue for blessings, he would never take shortcuts to make life easier for himself but would insist on doing exactly what was required without making a single concession to the situation he found himself in. At the same time he was not obsessed by the rules and regulations of ritual, and when it was necessary, I've even seen him use an apple as a ritual substance with absolute confidence.

Understandably, the majority of students are impressed by gurus who are disciplined and knowledgeable, and tend to be rather less interested in seeking a master just because he is kind. After all, kindness isn't as readily apparent—and anyway most people have their own definition of what constitutes kindness. And yet this third, *secret* quality of a spiritual master, kindness, although far less available or sought after than the other qualities, is both supreme and absolutely indispensable. If a master is very learned and disciplined but not kind, he's a waste of space on this earth. However even if he is not learned or well-disciplined but is kind, he will make absolutely sure that you get everything you need ultimately to attain enlightenment and make your life spiritually fruitful; therefore you can trust him completely. He may lack detailed knowledge and may also be a little temperamental, but as he has dedicated his life to Dharma and is sincerely concerned for your well-being, you are in safe hands. In Khyentse Rinpoche's case, it would be impossible even to begin to relate the apparently limitless examples of kindness that I have both personally experienced and witnessed.

I must point out that the kindness we're talking about here is beyond our ordinary way of thinking, no doubt because our concept of kindness is relative. Beings like us consider someone to be kind when they fulfill our wishes and cater to our whims, to the extent of not giving us what we really need just to keep us happy. As much as Khyentse Rinpoche would always encourage people, using all kinds of skillful means to guide them onto a spiritual path and away from a path that promotes wrong views, he would also be absolutely uncompromising and firm with practitioners to ensure they didn't make any mistakes in their practice. In essence, one way or another, directly or indirectly, Khyentse Rinpoche would always steer everyone who came to him toward the practice of the Dharma.

The great Rigzin Jikmey Lingpa wrote in his famous prayer of aspiration, *Entering the City of Omniscience*:

> Whatever my situation or circumstance, may I never feel the slightest
>   wish to follow worldly ways which run contrary to the Dharma!
> Even if, while under the sway of karma and habitual patterns, a
>   mistaken thought occurs to me, may it never succeed!

For me, this prayer of aspiration describes exactly the kind of courage Khyentse Rinpoche—who was, after all, the incarnation of Rigzin Jikmey Lingpa—showed by never doing anything that involved giving in to conventional expectations, however compassionate such actions might have appeared by ordinary standards. For a deluded being like myself, this tenacious reverence of Khyentse Rinpoche's for the Dharma and his refusal to concede to conventional expectations if it meant veering from this kind of aspiration is an attitude I can personally identify with. This very courage of not giving in to other people's expectations is, in itself, true kindness; giving in and doing what is expected of you is not kind at all.

Never once in all the time I spent with Khyentse Rinpoche did I see him turn away a single student without having fulfilled their requests and wishes. As Khyentse Rinpoche got older, many of those in his entourage, for the very best reasons, would try to limit the number of visitors he saw each day. It never really worked though because if Khyentse Rinpoche found out that there were people waiting outside to see him—and he always did—he'd simply go out to greet them. Days before he passed away in Bhutan—I'll never forget it—a group of devotees from Hong Kong requested from Khyentse Rinpoche an Arya Tara initiation. By then he appeared to be very sick and could hardly talk, nevertheless he didn't refuse them. In fact he made all the preparations necessary for the empowerment and in spite of everything had every intention of giving it.

I think in Buddhism we face two kinds of challenge, one easier to overcome than the other. First, there is the challenge of understanding the vastness and depth of Buddhist philosophy, which is very difficult but doable. By studying hard, reading a lot, and hearing the philosophical arguments again and again, it is possible to eventually gain a good understanding. The second is a far bigger challenge: to fully appreciate the simplicity aspect of Buddhism. Unlike understanding, this is extremely difficult to achieve because it's too easy. To accomplish the first challenge, we can use our rational mind and logic, but when we approach the second, we find that logic and rational thinking are almost powerless to help us. We may know theoretically what we should be doing, but because it's so simple, try as we might, we just can't do it. On a gross level, it is like knowing that smoking is bad for one's health, but when it comes to actually throwing away the cigarettes, which is the logical, commonsense thing to do, being unable to because the habit of smoking is so deeply ingrained.

The great Sakya Pandita said that in order to make a fire you need a magnifying glass, the sun's rays, and some kindling, and if even one of these elements is missing, you will not succeed. Likewise, the only way really to tackle this second challenge—and it's also the easiest way— is by receiving blessings from the guru. What better way to invoke the guru's blessing than by remembering him. And what better way to remember him than by reading his autobiography.

February 2007
Bir, India

Foreword by Sogyal Rinpoche

It is often said in the Buddhist tradition of Tibet that there is no greater source of merit and blessings than to speak about the master and to recollect his noble qualities. Hearing or reading about the great masters can so often bring us an experience of them that can be just as powerful as meeting them face to face. What I hope to do in this introduction to this wonderful study of Kyabje Dilgo Khyentse Rinpoche's life is to convey something of his essence, and of the feeling and atmosphere of his incredible presence. For I sometimes think that his greatest contribution, beside all his tremendous achievements, was the simple fact that he came and lived and taught in our time. An enlightened being actually manifested here and displayed his activity, and we were fortunate enough to witness it. As we will see in the pages that follow, Dilgo Khyentse Rinpoche was a miracle in himself, and his accomplishments, every bit as extraordinary as those of his predecessor Jamyang Khyentse Wangpo or his master Jamyang Khyentse Chökyi Lodro, were clearly the activities of an enlightened being. The honor of writing this brief introduction is mixed with an inevitable feeling of helplessness, faced with the impossible task of capturing in words Dilgo Khyentse Rinpoche's qualities and, above all, his being. I can only put down here some of my memories and personal feelings about how he stays within me and many others who knew him—impressions which I will try to share, with all my limitations, and yet with a mind, and heart, of devotion.

Who that has seen Dilgo Khyentse Rinpoche could ever forget him? Both in his spiritual realization and in his physical appearance and build, he was larger than life. In every sense there was something universal, even superhuman, about him, so much so that at one stage the young incarnate lamas he looked after with such infinite and tender care would playfully call him

"Mr. Universe." There is an occasion I will always remember from the mid-1960s, when Khyentse Rinpoche asked me to accompany him from the Darjeeling area in India to Nepal. Lama Urgyen Shenphen was attending him at the time. There were just the three of us, with about forty pieces of luggage packed with ritual implements and texts. We arrived at one particular railway station in India where we had a train to catch. At that point we decided to split up, in keeping with our responsibilities. Lama Urgyen had the task of finding porters to carry our baggage, while I was to go and try to reserve good seats on the train. We managed to pile all the luggage together on the platform, and then we asked Khyentse Rinpoche if he wouldn't mind sitting on it until we got back. He nodded in agreement and just sat down on this mound of luggage, with his long fingernails and his *mala,* just as if it was his own living room. He could not have been more serene or at ease. There we were in the midst of a busy Indian railway station, with the heat, the flies, and the utter chaos, and Khyentse Rinpoche was totally unperturbed, at peace, happy, and smiling. He looked like an oasis of tranquility; an almost hypnotic atmosphere of calm seemed to surround him and to still the clamor and the turmoil. A group of children started to gather around him, fascinated by his appearance and unable to fathom who or what he could be. Overcome with awe, they whispered to one other, "Who is this man? Where on earth is he from?" Finally, one child piped up, "Actually he's one of those Russian circus men. He must be the giant in the circus." When Khyentse Rinpoche got up to board the train, everyone scattered because he was so huge and his presence so impressive.

It's true that Khyentse Rinpoche's majesty would have been overwhelming had there not always emanated from him the most profound calm and gentleness, a rich, natural humor, and the peace and bliss that are the signs of ultimate realization. When he was very young, he was blessed by the great Mipham Rinpoche who gave him the name Tashi Paljor, the meaning of which combines auspiciousness, goodness, magnificence, abundance, and perfection. Chögyam Trungpa Rinpoche said, "Whatever he did was perfection of its kind. Even the way he walked into the hall showed this quality; all he said was expressed to perfection. In fact, he surpassed anyone I had ever met." Khyentse Rinpoche possessed that perfect discipline and conduct that distinguishes the greatest masters. I am sure that in his whole life he never did a single thing that was incorrect. Nor would he be swayed from taking the course of action that he knew was right; he would never, for example, reveal a teaching that was inappropriate. And everything he did bore the signature of his elegance and simplicity.

All of us will remember his generosity, his kindness, and his grandfatherly tenderness and warmth. In fact, Khyentse Rinpoche had a gift for making you feel special, as if you were the most important person he had met all day. He was effusive with his affection; he would just take your head gently in his huge hand and draw you next to his cheek. The great Dzogchen Khenpo Shenga gave Khyentse Rinpoche the name Rabsel Dawa, "brilliant moon," as if to single out, among his remarkable qualities, his compassion, and to depict its cooling moonbeams dispelling the searing heat of suffering. For compassion and kindness marked Khyentse Rinpoche's every action toward anyone he met.

Another of his qualities was humility. Never would he put on airs, exhibit his knowledge, or betray his realization in any overt way. When he spoke of the different stages and signs of spiritual attainment, he would simply say, "It is said that this is what you will experience when you attain such realization," not even hinting that he was speaking, as we knew he was, from personal experience. In this day and age, when lesser teachers boast freely of their realization and powers, he was an exemplary model of modesty and humility.

For example, Khyentse Rinpoche would never breathe a word about his visions. According to the tradition of *Heart Essence of the Great Expanse,* to be considered a holder of the lineage you must have received a vision of Longchenpa or Jigmey Lingpa. Now it so happened that Khyentse Rinpoche always had a special place in his heart for Orgyen Topgyal Rinpoche, whom he had known since Orgyen Topgyal was a child, and who, with his disarming forthrightness, had a way of eliciting answers from Khyentse Rinpoche that other people could never manage to obtain. Khyentse Rinpoche mentioned to him that while he was in retreat at Paro Taktsang, "the tiger's nest" (one of the most sacred caves of Guru Rinpoche), in Bhutan, he had received a vision of Jigmey Lingpa, who had transmitted to Khyentse Rinpoche the blessing of his wisdom mind, authorizing him as a holder of the lineage. At the time, Nyoshul Khenpo Jamyang Dorje was writing his great history of the Dzogchen lineage, *A Marvellous Garland of Rare Gems,* and when Orgyen Topgyal told him about this vision of Jigmey Lingpa, he was eager to include it in the chapter on Dilgo Khyentse Rinpoche's life. He approached Khyentse Rinpoche and asked him whether he had, in fact, had such a vision. Khyentse Rinpoche flatly denied it and told him that Orgyen Topgyal must have just let his imagination run away with him. But Orgyen Topgyal insisted that Khyentse Rinpoche had told him, and so Nyoshul Khenpo composed the following sentence in his draft manuscript: "In particular, at Paro Taktsang in Bhutan, Khyentse Rinpoche was graced with a vision of Rigzin Jigmey Lingpa, who entrusted him as a master of the *Heart Essence* teachings." He then returned to Khyentse Rinpoche and explained why he had written it, despite the earlier denial. He asked him to check whether it was accurate or not, promising to remove it should it prove incorrect. At first Khyentse Rinpoche seemed disinclined to look at the manuscript and did not say anything when Khenpo raised the question again. After a while though, he casually asked him to show him the page. He inspected it and then quietly told Nyoshul Khenpo there was no need to change it.

On one hand, Khyentse Rinpoche's enlightened qualities were so self-evident that no one could miss them, and on the other, he was forever humble, because he had tamed his mind and his whole being. He was always the same, stable and unchanging, his equanimity as steadfast as a mountain, his wisdom as endless as the sky, and his enlightened qualities as vast as an ocean. Whenever he taught, the teachings would pour out of him like poetry, perfect just as they were, and without ever a single superfluous phrase or interjection. They had the quality of revelation and could be written out exactly as he spoke them, without any need for editing. As he would begin to teach, particularly on *dzogchen,* he would lean back slightly and seem to become even more spacious, and then the words would just flow out of him like a mountain stream. There was no stopping him. I remember so often we would just look on in amazement. The neurobiologist Francisco Varela once told me that he simply could not fathom how Khyentse Rinpoche's mind or brain worked. He would speak for at least twenty minutes, and when the translation took place, he would rest, or, when he got older, take a nap. Then without any prompting, he would resume exactly where he had left off half an hour earlier and continue teaching without the slightest fluctuation or hesitation.

Khyentse Rinpoche's astounding achievements have been celebrated elsewhere, but they include his twenty-five volumes of collected works; his twenty-two years in retreat; the vast number of teachings and transmissions he both received and passed on; the colossal amount of practice he accomplished; the monasteries, temples, stupas, and works of art he created; the collections of teachings he had printed; the care with which he brought up and trained a whole generation of incarnate lamas; the terma treasures he revealed; his reestablishment of the tradition of drupchens (intensive Vajra-yana group practices); and so much more. He accomplished a vast amount, and yet did so with such consummate ease that he made it look absolutely effortless. Not a moment passed from morning till late at night when he was not teaching, practicing, or helping others, and yet he seemed to have all the time in the world. He was expert at not wasting a single second, while remaining completely at ease and, what is more, deriving the greatest joy and delight from everything. What was mystifying was how he managed something everyone finds so difficult: blending the everyday goal of getting an enormous quantity of things done with the spiritual ideal of staying utterly relaxed and free from the slightest stress or effort.

You will read much in this book, and elsewhere, about Khyentse Rinpoche's tremendous work, but what I came to realize was that perhaps his greatest achievement was that, more and more, he became an embodiment of the teachings. Even more than his words and his teachings, it was his very presence and his very being that communicated the truth of the Dharma. In short, just to think of him said it all. Great masters there may be who possess extraordinary teachings, but with Khyentse Rinpoche it was sufficient merely to look at him, or think of him, for the entire blessing of the lineage to be evoked. I often think of the life story of Guru Padmasambhava, which describes how all the buddhas convened and directed their blessing into Buddha Amitabha, who in turn emanated his blessing directly to the land of Uddiyana and Lake Dhanakhosha, where it took the form of this extraordinary manifestation of Guru Rinpoche. In the same way, I feel that the blessing of all the buddhas converged in Dilgo Khyentse Rinpoche.

I also believe that Dilgo Khyentse Rinpoche's great master Jamyang Khyentse Chökyi Lodrö had a very special vision of his destiny. As you will read here in this autobiography, in the early days at Dzongsar Monastery in Kham in eastern Tibet, Dilgo Khyentse Rinpoche was often present, receiving teachings from Khyentse Chökyi Lodrö. I remember that he was very tall and thin, and in those days he was known simply as "Tulku Salga" or "Tulku Rabsel Dawa." In any case, Jamyang Khyentse Chökyi Lodrö was held in such high regard that hardly anyone else was referred to by the title of Rinpoche. Dilgo Khyentse Rinpoche had been formally recognized at the age of eleven by Shechen Gyaltsap as the mind emanation of Jamyang Khyentse Wangpo, and this was subsequently confirmed by Jamyang Khyentse Chökyi Lodrö. At the time, Khyentse Chökyi Lodrö was regarded as the great Khyentse, the throne holder of the seat of Jamyang Khyentse Wangpo, and the emanation of his enlightened activity. By confirming Dilgo Khyentse as the incarnation of Jamyang Khyentse Wangpo, Khyentse Chökyi Lodro was stating in fact that he and Dilgo Khyentse were no different. Though they were both emanations of the same master, at that time Dilgo Khyentse became the student and Jamyang Khyentse Chökyi Lodro the teacher. Even so, Dilgo Khyentse Rinpoche gave many transmissions to Jamyang Khyentse Chökyi Lodro. So they became teacher and student to one another. It was Jamyang Khyentse Chökyi Lodro who urged Dilgo Khyentse to reveal his termas, and authorized him as a great treasure revealer. The affection they shared for one another was extraordinarily deep and warm, so much so that Jamyang Khyentse Chökyi Lodro used to weep when they had to part. Dilgo Khyentse wrote in his autobiography, "Whenever I went to see Lama Rinpoche [Jamyang Khyentse] at Dzongsar, he took care of me with such great affection that I felt like I was coming home."

Once, Dilgo Khyentse Rinpoche told me a particularly moving story about how he had been invited to a picnic with Jamyang Khyentse Chökyi Lodro. In Tibet, everyone used to carry their own bowl with them, and it was never the custom to share somebody else's. On this occasion, Dilgo Khyentse had forgotten to bring his bowl, and so Jamyang Khyentse offered him his own. This was an almost unthinkable honor, as he was held in such high esteem that nobody would dare to eat from his bowl. Out of respect, Dilgo Khyentse declined. Jamyang Khyentse offered it to him a second time, and again he refused. Finally, Jamyang Khyentse, appearing exasperated and somewhat stern, said, "Take it! It's not dirty!" When Dilgo Khyentse Rinpoche told this story and he came to those words, "It's not dirty," his eyes would fill with tears. Such was the depth of his love and devotion.

Over the years there were some who wondered why, when there were so many other great disciples, Jamyang Khyentse would treat Dilgo Khyentse so specially and keep him always so close during the teachings and transmissions. Not long after, that same generation of people came to witness Dilgo Khyentse transform and become not only like Jamyang Khyentse Chökyi Lodro, even in his personality, but also like Jamyang Khyentse Wangpo the Great. His presence seemed to become even more enormous. I remember so well the occasion at Enchey Monastery in Sikkim in the 1960s when Dilgo Khyentse Rinpoche gave the *Treasury of Precious Termas* empowerments to Dzongsar Khyentse Rinpoche, the reincarnation of Jamyang Khyentse

Chökyi Lodro, and many other incarnate lamas. I wrote about this in *The Tibetan Book of Living and Dying*:

> Many masters were there in a monastery in the hills behind Gang-tok, the capital, and I was sitting with Khandro Tsering Chödrön, Jamyang Khyentse's spiritual wife, and Lama Chokden, his spiritual assistant.
>
> It was then that I experienced, in the most vivid way, the truth of how a master can transmit the blessing of his wisdom mind to a student. One day Dilgo Khyentse Rinpoche gave a teaching about devotion and about our master Jamyang Khyentse, which was extraordinarily moving; the words flowed from him in a torrent of eloquence and the purest spiritual poetry. Again and again, as I listened to Dilgo Khyentse Rinpoche and watched him, I was reminded in the most mysterious way of Jamyang Khyentse himself, and how he had been able simply to speak and pour out, as if from a hidden inexhaustible source, the most exalted teaching. Slowly I realized, with wonder, what had happened: the blessing of the wisdom mind of Jamyang Khyentse had been transmitted completely to his heart-son Dilgo Khyentse Rinpoche, and was now, before us all, speaking effortlessly through him.
>
> At the end of the teaching, I turned to Khandro and Chokden, and I saw that tears were streaming down their faces. Chokden was usually a man of few words. "We knew that Dilgo Khyentse was a great master," he said, "and we know how it is said that a master will transmit the entire blessing of his wisdom mind to his heart-son. But it is only now, only today, only here, that we realize what this truly means."

I am certain that Jamyang Khyentse Chökyi Lodro knew he would not live beyond 1959. He said there was a prediction that one of the Khyentse incarnations would live a long life, and I believe that he put all his blessings into Dilgo Khyentse Rinpoche so that he would continue the vision and work of the Khyentse lineage. It was almost as if they had planned it out meticulously together, whereby Jamyang Khyentse Chökyi Lodro's work was to be in Tibet, and the most crucial part of Dilgo Khyentse's mission would be in exile in India and the outside world. Of course, the eventual fall of Tibet in

1959 was a devastating loss, but with Khyentse Rinpoche alive we did not lose everything, because in this one man all of Tibet's Buddhist heritage was embodied. He came to play a huge part in the survival of the rich spiritual and cultural legacy of Tibet. In Tibet he had been known as an outstanding teacher, and Jamyang Khyentse used to speak of him to everyone, yet it was after going into exile in India and the Himalayan regions that he really manifested. It was his time.

However many great enlightened masters came in the past, no one quite like Dilgo Khyentse Rinpoche, or of his caliber, has appeared in *our* time. What was extraordinary was that he took on his glorious manifestation at the very point when the Tibetan teachings were arriving in the West and spreading through the world. Khyentse Rinpoche stood out, along with His Holiness the Dalai Lama, Dudjom Rinpoche, and the other great masters, like a beacon for the teachings of Buddha, for all the Tibetan traditions and especially the ancient Nyingma school. He became the beloved teacher of His Holiness the Dalai Lama and countless lamas who are now teaching all over the world. How fortunate we were that a master such as he should have been with us for more than thirty years after the fall of Tibet, and that he should teach in India, Bhutan, Nepal, and the Himalayan regions, as well as in Europe, Southeast Asia, and North America.

Khyentse Rinpoche was a living example of the great masters, a testimony and a role model for us today. He served as a reference point, because we have not met buddhas like the Buddha Shakyamuni or Guru Rinpoche, masters like Jamyang Khyentse Wangpo, or deities like Vajrakilaya. Because Khyentse Rinpoche was an enlightened being, to see him was to imagine finally how an enlightened being could be. Chögyam Trungpa Rinpoche once said, "If Buddha Shakyamuni were alive, he would look like Dilgo Khyentse Rinpoche." When you marvel at what the legendary masters accomplished in the past, you can perceive in Khyentse Rinpoche exactly how they did it. All the stories of the great siddhas and saints and of their attainments: here was the living proof. To see him was to get a real, tangible idea of what Jamyang Khyentse Wangpo and the other great masters of the past were like. In a way, you could say that Khyentse Rinpoche validated the lineage of Tibetan Buddhism and rendered it unquestionably authentic.

Among all the great masters in exile, the special merit of Khyentse Rinpoche was that countless people actually came to know him and had the extraordinary experience of just seeing him and of being touched by his kindness and the enthralling aura of his presence. Once he arrived at the airport in Hong Kong, where he was met from the plane with a wheelchair. Hundreds of people were waiting at the airport for their relatives and friends to arrive. They were all milling around and talking to one another, so there was quite a din. But the moment the automatic doors of the customs area parted and Khyentse Rinpoche appeared in the arrivals lounge, everyone instantly rose to their feet, although they had no idea who he was. They all fell silent and stood there, in awe. He possessed that enchanting charisma and magnetism.

Not only did Khyentse Rinpoche inspire devotion in us, but he possessed unwavering devotion for his masters and the masters of all the different lineages, including His Holiness the Dalai Lama, the Sixteenth Gyalwang Karmapa, and the other great lamas of the time. He was an impeccable example of a Ri-me master, who continued the nonpartisan lineage and work of Jamyang Khyentse Wangpo and Jamgon Kongtrül. Thanks to his continuous transmission of the teachings—the oral transmissions, the empowerments, and the instructions—Khyentse Rinpoche was instrumental in safeguarding all the lineages of Tibetan Buddhism. The sheer number of transmissions which he sought out and of which he was the holder made him like a vessel brimming with teachings. Not only did he uphold these transmission lineages, but he revitalized them, composing liturgies, for example, or empowerments, commentaries, and supplementary texts for the terma cycles that were not complete, just as Jamyang Khyentse Wangpo and Jamgon Kongtrül had done. It is thanks to Dilgo Khyentse Rinpoche that such lineages flourish today, alive and unbroken. And it is thanks to his blessing that the younger generation of incarnate lamas have matured into the brilliant teachers that they already are.

Whenever I speak or think of him, I am filled with gratitude, amazement, and devotion—gratitude that someone like him came and showed us what he did; amazement that we were so fortunate to have known him; devotion because just to think of him is guru yoga, just to gaze at a photo of him is to reawaken the view of the nature of the mind. For me there was no one who, by simply being the way he was, expressed the view of *dzogchen* as vividly as did Khyentse Rinpoche. Through his very presence, he communicated the essence, the spirit, and the truth of the Great Perfection. Later in life he did not have to teach so much, because as time went by, he increasingly became himself an introduction to the nature of mind and to the heart of the teachings. One of my students, a middle-aged lady, told me about an incident in 1987, when Khyentse Rinpoche was coming to teach at my center in London. She had gone to say good-bye to him at the busiest terminal at Heathrow Airport, and while he was sitting there waiting in his wheelchair, she noticed that his shoelace had come undone. Without any second thoughts, she knelt down to tie it up. As she touched his feet, all her ordinary thoughts and perceptions suddenly came to a standstill. For her it was an introduction to the innermost nature of her mind. Just as she discovered, Khyentse Rinpoche's whole being communicated the perfection of *dzogchen*, without any need for words. Primordial purity, natural simplicity, spontaneous presence: he personified it all.

At this point in my life now, of all my masters, it is Dilgo Khyentse Rinpoche that comes to me most vividly when I think of the view of *dzogchen*, or when I practice guru yoga. He was actually "liberation upon seeing, upon hearing, and upon remembering." For in a single moment, in a flash, his presence was such that it communicated the absolute directly and yet with a totally human relevance. In fact, what was striking about him was his humanity: in one person, it seemed, a Buddha and a perfect human being coexisted. Khyentse Rinpoche was Great Perfection, completely natural, unfabricated—authenticity itself. Yet at the same time, he was never beyond our reach. To see the sheer perfection he embodied, while remaining only too aware of our own limitations, could have been disheartening. But with Khyentse Rinpoche, even though we realized we had so much farther to go, somehow his grace and his blessing infused us with hope and inspiration, as if he was implanting a little bit of himself in us, prompting us to aspire with even greater enthusiasm toward what we were striving to realize.

In some ways, I feel that if you really understand the Dharma, the Vajrayana teachings and *dzogchen* or *mahamudra,* just thinking of Khyentse Rinpoche is complete on its own as a practice. He was the Great Perfection, because everything was complete and perfect in him. As Khyentse Rinpoche once said, "Out of his great skillful means and compassion, the Buddha taught different aspects of the view through metaphors. He taught the emptiness aspect of the view through the example of the sky, the luminosity aspect with the examples of the sun and moon, and the aspect of pervasiveness throughout samsara and nirvana by the example of the sun's rays and beams of moonlight." Just as the Buddha could only describe the absolute by using metaphors, so we too can only portray Khyentse Rinpoche's profound simplicity and wisdom by likening him to the sky, the sun, the moon, or an ocean or a mountain. You could speak for a century and still not measure his qualities or express them adequately, because they cannot be described in ordinary terms.

Simply to be in Khyentse Rinpoche's presence transformed your mind, so much so that your whole perception and experience of the environment changed. Things and events appeared differently; even circumstances began to change. Around him, everything became heavenly, almost a paradise. Wherever Dilgo Khyentse Rinpoche was became like the palace of lotus light in Guru Rinpoche's pure realm, the Copper-Colored Mountain of glory.

What happens when we think of Dilgo Khyentse Rinpoche, his achievements, and his life, is that it brings into our small minds, just for a moment perhaps, the vastness of what an enlightened mind can be. Unfortunately, the trouble with us is that we are not able to think about the lama all the time. Kyabje Dudjom Rinpoche recalled that his master used to say, "An old man like me—with nothing to think about except the lama, with nothing to say except praying to him, with nothing to keep up except nonaction—it seems I've always been in this state. And now here I am: aimless, carefree, spacious, and relaxed." However, we are not able to have devotion all the time, and that is a sign of our delusion. But whenever we are inspired, it cracks open our ordinary way of seeing and perceiving. When we think of Dilgo Khyentse Rinpoche, the feeling he evokes in us cuts through the ordinary mind and reveals the innermost nature of our mind, the ultimate nature of everything. As it says in the guru-yoga practice, "recognize that the nature of your mind, your own *rigpa* awareness, is the absolute lama." Thinking of the master, you are ushered into a different space—the essential nature of your mind, your buddha nature. And because it is the master who has revealed it to you and made that connection, you feel such enormous gratitude. That is why whenever you even mentioned the name of Shechen Gyaltsap or Jamyang Khyentse Chökyi Lodro to Dilgo Khyentse Rinpoche, his eyes would cloud with tears of gratitude and devotion.

The heart of guru yoga is blending your mind with the wisdom mind of the master. But how exactly do you mix your mind with the master's wisdom mind? In his inimitable way, Orgyen Topgyal Rinpoche asked many lamas this question and found that they each had a different answer. One day he asked Khyentse Rinpoche, "How do you merge your mind with the wisdom mind of the master?" Khyentse Rinpoche replied, "It's like this. It is whenever, through some circumstance or another—it might be through prayer or devotion—a thought of your master arises that captivates your mind, so much so that you feel you are not apart from him for even an instant. The moment that thought arises, if you leave it right there and rest directly in its true nature (which is the nature of mind), without letting any other thought interrupt or distract you, then your mind is *already* merged with your master's wisdom mind. There's no need to make a special effort to improve it, as that would only be fabricated. Just remain in that state, without contriving in any way, but simply recognizing that the lama's mind and your mind are one. That is 'merging your mind with the wisdom mind of the master.'"

In a guru-yoga practice he composed at my request Dilgo Khyentse Rinpoche wrote:

> That which accomplishes the great purity of perception
> Is devotion, which is the radiance of *rigpa*. . .
> Recognizing and remembering that my own *rigpa* is the lama—
> Through this, may your mind and mine merge as one.

When devotion is aroused, all your ordinary thoughts and emotions cease, laying bare the innermost nature of your mind. If you think of the lama, or even just hear his name, that feeling fills your mind, *your* ordinary being dissolves, and you enter into *his* being. So simply to think of him is to become one with him, in other words, one with all the buddhas. You are infused with his blessing and transformed, so that you begin almost to feel him within you. That moment is when pure perception has conquered your mind. And that is where you build your faith and your trust.

I feel that the only way for us to arrive at transcendence is by being uplifted like this through devotion, so that we receive the master's blessing. In fact, when the Vajrayana is called the direct or swift path, I sometimes think that this is what it must really mean. Khyentse Rinpoche said, "Devotion is the essence of the path, and if we have in mind nothing but the guru and feel nothing but fervent devotion, whatever occurs is perceived as his blessing. When all thoughts are imbued with devotion to the guru, there is a natural confidence that this devotion will take care of whatever may happen. All forms are the guru, all sounds are prayer, and all gross and subtle thoughts arise as devotion. Everything is spontaneously liberated in the absolute nature, like knots tied in the sky."

Khyentse Rinpoche's cremation took place in Bhutan on November 4, 1992. It was an intensely moving occasion, as all his disciples were there. When the funeral pyre was finally set ablaze, I was, at that very instant, consumed with a sudden sense of the magnitude of our loss. That he was gone. My heart sank. And yet in the next moment, it dawned on me that Khyentse Rinpoche is not, and never will be, separate from us. Dudjom Rinpoche's words came back to me: "Since pure awareness of nowness is the real buddha, in openness and contentment we find the lama in our heart. When we realize that this unending natural mind is the nature of the master, there is no need for attached and grasping prayers or artificial complaints. By simply relaxing into uncontrived awareness, the free and open and natural state, we obtain the blessing of aimless self-liberation of whatever arises." I realized, with greater poignancy and conviction than ever before, that our master is alive within us, and whatever arises is his blessing. Even though his outer manifestation has dissolved into the nature of reality, his wisdom being lives on in the teachings he has given us. Therefore it is up to us. If we can remember Khyentse Rinpoche, if we can recollect and practice his teachings, he is never separate or apart from us, not even for a single instant. And as soon as this thought passed through my mind, my sadness was suffused with a feeling of blessing and confidence.

In the past, it sometimes happened that when a great master passed away, there was a lack of continuity in securing the future of his work. However, what was wonderful with Khyentse Rinpoche was that, through his blessing and his foresight, he established that very continuity. Here, I feel I must pay tribute to Shechen Rabjam Rinpoche, Khyentse Rinpoche's grandson, who is the living link in the continuous transmission of his vision and his enlightened activity. Khyentse Rinpoche brought him up with the greatest care and affection, and Rabjam Rinpoche, through his deep devotion and unique closeness to this great master, grew to hold his whole lineage and continue his work. Through him, Dilgo Khyentse's aspirations are now all being fulfilled. How inspiring it is as well to see the love, devotion, and respect with which he is bringing up Khyentse Rinpoche's incarnation, Khyentse Yangsi Rinpoche. To all appearances, it looks as though Rabjam Rinpoche never once had the feeling that Khyentse Rinpoche ever left, and he shows the same delight and exhilaration when he sees his reincarnation as he did when he saw Khyentse Rinpoche himself.

Khyentse Rinpoche's close disciples feel and know that Yangsi Rinpoche *is* their beloved master, and when they are beside him and he is out of the public gaze, he allows his qualities to show in a remarkable way. He also bears an uncanny physical resemblance to Khyentse Rinpoche. Not all reincarnations demonstrate such a clear and close association with their previous life. I hope and I pray that Yangsi Rinpoche continues his enlightened activity without any hindrance, and so unfolds a new chapter in the life of Khyentse Rinpoche and of this lineage, serving the Dharma and bringing present happiness and ultimate bliss to living beings everywhere.

Dilgo Khyentse Rinpoche was blessed with many exceptional disciples, all of whom maintain the spirit of his wisdom mind and carry his work forward with single-minded dedication. I think, for example, of the unwavering devotion of Her Majesty the Queen Mother of Bhutan, and of Matthieu Ricard and his phenomenal achievements. Let me offer a heartfelt prayer for all of Khyentse Rinpoche's disciples, that they may continue his lineage and his enlightened vision.

We all owe a debt of gratitude to Bhikshuni Jinba Palmo, a devoted disciple of Khyentse Rinpoche and many great masters, for compiling his life story. Many people met Dilgo Khyentse Rinpoche, and so there are numerous wonderful testimonies about him. Each of his disciples, for example his heart son Kyabje Trulshik Rinpoche, Dzongsar Khyentse Rinpoche, Rabjam Rinpoche, and Pema Wangyal Rinpoche, would have their own rich, personal story to tell about him, each one an entire biography. There must be hundreds of lives of Khyentse Rinpoche, so many emanations of him in the minds of those who knew him.

Everyone who met him had a powerful experience, and just to have seen him once, even for a moment, I believe, is to have had sown in you a seed of liberation that nothing will ever destroy and that will one day flower completely. If you had such great good fortune, be sure to remember that experience, treasure it, and keep it in your mind, because it is the Khyentse Rinpoche within you. The memory itself is his blessing. As he said:

> Do not forget the lama; pray to him at all times.
> Do not let the mind be distracted; watch your mind's essence.
> Do not forget death; persist in the Dharma.
> Do not forget sentient beings; with compassion dedicate your
>   merit to them.

Even in the case of those who have never met Khyentse Rinpoche, I have noticed that when we talk about his life, it brings them a sense of his presence, and they too are able to feel a real blessing. Because when you speak of the master and remember him, the power, the blessing, and the compassion of the lineage all come through. So I suggest you read this extraordinary account of Khyentse Rinpoche's life, *Brilliant Moon,* along with the words of His Holiness the Dalai Lama, Dzongsar Khyentse Rinpoche, and Rabjam Rinpoche, and even these few thoughts that I have shared here, and let what you read bring Khyentse Rinpoche into your mind and heart. Imagine that you were actually meeting him, because as the Buddha said, "For all who think of him with faith, the Buddha is there in front of them and will give them empowerment and blessing." Fill your heart with his presence, and let his blessings pervade your mind.

May 2007
Lerabling, France

Foreword by Shechen Rabjam Rinpoche

MY FIRST PERCEPTION of Khyentse Rinpoche was that of a wonderfully loving grandfather. In fact he was like my true father and mother in one person. As I grew up, my perception gradually transformed into deep respect and confidence and finally into unchanging faith. Khyentse Rinpoche thus became my spiritual master. When I started studying the scriptures, I found in him all the qualities they described for an authentic and realized master. After his death the strength of his presence, far from vanishing, became increasingly all-pervading. I now realize how fortunate I was to have met someone like him and spent twenty years of my life in his presence, as I lived with him since I was five years old, until his passing away, when I was twenty-five.

During that time I was very lucky to be present whenever he gave teachings and to go wherever he traveled. I think Khyentse Rinpoche was one of the finest examples of a perfect spiritual teacher. He was in fact a master of masters, and most of the twentieth-century Tibetan teachers received teachings from him.

His life was dedicated solely to helping others. If you saw the extensive list of books he had printed, you would have the impression that he spent his entire life publishing books. If you consider the twenty-five volumes of his writings, one of the biggest collections by a Tibetan master in the last century, it seems like he did nothing but write. In terms of practice, as he did more than twenty years of retreat, it seems that most of his time was dedicated to spiritual practice and that he did nothing else. As for the teachings he received, he had more than fifty different teachers and received teachings from all the different traditions in Tibetan Buddhism. And the teachings he gave consisted of all the different vast collections of teachings within the Tibetan Buddhist tradition, such as the *Treasury of Spiritual Instructions* and the *Treasury of Precious Termas.*

When Tibet was lost, the teachings of all the lineages were about to disappear, so Dilgo Khyentse Rinpoche did his utmost to preserve them by giving teachings whenever possible. According to the needs of his students, he was sometimes engaged in giving six or seven different minor teachings in the breaks during a major set of teachings. Directly and indirectly he built many temples and stupas in Bhutan, Nepal, and India, and his life was spent preserving the Buddhist teachings. These days, most of the young lamas are directly or indirectly connected to Khyentse Rinpoche because of the teachings they received through him or because of the books he printed. He was not only concerned about the Nyingma lineage; he also worried about other traditions such as the Kagyu, Sakya, Geluk, and Jonang; he was like the life force of the Tibetan Buddhist doctrine.

Khyentse Rinpoche himself never called his teachers by name but called them *kadrinchen,* meaning "kind one." When I asked him why, he said it was because they were so kind that he didn't want to say their names as they were the real Buddha in person. Only in teachings he would mention the names of his teachers.

During the twenty years I spent with Khyentse Rinpoche, I never witnessed him become either very depressed or extremely excited; his mood was always even. The second time we went to Tibet, in 1988, Rinpoche wanted to go to Shechen Gyaltsap's retreat house, so we carried him up there. He wanted to sleep in the ruins of the house, so we put a tent up there. It was then that he started to speak a little bit about Gyaltsap Rinpoche and shed tears; that was the first time I saw him cry in twenty years. Another time when Khyentse Rinpoche was giving the Kalachakra empowerment in Nepal, while remembering his teacher Khyentse Chökyi Lodro, he also cried. Seeing him cry these two times really affected my mind deeply.

After Rinpoche's fall shortly before he passed away, there was a blood clot on his knee that had to be removed, but the doctors couldn't give him anesthetics due to his age and heart condition. I went into the operating room with Khyentse Rinpoche; he was holding my hand and said, "Go ahead; cut it." So they started doing the operation without anesthetic and took out the blood clot, cutting the knee about three or four inches wide. I was amazed that Rinpoche's face didn't show any pain; he was just smiling all the time. Rinpoche was so courageous, not crying in such pain but shedding tears when he talked about his teachers. When it came to his teachers, Rinpoche couldn't utter their names as he saw them as the true Buddha, but under the knife he didn't cry. How can we understand his outer, inner, and secret qualities with our ordinary minds? All we can say about him is related to his outer appearance; we cannot get to the depth of his realization and inner qualities, as we cannot conceive of them.

Wherever Khyentse Rinpoche sat, his outer presence was so huge. Once in Nepal he was sitting in his room while a mother with her child came to see him. As the mother was doing prostrations, the child was looking at Khyentse Rinpoche and said, "Mommy, mommy, look, what a giant man!" The mother was so embarrassed and tried to keep him quiet, but the child kept shouting, "What a huge man!" Whenever you would sit near him, you would feel his blessings so strongly that you just wanted to dissolve into him.

Whenever Khyentse Rinpoche taught, his words never contained any extra additions or duplications; it was as if he was reading from a book. One special quality I found was that you didn't need to be a Nyingma follower to be his student, unlike with most other teachers, where to be their student one has to adopt their particular school.

Once I was traveling in Scotland in a car with Khyentse Rinpoche and Akong Tulku. Akong Tulku was asking a lot of questions, and when he asked, "Who is the best student among your students nowadays?" Rinpoche said, "Sengtrak Tulku." After Khyentse Rinpoche passed away, even many years later I still meet people that all have their own story about Khyentse Rinpoche; he made them feel that they were the most special. It would be impossible to collect all these amazing stories and fit them in this book.

Khyentse Rinpoche always placed great emphasis on the importance of mingling our mind with the Dharma and unifying the practice with daily life. He used to say, "It is not when things go well that you can judge a true practitioner. When adverse circumstances arise, then you can clearly see the shortcomings of someone's practice." He stressed upon the need to blend one's mind with the Dharma in meditation and to carry the quality of the meditation into all of one's actions. He encouraged us constantly to check whether we were becoming better human beings or not. Were we slowly getting free of the obscuring emotions? Were we enjoying the fulfillment of inner freedom and freedom from obscuring emotions?

He stressed that after years of practice, the measure of our progress should be to gain a sense of inner peace and become less vulnerable to outer circum-stances. Inner freedom and profound happiness is meant to be a result of Dharma practice. This can only happen when negative emotions and men-tal confusions disappear. He stressed that we would have missed the point of our practice if our mental poisons remained all-powerful, tormenting us con-stantly and causing us to remain preoccupied with ourselves.

This biography attempts to convey, without any exaggeration, who Khyen-tse Rinpoche was, how he spent his life, and what his day-to-day activities were, so that his life may inspire others. These days, authentic teachers are few, so when people read about Khyentse Rinpoche's life they may discover what the qualities of a great master are, and this may help them find a truly authentic teacher.

Although we can't meet Khyentse Rinpoche anymore, when one reads his teachings and writings, one can experience the profundity of his wisdom and compassion. Even those who have not yet achieved enlightenment can still achieve and radiate a kind of inner well-being, which is the sign of a good practitioner. A practitioner with a weak practice can be tense and difficult to be with. Such a practitioner experiences many disturbing thoughts and prob-lems without being able to handle them. In contrast, a practitioner whose practice is strong naturally becomes more open and experiences inner free-dom. Through the inspiring example of Khyentse Rinpoche we can seize the chance to tread the path of the bodhisattvas with joy, diligence, and compas-sion, confident and full of enthusiasm.

May 2007
Paro Satsam Chortèn, Bhutan

Translator's Preface

A FEW YEARS after Dilgo Khyentse Rinpoche's passing, around 1993, when his collected writings were being prepared for printing, Shechen Rabjam Rinpoche asked me to translate Khyentse Rinpoche's autobiography. Khyentse Rinpoche wrote this autobiography when he was in his seventies and left off writing at the period just before he left Kham for Central Tibet in the mid-1950s. Since the life story was not complete, during the years following Rabjam Rinpoche's request, I started collecting and translating interviews from those close to Khyentse Rinpoche, such as his wife, relatives, attendants, and close students, in order to complete his story. I also translated a number of audiotapes of oral stories that Khyentse Rinpoche had told to Dzongsar Khyentse and other close students. It was not until 2004, after publishing my translation of *The Life of Vairotsana*, that I finally started translating the actual written text.

A large part of the written text consists of descriptions of various teachings that Khyentse Rinpoche studied, received, and taught, as well as the many teachers he studied with. For the reader who is not familiar with these teachers and texts, it can be quite an ordeal to digest all this. Rabjam Rinpoche therefore allowed me to mingle the written text with Khyentse Rinpoche's oral stories in order to make it more accessible for the general reader. Though nothing was left out from Khyentse Rinpoche's written account, we combined it with his oral account to make it richer and more intimate.

In the autobiography, Khyentse Rinpoche often calls his various teachers Jamgön, which means "kind protector." He also calls the same teachers by different names, for instance Dzongsar Khyentse Chökyi Lodro is sometimes called Dharmamati, sometimes Lama Rinpoche, sometimes Pema Yeshe Dorje, and so forth, while Khenpo Shenga and other khenpos are often called

Khen Rinpoche. To avoid confusion for the reader, I have tried to use one consistent name for each teacher, and when a teacher is sometimes referred to with five different names following one another, I have abbreviated them to two or three, putting the remaining names in the endnotes. And, though some readers may be offended by this seeming lack of respect, I have mostly omitted the title of "Rinpoche," which means "precious," in order to avoid making the names of teachers even longer than they already are.

We also decided to divide the book into two parts. Part 1 contains Khyentse Rinpoche's own words, written and oral, and part 2, the recollections of his wife, grandson, and so on. There were many recollections of various close students and attendants, and it was impossible to include them all in this book, so I tried to choose the ones that were the most informative and relevant to the events in Khyentse Rinpoche's life. Several times I requested his closest student and spiritual friend, Trulshik Rinpoche, to relate some stories about his experiences with Khyentse Rinpoche, but he told me to translate the biography at the beginning of the index that he wrote for Khyentse Rinpoche's *Collected Works*. A large part of Trulshik Rinpoche's biography, which covers nearly half of the hundred-page index, consists of praises to Khyentse Rinpoche's different lives written in beautiful poetry that is very difficult to put into poetic English, and the rest of it relates events similar to Khyentse Rinpoche's own account. As it was impossible to combine the two biographies, I just chose a few anecdotes from that one, along with a story about Khyentse Rinpoche's plans to build a monastery in Nepal. I combined that chapter with Khyentse Rinpoche's written account about the building of Shechen Monastery in Nepal, which was translated by the late Ani Ngawang Chödrön during the eighties. Some of the stories told by Orgyen Topgyal Rinpoche were recorded at Chanteloube in France and translated by Erik Pema Kunzang. In my translation I have tried to adhere faithfully to Khyentse Rinpoche's exact words, and if the reader finds certain descriptions eccentric or notices an occasional interruption in logic, it is because I have kept as closely to his words as I could and have not taken any liberties such as moving information around, even if it might have seemed more logical.

The foreword by His Holiness the Dalai Lama and the forewords by Dzongsar Khyentse, Sogyal Rinpoche, and Shechen Rabjam Rinpoche already relate Khyentse Rinpoche's qualities in great detail, so it is needless to add anything more here. After completing the translation of the written autobiography and mingling it with Rinpoche's oral account, I spent nearly six weeks this summer in Bhutan checking every detail with Rabjam Rinpoche, who then made some important changes and additions. Khyentse Rinpoche's long-term attendant and translator Matthieu Ricard also reviewed the entire manuscript and made some useful additions in the oral stories. During the annual drupchen this year in Bumthang, Her Majesty Queen Mother Kesang Chödrön checked the account of Khyentse Rinpoche's activities in Bhutan written by herself, her secretary Loppön Nyabchi, and Loppön Pemala, and also made some valuable changes.

As for my personal experience with Khyentse Rinpoche, I had the opportunity to meet him in 1973, while he was performing the funeral rites for the late Neten Chokling Rinpoche in Bir, in northern India. From then, until his death in 1991, I had the good fortune to spend long periods of time with him. From the mid-seventies until 1981, I also served as his translator during various periods. In that way I became quite familiar with his accent, which is maybe why Rabjam Rinpoche, who I met when he was six years old, asked me to translate the autobiography. While working on the written account and the stories, going through all the details of his life, I got a much better understanding about who Khyentse Rinpoche really was and the extent of his activities, so it has been extremely beneficial for me. While Khyentse Rinpoche was alive, though I cannot claim that my feelings for him were genuine devotion, it was almost impossible to leave his presence, like a needle attracted to a magnet. Through Rabjam Rinpoche's kindness to let me work on this project, my devotion to Khyentse Rinpoche naturally increased; it was like a continuous shower of his blessings.

May well-informed readers exercise restraint in the knowledge that the translator takes full responsibility for errors that inevitably exist. I pray that whoever encounters this biography may develop faith in such a great being and feel inspired to follow such a way of life. I pray to the Buddhas, lineage masters, and Dharma protectors to forgive my inability to translate with accuracy, as well as any mistakes of omission or commission and any improper disclosure of secret teachings committed in preparing this book. By the virtue of this work, may the Buddhist doctrine spread in the ten directions, may the lives of the lineage holders be stable and long, and may all sentient beings, including all that come into contact with this text, attain happiness and enlightenment.

ACKNOWLEDGMENTS

First of all I would like to thank Shechen Rabjam Rinpoche for allowing me to work on this project, for writing his introduction, for recalling many stories, and for revising the entire manuscript with me. Secondly my thanks go to all those who generously gave their time to tell me their inspiring stories, such as the late Khandro Lhamo, Tenga Rinpoche, the Queen Mother of Bhutan Kesang Chödrön, Orgyen Topgyal Rinpoche, Tsikey Chokling Rinpoche, Khenpo Pema Sherab, Pewar Tulku, and many others. I would also like to express my gratitude to the unequalled Fourteenth Dalai Lama Tenzin Gyatso, for writing his inspiring foreword, and to the sublime incarnations Dzongsar Khyentse and Sogyal Rinpoche, for writing their outstanding introductions, expressing some of Dilgo Khyentse Rinpoche's amazing qualities in such a profound way. My special thanks go to Khenpo Yeshe Gyaltsen for correcting the entire written translation with me while in Bhutan during the summer of 2006, and to all the other lamas who helped clarify various passages, such as Changling Tulku, Jigmey Khyentse Rinpoche, Drugu Chögyal Rinpoche, Khenpo Pema Sherab, and Khenpo Gyurmey Tsultrim. I greatly appreciate my editor Michael Tweed, who read through the entire text many times, shaping the book into proper English. I am very grateful to the translator Matthieu Ricard for allowing me to use some of his remarkable photographs, reviewing the manuscript, and making valuable additions to the recollections. My thanks also go to the great translator Erik Pema Kunzang for translating some of the stories told by Orgyen Topgyal; to the late Ani Ngawang Chödrön for translating the section on building Shechen Monastery in Nepal; and to Vivian Kurz for her help with the contract.

Part One

The Autobiography

1. My Early Years

INTRODUCTION

Hands of wisdom and love that rescue me from the precipice of
    samsara and nirvana;
Lord of the hundred families, outstanding among the buddhas;
Precious master, glorious chief of the sea of refuges;
I shall constantly serve you within the ocean of my zeal.

Simply by arraying the flower of your name in the garden of my mind,
Its sweet fragrance, potent with benefit and bliss, dispels my torment:
Precious Triple Gem, splendid crest, crown of my hundredfold faith,
Always keep me feasting on the honey of perfect liberation!

On the hard rock of the karma and emotion within my being,
Spiritual qualities are just feeble creepers:
I am filled with shame that I have put into writing
The story of my life, a pretense filled with exaggerations.

GREAT BEINGS WHO are holders of the teachings and have attained the
level of a noble one are able to guide faithful disciples toward liberation through their lifestyle. They can directly or indirectly give instruction
through their oceanlike ever-excellent conduct of body, speech, and mind,
totally graceful. But in my case, the dung heap of my defects makes Mount
Meru look small, and even though I was able to grow a tiny sprout of the
appearance of holy qualities, it could not survive but has withered into a yel-
lowish green and is now on the verge of drying up. Constantly making a pig's

nest with undeserved offerings while polluting the wind with the stench
of my karma and emotions, aware of my flaws without hiding them from
myself—other than being embarrassed—I don't feel the slightest enthusiasm about writing my biography.

During this current final period, the splendid statements and realization
of the precious Buddhist doctrine are enveloped in darkness,[1] and the sun of
most of the genuine learned and accomplished beings has set. While the celebration of perfect teaching and practice diminishes daily, the irrational foreign occupation of Tibet has scattered most of the grandeur and goodness of
the Tibetans, like throwing peas on a drum, into foreign countries where no
one sees the value of Buddhism, and even I have reached the end of the line.
Due to the kindness of the matchless lords of the mandala I don't seem to be
lacking the treasury of great learning, but since I didn't take study and reflection to heart, the wild soil of my bad character remained rigid.

Without tasting the slightest flavor of the ten principles of a *vajra* master,
imitating the Dharma, I became the facade of a teacher with the Khyentse
Tulku name as a pinnacle on a victory banner.[2] Because of that dignified title,
thinking that it would perhaps be beneficial to resound the Dharma drum for
whoever showed up and requested the nectarlike gift of ripening and liberation, I distributed it everywhere at all times.

Due to that, I was regarded as an authentic teacher by beings upholding
the teachings according to name and meaning, and by Dharma followers,
who knew the characteristics of a teacher. With sincere faith and respect,
they suggested that I write my life story, and when they repeatedly encouraged me to do so, I remembered the words of my master. Previously, after
specifically requesting the omniscient Manjushri Chökyi Lodro many times
to write his life story,[3] he composed it himself, in verse, and said to me, "It
would be worthwhile if you could write your biography as well. Once Jamgön
Khyentse Wangpo said to his student the learned *vajra*-holder Dorje Rabten,
'It is very important that you request both Jamgön Kongtrül Rinpoche and
the great bodhisattva Patrul Rinpoche to write their biographies, and later I
will also write my own. You must urge them to write theirs as these will be
of great value and very auspicious.' Jamgön Kongtrül wrote his autobiography, but Patrul didn't promise to write it when he was requested, so Khyentse
Wangpo didn't write an elaborate autobiography." While remembering those
incidental words, I thought of what the world's spiritual Dharma guide, the
light of the world, Guna Samudra[4] wrote:

Having obtained the flawless support of freedoms and advantages, and naturally having acquired the favorable condition of the four wheels, the result of as much disciplined study, reflection, and meditation as possible is to accomplish the three spheres of reading and abandoning.[5]

Having consistently been accepted with kindness by noble masters endowed with unconditional compassion, it wouldn't be right for me to downplay or waste their words. And since those words may create auspicious circumstances for the absolute truth in the future, I will write down whatever virtuous actions I have engaged in.

MY BIRTHPLACE

To begin with, the place where this body came into existence was Mahabhota, the land renowned as Greater Tibet. Greater Tibet consists of three provinces, four districts, and three regions,[6] and according to that division, the place where I was born is called Mekham.[7] When known as the six ranges of Dokham, my birthplace is called Ngudza Zemo or Zalmo Range. The heavenly mandated universal monarch Genghis Khan offered Tibet as three provinces to Drogon Chophak Rinpoche, and, according to that division, it is called the Kham Province of Black-Headed People, a place owned by the great wealth god of the highlands, Gyogchen Dongra. This extensive land is pervaded by vast grassy valleys in which many rivers flowing from minor valleys create the form of a blooming eight-petaled lotus that is decorated by many homes at its center and surrounded by well-plowed fields adorned with grain. On its edge is a massive mountain, completely surrounded by forests, rocks, and well-shaped hills covered with green meadows. While the winter goddess guards the summit, it is bound by a white turban of snow encircling it like a rim.[8]

Of the four great rivers from Amdo, only the Yangtze, filled with gold, flows from west to east. On the right side of the Yangtze are hundreds of gently waving flags like victory banners conquering all directions. Like a blazing rocky gem on the summit of the majestic Mount Meru, this hilltop is adorned with the abode of the local deity that looks after the area, the awesome Barlha Tsegyal and his entourage. Below that, in a narrow gorge, is a river with myriad waves that appear to dance in space, flowing down from the southeast to the southwest. On the left side of this river is a hill in the shape of the auspicious symbol of embracing fish, and at the necks of the fish is the Dilgo mansion. Around that, the sky, the mountains to the right and left, the streams, lanes, and so forth, appear like figures of the eight auspicious signs.

Central Ga and Den produce an abundant fine banquet of both cultivated and wild grains and fruits, medicinal trees and plants, and the farmers and nomads have a prosperous share of wealth. The country has all the resources it needs and is known as Denma[9] because it is endowed with a wealth treasure and the gold-filled Yangtze River flows through its middle. The great district-controlling temple of Tare Pemo Jong is situated directly east of it.

Dokham has twenty-five sacred places that were visited by the Second Buddha, the ascetic Pema Gyalpo and his retinue.[10] Dokham of Greater Tibet consists of upper Kham, middle Kham, and Amdo. These three regions cover a vast area, with enormous distances between the upper parts of the valleys. There are many kinds of communities, people of diverse ethnic groups and dialects, and the fashion and behavior of each of these distinct tribes bear no similarity to the others. Some of them live spread out over the plains, and some of them live neatly clustered. They are like a multicolored variety of flowers in summertime.

My Family

At the junction of nine prominent districts in the center of Dokham lived the bodhisattva king of Derge with his subjects. The king had twenty-five governors of self-sustaining districts who were the chiefs in the large southern region. These governors were independent, they knew the government policies, and they were worthy of being the king's ministers. There were also thirty-five dignitaries who were the chiefs of twelve northern nomad tribes. All of them were descendents of the Zhakar family, wise and reliable, close to the king, and very concerned about the citizens.

I was born in a lineage of courageous and skillful noblemen, as mentioned in the treasure texts of Jamgön Khyentse Wangpo, "His lineage is Myo,[11] and his bloodline is Ga." My particular family line is called Dilgo, and there are three main branches of this family: the Terlung, Alo Rong, and Den Dilgos. These are all the same family line but they are now geographically separate. The Terlung Dilgo was the main family and the other two branched off from them.

I belonged to the Den Dilgos and my father was called Tashi Tsering. My grandfather was the Derge Governor, Tashi Tsepel. At Tashi Tsepel's request, thangkas of *The Wish-FulFulfilling Tree,* the stories of the successive lives of the Buddha Shakyamuni, had been painted.[12] That's why they also called him Pagsam.[13]

In our family history, one of the Alo Dilgo men died while fighting in a battle for the Derge king. As a condolence on behalf of the king, the Derge government gave the family a large parcel of very good land in Denkok. The Dilgo family used to send two of their servants, a man and a woman, to look after this land. The servants would work the fields and generally were in charge there. Every year the servants were sent in the spring and would then return in the winter. The servants traveled back and forth so much that the family eventually decided they should stay permanently in Denkok.

At that time, my grandfather, Tashi Tsepel, was one of many sons in the Alo Dilgo family. He was not what you would call a favorite son. In fact, there were so many sons that he was hardly looked on with any favor at all. The two servants, however, liked him very much and had, in a certain way, adopted him. He always slept in the two servants' quarters. The year that these two servants were about to go and live in Denkok looked to be a sorrowful one for Tashi Tsepel. They tried to keep their departure a secret from him to spare him the sadness of their separation, but the boy already knew. As they were leaving he gathered his things and followed after them. So the family decided to let him go along with the servants and stay in Denkok with them.

As he grew up, he became a very influential and, eventually, an important minister in the Derge government. Over time he came to own more land than all the other aristocratic families of Derge combined. He became known as "the Derge Governor" and was as famous for his honesty as for his intelligence and learning. That was my grandfather. His wife was an excellent Dharma practitioner and recited a large number of Avalokiteshvara mantras.

It turned out that the other sons of the Alo Dilgo family became peripheral members of society; some even became crooks. Now the gentlemen of the family came from Denkok. Nevertheless, the root of the family is still considered to be the Terlung Dilgo branch. Jamyang Khyentse Wangpo was from the family branch of the Terlung area, and in that area one can still see his room, bed, and the caves where he meditated, had visions, and revealed spiritual treasures.

There was also another incarnation of Jamyang Khyentse from our family, and he was a true incarnation. When Jamyang Khyentse the Great passed away, he promised that one of his incarnations would be born to the Bon religion. Of all the incarnations, this boy from our family was physically the most similar to Jamyang Khyentse, perhaps because he had the very same bloodlines. He even had Jamyang Khyentse the Great's unusually large eyes.

The main lamas for our family, especially for my grandfather, were Jamyang Khyentse Wangpo and Jamgön Kongtrül. In his youth my father hunted and killed a number of animals. My grandfather told him, "In our family no one hunts; if you kill animals, Jamyang Khyentse will scold you." One day the whole family went to see Jamyang Khyentse at Dzongsar, and when he called for my father to come to his room, he asked, "Have you killed any animals?" My father was very scared, but, as he knew one should never lie to a master, he said, "Yes, I have killed a few."

"The Dilgo family is very wealthy, so you don't need to hunt," Jamyang Khyentse told him. "Besides, I bet you couldn't bag anything even if you had to fill your stomach. Today you should take a vow to never go hunting again." Straight away he took a statue and put it on my father's head, who was feeling very uncomfortable and ashamed.

When he returned to his family's quarters, my grandfather asked him, "What did Khyentse Rinpoche say to you?" My father did not answer, as he was so upset. "Did he say you shouldn't hunt animals?"

"Yes, he did," my father replied.

My grandfather assured him that he had not told Jamyang Khyentse anything about it but that Jamyang Khyentse had great prescience. Then he added, "As you know, in our family it is Jamyang Khyentse whom we rely on for guidance, so it is not good for you to hunt anymore." And my father never hunted again.

As my father got older, Tashi Tsepel advised him to do Vajrakilaya meditation practice. Since my grandfather was especially fond of Jamyang Khyentse, the next year they went to Dzongsar to request the Vajrakilaya empowerment from him. They were disappointed, however, to discover that he was in strict retreat and not available to see them. Fortunately Jamgön Kongtrül happened to be visiting Dzongsar at that time, and my grandfather felt it would be auspicious for my father to receive the empowerment from him, so Jamgön Kongtrül agreed.

On the appointed day, as Jamgön Kongtrül finished the preparations for the empowerment, my father, uncle, and the rest of their entourage went to Jamgön Kongtrül's quarters. The entire party was composed of people from aristocratic Derge families, and Jamgön Kongtrül treated them with the appropriate hospitality, so before the empowerment began, they were to enjoy a picnic near Jamyang Khyentse's residence. Jamyang Khyentse's personal attendant unexpectedly arrived at the picnic to invite the party up to the great lama's retreat quarters. Though he was in strict retreat, it appears that Jamyang Khyentse knew what was going on down below at the monastery.

When they arrived at his quarters, the ritual master was standing outside the door with the vase of purification water, which seemed to indicate the beginning of an empowerment. Inside Jamyang Khyentse himself had begun the very same empowerment ritual that they had requested from Jamgön Kongtrül, and as soon as they entered into his room, Jamyang Khyentse Wangpo granted them the detailed *Quintessential Kilaya of the Hearing Lineage* empowerment, reading transmission, and instructions. Afterward he said, "From now on you should stop hunting wild animals; a religious boy shouldn't do immoral work. You should receive *upasaka* vows of formal refuge from Karmapa Kakyab Dorje."[14] So they received it from him, just as they had wished.

After the empowerment they went back to Jamgön Kongtrül's quarters where there was still a lamp burning in the window. Jamgön Kongtrül asked, "What did Khyentse Rinpoche want?" They said that he had given them the Vajrakilaya empowerment. "Oh, very good, there is nothing greater than to receive that empowerment from Jamyang Khyentse. Nevertheless, since I have already begun the preparations for the empowerment myself, I am going to go ahead and give it to you again!" So in one evening they received the Kilaya of the Hearing Lineage empowerment from the two founders of that very practice: the treasure revealer himself (Jamyang Khyentse) and the one who wrote it down (Jamgön Kongtrül).

Kongtrül advised my father to complete some mantra recitations for this Vajrakilaya meditation practice, so for three months he practiced in retreat. My father also received instructions on the union of the master and Vajrakilaya from Mipham Manjushri, who gave him his manuscript, which he had handwritten himself.[15] He accumulated a hundred thousand recitations of the six-line "Blazing like *Kalpa* Fire" prayer from the *Seven-Chapter Supplication* and received triple-refuge *upasaka* vows from Karmapa Kakyab Dorje, who gave him the name Karma Norbu Rigzin Tsewang.

My father only had devotion to a few special lamas, although he would never say anything bad about other lamas. Of all the lamas, he favored Onpo Tenga and Shechen Gyaltsap the most,[16] but he also had great devotion to Jamyang Khyentse Wangpo and Mipham Rinpoche. Gyalsey Shenpen Thaye's nephew Urgyen Tenzin Norbu, usually called Onpo Tenga, and other realized masters all cherished my father with great affection. He accumulated one hundred million six-syllable mantras with the *Self-Liberation of Suffering* Avalokiteshvara practice and did one hundred thousand recitations of the goddess Tara's mantra. Every year he accumulated many hundreds of thousands of Tara prayers and offered a few hundred thousand butter lamps. He funded the summer retreats at Benchen and Sakar Monasteries, and his religious and political education was not bad.

My mother, who was called Lhaga, was the daughter of a Derge minister. Unlike my father, who was somewhat strict, she was always very gentle. She met Jamgön Kongtrül and Jamyang Khyentse Wangpo, as well as Mipham Rinpoche, Khenchen Tashi Özer, and other masters, from all of whom she received many empowerments and teachings. Once she had received an empowerment from a master she would never disobey what that master said or disrespect him. Through her pure vision, generosity, and other virtuous deeds, she became known as being rich in virtue, and she lived up to her reputation.

MY BIRTH

The Derge prince once told me that Mipham Rinpoche had told my father, "I'm a sick old monk who is about to die, so I don't need a house; but you should build a hermitage on that hill behind your place. It will benefit the Dharma king and the Derge government. I won't go far away from the Derge people."

Concerning the outer geomancy, while observing that hill from the east, it had the distinct shape of a supine tortoise, with the omniscient Mipham Rinpoche's cabin Tashi Palbar Ling situated at its heart. A large juniper tree grew nearby, and Mipham Rinpoche said it was a bodhi tree. The tortoise's head faced west toward a mountain shaped like fire; to the right was a hill shaped like wood; on the left was a hill shaped like iron, and at its tail, a hill that resembled water.[17] The eastern side was wide open so that the sun and

Denkok Valley, Dilgo Khyentse's birthplace.
Photograph by Matthieu Ricard.

moon would rise early and set late, and the mountaintops looked like a vast many-spoked wheel in the sky. These were all excellent geomantic signs. Concerning the inner geomancy, the whole area was a perfect replica of northern Shambhala, with the central hill as the Kalapa Palace. All the surrounding plains were divided by rivers creating the shapes of lotus petals, and amid them was an array of villages. During the winter these were surrounded by a circle of snow-laden hills. It was here that the primordial Buddha Mipham Gyurmey Mikyo Dorje first turned the wheel of the Dharma with *Vajra Sunlight*, a detailed commentary on the concise Kalachakra Tantra.

When my mother was pregnant with me, my family went to visit Mipham Rinpoche. He asked right away if my mother was pregnant, and my father replied that she was. My parents then asked if it would be a son or a daughter. "It is a son," Mipham Rinpoche said, "and it is important that, the moment he is born, you let me know." He gave my mother a protection cord, and told them that on the day the child was to be delivered, they should send a servant to tell him. He also gave them some Manjushri pills and some other things.

I was born in the Dilgo family home at the foot of the mountain on a special day in the third month of the iron-dog year, 1910, while a thanksgiving feast offering was being held on the occasion of Mipham Rinpoche's successful explanation of the detailed Kalachakra Vajra Tantra commentary. It was a very auspicious Monday, the third day of the month. The omniscient Mipham Rinpoche sent a message telling my parents to call me Tashi Paljor, and to put a Manjushri pill dissolved in liquid on my tongue as soon as I was born, before even drinking my mother's milk. The moment I was born, they wrote the syllable DHI on my tongue with Mipham Rinpoche's sacred pill. From then until his passing Mipham Rinpoche gave me Manjushri pills and sacred medicine to drink daily.

Not long after I was born, my parents took me to see Mipham Rinpoche; he performed a cleansing and ransom ritual for me, with a blessing to attract longevity. He explained that it was a religious ceremony done in India when a child was born. He also gave me a piece of yellow silk and a vase with nectar. As I was born with long hair, my father said that long hair might harm my eyes and asked if it was all right to cut it. Mipham Rinpoche said, "Do not cut his hair. Instead, there is a Chinese custom of tying children's hair into five knotted locks like Manjushri; that's what you should do."

At my mother's request he wrote down my name Tashi Paljor in his own hand; my mother always kept this piece of paper in her prayer book. It is an Indian custom that when a child is born, a celebration is held, so Mipham Rinpoche served some wild sweet potatoes in melted butter to our family. Sometime later we went again to meet Mipham Rinpoche. He gave me a Manjushri empowerment and said, "Throughout all your future lives, I will take care of you."

Whenever I ate the slightest bit of contaminated food, it would get stuck in my throat, so Mipham Rinpoche himself would send me his leftover food blessed with the Arapatsa mantra.[18] Each month when my parents took me to see him, he would blow on me while chanting the Arapatsa mantra, and, to guard against infant death, he gave me handwritten protection circles. He told my mother to recite Palden Lhamo's mantra and gave her enough infant mineral-medicine made with three ingredients to last me until I was about five or six years old.[19] Just before he passed away, he specially gave me the body, speech, and mind blessings of the wisdom deity Manjushri, using the statue that was his practice support. He did prayers and promised to take care of my family until we all attained enlightenment. Because Mipham Rinpoche protected us with such infinite, great kindness, just before my father died, he dreamed that he was planning to go down to an obscure dark place, but Mipham Rinpoche was sitting in the interior part and said to him, "Don't go there; come here!" So my father went to Mipham Rinpoche.

Whenever I teach or study the Dharma, I still feel that the little understanding I have achieved is due to the kindness of Mipham Rinpoche, who was Manjushri in person—I have gained certainty about that.

> I pay homage to Manjushri,
> Whose kindness led to my virtuous attitude;
> I also pay homage to the spiritual teachers,
> Whose kindness made me progress.

Just like these words of Shantideva, as soon as I was born I met Manjushri in human form, and he took care of me without being asked, which could be considered the core of my life story.

They say that I am an emanation of many lamas. Dzogchen Rinpoche and Khenpo Shenga said I was an emanation of Onpo Tenga, who was my father's root teacher.[20] Onpo Tenga was quite a strict teacher and often stayed at my father's place for extended periods. Once, when leaving, his monks forgot one of his ritual objects at my father's place. So at night when the time of the evening ritual came, his attendant was quite worried, and expecting to be scolded, he explained that it had been left behind and that he was sending for it. To his surprise, Onpo Tenga told him that there was no need to do so because he would come back sometime to get it and that it was quite auspicious that it had been left behind. Onpo Tenga passed away not long after that, and people said that because of what he had said about the ritual object, he would probably be reborn as my father's son.

Sure enough my father soon had a son who was duly recognized as Onpo Tenga's incarnation. A delegation with Khenpo Yonga was sent from Gemang Monastery to invite the incarnation. The delegation reached the other shore of the river opposite to where my father and brother (the young tulku) were. The party decided to wait until morning to cross to fetch the young tulku. But in the evening there was a powerful earthquake and a wall collapsed in our house at Denkok, killing both the tulku and my grandparents.

The Fifteenth Karmapa, Kakyab Dorje, was staying nearby, so a servant was sent to request him to perform the funeral rites. The Karmapa replied that he was available to perform the rites, but as it was close to the New Year, if he would come to the Dilgo household he would have to perform the rituals and celebrations for the New Year there as well. So he wondered whether it would be all right for him to observe the New Year there in spite of the unfortunate events. He also explained that he would have a large entourage and asked if this would not be inconvenient. My father sent word back that the Karmapa was welcome to conduct the New Year's ceremonies at the household and that more than one hundred people could be accommodated. So one hundred people came and elaborate New Year's celebrations were observed in the Dilgo household. The Karmapa said that this would be very auspicious for the family in the future.

My father then asked Dzogchen Rinpoche where the tulku would be reborn. Dzogchen Rinpoche said that he could not tell clearly at that moment but that he would let my father know if he had any indication. Four days later, a messenger came with a letter from Dzogchen Rinpoche saying that the tulku had three emanations: one had dissolved into Guru Rinpoche's heart; one was reborn as a son of Raksha Thotreng, who was converting the cannibal demons on their continent; and one was going to be born again as my father's son. My mother soon became pregnant, and the child was expected to be this incarnation.

However, although there were many wondrous signs during my mother's pregnancy, the baby died in the womb. I was the next child, and, not knowing about the unborn child, people declared that I was Onpo Tenga's reincarnation. So, I became known as such by many lamas, such as Adzom Drukpa and Khenpo Shenga,[21] and when I was recognized as Khyentse Wangpo's incarnation at Shechen Monastery, the people of Dzogchen Monastery were not very happy.

In our house there was a temple, the main figure of which was a Buddha statue the size of the Lhasa Jowo. Around the sides there were statues of the thousand-eyed Avalokiteshvara, an almost life-size statue of Guru Padmasambhava, and a smaller one that had belonged to Jamyang Khyentse, as well as images of the Eight Manifestations of Padmasambhava, and many others. There was also an altar cabinet containing all the tormas of the protectors for the *Heart Essence of the Great Expanse,* and another one established by Onpo Tenga containing the tormas of Tseringma.

I used to study reading and writing for a few hours every day. As my family was rich, we had about seven or eight servants and all the instruments required for ceremonies. For fun, I used to dress up with a shawl and make all the servants dress up with raw-silk shawls; then we would make a big torma and play-perform the Vajrakilaya ritual. Many people used to come to visit my father, and when they saw us they would ask which monastery we were from.

In the summer when I was around seven or eight years old, after studying in the morning, I used to go up the mountain and pitch a tent. There were very nice meadows full of flowers where I used to stay the whole day and play in the water. In the late afternoon, around four, I would study some more. Our home was very big, like a palace, and had more than a hundred rooms. The western wing had a Sakya protector temple. My parents used to stay in the eastern wing; from there, they couldn't hear whatever noise we used to make with bone trumpets and other instruments in the protector temple. The house had five floors. We had about forty or fifty horses, about seventy or eighty mules, and about ten thousand *dri, dzo,* and so forth.[22] Some of them we would lend to people to take care of, and later they would give them back. As we had a lot of land, we had an enormous amount of grain. We had to sow about a hundred bags of barley every year. In the summer, our fields had to be worked for two months, and in the autumn gathering the harvest took another two months.

I had three brothers and several sisters. My eldest brother was relatively young when he died in the earthquake. The second brother was Shedrup; the third was Sangye Nyenpa Rinpoche;[23] and I was the youngest boy.

My Recognition

My father did not want any of us to be recognized as incarnate lamas. Before Sangye Nyenpa was born, our family's resident lama had a number of dreams that he related to my father. In one of them he dreamed that a famous pair of cymbals which was kept at Benchen Monastery was being played in our household and many people were there. He felt that this must mean that the next son would be an emanation of Sangye Nyenpa, whose seat was Benchen Monastery. My father got angry as he didn't want to lose his sons to the monastic system, and apparently he said that if the lama hadn't lived with them for so long and been such a good friend to the family, he would have whipped him a hundred lashes. My father also told him to keep quiet about his dream, and so the lama agreed to say nothing about it. However, some time later the Karmapa made a proclamation stating that this child was indeed Sangye Nyenpa. It was very difficult for my father to give him to the monastery, and he was concerned that if he had another son, he too might be claimed as an incarnate lama.

When I was one year old, another great lama, Vajradhara Jamyang Loter Wangpo, compiler of the infinite Vajrayana tantras of the great Sakya school, came to visit my home. He was the foremost disciple of Jamyang Khyentse, and he became the root guru to Khyentse Chökyi Lodro, as it was he who introduced Khyentse Chökyi Lodro to the nature of mind. At that time there was an epidemic in the area. As my parents were afraid that I would become ill, my mother took me to the top of the mountain where one of our nomads was staying. When Loter Wangpo came, my mother brought me down to see him.

As Loter Wangpo was staying in the protector's temple, we met him in the corridor. Upon seeing me sitting on my mother's lap, he was very pleased and said, "Oh what a nice boy. Please show me his hands." So my mother did. While he looked at the lines in my hands, he told my father that while in Dzongsar, Khyentse Chökyi Lodro had asked him to find the unmistakable Khyentse Tulku. "This is an emanation of Jamyang Khyentse Wangpo; you must give him to me." Because he kept repeating this over and over again, my father said, "I've asked Mipham Rinpoche about him, and he told me it would be better not to give the tulku a title or have him enthroned. He said that when my previous son was recognized as Onpo Tenga's reincarnation, collecting lots of donations for his enthronement caused him to become well-known, which created obstacles for the tulku's life, and so in this case it would be better to let the tulku do whatever he feels like later." After my father told him that, Loter Wangpo let it be and didn't tell Dzongsar that the tulku was at the Dilgo home.

Before Loter Wangpo came to the Dilgo home he had had some dreams, which he later told to his secretary Khenchen Jamyang Khyenrab Thaye. Lama Jamyang Dharmamati related to me what he said, "After dreaming for three days about my teacher Khyentse Wangpo, who was in a very good mood, the young boy from the Dilgo home was brought to me. Dzongsar Khyentrul Chökyi Lodro had told me to recognize a remarkable Khyentse tulku, and I've decided that it's this boy."

My mother wanted to take me back to the nomads, so Loter Wangpo gave me a protection cord blessed by his root guru, the omniscient Jamyang

Khyentse Wangpo. He also gave me a bead from the practice *mala* that Jamy-ang Khyentse had used during the *Path and Result*.[24] He told his nephew Losal, a very nice man who was also his secretary, that he wanted to give me a very good ceremonial scarf and Manjushri pills, and as we were sitting there, Losal brought him an old scarf. Loter Wangpo said, "No, not a used one, bring me a new one without any stains!" So Losal came back with a better scarf, but even that wasn't good enough, and Loter Wangpo again told him to bring a brand new one. My mother was very modest and said, "Oh, that one is fine," but then Losal brought a brand new one, and Loter Wangpo said that would do and put it around my neck. He told my mother to take good care of me. He also gave me a name, but it got lost.

Loter Wangpo stayed one month at the Dilgo family home. He went to see Mipham Rinpoche, who offered him a White Tara long-life ceremony in the guesthouse and did prostrations to him. Loter Wangpo offered Mipham Rinpoche a Manjushri statue which was a terma of Tertön Sogyal.[25] Mipham Rinpoche made the sword and the book for the statue out of gold that Drugu Tokden Shakya Shri had offered him.[26] Mipham Rinpoche then used it as his practice support and put it in a small wooden box that also contained a terma of Chokgyur Lingpa, as well as relic pills of the Kasyapa Buddha and Buddha Shakyamuni. He put five-colored brocade fabric on the box and carried it with him. Whenever he used to compose any texts, he would put the box in front of him and make offerings and then white light with syllables in it would come from Manjushri's heart which he would then write down. Sometimes the light would dissolve into Mipham Rinpoche's heart, and he would know what to write without thinking. When he was about to pass away, he had a bigger statue of Manjushri made, about the size of the Lhasa Jowo; he put the small Manjushri statue in its heart center and said to put it at Shechen. When the Chinese destroyed Shechen, this statue was taken to Derge Gonchen.

At that time, Mipham Rinpoche was staying on the mountain behind our estate, and when Loter Wangpo left, my father went to see Mipham Rinpoche and told him what Loter Wangpo had said. Mipham Rinpoche replied that Loter Wangpo was a very great lama and that what he said must be so, but that it was better not to do the recognition ceremony and offer ceremonial scarves now, as there might be obstacles. My father had great faith in Mipham Rinpoche and listened to him.

My father then went to Jeykundo to see Loter Wangpo and told him what Mipham Rinpoche had said. Loter Wangpo said that it was very good and that my father should give me to him. As I was a tulku of Jamyang Khyentse Wangpo, there was no way my father could not give me to him. My father didn't quite believe him and asked what signs he had that I was Jamyang Khyentse Wangpo. He said that before going to our home, he had visions of Jamyang Khyentse Wangpo for three days, and after that he met me and he was sure that there was no mistake. My father repeated that Mipham Rinpoche had also said that I was a tulku but I shouldn't be formally recognized yet, at which Loter Wangpo became angry and said, "Nobody can tell me not to recognize Jamyang Khyentse Wangpo!"

A close disciple of Jamgön Kongtrül's, named Drongpa Lama Tenzin Chögyal, was the tutor of my elder brother Chöktrul Sangye Nyenpa. Once when he was staying at our home doing a week's drupchen of the Dharma Lord Ratna Lingpa's *Secret Assembly Longevity Practice,* my parents, siblings, and I all had the privilege of receiving the essential empowerment.[27] That was the first empowerment I received in this body, and I think it might have been due to this initial auspicious coincidence that I lived longer than the rest of the Dilgo family.

On the twenty-ninth day of the fourth month in the water-mouse year, 1912, the omniscient Mipham Rinpoche passed away at his hermitage on the top of the hill near our residence. Just before Mipham Rinpoche passed away, he told his lifelong attendant and disciple Lama Ösel, "When I die, you will experience great pain, but it won't last." After Mipham Rinpoche passed away, Lama Ösel became almost like a madman. He would not eat, nor would he stay in one place but kept going in and out of his room. After one hundred days, he had a vision of Mipham Rinpoche in the sky. Wearing a *pandita* hat, Mipham Rinpoche was writing, and as he finished each page, he would throw it at Lama Ösel. The letters were not written in black ink but brilliant golden light. Lama Ösel looked at one of the pages and could read a few words, "Radiant light . . . rainbow body . . . adamantine . . ." Then Mipham Rinpoche pointed toward the sky with a mudra and said three times, "Indestructible, radiant light body!" After this, Lama Ösel was no longer sad.

Shechen Gyaltsap Rinpoche came to participate in the funeral ceremonies and was invited to stay with us. He was forty-three at the time. I visited with him regularly and one day he said to my father, "You must give me your son; he will benefit the Shechen teachings."

"Nowadays tulkus are mostly into business, collecting offerings," my father replied. "If that's not the case, and he can really serve the doctrine through study, contemplation, and meditation, I'll give him to you. But why do you think my son is a tulku?"

"There is a Tseringma statue in your family shrine room that was filled and consecrated by Onpo Tenga from Gemang," Gyaltsap Rinpoche, who would rarely speak of such things, explained. "I dreamed that it actually transformed into Tseringma who said, 'You should take care of that boy; he will benefit your teachings.'"

So my father, who was very direct, said that if this were really true, he would allow me to be taken to Shechen; but if I was merely to occupy a throne in Shechen or Dzogchen Monastery and be implicated in political and religious intrigues, he would not give me up. Shechen Gyaltsap assured him that I would be of benefit to the teachings and beings, so my father agreed to let me go. However, as I was still an infant, I was not sent to Shechen until I was a bit older.

Meanwhile all the senior Shechen monks thought I was an emanation of Rabjam Rinpoche, and even spread a rumor to that effect.[28] Three days after Rabjam Dechen Gyalpo passed away, his wisdom form appeared to Gyaltsap Rinpoche, who wrote down what he said in a poem with the words, "From three out of one, let the second be first" beneath it. Shechen Kongtrül Rinpoche said it meant that there were three emanations of Rabjam Rinpoche,[29] and the middle one should be enthroned at the monastic seat. I, born in the iron-dog year, 1910, was the eldest. The middle one, who was enthroned, was born in Golok in the iron-pig year, 1911.

A close disciple of the previous Rabjam Rinpoche and of Gyaltsap Rinpoche, Kachu Kunzang Nyentrak Gyatso from northern Gomey Dengkya, recognized the third one of Rabjam Rinpoche's emanations. This emanation was wise, pure, and noble-minded and had been enrolled in the unsurpassed Urgyen Mindroling Monastery for three years. During the later part of his life, he came to Shechen and stayed there for a while.

On another occasion, Dzogchen Rinpoche, Thupten Chökyi Dorje, visited us. "This child is a very important tulku of Dzogchen Monastery," he said.

"You should give him to us." But my father said nothing, and the incident passed. Later my father took my elder brothers Shedrup and Sangye Nyenpa, along with Lama Ösel and myself, to meet all the great lamas of that time. We went to visit Adzom Drukpa, from whom we received teachings on the preliminaries to the *Heart Essence of the Great Expanse* for ten days, and we met the Fifth Dzogchen Rinpoche, Thupten Chökyi Dorje, and others. When we went to Shechen, Gyaltsap Rinpoche was in retreat in the Cave of the Eight Herukas, so we were not able to see him.

When I was six years old, I received a long-life empowerment from Kunzang Dechen Dorje, who was the reincarnation of Jigmey Gyalwai Myugu, from the northern Dzagyal Monastery.

During the explanation of the empowerment, his consort, whom he called Apo, was holding the book, opening it to the right pages. When he came to read the history of the terma in which the author of the sadhana related his vision of the Copper-Colored Mountain, he began to relate his own experience and told us how he had gone to the Copper-Colored Mountain himself and met the three-headed, six-armed Raksha Thotreng in a pure vision. "When some people go to the Copper-Colored Mountain, they see Guru Rinpoche as the peaceful Tsokye Dorje, others as Padmasambhava. I however saw him as the wrathful Raksha Thotreng with nine heads and eighteen arms." Then, surprised at himself, he changed the subject, saying, "What am I saying? Apo, show me the page we are on."

After the long-life empowerment I said that we planned to go on pilgrimage to Central Tibet and Tsang the next year and asked for spiritual protection for my whole family. "I will pray for you," he said. "Usually I forget who to include in my prayers if my wife doesn't remind me, but I won't forget you, little dark-faced boy! You and I have been inseparable for many lifetimes. I remember a former life when we caught a frog together on the bank of a river. As the proverb says, 'In spring when there is nothing to eat, the frog keeps its mouth open; and in autumn when there is lots of food, the frog keeps its mouth shut.' When the frog sat there with its mouth shut, we would open it with a spoon." Then he turned to me and asked, "Do you recognize me?"

"Do you recognize him?" repeated my father.

"Yes, I recognize him," I said.

"I'm going to give him a nice present," Kunzang Dechen Dorje declared. He didn't really care for things; he only liked cups and had a rare and precious collection which he cherished a lot. Because he was the incarnation of Jigmey Gyalwai Myugu, he had some very precious relics. Sometimes when ordinary visitors, like villagers, would say things like, "Oh, what a nice statue," he would just give it to them, and occasionally the statue would turn out to be a terma. He would thus give away all kinds of precious things like rare books and so forth, as he just didn't care. One day he gave away all kinds of statues, so the lamas were going around collecting the statues to put back into the monastery. He just didn't care about any of this; all he cared about were his cups. They were always looked after carefully, and he would look at them one by one. He would hide the cups inside his robes, and when it was time to go to sleep he would remark, "What's this?" and would pull another cup from inside his sleeve.

At this time, he turned to Apo and said, "Bring my box of cups." He then sorted through it and presented me with a small blue china cup filled with the three sweets, and he looked at me with great affection. Apparently Kunzang Dechen Dorje told this same story to the previous Onpo Tenga, from Gemang.

Once Kunzang Dechen was giving some Dzogchen teaching, and when coming across terms like "lucid," "vivid," and "clear,"[30] he said, "I can't explain these terms; you should ask my little boy from Gemang."[31] But the next day he said, "Oh, I met Guru Rinpoche at the Copper-Colored Mountain in my dream and asked him the question, and he explained it." Later, when the disciples asked Khenpo Yonga, his explanation was practically identical to the one Guru Padmasambhava had given to Kunzang Dechen.

Apo was very devoted to Kunzang Dechen and served him all the time. He could never do anything without her and used to say that if she died, he wouldn't survive for a single day. One day she went to do retreat somewhere and passed away. Knowing how he felt about his wife, the local people thought it over carefully and decided that they couldn't tell Kunzang Dechen themselves, so they called upon his close friend Mura Tulku to perform the difficult task. Mura Tulku went to his house and said, "I have some difficult news to tell you."

"What?" asked Kunzang Dechen.

Mura Tulku told him, "Apo has passed away."

"What? Why are you making all these faces?" Kunzang Dechen said to everyone's surprise. "Aren't you a Dharma practitioner? You always say everything is the Dharma. Now look at you, what are you doing? What are you worried about? She died, that's all; everyone has to die."

So he was rather wild and unpredictable, never clinging to anything. When others suggested, "We should read some sacred texts for Apo," he agreed to read from the *Primordial Wisdom Guru,* but after a few words Kunzang Dechen started laughing and said, "What's the use? She's already in paradise, so let's just leave it."

When we were about to leave on pilgrimage to Central Tibet and Tsang, I had the privilege of receiving a long-life empowerment and the reading transmission for the *Oral Instructions in the Gradual Path of the Wisdom Essence* from the realized master Jamyang Trakpa. At Kilung Monastery I had the privilege of receiving teaching on the *Six Bardos* from the great bodhisattva Dzamura Jigmey Pema Dechen Zangpo, along with the awareness-expression empowerment in connection with the *Gathering of the Vidyadharas* and the maturing instructions of the *Primordial Wisdom Guru.*[32] Though these teachings were restricted, I received them together with my father when he went to the summer assembly, and because I was a tulku, I was regarded with pure perception.

Pilgrimage to Central Tibet

In the fire-dragon year, 1916, when I was seven years old, on the way to our pilgrimage through Central Tibet and Tsang we went to the northern Taklung, where we were admitted to an audience with Matrul Rinpoche, who strongly slapped me on the head three times. The next morning when he met us in his inner room, my father showed him his amulet box with protections against weapons. Among them was a ritual dagger, a treasure that the great Kyeyo Vidyadhara Lerab Tsal had revealed from a whirlwind.[33] After rolling it in his hands, Matrul Rinpoche said, "Your son needs this for protection," and gave it to me. He then turned to my father and said, "You should look after this child very carefully because he must be an incarnate lama. Do you plan to make him a householder or a monk?"

"He will be a householder," my father replied.

Matrul Rinpoche burst out laughing and said, "You watch how he'll keep the household. It will become clear when he is twenty years old!"

When we came back to the house where we were staying, my father said, "The lamas won't let me keep this son, but I am not going to let him become a lama. We have a large family, an estate, and a lot of land to look after. I want him to become a layman so that he can take care of all this."

In Tsang we received long-life empowerments from both the great *pandita* Chökyi Nyima and Sakya Gongma of Puntsök Palace, the great subjugator of this world. We also met Thinley Rinchen, the sister of the head of Drolma Palace.[34] In Tsurphu we met the Fifteenth Karmapa and Minling Trichen with his son, and also saw the Tsurphu torma-throwing ritual.[35] At that time I was close to death from the measles, and the son of Chokling Tertön, Chöktrul Gyurmey Tsewang Tenpel, told us to ransom as many lives as I was years old. For a few days he performed a hundred feast offerings from the *Heart Practice Dispelling All Obstacles* cycle and kept blessing me with a precious statue, a treasure revealed by Chokling Tertön, so I recovered from my illness. I felt that Matrul Rinpoche's slap on my head had also helped clear this obstacle to my life.

Together my parents, brothers, sisters, and I made an extensive pilgrimage throughout Central Tibet, Tsang, and the South, making offerings at the three doctrinal places and all the sacred sites and shrines.[36] Though our pilgrimage was very detailed, I was very young, and seeing temples as a child, I didn't think they were very useful. We also attended the feast offering at the Great Prayer Festival.[37] Then we went to Ngor Evam Chode where we met Khangsar Khen Rinpoche, who said to give me to him so that he could appoint me as one of the Zhabdrungs.[38] Later, when he came to Kham, he said the same thing, so my father asked why he kept insisting. Khangsar Khen Rinpoche said, "I had a dream of the Ngor monks performing an elaborate procession, at the end of which they welcomed a child. The next day, while I was wondering who this child was, he arrived in front of me. Your son was the very one that I saw the monks welcome in my dream, so he must be the emanation of a great saint."

2. My Studies

A T Peyul Monastery, they said I was a tulku of Karma Kuchen. The previous Karma Kuchen was my uncle, who once came for a lengthy stay at our home. He gave empowerments and teachings and did elaborate healing ceremonies that were helpful for this and future lives. When he returned to his residence, he left his *yadar* at my home,[1] but to his shrine attendant Gelek, a monk from Gyalrong, he said, "You don't need to get it back; it's a good sign for this old monk to go back there one day." He passed away the next year, and Katok Situ Pandita said that I was the reincarnation of Peyul Kuchen Tulku. When the shrine attendant Gelek was on his way to Central Tibet and Tsang, he stopped at our house and offered me his monk's staff and begging bowl and a copy of the *Treasury of Dharmadhatu* while I was still sitting on my mother's lap.

Just before Onpo Tenga passed away, he told my father to order a complete set of copper ritual utensils, so my father obeyed and offered them to him. While distributing his belongings among his circle of disciples, he gave my father Gyalsey Shenpen Thaye's dagger that he used to wear around his waist, and his *pudkong*.[2] Adzom Drukpa said that I was the reincarnation of Onpo Tenga, and gave Gemang Khenpo Yonten Gyatso an official letter stating that. [In response to all of the attention, the author composed this verse.]

> When the joyful prayers and aspirations of the noble ones
> Are transferred, the genuine qualities should manifest;
> But my mind is burdened with the heavy weight of karma and
>   emotions,
> So I am too embarrassed to even mention such qualities.

At the Sakar Monastery community, Lama Ösel, a close disciple and life-long attendant of Mipham Rinpoche, gave the *Chanting the Names of Manju-shri* and the instructions for Khyentse Wangpo's preliminary practices,[3] and Sangye Nyenpa gave the major *Kalachakra* empowerment according to Jona-ngpa's tradition, which I received. Around that time on an auspicious day Mipham Rinpoche's attendant, Lama Ösel, started to teach me a little reading, and the senior tutor Karma Chodzin from Derge continued to teach me reading. Since my father was the secretary of the Derge Dharma king, he taught me writing, and I worked hard at it; thus I learned both the ordinary and printed scripts without difficulty. Together with my brother Shedrup I received the empowerments and reading transmissions of Ratna Lingpa's *Kilaya* from the realized master Jamyang Trakpa, heart son of the two Jamgön Lamas.[4]

In the summer of the earth-sheep year, 1919, when I was nine years old, I went with my father and brother Shedrup to meet Adzom Drukpa. His encampment had been destroyed in a fight, so Adzom Drukpa and his entourage had settled near Shechen. He used to wear a white raw-silk shirt with a red brocade collar and a necklace of onyx stones. He looked very impressive; he had long black hair with a touch of gray, which he tied up with a scarf. It is said that he had perfected the four visions of *togal* and had unobstructed clairvoyance.[5]

My father was wearing a *chuba,* and Adzom Drukpa told him to put it up* as that was the way to wear *chubas.* He said that my grandfather also used to wear his *chuba* down. The next day, however, my father let his *chuba* down again. Adzom Drukpa scolded my brother Shedrup about wearing a monastic robe with patches and a long-sleeved shirt and said that even though my brother claimed to be a disciple of Mipham Rinpoche, he didn't know how to do prostrations. He also used to scold his son a lot, and so his son was very scared of him.

My hair had grown long, and I wore it wound around my head in the Derge fashion; I was also wearing a layman's robe. He asked if I was the son who would hold the family estates. When my father confirmed it, Adzom Drukpa laughed and said, "Yes, he will hold the family estates. But there is a big obstacle. Shall I look for it?" At that time there had been many bad omens—on the roof of our house were about fifty banners, and rats were

---

* I.e., place his arms in the sleeves instead of letting the top hang down from the waist.

found running around underneath them. Also, some containers myste-
riously broke, and a local bridge burned down. So my father said that he
should indeed go ahead and look for the obstacle, and Adzom Drukpa told
us that he would.

After a couple of days Adzom Drukpa said that the omens meant my
father would become ill and we would be cheated, but if we performed certain ceremonies we would be OK. He then added, "It would be better if you
made the boy a monk." My father replied that making me a monk would be
very difficult. "Then I'll dispel the obstacle," said Adzom Drukpa. He said I
needed a long-life empowerment and a proper *lalu* ritual,[6] so he performed
the empowerment for the long-life practice known as *Vase of Amrita*. A longevity arrow was brought, and they measured its length. Adzom Drukpa
recited a longevity invocation and then said, "Reveal the size of this longevity arrow," meaning that the life-force omens would appear. When he pulled
the arrow from my hands, it had become five inches shorter. Adzom Drukpa
had a son called Gyurmey Dorje who was the shrine attendant. At this point,
he asked whether the size wasn't mistaken. Adzom Drukpa got upset and
scolded him, saying, "How can you say such things? It is very precise! That's
the very obstacle I told you about—it is showing." My father was not particularly impressed. Adzom Drukpa once more concentrated on summoning the
life-force omen and recited the invocation again, three times. Then when he
pulled out the arrow it was five inches longer than originally. "I'm not just an
ordinary man," said Adzom Drukpa, "and again I say that it would be better if
you made him a monk." There was no response from my father, so every day
for seven days Adzom Drukpa gave me a long-life blessing.

One day he recited the *lalu*, putting a cup inside a pot with boiling water
and butter, according to the *Gathering of the Vidyadharas*. He fixed his gaze
on the *lalu* cup and it rotated by itself, turning toward me, so he said, "There
are a lot of obstructing spirits, but they are not malignant or hidden, so there
won't be much harm." After that he stopped worrying and said, "There was
an obstacle, but I have dispelled it."

He said he would now cut my hair and give me refuge vows and a long-
life empowerment. My father finally said that he could, but my brother Shedrup reminded him that Mipham Rinpoche had said not to cut my hair until
I was twenty. Adzom Drukpa asked if Mipham Rinpoche had really said that.
When Shedrup assured him that he had, Adzom Drukpa asked if he could
cut just a little snip, and my father said that was OK. So he gave me *upasaka* vows,[7] cut a lock of my hair, and, saying I had surrendered to Guru Rin-

poche, gave me the name Urgyen Kyab, "Protected by Urgyen Rinpoche." I didn't like the name.

He gave my father and Shedrup detailed maturing instructions in conjunction with a short teaching on the preliminaries of the *Heart Essence of the Great Expanse*, written by the omniscient Khyentse Wangpo. Adzom Drukpa himself had received the complete maturing and liberating instructions of the *Heart Essence of the Great Expanse* from Jamyang Khyentse Wangpo, and the omniscient father and son had appeared to him in a vision in which they gave him the additional teachings of the special short lineage.[8]

When I received the *Heart Essence* preliminary teaching from Adzom Drukpa, he was staying in a yak-hair tent in the forest. The side of the tent was put up when the weather was hot, and I sat there with my father. Like the previous Khyentse, he used to take tobacco when giving teachings. He used to put his ground tobacco in a steel box in front of him, and sometimes he would take a little and say, "Ah. . ." He told my father that I should receive the *Root Volumes of the Heart Essence* from Dzogchen Khenpo Luko, and my father remarked that this khenpo was the best lama at Dzogchen Monastery. When we left, I never saw Adzom Drukpa again.

Adzom Drukpa really was extraordinary. Khyentse Chökyi Lodro said that he met Adzom Drukpa when he was thirteen years old at Tromkuk. Adzom Drukpa had sent a message for him to come in the morning. He was going by horse, and as he was very small, he couldn't easily mount and had to climb up stacked pieces of wood to get on. He rode up to Adzom Drukpa's tent, and the latter came to receive him at the door with a ceremonial scarf. When they touched heads, Adzom Drukpa cried. Khyentse Chökyi Lodro stayed a few days and received part of the *Heart Essence* cycle. When he was about to leave, Adzom Drukpa told him, "I have very strong wrong views. Nowadays there are many tulkus, but since you received the name of my root master, I really wanted to meet you. When I first saw you, I didn't feel much devotion since you are but a small child, however the next morning, when you got on your horse, I actually had a clear vision of the previous Khyentse Rinpoche, so then I naturally got very happy. I really feel like making a large offering to you, but right now I don't have very much." So he offered him a vase made of gold and silver that he had received as a gift from Karma Kuchen, together with many other different things. Khyentse Chökyi Lodro had never received so many offerings before. Then Adzom Drukpa touched his forehead to Chökyi Lodro's and cried once again; he asked Chökyi Lodro to come often.

Khyentse Chökyi Lodrö later gave the vase to Dzongsar Monastery. Upon receiving it, the Dzongsar monks said the tulku would be very useful to the monastery, so they became known as "vase adorers."

My elder brother had requested the empowerment for the *Heart Essence of Chetsun* after Shechen Gyaltsap concluded his retreat, so we went to Shechen. There I met Gyaltsap Vajradhara and had the privilege of receiving, together with my brother Shedrup, the maturing and liberating instructions, along with the reading transmission, of *The Great Chetsun's Profound Essence of Vimala*. I did extensive prayers in front of Mipham Rinpoche's reliquary with his practice-support statue of the wisdom being of Manjushri, and I was given nectar pills that had descended from the statue. Because Adzom Drukpa had said I would have obstacles, Shechen Gyaltsap prayed for me in front of Mipham Rinpoche's preserved body relic. Gyaltsap Rinpoche touched my head with his daily practice books, which had become dirty from intensive use. At that time nothing was said about me staying there in the future.

Then we went to Tsering Jong, the hermitage of Rudam Dzogchen Monastery, where the great bodhisattva Khenchen Jigmey Pema Losal, also called Konchok Trakpa, gave us the major *Magical Display of the Peaceful and Wrathful Ones* empowerment from the *Nyingma Kahma* and the empowerments from the two root volumes of the *Heart Essence of the Great Expanse on the Great Perfection*, which my elder brother Shedrup had requested much earlier.[9] He gave the elaborate empowerment, along with the long-life empowerment, of the *Gathering of the Vidyadharas* written by Dodrupchen; the *Yumka* long-life empowerment; the empowerments for Lion-Faced Dakini, the Great Glorious One, and the four blood-drinking herukas. He gave the *Peaceful and Wrathful Ones Purifying the Lower Realms*, the *Self-Liberation of Suffering Avalokiteshvara*, Nyitrak's *Thousand Buddha* empowerment, the *Innermost Guru Sadhana*, and the maturing instructions of the *Primordial Wisdom Guru* with the awareness-expression empowerment; and the life entrustment of Ekajati, Maning, and Tseringma.[10] All of these he gave in great detail. Khen Rinpoche was very kind to me and each day gave me presents of sweets. The reading transmissions we received from Khenpo Thupten Nyentrak from Dzogchen. From the supreme incarnation of Gyalsey Shenpen Thaye, Shenpen Chökyi Nangwa, we received the *Amitayus Sutra* reading transmission. When I met Khenpo Shenga, the abbot of the Shri Singha Monastic College, he gave me a jade cup filled with nutritious things.

We also went to visit Dzogchen Rinpoche, who was having a picnic at the large rock in front of Dzogchen Monastery. He told me to stay one month, but we could only stay about ten days. Dzogchen Rinpoche said I would have obstacles and should free the lives of animals. Back home, since my father had many animals, we spared thousands of them from slaughter.

OVERCOMING OBSTACLES

By that time our home had become infested with rats, one following the other, joined like a rope. There were also some other bad omens, and, as I mentioned, when Adzom Drukpa and other lamas examined them, it seemed bad.

There was always a lot of work to be done on our estate, and we employed a large number of servants for whom soup was cooked in a huge cauldron. One evening my brother and I were playing beside a large hearth, throwing burning pieces of wood back and forth when one of them hit me on the head. I fell over backward, hitting the huge pot of boiling soup. The boiling soup spilled into my trousers and over my leg. The sheepskin *chuba* I wore stuck to my skin, burning me. My left thigh was completely covered with blisters, and the pain was excruciating. That night they invited Lama Rigzin Tekchok, who was a direct student of the two Jamgön Rinpoches, Patrul Rinpoche, Mipham Rinpoche, and Onpo Tenga. He had perfected a hundred million recitations of the *Mani* and *Arapatsa* mantras and possessed outstanding qualities of learning, discipline, and nobility. He had a mantra, of which he had done a few hundred thousand recitations, that was effective for many different diseases. He sprinkled blessed water over me a few times, which eased the pain.

In a way, the accident was fortunate, because afterward, my father asked many lamas for divinations and they all said I had to become a monk. Shechen Gyaltsap indicated that I would not live long if I was not allowed to become a monk, as I wished to do. Lama Ösel, who had been Mipham Rinpoche's main attendant, performed the ransom ritual of *Restoring Harmony to Disturbances of Phenomenal Existence* and a ransom ritual to avert death. Onpo Tenga's disciple Kunga Palden was invited to give me the *upasaka* vows of pure conduct and performed a month's longevity practice. Since I had started to decide things for myself, I had wanted to become a monk. My father asked me, "What healing ceremony do you think would make you recover from this accident? If you would just survive, I'll do anything necessary!" I said it would help to become a monk and get robes. My father promised and he was so happy that he ordered monk's robes for me, had a small hand drum and bell put on my pillow, and told Lama Ösel to cut my hair at daybreak the next morning. They said that my mother was crying because she was so afraid that I would die that very night. I was bedridden for six months, which was really difficult because I could only lie on my left side; my hip was very sore.

That next morning, I received vows from Lama Ösel, who cut my hair and gave me robes. Because Mipham Rinpoche had given me the name Tashi Pal-jor, Lama Ösel said that I didn't need to get a new one. He also did the *Stirring the Phenomenal World* ritual for me, as well as a ransom ritual to avert death.

Each monastic community did religious services; we ransomed the lives of ten thousand animals; and Kushab Gemang and Khen Losal Rinpoche were especially requested to do long-life practices.[11] In particular, my brother Sangye Nyenpa, who was in the midst of three years of strict retreat, did the White Tara recitation from Atisha's tradition on my behalf. In a dream he clearly saw a *sharawa* in a very clear sky,[12] with a blooming white lotus sur-rounded by white light in front. Toward the wild animal's tail, a white cloud in the shape of a clockwise swastika appeared. He made a colored drawing of it and sent it along with the water from the vase,[13] the long-life substances, and a letter saying, "The obstacle to my younger brother's life is now gone."

Without this accident, I couldn't have studied with Shechen Gyaltsap and all the other lamas. When I became a monk, my father asked where he should put me. Many lamas said that I had to be enthroned, but my father said he wanted to keep me at home. My father said that I was a tulku, but if he gave me to Shechen or Dzogchen Monastery, I would waste my time using offer-ings. So, after I became a monk, I stayed at home. There were two merchants from Dartsedo who used to come every year, and after I was scalded they gave me cups and sweets from their merchandise; they really liked me. When I had recovered and become a monk, the merchants cried and said that now that I had become a monk, the Dilgo family wouldn't have any sons. I spent that winter in retreat doing *Vajrakilaya* practice.

When I was almost cured, Khenpo Shenga came to visit my home. When I met him, he said, "The accident that caused Tulku's illness has stimulated good action. Do Khyentse mentioned Dodrupchen's secret name to his par-ents and said, 'I need to go see that teacher. If I can't reach him, I'm going back to my homeland. My native place is the Copper-Colored Mountain.' Likewise it's very good that Tulku became a monk, otherwise he could not have lived. I'm on my way to Dondrup Ling in Jeykundo, as Ngor Master Loter Wangpo told me to start a monastic college there. If you come that way, I'll teach you all the philosophical commentaries. When Do Khyentse Yeshe Dorje was young, he lived in Drikung, and during that time the great protector Rahula actually came and told him to study texts. Since you are a holder of the teachings just like him, you certainly need extensive study and reflection from now on."

Because he kept saying that, I went to Tashi Palbar Ling, the omniscient Mipham Rinpoche's cabin, when I recovered from my illness. There, my brother Shedrup and I did over a week's secluded retreat on the *Innermost Hidden Secret Assembly Longevity Practice*. After that I went to Dondrub Ling in Jeykundo, together with my brother Shedrup, who was my second spiritual teacher.

PHILOSOPHY STUDIES

When I arrived in the presence of Khenpo Shenga, whose qualities of learning, discipline, and nobility were peerless, he took care of me with immense affection, and I had the good fortune to study and reflect on the impressive text of *The Way of the Bodhisattva*, a wish-fulfilling gem.[14] When I first started studying *The Way of the Bodhisattva*, he sent a student to check on my understanding three times. The next day when I took examination, he was delighted. Khenpo Shenga said that when Patrul Rinpoche was studying *The Way of the Bodhisattva*, he wasn't able to study much more than one stanza a day, therefore Khenpo Shenga wouldn't teach me more than one page a day. Using what he taught daily as a commentary to the root text, my tutor made me read it a hundred times. At noon I was allowed to play for about an hour; I don't know whether it was because of that hour, but I never felt bored at all.

Every afternoon, one of Shenga's learned disciples, Aku Sotruk, would help us review the teachings. I had to take daily tests in front of Khenpo Shenga, but since my reading was good, my examination results were never poor.

I think it was on the full moon of the fourth month in the sheep year, 1919, that Khenpo Shenga, with the help of the traditional five monks, gave novice ordination in front of the Jowo statue at the Jeykundo Monastic College.[15] I received it along with my Dharma friend, a young monk from Tharlam Monastery in Ga, named Jampa Rinchen. Khenpo Shenga gave me a brocade robe with a swastika design and the name Jigmey Rabsel Dawa Khyenrab Tenpa Dargye. He said that I was highly intelligent and would become very learned in the scriptures. Although he praised me directly and indirectly, when I evaluate it now, I was very young and didn't really acquire a good understanding of the scriptures, but merely mastered the words.

Though I had recovered from the burns, my skin was still itchy from pus. Khenpo Shenga said that at Dothi Gangkar, a special place in Gyam blessed by Guru Rinpoche, there were hot springs that could improve my condition, and he suggested finishing *The Way of the Bodhisattva* there. So that is where we went, and we concluded the teaching near that sacred place.

Meanwhile Drongpa Lama Tsewang Gyaltsen from Benchen, who was very kind to me, said, "It's good that you became a monk. I hope you'll become a good lama," and gave me a small begging bowl of good quality metal in a cloth case, which made me extremely happy. When I called on Lama Tenzin Chögyal, he gave me a jar full of raisins and said, "Now you are a lama!"

A few months later I went to Khenpo Shenga's retreat place at Gyawopu. Khenpo Shenga had been in a strict solitary retreat, but when I arrived, I saw that all the monks from the Dzogchen Monastic College were assembled as if they were about to receive teachings from him. When I entered, he told me to sit on the throne where his root teacher used to sit and he sat on a lower seat. Before he began the teachings, he announced to the congregation that I was the incarnation of his own teacher and that they should pass by for my blessing.

As Khenpo Shenga told me to teach my mother the first four chapters of *The Way of the Bodhisattva*, I taught it to her as soon as I arrived home in the winter. He said that when I settled at Samdrupling, which was near our home, I could say that I had taught *The Way of the Bodhisattva* from the age of eight. Samdrupling was the Sakar Monastery residence in Den that had been established long ago by the Sakya translator and editor Tsultrim Rinchen. Khenpo Shenga sent a teaching assistant along with me, a monk from Palpung called Karma Tsultrim who was humble and very talented. Teaching the text in great detail, I felt that the name of the chapter presenting the benefits of the enlightened attitude truly corresponded to its meaning. Growing confident about it, my understanding improved a little. When I took a test, giving a detailed explanation of the difficult points from the wisdom chapter of *The Way of the Bodhisattva*, Karma Tsultrim was very pleased and said, "Tulku, the fact that you learned this text so well makes me happier than getting a lump of gold!"

There was a replica of the Copper-Colored Mountain in our home shrine room, and I visited it frequently. One day it seemed to remind me of something. I said to one of my playmates, "Tonight I'm going to the Copper-colored Mountain." Even though I didn't think about the buddhafield and didn't remember it when I went to bed that night, in my dream I arrived at a palace that was said to be the Copper-Colored Mountain. I briefly met Padmasambhava and Mipham Rinpoche, and below Mipham's throne was an empty seat with a square carpet where he told me to sit. I remember that as soon as I sat down, he said, "This is your *yidam* deity," giving me a five-inch high golden statue of the longevity lord Yamantaka, which he put on the table in front of me. At that time I didn't know much spelling or grammar, but Sangye Nyenpa said that after I had studied *The Way of the Bodhisattva,* there were never any mistakes in the letters that I sent him.

In the monkey year, 1920, I went back to Jeykundo. Khenpo Shenga was teaching a commentary on *Entering the Middle Way* to a monastic community of over three hundred students, and I received it with them. Every day I took examination alone, but a few times I had to offer examination among many students, which was very pleasing to Khenpo Shenga, and my fellow practitioners were amazed. My tutor, Karma Tsultrim, also gave me an extensive teaching on the text, and I read the excellent notes that my brother Shedrup had made; otherwise I had absolutely no capacity or understanding to get to the bottom of the extensive commentary on my own.

My brother Shedrup told me, "Patrul Rinpoche's students would first gain a thorough understanding of the root text by using a word-for-word commentary. When beginners start by studying the detailed explanation of a text, their understanding is scattered. By memorizing the outline, one can understand the general meaning, and when reviewing the commentary from there, one's study will be effective. Nowadays there are too many annotated commentaries which lack an outline and so don't produce a good understanding." He thus gave me some important instructions about the earlier way of studying texts, which were extremely helpful. My father sent a letter to the kind Lord Situ Pema Wangchok, requesting two books of notes on *Entering the Middle Way,* and Situ Rinpoche gave me a pair of high-quality books.

I accompanied Khenpo Shenga to visit the Gyanak Mani, a beautiful heap of stones that are carved with Avalokiteshvara's six-syllable Mani mantra, piled up like a mountain. It is said to liberate those who see it.[16] And there

I received the reading transmission from him for the *Sutra Designed like a Jewel Chest*. Meanwhile Khenpo Shenga had given me a Buddha Shakyamuni statue made of metal from East India;[17] Onpo Tenga's copy of essential instructions on the Great Perfection, *Resting in the Nature of Mind*; a manual on the development and completion stages of the Great Perfection with the chö practice from the *Heart Essence of the Great Expanse* cycle;[18] a book of Jamyang Khyentse Wangpo's spiritual songs with many notes in Onpo Tenga's hand; a handwritten copy of outlines of the major philosophical texts; a high quality Indian vajra and bell from Ngor Sharchen Migyur Gyaltsen that Khyentse Chökyi Lodro had given him; and an ivory small hand drum with a golden sash. He gave me all these things in confidence and requested me to visit him again to continue taking teachings from him.

That winter Khenpo Shenga vowed to stay in solitary retreat at Gyawopu for the rest of his life. Gyawopu is near Trö Ziltröm in Derge and was the meditation place of the Mahasiddha Thangtong Gyalpo's disciple Kunga Gyaltsen, who was a relative of the Derge king. But Khenpo Shenga said that it didn't feel right not to finish teaching me and told me to get there in the first month, on the anniversary of Onpo Tenga's death. He told my father, "You should a build a hermitage in this retreat place." Following his advice, I went to the Gyawopu retreat place that day and was welcomed by Khenpo Gelek Namgyal from Dzogchen Monastery and a procession of all the monks from the Shri Singha Monastic College.

When I entered his room, Khenpo Shenga washed my whole body with blessed water from the *Metsek* practice that he always did there in winter and gave me a full set of new clothes.[19] That day he did a very elaborate *Supreme Heruka Assembly* feast offering and placed me on a seat higher than his own.[20] He told whoever came to see him—high, low, learned, or noble—to go meet the reincarnation of his teacher. After Kunga Palden, a great renunciant yogi who was a close disciple of Onpo Tenga from Gemang, had given me a beautiful, large bronze mandala, including the rings and top ornament, I was put up in a yak-hair tent in a meadow, where I stayed.

Khenpo Shenga taught *The Words of My Perfect Teacher*, an explanation of the preliminaries of the *Heart Essence of the Great Expanse*, and when he reached the *bodhichitta* section,[21] he said it was traditional to give some teaching on the nature of mind in conjunction with absolute *bodhichitta*. When he asked us to observe what was the most important among body, speech, and mind, I answered, "Mind is the most important." Then he said, "Observe the nature of mind!" Near my yak-hair tent was a charming meadow below a rocky shelter where I sat and pretended to watch my mind a little. When the perception of identifying cognizant emptiness occurred, I told Khenpo Shenga about it. Later on, while my master Khenpo Shenga was talking to his Dharma friend Kunga Palden, a Dzogchen practitioner, both lamas said that my words were from former training and praised me as extraordinary. But I felt that the sudden thought of mind being cognizant emptiness might just be due to learning a little from the *madhyamaka* training I had done before and probably wasn't a recognition but just an experience of the all-ground consciousness.[22] By that time I had a servant and told him to bring me many white and black pebbles. Giving in to a few positive habitual tendencies, I decided that I should train as described in the life story of Brahmin Rahula.[23]

Whenever I went to see my teacher Khenpo Shenga, he used to give me things like the three sweets, and he would engage in cheerful conversation. In front of his residence was a flower garden and sometimes, in the afternoon, he would take me to play. There was a big rock in the front part of the garden where ground squirrels would always be scurrying about. Khenpo said, "Let's sit down here and throw some pebbles at the ground squirrels. Would you get some pebbles?" I went to gather the pebbles, but the stones I returned with were too big for the little squirrels and Khenpo asked me to bring some smaller ones. He began to lob his little pebbles gently at the ground squirrels. His pebbles would come very close to them, and they would all rush off. At one point he chuckled and said, "Maybe I am better at throwing these pebbles than you are!" I think he wanted to entertain me so that I wouldn't get bored with my studies. He also used to give me treats such as hard candies made with milk and a special kind of Tibetan vitamin that he made himself from many medicinal herbs.

He told us a story about Onpo Tenga walking the outer circuit of Dzogchen Monastery one day. When Onpo Tenga saw a tutor beating a novice monk, he said to Khenpo Shenga, who was his attendant, "After I die, they'll give my name to some child, saying it's my reincarnation, and a tutor without compassion will make that child miserable, just like that guy is doing." Then Khenpo Shenga explained, "Even though you were born as the favorite child in a powerful, wealthy, and high family, you are not spoiled. It makes me feel at ease that your brother trains you properly. I couldn't be severe and am not suitable to teach you anything."

Shechen Gyaltsap Pema Namgyal. Photograph by Matthieu Ricard.

Khenpo Shenga frequently said that from the monkey year, 1920, onward he would drop everything, not associate with anybody, and stay in solitary retreat. Even though he intended to do so, since he had named me the reincarnation of his root guru, hoping that I would uphold Onpo Tenga's teachings, he taught me the scriptures. His disciple, Dechi Tsangda Kyungram, was building a retreat house for Khenpo Shenga there, and when the hermitage was finished, complete with monastic offering utensils, Khenpo Shenga said to his Dharma friend Kunga Palden, "I've collected lots of offering tools at my retreat place. When Tulku is twenty years old, he'll either be a great teacher and it will be useful, or else he'll become a renunciate and by that time he'll let go of it."

After completing *The Words of My Perfect Teacher*, he taught the *Fundamental Treatise on the Middle Way*, the *Refutation of Criticism*, the *Seventy Verses on Emptiness*, the *Sixty Stanzas on Reasoning*, the *Finely Woven*, and the *Four Hundred Stanzas on Madhyamaka* one after the other, using the learned and noble Mewa Sonam Gonpo as his teaching assistant. I used to attend the feast gatherings on the tenth and twenty-fifth days of the lunar month. My brother Shedrup said, "It would be good to offer each of the clothes that the lamas gave you as presents to important teachers and ask them for spiritual protection, so you won't have obstacles in your life and Dharma practice." So I didn't even wear them once but gave them all to my teachers.

Left: The Sixth Shechen Rabjam. Shechen Archives. Photographer unknown.
Right: Shechen Kongtrül. Shechen Archives. Photographer unknown.

Khenpo Shenga's retreat house was a solitary place. Nearby was a snowy mountain range below which was a natural lofty rock mountain with a roaring waterfall. Due to constant dense fog, the sun was never visible and most of the summer rainfall would blend with snowfall, so the twigs on the ground were covered with dewdrops; yet I never felt depressed or bored. Khenpo Shenga had composed a song to the Lords of the Three Families, Guru Rinpoche, Tara, and all the Indian and Tibetan *panditas* and siddhas, which resembled a song for calling the guru from afar.[24] He said it was for laypeople to chant while circumambulating the stupa at Gatod Dzomnyak. Using this as an example, I wrote a whole sheet full of devotional verses, some of which related to each other and some of which had no relationship whatsoever. I often watched the wonderful presence of young wild sheep playfully dancing on the smooth rock surface of that secluded place. Occasionally, when it rained very hard, a continuous stream of water came down between the cliffs. Seeing all this, I felt like writing a praise to the site. I think I wrote that the cliffs were like deities of the pure regions and the streams like banners honoring them, but at that time I had not yet studied poetry and didn't know how to write in proper verse.

When one of my sisters died, I thought it might be an obstacle to my life.

Left: The Fifth Dzogchen Rinpoche, Thupten Chökyi Dorje.
Photographer unknown.

Right: Palpung Situ Rinpoche. Shechen Archives. Photographer unknown.

This suspicion caused me to dream that I went to a temple that was said to be the Trö Ziltröm Palace. Inside the temple was a lama wearing a lotus hat who gave me a long-life empowerment.[25] When I told my brother about the dream, he felt relieved.

I had a bowl with a silver lining that I got when I went home during the winter, and when Khenpo Shenga saw it, he said to me and my tutor, "Until you are fifteen years old, you can do whatever you like. When you reach the age of fifteen, you should only eat before noon and not have things like silver-lined bowls and decorated *malas*. Your whole lifestyle should be in accordance with the monastic discipline."

The Dharma king of Bhutan, Urgyen Wangchuk, sent five educated monks, including Tenpa Rinchen, to study with Khenpo Shenga. Together with them I received the oral transmission of a commentary written by Khenpo Shenga himself on Patrul Rinpoche's *Virtuous in the Beginning, Middle, and End*.

On my way home, I stopped at the Namdroling Zalung hermitage, where I met the renunciate Dharma lord Damchoe Rinchen and the Zurmang Trungpa Rinpoche, Karma Chökyi Nyinche, and received the *Gesar Longevity Blessing* that the latter had composed. I often thought I should constantly

Khyentse Chökyi Lodro, Situ Pema Wangchok, Khenpo Shenga, Khamche Khenpo. Photographer unknown.

endeavor in studying texts and so moved to Sakar Samdrupling, which was near the home of my parents and siblings. There was a new house at Samdrupling where, upstairs, Shedrup and I did a one-month retreat on Mipham Rinpoche's *Tantra System Kilaya*.[26]

I was very fond of stories and would specifically inquire about legends from all my elders. While listening to Milarepa's biography, when I heard how successfully he practiced black magic on his uncle and aunt, I stared and bit my lower lip. I often heard that Mipham Rinpoche liked subjugations, and it was customary at our home to have some selected Sakya lamas perform an annual *Kilaya* exorcist rite from the Khon tradition, along with rites for subjugating recurrent enemies, family deaths, and misfortune.[27] Because of that, I used to get together with lots of children my age and spend the evenings playing drums, cymbals, and thigh-bone trumpets while pretending to enact various rituals such as destroying the clay effigy of a malign torma, burning the torma, performing ceremonial dances, and so forth.

When I heard Drongpa Lama Tsewang Gyaltsen from Benchen and my brother Shedrup offer lots of praise to Vajrakilaya, I developed faith and became very fond of Kilaya. While I was in retreat, my young servant ran away, and even though I didn't know any of the other visualizations, I kept visualizing him being squashed under Kilaya's feet. He got into a lot of trouble because he lost his way, and his eyes got inflamed from the reflection of the sunlight off the snow, and so forth, and I felt proud thinking it was due to my power.

At home we annually performed the accumulation of a hundred thousand repetitions of the "Seven-Line Prayer," and I participated. Our shrine room had a three-foot tall Guru Rinpoche statue, and as I kept admiring it, I felt that his presence became so overwhelming that I ended up wondering if it wasn't Guru Rinpoche in person. Shortly after that, when I saw Mipham Rinpoche's *White Lotus Commentary* on the "Seven-Line Prayer" that Lama Ösel had carved onto woodblocks and saw the colophon that Gyaltsap Rinpoche had written, I found the words so inspiring that I was fascinated.

When I finished my retreat, we invited Bathur Khen Rinpoche from the Changma Hermitage in northern Dzachukha.[28] He was glad to come but wouldn't ride a horse, so he had a lot of trouble on the way due to snowfall and rain. From him I requested Maitreya's treatises of the *Two Ornaments,* the *Two Analyses,* and the *Unexcelled Continuity.* My brother Sangye Nyenpa received the explanation of Mipham's' detailed commentary on the *Ornament of the Middle Way.* By that time my elder brother fell ill with fever and dysentery, and every day Khenpo Shenga recited the *Metsek* cleansing and ransom ritual for him. Incidentally I asked Khenpo Shenga about the purpose of the vase, mantra thread, and vajra, to which he answered, "These symbolize the three vajras of the mandala deity: the vase is the body, the mantra thread is the speech, and the vajra is the mind."[29]

When my father had offered funds for the rainy season retreat at Sakar Monastery, Khenpo Shenga went there to start the summer retreat, and on my own initiative I promised to stay too. During the auspicious restoration and purification ceremony,[30] Patrul Rinpoche's *Praise to the Vinaya* was explained, and I too received this teaching. Shedrup and I spent the winter at a small hermitage doing the recitation of Mipham Rinpoche's guru yoga; the *Innermost Sealed Essence Guru Sadhana;* and the *Secret Assembly Longevity Practice.* At that time I met Khen Sochoe Rinpoche from Dzogchen Monastery, who was returning from a pilgrimage to Central Tibet and Tsang. He told me I had an obstacle coming and said he would remove it. He gave me the empowerments for the Three Roots of the *Heart Essence of the Great Expanse* and the empowerment and reading transmission for Do Khyentse's profound treasure *Self-Liberation of Clinging,* which Shedrup had requested. He also gave us sacred medicine that had been created at Crystal Cave.[31]

Usually my father only had faith in monastics and thought that ordained lamas and tulkus shouldn't use high seats or indulge in frivolous behavior such as singing folk songs. Since my father and brothers lived according to the *Vinaya,*[32] they became my spiritual teachers. I also believed in pure conduct and kept the three Dharma robes, the begging bowl, the sieve, and the water vessel by my side.[33] I memorized the verses of the monastic, bodhisattva, and tantric rules and used to chant them. I didn't like to watch performances, and when I think about it, I feel that it was extremely helpful that my father and brothers were my Dharma companions.

My brother Shedrup's personal deity was Sarasvati, and the omniscient Mipham Rinpoche had told him to have a white Sarasvati thangka painted as a samaya support. This thangka had been consecrated by Mipham Rinpoche and was hanging beside his bed, and one night when I went to sleep, I dreamed that Sarasvati herself appeared in the sky, surrounded by swirling five-colored rainbow lights.

That spring Lama Ösel, a renunciate from Dzogchen who had perfected the three ways to please his guru Mipham Rinpoche and who had trained in the four visions, gave us the transmission and explanation of Mipham Rinpoche's *Gateway to Knowledge.* We also had the privilege of receiving the reading transmissions for its "Summary Text" and "Table of Contents"; the *Collection of Hymns;* the general and specific *Sadhanas of the Eight Classes of Heruka;* the *Oral Instructions* cycle; the *Great Perfection* cycle; the commentary on the *Eight Sadhana Teachings,* and other texts.[34] Shedrup always told me how important it was to receive the omniscient Mipham Rinpoche's entire *Collected Works* from both the venerable Lama Ösel and Shechen Gyaltsap, so I was hoping to receive it.

On my way home from Dzogchen, I stopped at a place called Sara Monastery, where I went into retreat for about three months. Afterward I continued my journey and stopped at the Namgyaling Hermitage in Den to meet the highly learned and accomplished Damchoe Özer, heart son of the two Jamgön Dharma lords, who said, "It would be very good if you receive the *Nyingma Kahma,*" and while praising it, he insisted that I receive it.

3. Meeting My Root Teacher

THEY SAY THAT it is very important to have a spiritual friend as an example, and my brother Shedrup, confident that I would become a sublime being, told me, "You should follow an authentic great master and enrich yourself with the empowerments and transmissions of the kahma and terma.[1] With the qualities of study, reflection, and meditation, you should continue the example of the holy masters; and through learning, discipline, and goodness, you must be able to uphold the teachings." He also constantly instructed me how to do so, telling me, "They always say that the actions and behavior of Jamyang Khyentse, Mipham Rinpoche, Shechen Gyaltsap, and Gemang Khenpo Yonga were more remarkable than those of other doctrine holders. So now you need to enrich your mind by receiving the empowerments and teachings of the kahma and terma of the Nyingma tradition from Shechen Gyaltsap. It is important to get to the core of the practice like Mipham Rinpoche did—that's what's essential. Generally speaking there are many disciples of the three Jamgöns that are remarkably learned, disciplined, noble, and accomplished,[2] but among them Mipham Manjushri paid unusual attention to Shechen Gyaltsap. When he was about to pass away, his last will was to give all his books to Shechen Gyaltsap, considering him as exceptional. So you should rely on him as your root teacher."

At that time we were living in a tent with two servants, one of whom was a monk and an excellent long-distance walker, who was sent to Shechen with a letter asking Shechen Gyaltsap when it would be suitable to come for an audience. The supreme refuge, lord of the mandala, was seriously ill; and as he was getting older, he wasn't staying at his residence in the monastery at that time but was in retreat in a cave on the hill behind Shechen. This cave was a shrine room of the *Eight Commands: Union of the Sugatas,* and he lived there like a renunciate, free of all activity. He answered with a letter saying, "I am a sick old man, and, waiting for death, I have let go of all activities. If I eventually happen to recover from my illness, I'll try my best to perform the empowerments and teachings." When my brother got this news, he was quite happy and said, "Now we have accomplished something!"

My father had decided that I should definitely go and stay at Shechen Monastery with Gyaltsap Rinpoche. At that time my brother Sangye Nyenpa had just finished a three-year-and-three-month retreat, and he also wanted to meet Shechen Gyaltsap. So in the summer of the wood-mouse year, 1924, when I was fifteen years old, my brother Sangye Nyenpa, my tutor Shedrup, and I all went to Shechen in order to attend to the perfect realized master Gyaltsap Rinpoche, unique lord of the family, at Shechen Tennyi Dargyeling. We stayed in Gyaltsap Rinpoche's Immortal Lotus Heaven cabin at the Lotus Light retreat center, which was located between the monastery and his hermitage. The venerable master was staying in strict retreat within the boundary of his Chakrasamvara Hermitage.[3] He sent us two ceremonial scarves with his attendant monk Shingkyong and a message saying that, since Shedrup had met him previously, he could see him the next day. However, as this would be our first meeting, he would meet Sangye Nyenpa and me on an auspicious date about three days hence. I wanted to meet the master immediately, so those few days seemed like a long time.

When we arrived at his retreat quarters on the proper day, Shechen Gyaltsap was not wearing the usual monastic robes, but a yellow, fur-lined jacket. His hair came down to his shoulders and was curled at the ends. When I first saw his precious countenance, he was very cheerful and asked Sangye Nyenpa what major and minor teachings he had received, and so forth, talking about Dharma for a long time. While the attendant was serving tea and rice to teacher and pupils together, he asked Gyaltsap Rinpoche for his wooden bowl, to which he replied in jest, "This is my gem box!"

Before we left, I requested the transmission and explanations of Mipham Rinpoche's *Collected Works*. Shechen Gyaltsap was quite sick but said that if his health permitted, he would give us the empowerments and the transmissions of Mipham Rinpoche's *Collected Works*.

Khamgo, a senior attendant of my venerable master who was staying in the same place we were, told us, "In the past, after Vajradhara Khyentse Wangpo had given the complete cycle of *Vajrakilaya* empowerments from the orally transmitted and revealed treasure teachings, he told Gyaltsap Rinpoche, 'Since you are an emanation of master Prabhahasti and Langlab Changchub Dorje, when you go to Shechen you must do an intensive Kilaya retreat in your residence until you perfect all the signs, and then do the fire ceremony.'[4] In accordance with these words, Gyaltsap Rinpoche did retreat in the Barchung residence of the Shechen Hermitage. After one hundred days, although he hadn't completed the recitation due to illness, he had acquired all the signs and so performed the fire ceremony. It was then that he left his footprint on a rock near his door." Fearing that people would find out, he threw the stone far away, but Khamgo found the stone and placed it on his shrine. When I heard that story, I was overwhelmed with faith and felt even more confident in Shechen Gyaltsap than usual.

One day we received a message saying that we should visit Shechen Gyaltsap on a certain date. On the appointed day, we went to his quarters again and he said that day would mark the beginning of the teachings and empowerments. We began with the maturing empowerment of the Dharma king Terdak Lingpa's profound *Mindroling Vajrasattva* treasure, core of the ocean of great secret tantras. He gave it in full detail according to Jamgön Kongtrül's empowerment ritual, and the next day he gave an explanation of the root text. He also gave the auxiliary instructions and the reading transmission of the root volume. Then a disciple of the same Dharma lineage arrived and also requested the *Vajrasattva* empowerment; according to his humble request, Rinpoche gave it based on the empowerment manual by Gyaltsap Tenzin Chögyal. We also got the reading transmission for the empowerment manual, and I copied the text.

Gyaltsap Rinpoche's personal *yidam* deity was Guru Chowang's profound *Innermost Razor Kilaya* treasure,[5] for which he gave us the empowerment according to Jamgön Kongtrül's writings, including the instructions on the view. Then he gave us the instructions on his own *Words of the Vidyadharas* commentary on Kilaya, with the maturing empowerment. At the end he said that he had received the complete maturation and liberation from the two Jamgöns, and that by means of this personal deity he had attained a few signs of blessing. After that he gave us the empowerment of Khyentse Wangpo's profound *Quintessential Kilaya of the Hearing Lineage* treasure, with the explanation of the four daggers.[6] Then we had the privilege of receiving the reading transmissions for the *Ever Perfect Path of Bliss,* a Kilaya sadhana that he wrote; along with the *Kilaya Descent of Blessings;* the *Kilaya Ritual for Summoning Longevity;* the *Kilaya Ritual for Summoning Prosperity;* and so forth. He told

Shedrup, "It would be good to rely on these two revered *yidams*,"[7] and, following his words, I recited the daily practices.

Then we requested Shechen Kongtrül[8] for the life and heart of the Early Translation School—the major empowerment of the *Magical Display of the Peaceful and Wrathful Ones*; as well as the two *Dongtruk* empowerments; *Vishuddha* from the So tradition; the *United Assembly* empowerment connected with the nine gradual vehicles and its major empowerment of the main practice with the supportive teachings, along with the reading transmissions for the sadhana mandalas of the kahma.[9] Then we received the complete empowerments and reading transmissions of both the mind class and the space class of the Great Perfection;[10] the *Heart Essence of Vima*; the *Guru's Innermost Essence*; the *Heart Essence of the Dakinis*; the *Quintessence of the Dakinis*; and the *Profound Quintessence*.

Even though I didn't understand anything about the purpose of empowerment because I was still quite young and my intellect was immature, Shedrup always talked about mind essence and it really inspired me. While abiding in meditation during the fourth empowerment, my precious master directed his gaze and pointed his finger at me, asking, "What is mind?" I thought, "Such a great yogi, he has actually realized the ultimate nature!" and, feeling deep faith, I even got some idea about how to meditate.

Gyaltsap Rinpoche then gave us the reading transmissions for Mindroling Jetsun Migyur Paldron's *Excellent Path of Bliss*, a commentary on the *Heart Essence of Vima Unifying Mother and Son*, and the liturgy for the *Heart Essence of Vima* preliminaries written by Khyentse Wangpo. He also gave the complete empowerments and reading transmissions for the Three Root sadhanas of the *Heart Essence* and the *Wishing Vase*.[11] Then he gave the vase empowerment of Minling Terchen's [Terdak Lingpa's] *Embodiment of All the Sugatas* followed by the supreme three higher empowerments, the instructions of the *Profound Unsurpassable Meaning of the Great Perfection*, and the protector Tsokdak according to the Kham tradition of the kahma.[12] In particular, on the anniversary of the peerless Gampopa's passing, he gave us the bodhisattva vows according to both the Vast Activity tradition as well as the Profound Middle Way tradition.[13]

As my venerable master was quite old and his illness quite severe, he was not inclined to elaboration. But that day he wore the three Dharma robes with the *pandita* hat and was quite cheerful when he put on Khyentse Wangpo's hat.[14] From that day on my brother Sangye Nyenpa kept offering our precious master the three whites [curd, milk, and butter] and the three sweets [sugar, molasses, and honey]. My brother said that we were extremely fortunate to receive the bodhisattva vows from such a great bodhisattva and should develop faith and inspiration, and he specifically advised me to take the bodhisattva vow every morning without interruption from that day onward.

On the tenth day of the monkey month, the fifth Tibetan month, an elaborate intensive sadhana with sacred dances was performed at Shechen Tennyi Dargyeling, and as the Fifth Dzogchen Rinpoche came to watch the dances, I had the opportunity to meet him.

In addition to receiving teachings from my master, Shechen Gyaltsap, I memorized the Guhyagarbha root tantra. I had not studied any Vajrayana texts prior to this, so I didn't understand it and had a little trouble remembering it, but in the end I became familiar with the words.

I don't remember the exact time, but in the early morning of an auspicious day, all of us, Shechen Gyaltsap and students, together chanted the *Auspicious Manjushri Offering* liturgy in preparation for the reading transmission of the *Collected Works* of Mipham Rinpoche, lord of inherent wisdom and compassion, in order to resound the lion's roar of the supreme vehicle in the Dark Age. To give the reading transmission, he used the Ka, Kha, and Ga volumes of the long printing blocks and the OM A RA PA TSA NA DHI volumes of the medium printing blocks from the Lhundrup Teng Printing Press in Derge.[15] From the Dzogchen Monastery prints Gyaltsap Rinpoche gave us the transmissions of the *Ketaka* commentary on the wisdom chapter of *The Way of the Bodhisattva*; the *Commentary on Valid Cognition*; the *General Meaning of the Secret Essence: Core of Luminosity*; the lineage supplication; Mipham Rinpoche's analysis of the detailed *Wish-Fulfilling Treasury* commentary; the word-for-word commentary on the eighteenth chapter; the tenets, table of contents, and the detailed explanation of the *Commentary on Valid Cognition*.

From the Lakar prints we received the *Shakyamuni Liturgy* and the *White Lotus Supportive Teaching*. From the Shechen prints we received the *Medicine Buddha Worship Liturgy;* from the Katok prints, the commentary on the *Secret Vishuddha Manual;* from the Dzongsar prints, the *Collection of Hymns,* the cycle of sadhanas, the cycle of advice, the *Profound Instruction* cycle, the *Completion Stage* cycle, the *Great Perfection* cycle, the *Prayer* cycle, and the *White Lotus Commentary* on the "Seven-Line Prayer." Then my precious master gave us the reading transmission of his compilation of teachings on natural mind, its analysis, and the difficult points of the common philosophical scriptures.

Looking through the texts that had not been printed, he gave us the complete reading transmissions for the special sadhanas of *Marici Goddess* and *Kurukulle;* the *Torma of the Four Elements* with its application; the chart for doing divination through *Arapatsa;* the peaceful *Vajrasattva* fire ceremony; the enriching *Mahottara* fire ceremony; the magnetizing *Hayagriva* fire ceremony; the wrathful *Yamantaka* fire ceremony; and the *Vajrakilaya* fire ceremony for all activities.[16] He also gave us the entire reading transmission for the *Pure Gold Great Perfection* cycle and so forth.

When my master started the reading transmission of Mipham Rinpoche's commentary on the invincible Maitreya's *Two Analyses,* I was still a child with immature understanding, but hearing the amazing words of his *Auspicious Offering Ceremony* instilled faith and inspiration in me.[17] My elder brother Sangye Nyenpa copied the text immediately, and due to that, while searching through my master's writings, we coincidentally received the reading transmissions of the *Offering Ceremony of the Thousand Buddhas of the Good Aeon;* the *Mending-Purification of the Three Vows;* the *White Manjushri* according to the Mati tradition; the *White Sarasvati* sadhana with the recitation manual; and the recitation manual of the great scholar Manjushri Lodro Thaye's secret treasure *Innermost Trolo Sadhana Subduing All Evil.*[18] Inspired by that incident, an exceptional confident faith dawned in me, and from then on, before doing anything important, I have always recited the *Auspicious Offering Ceremony.* At that time Sangye Nyenpa also received the reading transmissions for the *Profound Inner Topics;* the *Two Segments;* and the *Unexcelled Continuity,* along with two minor texts for which he had received the root text from Lama Kewang Trapel from Palpung Monastery.

Offering my master about ten sheets of saffron-soaked paper, two pens, and a silk scarf, I requested some oral advice and then memorized all the words of the essential instructions he gave. Reciting them by heart each day, I felt I should act accordingly, and deliberately kept them in mind. My father had gone to visit Jigmey Gyalwai Myugu's remains in the Dzachuka region, as well as Changma Khen Rinpoche, Gemang Monastery, Kilung Monastery, and other places, and he arrived at Shechen when the teachings were nearly finished. Shechen Gyaltsap kindly gave him teachings on the *Perfect Honey Vase,* his own detailed guidebook on the *Seven-Point Mind Training,* as well as the essential instructions on *Finding Rest from Illusion.*[19] At the end of our teachings and empowerments, we did a three-day thanksgiving offering according to the longevity practice revealed by Ratna Lingpa. Shechen

Gyaltsap also performed the short and the elaborate empowerments of the same cycle of rediscovered teachings, the *Secret Assembly Longevity Practice.*

I went to see Shechen Gyaltsap Rinpoche quite often after that. He was fond of children and he seemed to enjoy joking with me whenever I went there. He was always gentle, considerate, and soft-spoken. During empowerments and at other occasions, he would make a point to play with the young tulkus and monks and tell them stories.

STUDIES OF GRAMMAR AND POETRY

Then we went to Rudam Dzogchen Monastery where we made offerings to Khenchen Losal's precious reliquary, which was concealed in the mountain. From Gemang Rinpoche we received the *Amitayus Sutra* as a Dharma connection, and Sangye Nyenpa and I received gifts of body, speech, and mind representations.[20] I met the Fifth Dzogchen Rinpoche, who was a great siddha, from whom I received a long-life empowerment one hundred times and the transmission of a Vajrakilaya tantra.

I also went to the Dzogchen Monastic College, where I received the *Amitayus Sutra* transmission again and met Khenpo Lhakong, who had come to take care of his nephew's funeral rites. I received the transmission of the *Three Lines That Strike the Vital Point* from him. He also presented me with a copy of the text and joked a lot with me; I liked him very much. After Dzogchen I went to Karling Monastery where the famous hermit called Kunga Palden lived, and from him I received the longevity blessing from the *Gathering of the Vidyadharas.* After that I returned to Gyawopu and Khenpo Shenga gave me this teaching again.

Then we went to Palpung Thupten Chokor Ling and stayed in the Alo Dilgo monks' quarters, where my uncle Lama Tradon from Palpung very lovingly took care of me. He gave me a set of new clothes and an antique cup in a case. He had a summer cottage where he put us up for studies.

It seemed that Situ Rinpoche was going to be in retreat for three years and would not be able to see us at all. He was a good scholar and had received the teachings contained in the thirteen major Indian philosophical texts from Khenpo Shenga. Situ Rinpoche told us to wait until the New Year when he would interrupt his retreat so we could meet him. We were also invited to stay after the New Year to see the dances and the tenth-day festival dedicated to Padmasambhava. So my uncle Tradon requested the senior chant master, called Tenzin Dorje, who had been one of Jamgön Kongtrül's close disciples, to teach me the five traditional sciences, including grammar and poetry.[21]

Tenzin Dorje possessed the qualities of knowledge and realization, and was doing retreat on the *Wrathful Guru Ablaze with Wisdom* for the general stability of the Kagyu doctrine in the monastery. We visited him in retreat and he gave us detailed explanations on grammar and spelling based on the *Perfect Vision of Elegant Description* commentary. He said that he had studied grammar with Jamyang Lekpai Lodro, also called Tsering Tashi, who had been Khyentse Wangpo's secretary. He said that his way of teaching the three tenses, verb, subject, object, and so forth, was based on the oral instructions of his teacher.

Situ Rinpoche had a secretary who was extremely skilled in spelling, and even though he tested me a lot, there were only one or two questions that I couldn't answer. He said that my level of education was very high and that he really appreciated it.

Even though Sangye Nyenpa had already studied the subject before, he took the teaching again and said that most of the examples were excellent. Tenzin Dorje also taught the *Lamp of Speech Grammar* and the *Detailed Analysis of Suffixes*. Then he gave detailed teachings on all three chapters of the *Mirror of Poetry*, using the principal commentary by Dokhampa Chökyi Nyima, who was the heart son of Jamgön Chöjung, and his equal.[22] I borrowed the analogies that my teacher had written in conjunction with White Tara, using examples of the thirty-five ornaments of meaning and giving examples of synonyms, and studied them. Then I took examination in composition. Tenzin Dorje said that because I had studied a little inner science before, I was already quite knowledgeable. The omniscient Jigmey Lingpa and Khyentse Wangpo's collection of spiritual songs and hymns especially suited my temperament, and I studied them in great detail. Any praise or prayer to Jigmey Lingpa that I wanted to write would quickly occur in my mind and was quite easy to compose. When we reached the middle chapter, my teacher gave me many compliments in verse about my vast insight in writing examples. He said that in general, having studied the *Mirror of Poetry*, each person's composition would be in accordance with their own character and not according to the rules of poetry. Tenzin Dorje was happy about my progress, and he really wanted me to stay there after completing my studies, but my father wouldn't consent to this.

Preceded by teachings on the Shechen secretary's *Fivefold Science of Language*,[23] Tenzin Dorje gave a detailed explanation of the complete Kalapa and

Tika language texts. He said he had received these from Lama Sherab Özer of Peyul, who was a student of Khyentse Wangpo's secretary, Tsering Tashi, living at Dzongsar. He kept saying that I had properly mastered the language patterns, but that nowadays it was very rare to understand language theory. He said that those who had understood language theory were beings like the past translators and the two Jamgön lamas.

Sangye Nyenpa had studied poetry before, so his compositions were good. While he was studying it once more together with me, imitating the composition technique of his writings proved to be very helpful for me. When Sangye Nyenpa composed a traditional Tibetan acrostic to Mipham Rinpoche by means of the ten topics of learnedness and the four types of right discrimination, I also wrote an acrostic by means of the eight great treasuries of courageous eloquence and the four types of right discrimination.[24]

Sangye Nyenpa tutored me, correcting my writing and training me. We took examination with the learned Lama Trapel, heart son of the two Jamgön Rinpoches, and, needless to say, Sangye Nyenpa's test was excellent. As for my own, our examiner said, "The younger tulku's poetry presentation is certainly excellent," and gave me back the composition scroll adorned with a silk scarf. When Sangye Nyenpa went to see the learned Lama Trapel as he was about to pass away, Lama Trapel had his attendant write down the names of his teachers in big letters and put it where he could see it. He said, "This is to remind me of my teachers." After Lama Trapel passed away, Sangye Nyenpa took this list and it turned out to be the *Heart Essence of Chetsun* lineage. When I wrote a praise to the omniscient Jigmey Lingpa, it turned out to be the best of all my compositions from that time. I showed it to several great khenpos who said the writing was very good, and when they showed it to others, I heard a lot of flattering words.

During the fourth month, Gyalsey Chöktrul came to preside over the drupchen of the *Secret Gathering of Avalokiteshvara*, a treasure of Ratna Lingpa. I met Gyalsey Chöktrul and also had the privilege of receiving the essential *Secret Gathering of Avalokiteshvara* empowerment. In the fifth month, when the Prince of Derge, the Central Tibetan official Trethong, and all the Derge ministers, came to attend the tenth-day festival at Palpung Monastery, Khyentse Chökyi Lodro, Lord of the Ocean of Teachings in Tibet, came to Palpung. That is when I first met him, and I felt a natural, genuine faith and affection, like a son meeting his father. While talking with me, he said that before long he would go to receive the *Treasury of Spiritual Instructions* empowerments and transmissions from Shechen Gyaltsap Rinpoche.

Each incarnation of Palpung Situ Rinpoche expected a lama from the Dilgo family to serve and support the establishment of the teachings in a religious and political way, which was a good system that had remained uninterrupted. On New Year's Day of the wood-mouse year, 1924, I met Situ Pema Wangchok, and whenever I went to see him, he always gave me presents of fruits, the required Chinese brocade boots that lamas wore, and other things. When my brother Shedrup and I had to leave for Shechen, he sent four pack animals and two servants. He always gave us whatever provisions we needed and was extremely kind.

When I heard that Khyentse Chökyi Lodro had decided to leave to take the *Treasury of Spiritual Instructions* from Gyaltsap Rinpoche, I went to see him and inquired about the empowerments. As he confirmed the news, we requested leave from Palpung Situ. Situ Rinpoche, however, wanted my brother Sangye Nyenpa to stay with him, as it was traditional for a man from Denkok to share in the monastic life at Palpung, but he gave leave to Shedrup and me. He most kindly provided us with several *dzo* and yaks, all our provisions, and many other things. We reached Shechen some days before Khyentse Chökyi Lodro arrived, and went to meet Gyaltsap Rinpoche. At the Shechen Lotus Light retreat center we stayed in the Barchung Lama residence and had the great fortune to spend time with Shechen Gyaltsap and receive the nectar of his guidance. I asked him to check my newly composed acrostic and a praise to Mipham Rinpoche, and he reviewed them closely for a few days. One day he said that it was very good that I had studied and trained so extensively and that my writings were also excellent; smiling, he then put an auspicious silk scarf around my neck. When my brother Shedrup said, "Rinpoche, instead of praising and putting scarves around his neck, please be so kind as to show us how to improve his compositions"; Gyaltsap Rinpoche answered that my literary work was really good and that my poetry would become excellent.

RECEIVING NOVICE VOWS FROM SHECHEN GYALTSAP

Previously I had received novice vows from Khenpo Shenga, whose beneficial qualities of steadfast discipline and learning were peerless. But since his precept lineage was the upper lineage of *Vinaya* and this period coincided with my revered master Shechen Gyaltsap giving novice vows to a number of people,[25] my brother Shedrup asked permission for me to receive them again, to which Gyaltsap Rinpoche kindly agreed.

So I received the lower *Vinaya* ordination from Gyaltsap Rinpoche, together with Shechen Gönto Chöktrul, and my master's nephew Khenchen Lodro Rabsel. In the Chakrasamvara Hermitage, our novice vows were established as real by a gathering of five: my revered master Shechen Gyaltsap, the unique heir of the Sakyas; Shechen Kongtrül; Shechen Khenpo Gyurmey Loden, and the assistant preceptors. My abbot, Shechen Gyaltsap had received the vows from Khenchen Pema Vajra from Dzogchen, who was also called Pema Damchoe Özer and was the heart son of Gyalsey Shenpen Thaye, the Single Eye of the Doctrine from Amdo.

Because he used to get seriously ill from obscurations, my master wore a metal ring, made from a knife that caused sudden death, on the ring finger of his left hand for protection.[26] When I went to see him that morning, he said, "Today this old monk also needs the *Vinaya*," and removing the metal ring from his finger, he put it in a bowl in front of him.[27] Though he was a perfect monk, he said that he had damaged many precepts.

While my master was getting dressed, Shedrup asked if I had to give back the novice vows I had taken before, and his answer was, "There are two views according to the greater and lesser vehicles, respectively. According to the Mahayana, when developing the mind set on supreme enlightenment for the twofold purpose of benefiting oneself and others, it is not necessary to give back the vows, just like one may put several layers of gold upon a stupa." Gonto Chöktrul received the name Gyurmey Shedrup Gyaltsen; Khenpo Lodro Rabsel received the name Gyurmey Thupten Gyaltsen, and I received the name Gyurmey Labsum Gyaltsen. I also had the privilege of receiving the expository transmission of the general tantric preliminaries composed by my master, the *Guide to Liberation: Oral Advice of the Omniscient One;* and the *Tantra of the Definitive Meaning* with its summary.

THE TREASURY OF SPIRITUAL INSTRUCTIONS

Soon after that the omniscient Khyentse Chökyi Lodro arrived. He was welcomed by the Shechen monks assembly who went to meet him by horse. While he was approaching the monastic community, they played musical instruments, and when he arrived at Shechen Kongtrül's quarters at the Lotus Light retreat center, he was greeted with various types of incense and blowing horns. After having tea and rice, he was put up at Rabjam Rinpoche's quarters, which were near my revered master's apartment. Khyentse Chökyi Lodro had been invited by Khenchen Wangdu to perform the enthronement of a *khenpo* from Ngor, but he said he didn't want to perform the enthronement and took the *Treasury of Spiritual Instructions* from Gyaltsap Rinpoche instead.

Khyentse Chökyi Lodro had told Gyaltsap Rinpoche, "I have met this child before and feel strongly that he is an incarnation of Jamyang Khyentse Wangpo. It is very good that you are now taking care of him. I will also do whatever I can to serve him. I beseech you to give him the transmission of the *Treasury of Spiritual Instructions* and the *Four Parts of the Heart Essence*. In the future I shall also offer him the transmission of the *Treasury of Precious Termas*."[28]

To the entire faithful gathering that had specially come for maturation and liberation, Gyaltsap Rinpoche then gave a detailed explanation about the need and purpose of the great *Treasury of Spiritual Instructions*[29] compilation from the eight great chariots of the Practice Lineage by the omniscient Khyentse Wangpo and the Dharma king Jamgön Kongtrül, who were like sun and moon.[30] He also explained the authentic lineage of Shechen Gyaltsap, the perfect master himself, universal lord of the mandala, and taught about the right attitude and conduct for receiving the teachings. He explained that the *Treasury of Spiritual Instructions* was only for khenpos and serious practitioners, and he wouldn't see anyone else. So he wrote down the names of those who could take the empowerments, and we put up a sign to mark the boundaries.

On a special day, I don't remember exactly when, we did the amending and averting ritual from Ratna Lingpa's *Secret Vajrakilaya* sadhana to eliminate obstacles. For two days we did the elaborate *Ocean of Accomplishment* according to the Mindroling tradition with elaborate chanting and music. Preceded by the elaborate *Spontaneous Fulfillment of Wishes* offering liturgy and the *Tara* liturgy, the teachings started on an auspicious day with the reading transmission of the list of contents, called the "Auspicious Banner of Fame." My precious master then put on his Dharma robe and started with the Kadam teachings. Over a period of three months my precious master gave the empowerments for the *Treasury of Spiritual Instructions* at his retreat place to about twenty people. I had the good fortune to receive the entire maturation and liberation, from the beginning of the threefold guidance on the *Parting from the Four Attachments* mind training up to the *Three Classes of the Great Perfection.*[31]

During the chö empowerments from the *Treasury of Spiritual Instructions,* Khyentse Chökyi Lodro couldn't blow the thigh-bone trumpet very well and neither could I. Sotar, a student of Özer Dongnak, who in turn had been a disciple of Patrul Rinpoche, used to sit near me. He spent most of his time in solitary places doing chö practice and blew the trumpet very well, but Gyaltsap Rinpoche's ritual master thought that he was showing off.

Generally speaking, my teacher Shechen Gyaltsap appeared to genuinely possess all the qualifications of a master that are taught in the sutras and tantras, and he was especially grounded in the experience of the highest view of the Great Perfection as it is. Subsequently, when I studied, reflected, and pretended to teach these aspects, I felt that having the good fortune to actually receive such a golden doctrine like a wish-fulfilling gem from my precious master, the perfect Buddha, made gaining a human birth worthwhile, and I felt even more devoted and inspired than usual. Even nowadays, while pretending to teach these aspects, I keep my precious master in mind and feign to invoke him to make the exposition and study meaningful.

My master gave the permission blessing for the Shangpa Kagyu protector Nyingzhug and the yaksha Kshetrapala as a secret teaching to the two Jamgön Chöktruls who were like sun and moon, to Gontoe Tulku, the retreat master Kardrup, and some more of us.[32] While performing the feast offering of the Shangpa Kagyu liturgy of guru worship, they sang the spontaneous spiritual songs of Jamgön Kongtrül, the Lord of Secrets, with a joyful expression.[33] Khyentse Chökyi Lodro had given my master a monkey skull lined with silver, which my master gave to me. When the retreat master, Kardrup, requested the method of visualizing the wisdom protector inside the central channel at one's heart, Gyaltsap Rinpoche, with a smiling expression, gave a detailed explanation on the symbolism, meaning, and reason of the central channel with many quotations from tantras. When the teachings were finished, Shedrup said as we were going back home, "When you teach, I hope you'll be able to teach like Rinpoche did today."

During a break between the teachings, Shechen Kongtrül said that he had previously received some teaching on poetry that wasn't finished and wanted me to explain the remaining middle chapter to him. My brother Shedrup said to Gyaltsap Rinpoche, "Since my brother doesn't know anything about the meaning of difficult points in poetry, it wouldn't be appropriate for him to teach poetry to Kongtrül Rinpoche. So what should we do?" Gyaltsap Rinpoche replied that just the same, it would be good to obey and teach Shechen Kongtrül, so I explained whatever I knew from the middle chapter.

I was naturally disposed to inquiring about and exploring in detail how to do the liturgies and make the specific tormas. So during that time I kept requesting Shechen Kongtrül and my venerable master's shrine attendant, Jamyang Losel, a great practitioner, for their kind direct and indirect instructions on how to make tormas, perform the rituals, and so forth.

Gyaltsap Rinpoche was in the process of establishing a monastic school at Shechen, and on one astrologically favorable day, he said they should hold the opening ceremony. For a few days Khyentse Chökyi Lodro gave elaborate teachings based on a commentary written by Khyentse Wangpo on *Chanting the Names of Manjushri,* and together with Shechen Kongtrül, Gontoe Chöktrul, Gyaltsap Rinpoche's nephew Khenchen Lodro Rabsel, and Khenpo Phakang, it was attended by all the participants of the *Treasury of Spiritual Instructions.* Later they all became unrivaled practitioners of sutra, tantra, and science, endowed with learning, discipline, and goodness.

Through the kindness of a chant master from Ba Lingkar, who requested Shechen Kongtrül for the reading transmission of the great tertön Dharma king Gyurmey Dorje's entire *Collected Works* and the essential empowerment from Jamgön Tennyi Lingpa's profound *Embodiment of Realization of the Three Roots* treasure, I was able to receive these as well. Owing to the request of Kardrup, the retreat master from Tsatsa Monastery, I received the blessing empowerment of the eight close sons from Khyentse Chökyi Lodro.[34] And due to the request of another faithful disciple, I also received the *Supreme Heruka Assembly* empowerment from the *Heart Essence of the Great Expanse* and the *Kilaya Subjugating the Hordes of Mara* empowerment. These were my first Dharma connections with Khyentse Chökyi Lodro.

At intervals, when the revered master Gyaltsap Rinpoche was a little sick, he would listen to Khyentse Chökyi Lodro giving the reading transmission for the five volumes of Tsele Natsok Rangdrol's *Collected Works,* three volumes of Indian scriptures on Mahamudra, sections of the *Openness of Realization Tantra,* one volume of Dorje Lingpa's *Cycle of Hung Heart Essence,* and a collection of texts from the *Heart Essence of the Vidyadharas.* I also had the good fortune to receive all of these at that time. Due to Khyentse Chökyi

Lodro's extraordinary affection for me, he would invite me to stay to have lunch with him during heavy rain, since my lodgings were quite far away from where the teachings were held. As a Dharma connection, he asked me to give him the reading transmission for the *Collected Works* of Mipham Rinpoche, the *Important Notes on the Four Tantras,* and some other texts, which I did. While receiving the teachings, he would do things like let me read the text together with him. At such times, the sun of his extreme kindness dawned on me.

Generally speaking, all the people that received the teachings during that time were learned and righteous wise beings, so while the Vajradhara Shechen Gyaltsap was preparing the empowerment, the two Jamgön Chök-truls would give teachings, and other disciples would accumulate a hundred thousand prostrations or meditate on Mahamudra and the Great Perfection. The two Chöktruls and others would exchange their compositions. One day, while engaged in proper teaching, debating, and writing, Gyaltsap Rinpoche, the lord of the mandala, said that in view of the behavior of the Jamgöns, through interdependent connections, in the future their explanation, debate, and composition would be like that which once flourished at glorious Nalanda.[35]

During a break, when I met my venerable master on his way to the toilet, he smiled, took my hand in his, and (referring to my taking of a consort in the future) jokingly said, "Bees wait to unite on unopened flowers!" all the while caressing my head with his hand.[36] Though I was still a child at that time, I had confident faith in my master, and since I wasn't involved in any such behavior at that time, I wondered what he meant. I got quite worried, assuming that through his wisdom he might see that in the future I would become a wicked old grandpa.

Whenever my precious master would give a profound empowerment, his face was resplendent. On one occasion, while directing his gaze and pointing his finger toward me during the pointing-out instruction, I felt that due to my limited devotion, I saw my master as a human being while in fact he was Guru Padmasambhava, the Second Buddha, from Uddiyana, giving empower-ments to his twenty-five main disciples. Quite often I believed that there was no difference of high or low in the realizations of the view of Padmasambhava and my master, and I supplicated my master accordingly. My brother Shed-rup kept talking about Mipham Rinpoche's life story, and Sangye Nyenpa also faithfully spoke of nothing but the great qualities of my tutors. Due to hearing such things, I felt faith and devotion toward all my spiritual friends and apparently knew how to see whatever they did to be nothing but good.

While I was reading a set of instructions that my precious master wrote on this topic of devotion to the guru, I came across a verse that he had written to the omniscient Mipham Rinpoche, praising him as having realized the essential meaning of the profound and vast sutra and tantra teachings of the eight great chariots of the practice lineage. Mipham Rinpoche had written an answer in verse. After reading this, I was inspired to write about ten verses that were like an offering of my realization, and when I showed it to my master, he was pleased to receive it. But when I thoroughly inspected it later, they weren't even words of experiencing the nature of the mind, let alone realization. Generally speaking, since I was a member of a noble family and had a tulku title, the lamas that guided me had nothing but affection for me and never scolded me or exposed my hidden flaws, so I turned out to be exceedingly conceited and pretentious. Wondering if my precious master was utterly unconcerned about this, afterward I felt terrified. Although it would have been appropriate to add these verses here, I made the mistake of losing them.

Khyentse Chökyi Lodrö performed the *Liberation with a Golden Key* rite for averting curses for my revered master, and I had the privilege of receiving it too.[37] When Dharmamati offered my revered master the empowerment for Mipham Rinpoche's *Red Manjushri,* which increases wealth and life span and is a combined empowerment of Sangye Lingpa and Dudul Dorje based on Mipham Rinpoche's writings, I had the good fortune of receiving it as well.

At that time my revered master was having a set of his own writings, the *Collection of Advice,* carved into woodblocks and told me to correct and supervise the carving, so I read it thoroughly. When I read the *Ornament of Renunciation,* a reminder to stay in seclusion, it transformed my perception and made me wish to give up all mundane concerns of this life and stay in solitude like my precious master to realize the Great Perfection. This idea became irreversible and often arose in my mind as I repeatedly read the text with faith and yearning while sitting on a patch of dry grass on the mountain slope, so I wondered if perhaps it was a habitual tendency of the past. I also wrote many scattered songs, both relevant and irrelevant, and offered the reading transmission of selected works from Mipham Rinpoche's *Collected Works* to Khyentse Chökyi Lodrö.

4. My Enthronement

AT SOME POINT during the teachings, Khyentse Chökyi Lodro had to attend the enthronement of the Lingkar Prince at Kyisoyak, at the confuence of three valleys where King Gesar of Ling was born, and when I went to see him off, he gave me his own handwritten copy of the line of masters who held the transmission for the condensed *Prajnaparamita*. Meanwhile, I had some blood-pressure trouble and asked Gyaltsap Rinpoche for a blessing to get rid of obstacles. Gyaltsap Rinpoche placed a ritual dagger on my head and put his thumb and then his foot on my heart. He then asked me to come to his retreat place again.

During a break when my master was giving Khyentse Chökyi Lodro a record of Manjushrimitra's short and long transmission lineage, in the early morning of an astrologically auspicious day, he asked me to come to his unsurpassed Chakrasamvara Hermitage. When I arrived, Shechen Kongtrül, who was very young at that time, welcomed me at the entrance of the cabin with a silk scarf and a variety of incense, and as soon as I stepped inside, they put me on a throne with four piled-up cushions and a white carpet with a vajra and swastika design. There were only a few people in the room.

Preceded by a purification and cleansing ritual according to the liturgy for enthroning tulkus written by my master, the ceremony for longevity and the enthronement itself were elaborately performed by means of Minling Terchen's *Profound Teaching on the Essence of Immortality* from our own tradition. After that, when Gyaltsap Rinpoche personally read the list of things to be offered, he mentioned that I was the reincarnation of Jamyang Khyentse Wangpo and described how my father had offered me to him. He then recited my name, Gyurmey Tekchok Tenpei Gyaltsen, "Immutable Victory Banner of the Supreme Vehicle," with a prayer in verse for the stability of my life.

As a body support he gave me a priceless blessed statue of Buddha Shak-yamuni made of metal from East India, which Mipham Rinpoche had given him when he gave him the explanation on *Gateway to Knowledge* in the Small Forest Hermitage at Dzogchen.[1] As a speech support he gave me the root text of the precious *Wish-Fulfilling Treasury* with Mipham Rinpoche's hand-written annotations. As a mind support he gave me an Indian vajra and bell imbued with Mipham Rinpoche's blessings from his personal use. As a qual-ity support he gave me Mipham Rinpoche's silver grain container that he used throughout his life; and as an activity support he gave me Mipham Rin-poche's skull hand drum decorated with gems and a silk tassel, and a maroon-colored square seal made of gilded metal, as well as horses, gems, and many other articles.[2]

Then he presented me with a certificate that he had composed in verse, installing me as a doctrine holder of Shechen Tennyi Dargyeling; holder of the three Dharma lineages of So, Zur, and Nub—lords of the kahma and terma, the essence of the Early Translation School; holder of the teachings of Lord Pandita and his brother;[3] of the omniscient father and son; of the Minling brothers; the two Jamgön Dharma kings—masters of the Buddha Shakyamuni's entire doctrine; and of Mipham Rinpoche, spiritual guide of the supreme vehicle. The certificate also said that if I would benefit the doc-trine and sentient beings through teaching, practice, and activity with the twelvefold good conduct according to my master's advice, his actions of this life would be accomplished and his wishes would be fulfilled. It also men-tioned that the masters, the Three Jewels, the Three Roots, and the protectors needed to perform enlightened actions, and that good celestial and human beings should turn all directions and times into virtue like beating the auspi-cious victory drum.

While sitting on the throne, it occurred to me that since I was enthroned as the reincarnation of Khyentse Wangpo, I should remember my past lives. As I pondered this, I remembered a mountain rock cavern that had a young tree in front with thick foliage, where the sun and moon could be seen in the sky from the opening in between. This image clearly appeared in my mind, but I didn't tell anyone about it. Later in my life I visited Yangleshö in Nepal and discovered that, for whatever reason, this was the very place I had seen in my vision.[4]

My master told Shedrup that we should return home and come back later to stay at his hermitage. He said it would be good to do a *Vajrakilaya* retreat, and as he was giving the empowerment and instructions based on the recitation manual to a fellow practitioner, I had the privilege of receiving them again. Shedrup told me to request some mind teachings, so Gyaltsap Rinpoche gave me vast and profound instructions. Later on, whenever receiving oral instructions on the Great Perfection from the *Seven Treasuries* or other texts, I clearly remembered those all-pervasive words from the primordial lord. When I told him that my mind was empty and aware, he told me to relax in that state.

One day while Khyentse Chökyi Lodro and I were having a meal together after he had returned, he told me what he had said about me to Ngor Loter Wangpo and his secretary Onto Khen Khyenrab. He gave me a detailed account about why they truly believed that I was the reincarnation of Khyentse Wangpo and their conversation about it. Loter Wangpo had sent a letter saying that I was Jamyang Khyentse Wangpo's tulku, and accordingly Gyaltsap Rinpoche gave me the name, Immutable Victory Banner of the Supreme Vehicle.

As Gyaltsap Rinpoche had made it public, Khyentse Chökyi Lodro also said, "From now on, when you and your brother come to Dzongsar, you can stay in the Khyentse lama residence. I feel that I should give you the reading transmission for the *Hundred Thousand Nyingma Tantras* and the empowerments and transmissions of the *Compendium of Sadhanas*."[5] He cared for me with great kindness and gave me a silver mandala with the sacred objects symbolizing enlightened body, speech, and mind, and a dotsey of Chinese silver.[6] He also lent me the revered Gyaltsap Rinpoche's manuscript on natural mind that he had always kept with him.

I gave back the presents of horses and goods that Gyaltsap Rinpoche had given me earlier, and Shedrup told him, "If Tulku is capable of keeping pure discipline and serving the doctrine, since he has no master other than you, he will obey whatever you say." Then we went to Palpung. Because Situ Rinpoche was not feeling very well, Sangye Nyenpa stayed there for a while. My brother and I received presents of a gilded vajra and bell and other things, and then headed home accompanied by the Dharma lord Dulmo Chöktrul from Damkar.

I continued to receive teachings from Shechen Gyaltsap intermittently for about five years. I didn't stay at the monastery itself; my quarters were always at the retreat center, about twenty minutes' walk above the monastery. It was there that I received all the teachings I have already mentioned. My father was a very straightforward person and never scolded me. When I was studying well, he was always very pleased and would give me fruits and small presents. If I went to gathering places, he would be displeased.

Around the time of my enthronement I had a tutor called Damchoe, who had a pure motivation and was very kind to me. He said he needed the *Quintessential Kilaya of the Hearing Lineage* empowerment and instructions; I had received the empowerment from the kind Gyaltsap Rinpoche, but there was no one to teach me how to do the empowerment ritual. I only had the *Quintessential Kilaya of the Hearing Lineage* daily practice and empowerment text, and I added the accumulation of merit, preparation, and conclusion from the *Profound Essence of Vishuddha* according to his need. When I think about it now, it seems like I didn't omit or add much. I boasted at random about the four daggers as explained in the outline.

Zurmang Trungpa Chökyi Nyinche also came and received Khyentse Wangpo's direct lineage of the great treasure revealer Dorje Lingpa's cycle of teachings from Lama Damchoe Özer. From Lingkar Jetsunma Jamyang Tsultrim Zangmo he received Jamgön Kongtrul's transmission lineage of the Lord of Secrets Taranatha's *Collected Works*. I went to see Trungpa Rinpoche to request a longevity blessing and received a Dharma connection of the *Gesar* longevity ritual that he wrote. On the way I also sought an audience with Lama Damchoe Rinpoche, who persistently told Shedrup that it would greatly benefit the doctrine and beings if I would do the recitation practices from the profound treasure cycle of Khyentse Wangpo and Jamgön Kongtrül.

Then we went home, and I started a *Vajrakilaya Innermost Razor* retreat. I consulted my master's oral instructions and the recitation manual, the *Kilaya* commentary, and Mipham Rinpoche's *Three Roots Recitation Manual*, and I kept the visualization as vivid as possible during my sessions. During breaks I studied the annotated commentaries with Shedrup, and though it was easy to teach and study as *khenpo* and student, my understanding didn't get to the bottom of it. Shedrup told me, "You must thoroughly know how to master both the words and meaning of the root text according to Patrul Rinpoche's tradition. So train in memorizing the root texts of the *Five Treatises of Lord Maitreya*, and especially look through Patrul Rinpoche's outline and word-for-word commentary on the *Prajnaparamita*." I had the annotated *Prajnaparamita* root text, outline, word-for-word commentary, and so forth, of

Lama Trelo from Dzagyal Monastery, who was a close student of both Patrul Rinpoche and Gemang Onpo Tenga and had spent his whole life in solitude, and I pretended to study these.

Studies of the *Guhyagarbha Tantra*

That summer I invited the great vajra master Khenchen Thupten Choepel from the northern Changma Hermitage, where there was no monastery, only tents. He didn't ride a horse, and disregarding the hardship of traveling by foot, he arrived joyfully. When I met him I took a test based on the root text of the *Prajnaparamita Ornament of Realization*. He was pleased and said that I had trained well and studied hard. Though I didn't gain certainty in my understanding of the three knowledges and the four applications, I was clever in remembering words and was able to connect all the terms of the word-for-word commentary to the root text, thus pleasing Khenpo Thupten.

One day he said, "The reason for my coming here at present is to teach Tulku the *Dispelling the Darkness of the Ten Directions* in six months," and then he arranged the overview with the tantric liturgy according to Patrul Rinpoche's tradition for Shedrup, Changma Khenpo Tsulu, and me. Khenpo Thupten knew the entire root text and commentary by heart and taught it in ten days. He did stay for six months, teaching it three times altogether. Then he performed the elaborate *Peaceful and Wrathful Deities* thanksgiving feast offering and fulfillment ceremony.[7] My brother Shedrup made him start again from the beginning, and he gave detailed teachings on two-and-a-half pages a day. Then Khenpo Thupten gave it yet again, teaching five pages a day.

Khenpo Thupten's physical, verbal, and mental conduct was entirely according to the Dharma. His discipline was extremely precise; during meals he didn't speak, while chanting he remained silent, and when he was free, he never wasted a moment—he did nothing but read, write, teach, or study the Dharma. He didn't hoard anything whatsoever and just kept the bare necessities for clothes and provisions, using everything else for making offerings and benefiting whomever he encountered. Even though the Fifth Dzogchen, lord of siddhas, said that Khenpo Thupten was an emanation of Patrul Rinpoche, I heard that Khenpo himself asked him not to make it public, staying true to what it meant.[8]

By then I had made a promise not to eat meat from animals that had been killed at home or from freshly slaughtered animals, which seemed to please

Khenpo Thupten. While I listened to his detailed explanations of the tantric commentary three sessions a day, I made a note to ask questions about any quote he mentioned that I didn't remember immediately. Other than that I memorized everything without leaving out a single word and was allowed to take an examination the next day. I gained a precise understanding of the section on elaborate and abridged sadhana practice, the arrangement of self and front mandalas, the purpose of the threefold *sattvas* and the meaning and purpose of the four aspects of approach and accomplishment.[9] And, my direct understanding of the vast and profound points of the four axioms, the indivisible two truths, and so forth, improved.[10] I thoroughly enjoyed studying and reflecting on sutra and mantra texts such as writings on the evaluation of empowerment and samaya,[11] and among all the study I did, I felt that this was the most worthwhile and satisfying for my mental aptitude.

Khenpo Thupten only talked about Dharma, and I visited him around the clock. With his teaching he knew how to direct my body, speech, and mind toward the Dharma, for which I was very grateful. Shedrup had offered him a copy of the *Treasury of Dharmadhatu* root text in very fine handwriting that Khenpo Thupten used to chant from. Subsequently this provoked in me a strong interest in the practice, and I requested the reading transmission for the root text. After hearing Khenpo Thupten speak about the great benefit of chanting the omniscient Longchenpa's writings, I started to recite a chapter a day from then onward, which had the effect of greatly improving my Vajrakilaya recitation practice. The thought of wanting to reach the bottom of my study, reflection, and meditation on the Guhyagarbha tantra, like Khenpo Thupten had, often occurred in my mind.

Khenpo Thupten said, "When the Dharma lord Patrul Rinpoche stayed in Khenpo Yonten Gyatso's quarters at Gemang Monastery doing a year's recitation of *Shaken from Its Depth*, Khenpo Yonten Gyatso was his retreat attendant.[12] For six months Patrul Rinpoche taught him *Dispelling the Darkness of the Ten Directions,* and for six months he taught the *Adornment of Realization of the Lord of Secrets* and the *Oral Advice.*

"He said not to interrupt the flow of the tantra explanation, so Khenpo Yonten Gyatso memorized the entire *Dispelling the Darkness of the Ten Directions* tantric commentary. He realized the meaning of the tantra like the three Lords of Secrets Zur, Mey, and On.[13] When one receives instructions on *Dispelling the Darkness of the Ten Directions* from such a master, one fully comprehends the *Adornment of Realization of the Lord of Secrets,* the *Oral Advice,* and the *Three Jewel Commentary.* On whatever commentary Khenpo Yonga would base his explanation of the tantra, even though each of his students would use a different commentary, it seemed like he was explaining their chosen commentary, which was really amazing.

"While On Tenzin Norbu and Yonten Gyatso were teaching and studying the *Guhyagarbha Tantra* together, both master and student contracted an eye disease that became a big obstacle. When they told the omniscient Mipham Rinpoche about it, he said that when teaching *Dispelling the Darkness of the Ten Directions,* one should do so in a secret way for ten days, like setting outer and inner retreat boundaries; if so done, when repeating the study afterward, no matter how many years or months they would teach or study it, there would be no obstacles. He gave Khenpo Yonten Gyatso an offering vessel for the first portion and said that he issued a command to the Dharma protectors. They continued to teach and study in this way and never encountered obstacles in teaching and studying the tantra again.

"Khenpo Yonten Gyatso taught the *Guhyagarbha Tantra* once a year and never missed a year throughout his life. I also memorized the words of *Dispelling the Darkness of the Ten Directions* and never interrupt the yearly ten-day period of teaching. I hope that my present explanation benefits the continuity of this teaching, and you should also study it that way." He earnestly told me this many times and said that even though he felt anxious about disclosing the profound secrets of this tantra, he had obtained permission to do so.

After completing the detailed explanation and study of the tantra, he insistently said, "From now on don't interrupt your study and exposition of this tantra, but memorize *Dispelling the Darkness of the Ten Directions.*" Then Khenpo Thupten went north to receive the *Tantra of the Two Segments* from Kargo Jamyang Trakpa based on the teaching tradition of Jamgön Kongtrül's great commentary.

That winter I invited Khenpo Rigzin Özer from Dzogchen to my retreat place. He was a close student of Khenpo Yonten Gyatso from Gemang. From him I received the root text, summary, and outline of the omniscient Mipham Rinpoche's *Gateway to Knowledge,* as well as detailed teaching of the *Treasury of Precious Qualities* based on Changma Khen Rinpoche's annotations, and thorough guidance on *The Words of My Perfect Teacher,* the commentary on the *Heart Essence of the Great Expanse* preliminaries. In addition to these, he taught Patrul Rinpoche and Mipham Rinpoche's exegetical traditions, difficult philosophical key points, and so forth, in great detail, which was very useful for clearly distinguishing the different philosophical systems.

Through previous extensive explanations of the *Magical Net* I had gained a certain degree of understanding of the Vajrayana empowerment, the categories of samayas, as well as the system of the development and completion stages and the Great Perfection, and the oral instructions helped me understand them more clearly, which was like opening the door of my awareness. Later, when I told the realized Khyentse Chökyi Lodrö about this, he said, "The *Treasury of Precious Qualities* has very powerful blessings. Even when the omniscient Mipham Rinpoche himself studied it, it opened his door of wisdom like the sun rising at daybreak."

I sent the lord of the mandala Gyaltsap Rinpoche a letter in verse about my progress in studying the *Magical Net,* the *Guhyagarbha Tantra,* and the *Treasury of Precious Qualities.* Together with a Tibetan painting of the eight auspicious symbols,[14] he replied with a letter saying, "It is very good that you, noble one, are extensively engaged in praiseworthy study and training," and these became his final words to me.

In general all the masters that I relied upon were renowned like sun and moon for their matchless qualities of the sacred Dharma, and all of them had given up concerns with social affairs. Due to their kindness, it also became my character to have little interest in society. Due to the kindness of my noble parents, I had sufficient resources to do nothing but study and contemplate under authentic masters, and didn't need to engage in a Dharma career like being head of a monastic household or a monastery. Shedrup, who was still tutoring me, advised me, "You must act like our teachers and perfect the qualities of the Dharma by properly abiding in study, reflection, and meditation. I can take responsibility for all the social affairs; you just stay like a mute." Due to his kindness, I didn't need any donations even when I was young, and so I committed myself to study, reflection, and meditation, promising not to waste even a single hour. Every day, acting as my tutor, my brother encouraged me to write various poetic praises, supplications, discourses, songs, and so forth, telling me that it would help both my writing and composition. So I composed various relevant and irrelevant writings. When I had difficulty remembering certain things, I would look through collections of hymns and advice by Patrul Rinpoche and many other realized masters, and thus constantly practice my writing, which was evidently useful for my compositions. Even so, my handwriting never became very good.

Around that time, as the Sakar Samdrupling community annually performed the *Realm of Great Bliss* sadhana, I went there to preside over the assembly and taught the *Realm of Great Bliss* practice for three days, and everyone perceived the teaching as a great wonder. I also chanted the empowerment for the *Swift Path of Amitabha* liturgy from the *Heart Essence*. From Lama Rigzin Tekchok, I received Mipham Rinpoche's exegesis of the *Novice Aphorisms,* as well as Dodup Tenpai Nyima's guidance on *Chanting the Names of Manjushri.*

Upon completing my one-year *Kilaya* recitation, around the spring of the fire-tiger year, 1926, I concluded my retreat with the fire ceremony. I then went to see Dru Jamyang Trakpa and received Longchenpa's *Seven Treasuries,* the *Trilogy of Natural Ease,* the *Selected Works,* and the *Novice Aphorisms,* which he gave to several people. He said it was best to stay in a retreat place.

That summer my former cultural teacher Tenzin Dorje, who was the senior chant master at Palpung, went to Benchen Puntsök Dargyeling to check on the tantric practices, chanting, and music of the sadhanas, the tenth-day ceremonies, the ritual for the twenty-ninth day of the twelfth month, and so forth, according to the Marpa Kagyu tradition.[15] So I went there, too. I resumed the remainder of my previous training with him and extensively studied the chapter on melody from Jamgön Kongtrül's commentary, the chapter on divination from Karma Chagmey's *Soaring Balmo Hindrance Astrology* manual, the *Pine Tree Calculation of Illness,* the *Horoscope about the Dead,* and so forth.[16]

My Guru's Passing

One day when I was eighteen years old, while at Gakok, I received a letter from my father relating how Gyaltsap Rinpoche, the lord pervading all families, had passed away on the eighteenth day of the fifth month in the fire-tiger year, 1926. He was only fifty-six years old. My mind was in such a state of grief that I felt like my heart had been torn out. After finishing my petition-offerings to the dharmapalas that evening, it didn't feel right to chant my precious master's long-life prayer. I couldn't let it go either, so I turned it into a supplication that I chanted while crying and went to sleep feeling upset. To console me, Shedrup said, "Don't mourn your teacher's passing like an ordinary person; mingle your mind with his! You two are both tulkus, so you will receive the blessing of mind-to-mind transmission after death!"

The next morning I sat in the cool shade of the meadow behind the house in order to study. While pretending to watch mind essence, whenever I thought of my master, an unbearable sorrow rose in my mind. Bursting into uncontrollable tears, I wrote this sorrowful song:

Alas, qualified master,
Though I followed you, the Buddha in person,
I haven't come to a true understanding about the instructions;
How can you leave me behind like an abandoned orphan?

The smiling eyes in your white moon-like face
Watching me with loving-kindness
Can't be seen with the eyes of my bad karma;
Your son can't bear to be without his father!

Your sweet, clear voice, subtle and inspiring,
Is simultaneous with the vast and profound Dharma nectar,
But its clear strength can't be heard by my ears;
Your son has no choice but to cry out for help!

Your smooth hand caresses the top of my head
With a vase of blessed *amrita* and nectar;
Feeling that I won't have the chance to enjoy its taste,
How can anyone not sigh from sadness?

Your lucid power of realization shines forth
While gazing at me with your vivid eyes;
When will there be a chance for you to watch me?
I can't help but cry out with intense hope!

When the Chakrasamvara Hermitage
On the hillside of the unsurpassed Lotus Light retreat center
Appears in my mind, I feel delighted;
Yet why did you leave it empty now?

The noble group of learned and virtuous realized meditators,
Harmonious like children of the same parents,
An assembly of vidyadharas that act in accord with the Dharma,
Has dispersed, like birds at dusk.

Each empowerment and word of advice was more amazing than
    the other,
Dharma lord, you and your spiritual sons had all you desired;
Like the gate of a fence when losing a battle,
How could you close the door now?

As the khenpos, tulkus, and monks—both old and young—
From Dongnak Tennyi Dargyeling Monastery
Exclaim how kind you are;
Why did you pass into the realm of the invisible now?

On the high summit of the divine Lotus Mountain,
In rock caverns and wooden huts,
With whom will all those relaxed and carefree yogis
Discuss their experiences and realization?

Though living at home, male and female householders
Are bound by the golden rope of samaya
Adorned with the gem of faith;
Who will help them during birth, death, and the bardo?

In the past I wondered whether your place wasn't
The real Glorious Copper-Colored Mountain;
But when your appearance comes to my mind now,
Feeling sad, I shed an incessant stream of tears.

Master, abiding in the pure lands of the ten directions,
Though you are refreshed by unconditioned bliss,
Look upon your abandoned student with your wisdom eyes,
And rest your broad loving hand on my head!

Your disciple living in this impure realm,
Is daydreaming and pondering about how you dwell
Amidst the buddhas and bodhisattvas;
Kind only father, I can't bear it any longer!

Though you have dissolved into primordial inner space,
Unique protector, throw the hook of your natural compassion
Right now, without increase or decrease,
And draw me into your delightful presence!

During a break in my studies I went for a picnic, and upon reaching the top of a rocky height, I was exhausted and sat down to catch my breath. Though I didn't deliberately watch my mind, an experience of empty cognizance like space without limit or center spontaneously occurred. I had never experienced anything like that before and sat there until it vanished.

When Tai Situ Pema Wangchok came to Benchen, I received many Dharma connections from him, such as the crown ceremony, a *White Tara* empowerment that was his personal practice from the Karma Kagyu tradition, and so forth. Then I returned to my own place, and in autumn I went back home. That winter I did a recitation retreat on Chowang's *Kilaya* in a hermitage and studied a bit of *Dispelling the Darkness of the Ten Directions*. I also pretended to give a detailed teaching on *The Way of the Bodhisattva* to about ten monks from Sakar Monastery.

Not too far from my home was a hermitage called Draktsa, a beautiful, high, rocky mountain with many juniper trees. At its center was a cave with enough space for the four types of daily activities, and as I felt attracted to it, I went there for a visit. Even though it was winter, there was a small spring where all the ice melted and the water rose like in summer. The local people all said that it was a sign of the local deities being happy about my going there.

Before dawn I would first do the preliminaries in bed, and one day, in front of where I was sitting, a brief flash of a woman holding a long-life arrow clearly appeared before my eyes. I wondered if it was the medicine lady Tseringma, and assumed she was the local deity. Many disciples of the Gyalwa Drikungpa had stayed at that sacred place in olden times and seemed to have abandoned it. One monk who sometimes stayed there asked me to write a smoke offering liturgy, which I did.

I read the omniscient vidyadhara Jigmey Lingpa's life story quite often, and at that time I was reading the spiritual songs about his practice; Patrul Rinpoche's advice about solitude, *Divine Drum Beat*; his *Praise to the Vinaya*;

Gemang Onpo Tenga's *Praise on Discipline* and spiritual songs; and my venerable master Gyaltsap Rinpoche's advice on seclusion, *Ornament of Renunciation*. Shedrup often talked about how Mipham Rinpoche only did practice during the latter part of his life, reminding me that I ought to just spend my whole life doing practice in a secluded place.

After that I went to see the learned and righteous lord of siddhas Jamyang Trakpa, who was the heart son of the two sun- and moon-like Jamgöns and Dokhampa Tenpai Nyima. From him I received the oral transmission of the omniscient Longchenpa's writings of the *Seven Treasuries*, the *Trilogy of Natural Ease*, *Dispelling the Darkness of the Ten Directions*, and the *Tantric Overview*, all of which he had received from Jamgön Kongtrül Lodro Thaye. I received all these texts in great detail, along with the table of contents written by Shedrung Pandita. Lama Jamyang Trakpa finished it by the end of the fire-tiger year, 1926, and on New Year's Day of the fire-rabbit year, 1927, he said, "This is the fifth time I have given the reading transmission for the *Seven Treasuries*, and it is very auspicious that you brothers received it," thus complimenting us and putting silk scarves around our necks. Because we needed it, we also received the empowerment and reading transmission of the great treasure revealer Sangye Lama's *Combined Sadhana of the Three Roots*: a treasure rediscovered by Jamyang Khyentse Wangpo, and a blessing of the *Five-Deity Kurukulle* contained in the *Compendium of Sadhanas*.

I studied the *Collection of Five Branches of Astrology* with the master's niece, Lady Yeshe Chödrön. Although we finished it in a week, because I didn't persevere with it afterward, my knowledge of it turned out to be the worst of all the texts I studied. While I taught Lady Yeshe Chödrön the *Novice Aphorisms*, in front of the hermitage where she lived was a high mountain about which hovering vultures circled, and when I saw the forest with beautiful flowers, I yearned for solitude and felt like I couldn't bear it any longer.

5. Yearning for Retreat

AROUND THAT TIME my mind got busy thinking about getting my own
cave. Because I couldn't leave for a while, at night I would prostrate in
the direction of Lama Vijaya's residence from the terrace of my home, while
supplicating and promising again and again to engage in practice.[1] Praying to
fulfill that promise, I also sang this spontaneous song:

In the delightful temple of the eight great deities
On the high summit of Crystal Lotus Mountain, a sacred abode,
Father, Pema Vijaya, lord who pervades all families,
I long for your full smiling face!

Though your mind is free of confusion, you stay in solitude
With your faithful retinue of learned and accomplished supreme
   incarnations,
Released from the fetters of involvement in this life's phenomena;
I long for living in a carefree, natural way!

In our splendid, elegantly structured, lofty home,
A pleasant place amidst well-plowed grain fields,
Whatever recreation, tasty food and drink,
And soft, fine clothes I receive, my mind never feels happy!

A beautiful self-arisen cavern, untouched by humans,
With a cool shelter of trees swaying to and fro,
Embraced within gently drifting, misty clouds above:
I feel like taking such a sacred rock cave as my home!

Surrounded by intimate parents, brothers, and sisters
Who respect me with affection and smiles, I am not satisfied;
Though they give me whatever I need right away,
Your son's mind remains discontent!

The company of bucks and does, little birds, and wild animals,
Is an imminent reminder of joyful loving-kindness;
No matter how much time one spends with them, the passionate
    distracted mind
Should stay free of hope and fear; this is your young son's aim.

Managing gold, silver, cattle, horses, and cows,
An overload of well-plowed fields, harvests, and farmers,
Horses, yaks, *dzo,* and mules to fill the innermost storeroom;
I have no desire for business and agricultural wealth.

A full stomach and shelter from cold can be gained by alms,
Free of desire for tasty food like meat, blood, and wine;
Wandering in random places to practice whatever virtue,
My mind feels irrevocable about the thought of leaving.

On a throne decorated with fine silk and an ornate back
In the interior part of our fancy mansion,
Many people respect me, requesting audience and blessing;
Getting rid of a hundred attracts a thousand,
And I have no hope of being a great lama.

In a self-arisen, beautiful cavern containing the four activities,
With a small book of ultimate instructions from the hearing lineage,
    and a begging bowl,
And the three Dharma robes—the victory banner of liberation[2]—
I wish to engage in the ascetic practice of wearing tattered clothes.

My present heavy burden of wrong livelihood, love, hate, and
    competitiveness,
Causes acts contrary to the Dharma, the violation of precepts, and
    wealth spirits for the future;

I have no desire to accumulate perverted actions
Through the trouble of enjoying a wife and alcohol.

Inspired to gather the harvest of renunciation
In the citadel of samadhi, free of distraction,
I want to be like Milarepa,
Never content with the wealth of experience and realization.

Thoughts of the three times, emotional reaction, and pretense:
The cunning mind wavers like a potter's wheel;
Along with the disguise of shiny clothes,
I let go of cleverly deceiving people.

Bidding farewell to this enemy, samsara,
I'll embrace desolate areas like a wild animal;
In a rustic cave amidst drifting clouds of mist,
I am eager to witness the play of experience and realization.

Making random places my hermitage,
Whatever is available right now is enough for the darling child of all
    beings;
Capable of giving up all mundane actions,
Lord, bless me that I may be like you!

Another time I thought about leaving a message for my family, and then
departing for a hermitage, and I wrote this:

Alas, beloved parents, who produced this well-favored body!
Nurturing me with loving-kindness from childhood until now,
You were so kind to introduce me to a qualified master
Who handed me the way to freedom—the perfect teachings.

Wanting to follow the example of my authentic master,
The accomplishment of Dharma study and reflection,
Completely letting go of the affairs of this life,
I feel like wandering in remote places.

Parents, you stay in this lofty, beautiful home!
Your young son is overly fond of empty caves!
Though you are very kind to give me soft, elegant clothes,
I prefer a white felt robe, so they're useless to me.

Letting go of valuable belongings,
I'm content with my monk's staff, begging bowl, and robes;
Giving up all desirable possessions without regret,
I feel like gathering books full of profound instructions!

Abandoning this beautiful flower garden,
I prepare to go alone to a remote rocky shelter;
With no need of attendants causing emotional reactions,
I feel like keeping company with birds and wild animals!

Previously, in the presence of my all-pervading master,
While he gave the *Innermost Essence* empowerment,
I promised to give up the schemes of this life
And commit myself to act according to the Dharma.

I have no choice but to pursue mountain solitude,
The desire for this appears like an engraved rock in my heart;
Remembering the life stories of the ancestors,
I can't bear not to practice any longer!

Our joyful relationship in this life
Will definitely be severed by the Demon of Death;
Though your young son will hide in the mountains for a while,
It's impossible to part with your cheerful, smiling faces!

While remembering your unforgettable kindness,
When I capture the kingdom of experience and realization,
I will certainly not forget to show my gratitude
And repay your graciousness!

In this age of degeneration, attachment, aversion, and jealousy
Blaze like fire, even inside the monasteries;

Trying to act according to the Dharma is hard,
So I feel like setting out to stay alone, like a unicorn!

Disgusted with praise, the resounding thunder of fame
Is nothing but meaningless noise, expressed momentarily.
Obtaining it doesn't enrich; like products in the market,
Without a clue as to when they'll vanish, it will be lost like gathered
  honey.

Though married, conflict can't be avoided throughout one's life;
By the end of autumn the bee's birth or death is unpredictable;
One might be happy, but my aim of lasting happiness without
  attachment
Is solely the sacred Dharma that gives present peace and future
  delight!

Tired in body and mind from achieving worldly success,
It seems like I'm wasting the freedoms and advantages I have
  obtained!
Taking a cave just large enough for one person as my home,
I yearn to be a carefree renunciate without any concerns,
Committing myself to the guru and the Three Jewels;
Please fulfill your young son's wishes!

LEAVING FOR RETREAT

After writing this, I showed it to Shedrup, who said, "Your strong dedication to practice is a good resolution. By spending your whole life practicing, you will also fulfill my own aspirations. But you are still very young, so don't start bragging about it now, otherwise nothing would be more embarrassing than not succeeding in your practice. Before long, the two of us can go to a secluded place to alternate study, reflection, and meditation. Then our parents won't be displeased either and won't stop you from going." This made me feel at ease, and in no time at all, in the fire-rabbit year, 1927, when I was eighteen, I went with him and two retreat attendants to stay in a secluded, rocky shelter that we made suitable to live in.

In the morning I would recite about a thousand mantras of Ratna Lingpa's

Innermost Hidden Longevity Practice, as well as a thousand mantras of the omniscient Mipham Rinpoche's Manjushri sadhana, *Sun of the Intellect*. At the beginning of each session, I would alternate between chanting Mipham Rinpoche's supplication to the twelve Dzogchen masters and the prayer and homage from the *Wish-Fulfilling Gem of the Guru's Innermost Essence*.[3] At the end of my sessions, I chanted some prayers by the omniscient Longchenpa. After that I would concentrate one week on each visualization aspect of the *Three Topics and Three Virtues*, the essential guidance text on the Great Perfection from *Resting in the Nature of Mind*. In between sessions, I would memorize a page from *Dispelling the Darkness of the Ten Directions*, the detailed commentary on the *Guhyagarbha Tantra*. Frequently I would study and reflect on the root text and commentary of *Resting in the Nature of Mind*, as well as the root text of the *Treasury of Precious Qualities* and its commentaries, *The Two Chariots* and both the *Refulgence of the Sun* and *Radiance of the Moon*.[4] While contemplating the visualizations of the four mind changings in separate sessions,[5] I would read one chapter of the *Treasury of Precious Qualities* root text and reflect on the meaning, and as the one benefited the other, I was able to slightly infuse my mind with true Dharma. At that time I composed a song of praise to that sacred place:

> Lord Vijaya, perfect Buddha,
> I pray to you from the core of my heart;
> By turning my mind to the Dharma,
> Bless me to devote my whole life to spiritual practice.
>
> The adamantine protrusion in this wondrous place,
> Its rock like a heart suddenly rising into the sky,
> Shaped into a pair of charming caves
> With patches of grass and trees at its borders,
> Hangs down like a precious necklace ornament.
>
> The *sala* tree on top is like an umbrella,
> With cool trees fluttering on either side,
> Where small birds utter pleasant sounds;
> On the fully grown branches of the tree in front,
> Dewdrops on the flowers are like pearls.

Around it is a large juniper forest
Where wild beasts roar and wolves cry;
On the young branches of the lofty peak in front,
Carefree birds and wild animals sweetly sing.

Amidst a profusion of lovely, bright-colored flowers
Where bees fly around singing songs,
This lovely cave with room for the four aspects of living,[6]
Cool in summer and warm enough in winter,
Is adorned with a splendid, indestructible rock staircase.

In the East appear the radiant lamps of sun and moon,
In the West a magnificent rock glacier;
Its mist-shrouded slope suspended in white ice
Is illuminated by bright rays of sun and moon.

Birds large and small hover and drift above
The clean water in front, drinking divine water offerings;
How joyous is this place, without involvement and attachment!
How nice it is to be without distractions and diversions!

In this meditation hut conducive to Dharma,
While staying carefree and feeling at ease,
Without relaxing my endeavor of the three doors,
Grant your blessings that the Dharma takes birth in my being!

I stayed seven years in a very nice cave at Denkok. Below the entrance was a round rock, and I had to climb up some stairs to get in. There was also a house, so Shedrup and the two attendants made food there, but the door was not very good. Small bears used to defecate at the door to the house, but couldn't come up to the actual cave because of the ladder. There was also a small cuckoo which acted as my alarm clock. Whenever I heard it, I used to get up.

I only wore robes made from raw silk. I would sit in a box, and sometimes stretch my legs. I didn't have to get up from where I was sitting and only had to bend over to stoke the fire and make tea. I didn't have a proper tea kettle, but

Dilgo Khyentse at Karpuk in his twenties. Shechen Archives.
Photographer unknown.

just used to take the tea straight from the pot. In the evening I used to let the fire burn slowly so that in the morning I didn't need to start a new one. In the morning, I would get up around three o'clock and do a session until around five o'clock. I used to make my own tea, and thus I would not see anyone till lunch. Once my attendant's father came while my attendants were still asleep and told them to get up, as I had already made tea.

When I stood up, my head didn't touch the ceiling—it was quite high— but the cave was very humid. All the caves in Kham are cool in the summer and warm in the winter. I stayed in that cave for seven years without breaking my retreat, but my family would come to see me. Nobody else could come. In front was a forest with many foxes and all sorts of birds. There were also leopards, which ate a small dog that I had.

When I did the petition-offering to the dharmapalas, there were always some crows that used to make noise, and when I offered the torma, they just took it away. There were also many small birds that came into my cave. I used to put butter on my finger, and they would come and eat it. There were two mice that I used to feed tsampa;[7] they would run around on my lap. There were also about twenty or thirty blackbirds.

Dilgo Khyentse's retreat cave in Bhala. Photograph by Matthieu Ricard.

In front of my cave I put many clay pots with flowers, and the nomad children used to come and look at them. I used to put a cloth in front of my window so no one could see me. All my food was brought by my attendants from my home. I never used to just rest; I had a lot of books, and after lunch I would read. My brother Shedrup often asked me to write prayers and things, and I had no trouble writing. He thought that by writing, I would get used to composing. While I was in retreat, my hair grew quite long. I would occasionally wash it, but otherwise I didn't bathe much.

Other than going to sleep at night and going to the toilet at midday, I would not take a break even for a short while, but would write or read texts, keep meditation sessions, and arouse great diligence in doing prostrations and mantra recitations. My elder brother Shedrup kept saying that unless I would occasionally take a little break, I might become depressed, and when my parents came from time to time, they said the same thing.

My father said, "Son, you said that you wanted to become a monk. Moreover you were given the title of an incarnate lama and received extensive empowerments and transmissions. Since you are able to put so much effort into studying the texts and putting them into practice, I'll feel at ease when I die. But if you continue to meet masters with exceptional experience and realization, you will come to a true understanding, which is very important."

Shechen Monastery in Eastern Tibet. Photograph by Matthieu Ricard.

Though my perseverance was unremitting, due to the kindness of my venerable master, the vajra holder Shechen Gyaltsap, I didn't encounter any obstacles. As a recreation I would read songs of realization by the precious lord Milarepa and the chapters on persistent practice from the biography of the omniscient Jigmey Lingpa, and this caused me to feel intense faith and inspiration.[8] The omniscient, great Jigmey Lingpa took seven commitments while engaged in spiritual practice at Palri and followed them as much as possible;[9] when I read this story and the story about how compassion arose in him while staying at Samye Chimphu when a wildcat killed big white birds and when a faithful benefactor offered him sausage made of the entrails, flesh, and blood of slaughtered animals, I developed a strong renunciation and compassion, and took a vow to eat meat only once a day.[10]

When the harvest in that area was destroyed by frost, and rain was so scarce that the farmers got worried, I thought that if I were a powerful bodhisattva, I would display the miraculous power of covering the sky with clouds and bring rain; and I kept hoping for this to happen. We had a rooster to keep track of the time and an old dog, and as I prayed to Guru Rinpoche over and over again, when they were wounded from being caught and bitten by wild animals, they wouldn't bleed. Even when nomads lost their cattle, goats, and sheep in the vicinity of my secluded dwelling, the livestock were never killed by wild animals. Though I always practiced the recitation of Manjushri, I felt that this was also due to my one-pointed recitation and visualization at that time. My understanding of the profound teachings of sutra and tantra got better than before, and my poetic compositions also improved. I contemplated staying alone in remote mountains from then on, regardless of the comfort of food and clothes, living in hiding like a wounded deer. Planning to carry through with the lifestyle of the revered Milarepa, I felt such an irreversible yearning that I wrote this song:

> Though you perfected the qualities of the three kayas,
> In order to liberate beings of the impure realms
> You manifested as a supreme renunciate;
> Lord Pema Vijaya, I miss you from the depth of my heart!

> The feeling that this precious support, a free and blessed human body,
> Will be lost to the enemy, the bandit Lord of Death,
> Overwhelms my mind with anguish,
> Like a frightened little bird falling to the ground.

> The abyss of the lower realms is hard to fathom, and
> This present comfort and happiness in the higher realms
> Is like a rainbow in the sky that's about to vanish;
> Remember the spreading, dense rain clouds of wrongdoing!

> A delightful palace may be magnificent,
> But it can't guard against fear of the Lord of Death!
> All food and drink may taste delicious,
> But it might become the cause of drinking melted copper![11]

> No matter how much I cherish this body covered in soft clothes,
> It's uncertain when it'll start to smell like a rotten corpse;
> A handsome, youthful body may gladden my heart, but
> When the eyes dissolve into the skull, it's useless.

> My shiny jewelry may be a charming object,
> But it can't seduce the wrathfully grimacing Lord of Death;

Though my fame may pervade the whole country,
It won't help me when body and mind separate!

Though prestige and power may frighten everyone,
They won't protect me when going alone;
A powerful rank and status may be impressive,
But it's impossible to avoid the Lord of Death's court of law!

Large crowds of people are the cause of like and dislike;
By the time I go to the bardo I'll be alone.
Remaining far away from the affairs of this life,
I'll stay alone in a secluded, rocky shelter!

Living like a wounded deer,
My heart's desire is to watch the show of mind within;
All past siddhas stayed in remote rocky mountains too,
Capturing the kingdom of experience and realization.

Remembering the life story of Lord Milarepa,
When I'm hungry I'll eat the food of samadhi,
When I'm cold I'll wear the cloth of mystic inner heat;[12]
In the company of birds and wild animals,
I'm going to cloudy, mist-shrouded mountains!

In a cave that's not altered by people,
Nourished by leaves that need no cultivation,
Drinking the clear and cool water from rocks,
My heart's wish is to just be with mountain birds.

In the cool shade of excellent trees,
In a relaxed and carefree state of mind,
With the cool shelter of a fresh breeze, my health will be good;
All by myself, my activities will be in accord with the Dharma!

On the summit of a high rock in the immense sky,
Developing strength in the realization of aware emptiness within,
When rays of the smiling sun and moon above reach my heart,
I enter the inner space of the six lamps of space and awareness.[13]

Sometimes clouds and mist appear,
Thunder and red lightning flash like a playful dance,
Roaring wind swirls around black clouds,
Reflecting the sounds, lights, and rays in the threatening bardo.

In the pure meadow, around gently moving water,
My companions, young wild sheep, play and climb the rocks;
Sweetly singing, shiny blackbirds develop strength in flying,
And white vultures circle around at leisure.

Except for the mother dakinis that gather here,
Wicked people never pass by;
The vast expanse of a blue lake full to the brim,
Indicates the four modes of freely resting awareness within.[14]

The company of small swans,
Sweetly singing and training their wings,
Reminds me of practicing the different types of loving-kindness;
In my estate of this empty valley,
Relying on the pure, cool water from snow mountains,
I'm going to capture the kingdom of experience and realization!

I decided that from now on I don't need anything;
The countless joys and sorrows of this life,
Whatever I experienced in the past, are like a drawing on water.
Except for accumulating habitual tendencies for samsara's depth,
Look at this present body to see if there was any benefit or not!

With hope and fear of making a living for the future,
Life runs out with a stock of karmic activity;
The very moment one is captured by the foe, Yama's rope,[15]
Reflect on whether it is any use when you exhale your final breath!

Though I am naive and immature,
As my father, the Dharma lord Lama Gyaltsap,
Let his blessing enter my heart, I conceived the urge to escape,
And see activities for this life as confusion.

Unable to bear that all-consuming thought, the urge to escape,
I wrote it down as it slipped from my mouth;
Though thoughts in an ordinary person's mind are
    impermanent,
Bless me to be free of adversity and obstacles.

With the root of all Dharma, renunciation,
Steadfast like an engraved rock,
May I become like the protector Pema Vijaya,
The master of nonaction, yogi of the sky!

I read the vajra holder Khyentse Wangpo's spiritual songs and had written a book of songs that was like my own interpretation of his songs. When I showed it to the omniscient Khyentse Chökyi Lodro, he said, "Nowadays you and Dudjom are unrivaled in writing songs like the omniscient father and son."[16]

Most of the vidyadharas of the Nyingma school in general and in particular the three Jamgöns and my great teachers had all studied, contemplated, and meditated while exclusively staying hidden in secluded places. They were my main examples, showing me how to benefit the doctrine and sentient beings, Feeling that I should act like them, I didn't allow anyone except my parents to meet me. Letting go of the ordinary concerns for this life and leaving flattery and pretense far behind, except for minimal conversation, I didn't say anything unnecessary. My livelihood was no problem at all, and I felt like spending my whole life in such happiness.

Following Khenchen Thupten Choepel's instructions, I kept struggling to memorize the *Dispelling the Darkness of the Ten Directions* commentary on the *Guhyagarbha Tantra*. For a few years I also stayed in a meditation hut in a charming forest with meadows. My brother Shedrup was my tutor and said that unless I would go out a little, my mind would get disturbed. So one time Sangye Nyenpa and I went to a place known as Padampa Sangye's meditation cave to make a connection with that sacred spot. Nonetheless, although it was surrounded by snow mountains, it wasn't a very nice place.

Once on the tenth day, an astrologically favorable Monday, in the seventh month, we did the feast offering of the *Heart Essence of the Immortal Arya* sadhana. While we were doing the ceremony, I wrote a supplication based on

Khyentse Wangpo's *Five Visions* pure-vision treasure in conjunction with the profound meaning of the five herukas.[17] As soon as I had written it down, the river in that small valley suddenly swelled and became like a river in spring and summer.

Around that time Khenchen Tekchok from Gemang and various other khenpos came to stay at the hermitage, and I received teachings from them on the *Heart Essence of the Great Expanse,* the *Adornment of Realization of the Lord of Secrets* commentary on the *Guhyagarbha Tantra,* the *Oral Advice,* the *Three Jewel Commentary,* teachings on the *Six Bardos,* the *Collected Works* of Onpo Tenga from Gemang, the empowerments of *Abhirati Vajrasattva,* and Atisha's *White Tara* from the *Heart Essence,* and so forth. The two Khen Rinpoches showed me unusual affection, and when they left it seemed like they couldn't bear to part with me. Khenpo Tekchok gave me his own hand-written copy of the *Refulgence of the Sun* and *Radiance of the Moon* texts, which are the detailed explanation of the *Treasury of Precious Qualities.*

Meanwhile some of the servants from my home, who were amazed that the son of a governor, the favorite child of rich parents who had experienced nothing but comfort before was able to stay in a cave at such a retreat place, were saying that I was an unusually sublime being. Other practitioners at that mountain retreat who were enduring austerities also thought that if even the darling child of a rich governor could live that way in a hermitage, why shouldn't they be able to tolerate hardships? I heard that this worked to their advantage. Generally speaking, someone who always stayed in mountains during his past life, like a hunter or whoever may be born in the mountains, will, whatever body they take on in this life, feel happy and relaxed at the sight of a pleasant cave or a hut in a nice-looking forest. This is due to their habitual tendencies, and the thought of staying quiet and secluded in such a place will naturally occur to them.

STUDIES OF THE *GURU'S INNERMOST ESSENCE*

By that time about twenty monks were doing the rainy season retreat at Sakar Monastery, and I taught them the visualization of the *Hevajra* sadhana.[18] I just wanted to practice the heart of the matter, the Great Perfection, and spend the rest of my life practicing in a solitary place. For that purpose, in the iron-horse year, 1930, I invited Kunga Palden Rinpoche to my hermitage in order to receive guidance through personal experience. He had been a close student of Onpo Tenga and had spent his entire life in secluded places, letting go of anything to be done, and exclusively practicing *Resting in the Nature of Mind* and the *Guru's Innermost Essence* combined into one.

This master gave me detailed explanations on the liberating instructions of the *Wish-Fulfilling Gem of the Guru's Innermost Essence,* which he had practiced his whole life. He also thoroughly taught me the exercises for the yogic techniques of the channels and energies according to the *Heart Essence of the Great Expanse.* After teaching the *Minor Oral Transmission of the Natural Manifestation of Wisdom* from the *Guru's Innermost Essence,* he gave me the highly valued, vast oral instructions. During that time he gave me some additional advice:

"When I received the *Guru's Innermost Essence* empowerment and liberating instructions from Onpo Tenga Rinpoche, I promised to practice daily the *Ocean of Accomplishment Stages of the Master* guru yoga and the guru yoga from the *Minor Oral Transmission* without interruption. I kept the *Wish-Fulfilling Gem of the Guru's Innermost Essence* book inseparable from me and exclusively relied on that. I have practiced it my entire life, and though I don't feel confident about my experiences and realization, even in my dreams I never thought that these instructions were deceptive, and I have always had irreversible trust in them.

"When I was doing a darkness retreat for a while, even though I experienced some extremely frightening visions of the intermediate state, it only increased my faith in the Dharma and my master. I suffered from a nerve disease, and by endeavoring in my practice for a long time as a way to remove my physical obstacle, I recovered from my illness. Though members of my family normally don't have long lives, by doing my personal meditation of the *Wish-Fulfilling Gem* recitation practice every year without interruption, my life was carried to the end.

"In the past, when Onpo Tenga Rinpoche gave us the empowerment and teachings of the *Guru's Innermost Essence,* he said as he finished it, 'It was an auspicious coincidence for the Dilgo son to give me a thangka of the omniscient Longchenpa.' And he gave me the thangka as an object of reverence. Now that I have given you the detailed explanation, you should make it the core of your practice. In addition to that, when faithful people show up, you should always give them the common and extraordinary teachings."

He explained the need to benefit the doctrine and sentient beings, and with great affection gave me his books of the *Seven Treasuries* and *Resting in the Nature of Mind* that he had kept as an object of worship his entire life. He told me to continuously study, reflect, and meditate on these texts. According to his advice, I have pretended to diligently study and contemplate them as much as possible since.

Both my revered masters said, "When flourishing and becoming more and more widespread, the land is filled with cotton-clad yogis. When declining and weakening more and more, there is no lineage holder except Lama Palge."[19] Patrul Rinpoche specifically received the teaching on the yogic techniques of the channels and energies from the *Heart Essence of the Great Expanse* that Dodup Jigmey Thinley Özer gave to Rogza Palge,[20] and while he trained in yogic exercises in the middle of his tent, his head would hit the central pole, which got a little dirty. Onpo Tenga and Adzom Drukpa received these teachings from him, and Onpo Tenga practiced it his whole life without interruption.

Since both of them had received and practiced it and frequently mentioned its great importance, I endeavored in the yogic exercises in my hermitage for a long time. Even though I never got any signs of my energy and mind attaining pliancy, my proficiency in the instructions of the yogic exercises became solid, and Kunga Palden, who had spent his whole life meditating on the Great Perfection in solitude, told me, "Son, your stay in mountain retreat has not been in vain."

Meanwhile I performed about three hundred thousand feast offerings according to the *Auspicious Offering Ceremony* and *Manjushri's Perfect Generosity Vajra Liturgy*. At the sacred springs symbolizing the main local guardians of my dwelling, I buried treasure vases to enhance the fertility of the earth, prepared a symbolic abode for the guardians, and performed a smoke offering and a cleansing ritual. Then I relaxed for a while. During breaks between my sessions I gave Sangye Nyenpa, Kargo Rabdzey Tulku, and about ten students the reading transmission for the *Seven Treasuries* and the *Trilogy of Natural Ease*, and taught the *Treasury of Precious Qualities* to Karma Guru, a *khenpo* from Benchen.

Generally speaking, all my authentic teachers frequently told me, "You should properly abide in study, contemplation, and meditation, and then uphold, preserve, and spread the doctrine by maintaining disciples. From now on you should give empowerments and teachings to the faithful." Accordingly

I taught the *The Words of My Perfect Teacher* and the *Primordial Wisdom Guru* a few times to some humble people yearning for teachings.

Later, when I asked Khyentse Chökyi Lodro how to teach and propagate the great empowerments and transmissions such as *Sutra, Illusion, and Mind,* the *Eight Sadhana Teachings,* and the *Embodiment of Realization,*[21] he said, "By continuing the omniscient Jigmey Lingpa's activities, you will grant extensive maturing and liberating teachings to countless beings, as if they were transferred to the highest buddhafield." He frequently gave me amazing poetic verses. As I grew up, while unable to subdue my own mind, I nevertheless had to, in the unceasing guise of a teacher, deceive many people, and I wondered if that was what Khyentse Chökyi Lodro was referring to.

From Lord Kangyur Karma Ösel Lhundrup, I had the privilege of receiving the *Six Volumes of Jatson;* the reading transmissions he had received from Tsentrul Jampal Norbu; the *Sky Teaching* in thirteen volumes; Chagmey Rinpoche's biography; stories about the incarnations of Tulku Migyur Dorje and Chagmey Rinpoche; the *Chagmey Retreat Manual* and its supportive teachings; *Practical Guidance on Avalokiteshvara* and its preliminaries; the eighteen auxiliary teachings of the *Heart Essence of Yuthok;* Karma Khenchen Rinchen Dargye's manual on Yonge Migyur Dorje's *Trolo;* the *Chronicles of Padma;* the *Five Chronicles;* and the *Chronicles* and the *Life Story of Yeshe Tsogyal* revealed by Taksham, of which he had received the reading transmissions from Drung Rinchen.[22]

Once, when I was about twenty years old, while I was staying in solitude, I dreamed that I was sitting in the sky amid thick clouds and fog above a great sea. My body was colored yellow, adorned with hooded snakes and jewel ornaments, my lower body coiled into a snake, and I dreamed that I moved through space with great joy. Later I told Dharmamati about it, and he replied, "You are the son of Naga Jasuki in disguise."[23] I asked him to compose a petition-offering, which he kindly did. When I observed my own character, I found that my health was much better when my sleep was very deep, when it rained heavily with dense clouds and fog, and when the ground was very humid with lots of green grass and plants, and the weather was cool and clear. When my body came in contact with hot sun rays, when rain was scarce and the sky was clear, it didn't suit my health and my shoulders would always break out into a rash of many small pocks like a toad's skin. When I thought about it, I felt that I must have been some type of animal that lives in wet places and incidentally just wrote it down. I felt that my expanse of realization of the Great Perfection should reach fullness around the age of twenty, but though I pretended to practice the heart of the matter while keeping that hope in mind, it was nothing other than boasting; even now that I'm seventy, I still haven't even attained stability in concentration on calm abiding.[24]

I received the empowerment, reading transmission, and teaching on the guru sadhana of the revered Milarepa from Sangye Nyenpa. Then I received some teachings on mirror divination and astrology from a *khenpo* at Benchen. The *khenpo* was also the chant master, and I learned mirror divination and astrology very well.

Upon coming out of retreat, I first went to Dzongsar. I was around twenty-seven years old then. Khyentse Chökyi Lodro had told me to come as he wanted to give me the reading transmission of the *Hundred Thousand Nyingma Tantras* and the *Treasury of Precious Termas*. When I arrived Khyentse Chökyi Lodro said, "It is a very auspicious sign that you have come today." That first time I only stayed about two months. Gradually I began to go there every summer, and during the winter I would go back to my home in Denkok or elsewhere, such as Chokgyur Lingpa's monastery at Tsikey, to receive transmissions from various teachers, such as the *Chakrasamvara of the Hearing Lineage* at Zurmang Monastery from Drungram Gyatrul.[25]

Dangtok Rinpoche was staying in the Khamche Monastic College,[26] so I met him, and he asked me to give him the reading transmission for Mipham Rinpoche's *Oral Transmission Scriptures*. Tarthang Tulku came when Sakya Gongma of Puntsök Palace was giving the *Compendium of Sadhanas* empowerments.[27] At that time he was an ordinary monk and used to get very angry if he didn't get to see Khyentse Chökyi Lodro because there were so many visitors that the attendants wouldn't let him in. Shechen Rabjam wrote a letter of introduction saying that Tarthang Tulku was very intelligent and to let him see Khyentse Chökyi Lodro, so eventually he got to meet him. Later Tarthang Tulku went to Gyalsey Gyurmey Dorje's encampment and received the *Guhyagarbha* from him, which was very good.[28]

6. The Reincarnation of My Guru

WHEN I WAS TWENTY-THREE, coinciding with the tenth-day celebration of the seventh month in the water-monkey year, 1932, the omniscient Jamyang Chökyi Lodro, quelling the anguish of samsara and nirvana, perceived, through his unobscured wisdom, the fourth incarnation of Gyaltsap Chöktrul, the one unequalled in kindness, and genuinely recognized him. The incarnation was born near the small, white stupa at Dowam in Nangchen and was enthroned on the lion throne in my unsurpassed master's residence at Shechen Tennyi Dargyeling.

When I went there on foot to meet him for the first time, the monastery paid extensive respect to me, playing the instruments on the roof and so forth. Headed by the main lamas—the Sixth Rabjam, Lion of Speech; Jamgön Chöktrul Pema Drimey Lekpai Lodro; my Dharma brother Gontoe Chöktrul with whom I received the *Vinaya*, bodhisattva, and Secret Mantra vows; Barchung Chöktrul; Lochen Tulku; and master On Gelek Gyatso—along with the other lamas and monks, they all took care of me with great affection, like an encounter of father and son. When I performed a feast offering at the tomb of my omniscient master and supplicated him, the sky became covered with rainbow-hued clouds. In front of the Manjushri statue with Mipham Rinpoche's practice support inside of it, I did the feast offering prayers over and over again.[1]

I went to join the row of participants in the feast ceremony of the elaborate tenth-day celebration, and Rabjam Rinpoche, Shechen Kongtrül, and the others went to welcome the supreme reincarnation at three distances.[2] Monks from Dzogchen and many other Kagyu and Nyingma monasteries rode on horseback to welcome him. When the lord of the families was seated in his residence, they made the most elaborate clerical procession to meet the youthful, radiant countenance of the master's graceful appearance.

His enthronement on the immutable lion throne was performed according to the *Innermost Essence of Immortality* long-life practice from our own Minling Terchen tradition, and the ceremony for longevity was done following my omniscient master Pema Vijaya's writings, according to the tradition of the former realized masters. We had a stylish feast for the occasion, and the lamas and tulkus from my monastery offered an elaborate thanksgiving.

From both Jamgön Chöktrul Khedrup Wangpo and the great practitioner Lama Jamyang Losal, who had perfected the three ways of service to please his revered guru, I received all the reading transmissions from the *Collected Works* of my omniscient master that I had not received from him in person. From Shechen Kongtrül I received the major empowerment of the *Eight Commands: Union of the Sugatas,* while from Rabjam Rinpoche I received his personal practice, Minling Terchen's *Yama Destroying Arrogant Spirits;* as well as the complete reading transmissions and empowerments for Khyentse Wangpo's cycle of profound treasures. From the lord of siddhas Dzogchen Thupten Chökyi Dorje, I received the major empowerment of his personal practice, the omniscient Jigmey Lingpa's *Tantra System Vajrakilaya.* At the Yamantaka Cave I met Khenchen Pema Tekchok Loden from Lhakang, who had perfected the four visions, and received a spiritual connection from him. When Shechen Rabjam invited the Lingkar Dharma king Wangchen Karma Tenzin for a party, I requested him for Lharik Dechen Rolpa's pure vision *Life-Entrustment of Gesar* through Mipham Rinpoche's lineage. I persistently investigated the teacher's oral instructions on the ritual traditions at Shechen.

In Rabjam Rinpoche's cabin at the Lotus Light retreat center, I made a brief connection with the *Razor Kilaya* recitation, and at that time Rabjam Rinpoche cared for me with unusually sincere affection and said, "Nowadays the vajra holder Jamyang Khyentse Chökyi Lodro is incomparable, like the Buddha who appeared in this world. Other than him, among all the supreme reincarnations of the two Jamgöns in Dzogchen, Palpung, Sakya, and so forth, there is no one more wise, pure, or noble-minded than the Khyentse and Kongtrül tulkus at Shechen Monastery. Compared to others, the character of Gyaltsap Rinpoche's supreme reincarnation should especially become like a peerless holy being, so you two foremost spiritual sons of the previous master should mainly look after Gyaltsap Rinpoche's reincarnation, as well as us and the monastery." He repeatedly said this and talked about his personal experience and realization in great detail.

Meanwhile I pretended to teach Rabjam Rinpoche the middle chapter on poetry and to explain the grammar and spelling from *Sublime Light of Excellent Discourse* to Mipham Chöktrul and my spiritual friend Lochen Tulku. I offered Gyaltsap Chöktrul and Khen Lodro Rabsel the authorization for Mati's *Manjushri*, Padampa's *Lion of Speech,* and *White Sarasvati.* When my revered master's supreme reincarnation returned to his family's estate, I saw him off, and though I promised to give him the *Treasury of Spiritual Instructions* later, the opportunity never occurred.

Meanwhile unrest broke out between China and Tibet, so I went home for the winter. On the way I stopped at Palpung to see Situ Rinpoche, who had just come back from Central Tibet. During that winter, in the tenth month of the water-monkey year, 1932, my father passed away. My whole family— Sangye Nyenpa, my other brothers and sisters, and my mother—performed extensive virtuous deeds for his sake.

At that time I met Drungram Gyatrul Rinpoche, a spiritual teacher in accord with sutra and tantra. Together with Sangye Nyenpa, I requested him for Gampopa's *Jewel Ornament of Liberation* and instructions on *Kalachakra,* while he kept looking after me with great affection. Meanwhile a severe black pox disease broke out in my home region, but the Manjushri statue in the Dharma lord Mipham Rinpoche's reliquary took on the pox disease, which stopped the epidemic. I went back to my previous hermitage to do retreat and sealed off the entrance with mud.

The night that I started the *Vajrasattva* recitation I dreamed about a beautiful five-pronged vajra wrapped in a long silk scarf covered with symbolic script and heard a voice saying, "This is a sign that you are Jamyang Khyentse's mind emanation." The next year, the water-bird year, 1933, I established an annual, elaborate seven-day drupchen of the *Vajrasattva* heart sadhana for the anniversary of my father's death. We went for a picnic to the mountain peak called Barlha Tsegyal, the main local deity of my home, where I did an elaborate cleansing ritual and smoke offering, and buried treasure vases for enhancing the fertility of the earth and for the symbolic abode of the local guardians. At that time, I sang this song:

On this high mountain, a pillar raised in space,
Reaching to the peak, below the eastern sky,
Abides my father, the perfect Buddha named Pema,
Surrounded by a group of realized masters;
Smiling happily, he causes the fall of a pleasant nectar rain
Of maturing and liberating teachings.

I miss the Lotus Light retreat center
On the glorious mountain of Tennyi Dargyeling;
Remembering my father, no matter how much
His young son grieves, what's the use?

Confident that I'm beyond meeting and parting with
The luminous mind of that *dharmakaya* master,
To practice my father's heritage of vast and profound secret
    teachings,
Is like enjoying a king's treasury.

If I don't waste time while studying, reflecting, and meditating,
I don't think that the profound path will deceive me;
In the style of the forefathers of the practice lineage,
Taking my whole life as the limit,
I'll rely on rocky shelters in secluded places.

Lord, while thinking of your determination to be free,
I feel like casting the foe of the eight worldly concerns to the wind.
Though still young, I'm afraid of death;
Without hope of acquiring prestige,
May I attain lasting happiness in my next life!

Lord, when seeing your assiduous practice,
My heart's desire is to spend my whole life in retreat, and
Merge the approach and accomplishment of the *Eight Great
    Sadhana* tantras
and their branches together as one practice.

Lord, when hearing about your diligent style of practicing
The path of the channels, winds, and essences,
I wonder if through the non-dual paths of means and liberation
I will realize the view of the innate truth!

Lord, when discovering your supreme realization,
I have no trust in mind-created Dharma;
In the innate essence of naked empty awareness,
I long for view, meditation, and action to be of one taste.

Lord, while thinking about your advice,
Though I'm without power or ability, my heart's desire
Is striving to spread the Buddha's doctrine all over the world,
Through teaching, practice, and activity.

Father, with kind and genuine affection,
You focused on me with unusual attention;
To show my gratitude for giving me your confidence,
I hope to repay it in this lifetime.

Lord, while pondering your supreme qualities,
I deeply feel a firm conviction;
From now until I attain enlightenment,
Though not separated from your company for an instant,
Having become your close heart son,
May father and son's minds be mingled!

Having realized outer phenomena as an illusion,
Good and bad conditions are alike in the great bliss of *dharmakaya;*
The inner mind's confused thinking is purified in basic space,
Free of clinging to experience in ultimate great wisdom.

Amidst undirected meditative experience in the *dharmadhatu*
    expanse,
Where involvement with the thought of comfort falls apart,
The luminous nature of sun and moon is unceasing;
May I spend my whole life in peace and happiness!

May whatever I do benefit the doctrine and sentient beings,
May the Dharma be effective, so grasping and fixation fall apart,
May the supreme mandala of awakened mind expand,
And may I attain the ten powers to be able to deliver
Whoever encounters me to primordial basic space!

At that time my brother Shedrup went to both Shechen and Dzongsar Monastery to ask if he could borrow any books by Mipham Rinpoche that they might have. At the Tashi Palbar Ling hermitage where Mipham Rinpoche passed away, his close student and lifelong attendant Lama Ösel gave us the reading transmission and authorization blessing of the recitation manual and appendix for the *Longevity Lord Yamantaka;* the *Trochu* recitation manual; the *Yamantaka Thread-Cross Ceremony* practice; the *Fierce Mantra* commentary; the *Expression of Awareness* cycle; the detailed and concise *Palden Lhamo* supportive practice from the set of sadhanas printed at Dzongsar; *Instructions on Rahula;* and the *Yudron Mirror Divination* practice and fulfillment-offering.[3]

Meanwhile, once when I was writing a letter, my precious master Chökyi Lodro jokingly asked if I was writing down a mind treasure, and I wondered whether that was a divination for the future. I made a revised edition of the copied manuscripts of Mipham Rinpoche's writings, the sevenfold profound treaty on empowerment, two books of miscellaneous instructions on wrathful mantra, the cycle on magical display, and Mipham Rinpoche's biography, and asked the omniscient Jamgön Dharmamati to look over the draft. He gave me a silk scarf with a poem gracing and honoring the treatise as well done, a vajra and bell, a piece of red Chinese satin, and the Vajradhara Khyentse Wangpo's treasure box with yellow scrolls.[4]

SERIOUS ILLNESS AND TAKING A CONSORT

I went to stay in a cave on the slope of a very high rocky mountain called Barlha Tsegyal, and when I reached it, the appearance of a rainbow and other good omens occurred. To dispel obstacles, I did a month's recitation of the *Supreme Heruka Assembly* and the secret sadhana of Jamgön's profound *Trolo* treasure. When Sangye Nyenpa received the exegetical transmission of Ngok Zhedang Dorje's *Like a Jewel Ornament,* a commentary on the *Two Segments,* from Nesar Lama Trapel, I also received it.

Later during the wood-dog year, 1934, when I was twenty-five years old, I contracted a type of colic that caused fever and chills and covered my mouth and orifices with sores. The pain from my fevers often brought me to the verge of death. At that time I endeavored in the recitation of the Dharma lord Chokgyur Lingpa's profound *Vajra Club of the Lord of Secrets* treasure, through which I experienced some improvement.[5] I especially focused on a hundred thousand feast offerings according to the female deity *Queen of Great Bliss* and the *Longevity Ceremony Averting Time,* and practiced the omniscient Jamgön Dharmamati's transmission of the *Mahakala and Mahakali Ransom Offering for Averting War* in detail.

Some ill omens occurred in my hermitage, such as rats taking away an entire rosary, eating my books, and so forth. When I did the recitation of the *Kurukulle* sadhana cycle that manifested from Mipham Rinpoche's realization, my previous deluded idea of meeting a consort to reverse the obstacles to my life and live for a long time reoccurred, and I decided to become a *ngakpa.*[6] Several lamas had told me that, being a tertön, I should take a consort. Mipham Rinpoche's closest disciple and lifelong attendant, Lama Ösel, recounted that Mipham Rinpoche had once told him that, in similar cases, if one were to burn hair of the consort-to-be next to the tertön, he would get better. So Lama Ösel said to take some of Lhamo's hair and burn it near me, but they told me it was Mipham Rinpoche's hair. After doing so, my health noticeably improved.

I did the detailed recitation of the peaceful Manjushri practice from Mipham Rinpoche's *Expression of Awareness* cycle, and in the third month of the wood-pig year, 1935, I went to see my unsurpassed teacher Chökyi Lodro at his residence, Dzongsar Tashi Lhatse. On the way, when I stayed below Marong Drugutil for a day, due to my dreams I wrote a guru sadhana of Saraha.

Whenever I went to see my precious master at Dzongsar, he took care of me with such great affection that I felt like I was coming home. This time he seemed even more delighted than usual and came to welcome me at the gate of his residence, holding long incense sticks. As soon as he saw me, he prostrated, put me on a high seat, gave me tea and rice, and said, "Last night I dreamed about the omniscient Khyentse Wangpo looking radiant and extremely happy, which was a sign of your arrival today. I remember the appearance of the Khyentse mind emanation in my awareness state, and that is who you are."

I requested him to give the *Treasury of Precious Termas*, which I had asked for in the past. Though he really wished to give it, due to the foreign invasion there was too much unrest in Amdo, so he postponed it for a while. He gave me Ra Lotsawa's lineage of *Yamantaka; White Tara* from the Tsar tradition; the *Heart Essence of the Lotus-Born*; the *Secret Gathering of the Dakinis* with the four *dakini* families; the *Heart Essence of the Immortal Arya* and other teachings in a very extensive way. He then told me, "These teachings definitely need a commentary, and you are qualified to write it." He gave me a silk scarf, a vajra and bell, over a hundred sheets of good quality paper that had been the writing paper of the former master, Khyentse Wangpo, a Chinese ink pot, and some pens.

I requested the entrustment of Thangla's life-force from the *Northern Treasures*, and though this doesn't have any seal of secrecy, he said to put it off for the time being.[7] To improve the changing circumstances, he performed the torma-exorcism of the *Lion-Faced One* from the *Heart Essence*, the *Wish-Fulfilling* smoke-offering reward, and the mountain purification—all in a tent on top of his house.[8]

That evening, though it was the second Tibetan month (corresponding to March), the Mechu River swelled as much as during the summer, and I felt that the revered master was pleased. He did an elaborate consecration of his residence from top to bottom and also subdued a dangerous place above the Khamche Monastic College. He showed me all the sacred representations in his house and explained their history in great detail. Then he told me to give him a long-life empowerment of the inner female deity practice from the *Heart Essence of the Great Expanse*, as well as the reading transmission of the *Treasury of Words and Meaning*, so I did as he told me.

Just before I was to depart he gave me a beautiful metal Shakyamuni statue from India, which had been Jamyang Khyentse Wangpo's practice support in the interior part of the room where he passed away. He also gave me many other presents, such as Yakchar's *Tara* treasure text handwritten by Khyentse Wangpo; the master's vajra and bell that he had used throughout his life; the Image of Emptiness hat that had belonged to both the former master's paternal uncle Mokton Jigdral Choying Dorje and Khyentse Wangpo; a full set of clothes that had belonged to Khyentse Wangpo; and other things. Then he said, "Don't ignore your profound treasure transmissions; they will truly benefit this degenerate time. Your decision to take a consort surely makes you greater than a hundred disciplined monks."

When I requested him to inspect my newly written commentary on the *Quintessential Kilaya of the Hearing Lineage,* he was delighted and said, "You must write such a commentary for each of Khyentse Wangpo's five cycles of the *Hearing Lineage.* You should compose a detailed manual of Khyentse Wangpo's treasure-teaching cycle that contains the entire path, like the writings of Mindroling Terdak Lingpa and his brother; I think it will become widespread. You should also write empowerment rituals for the specific sadhanas of the four classes of herukas from the *Heart Essence of the Great Expanse* and an empowerment outline for the *Innermost Sealed Essence Guru Sadhana.* Nowadays, among the four main schools in Tibet, the Nyingma school has about four great masters that are able to write commentaries, which is amazing."[9] He told me to establish an intensive sadhana ceremony at Sakar Monastery in Den for the remarkable and much-needed *Offering Liturgy to the Buddha Shakyamuni and his Eight Closest Sons* written by Jamgön Kongtrül, which I did. Then I went to Palpung where I met Situ Rinpoche and Khyentrul Rinpoche, and received a longevity blessing and a protection ceremony.

After that I returned to my own place, and while I was staying in my hermitage like before, the Tenth Zurmang Trungpa, Karma Chökyi Nyinche, came specifically to see me. He relaxed for three days and gave me the empowerment and reading transmission of the four practices of *Achala,* a Chokling treasure.[10] He told me, "By becoming a tantric practitioner, you will definitely have profound treasure transmissions that will truly benefit these degenerate times. It is an auspicious coincidence and aspiration for uniting the spiritual careers of Khyentse, Kongtrül, and Chokling." He then gave me a long-life prayer in verse and continued, "We will often meet again, and later I'll also give you the *Chakrasamvara of the Dakini's Hearing Lineage* empowerment and reading transmission from the Zur tradition." He also advised my consort and gave her a profound, short instruction on the Great Perfection. Drungram Gyatrul Rinpoche also came to my hermitage, so I requested a long-life empowerment from him. He said, "This is an auspicious coincidence to be enthroned as Guru Padmasambhava's regent," and presented me with a shirt.

Around that time I was doing recitation of Khyentse Wangpo's rediscovered *Hayagriva's Thunderbolt Fire Wheel* treasure. According to my request, in the fire-ox year, 1937, my mother and I had the fortune to receive the lucid, well-enunciated, and pleasant-sounding reading transmission of the precious *Kangyur* from Lama Karma Ösel Lhundrup. He was remarkably wise and kind, and had been sent for this purpose. He was so gracious as to also give us the exegetical transmission of Jamgön Kongtrül's *Extensive Treasury of Instructions* and the great *Treasury of All-Pervading Knowledge*. I made an offering of a hundred thousand feast offerings according to the *Secret Gathering of the Dakinis* liturgy with the elaborate *Fulfillment-Offering of the Five Elements*. He asked for instruction on *The Great Chetsun's Profound Essence of Vimala,* so I wrote a guidance text. Then I did the *Nagaraksha* recitation from Mipham Rinpoche's *Expression of Awareness* cycle.

When the Panchen Lama came to Jeykundo Dondrup Ling in Gatod, I went to meet him and received a Dharma connection, and as Karmapa Rangjung Rigpai Dorje came to Benchen Monastery, I met him as well and saw the black-crown ceremony that gives liberation upon sight. From Sangye Nyenpa I received explanation and guidance on the *Four Medical Tantras* and also received the instructional transmission of Mipham Rinpoche's detailed *Kalachakra* commentary. From Lord Kangyur, I learned how to recognize the different medicinal herbs and so forth in great detail.

Meanwhile, as I got the deluded perception that the mountain behind Benchen Monastery was a sacred place of Avalokiteshvara, some good omens also occurred, such as the increase of the community's vase consecration pills and so forth. I didn't get to circumambulate the mountain or write a guidebook for it. At the sacred Crystal Lotus Mountain in Gyamgyal I did a feast offering at the Dakini Lake and offered gifts. When I returned to my hermitage our first daughter was born, and Khyentse Chökyi Lodro gave her the name Chimey Dronkar.

From Muksang Khenpo Kunzang I received the reading transmission of the nine treasure volumes from the *Eight Sadhana Teachings*. Around the earth-tiger year, 1938, I went to the Benchen retreat center. In the inner apartment I received the empowerments and reading transmissions with the instructions of the *Secret Mantra Treasury of the Kagyu Lineage* from the Ladro Norbu Tulku through Karmapa Kakyab Dorje's lineage.[11] I also received the complete reading transmission of the Fifteenth Karmapa's entire *Collected Works*.

From Sangye Nyenpa I received the *Vajravarahi* empowerment according to the Karma Kagyu tradition twice; he said he had received it from Khenchen Tashi Özer, the Fifteenth Karmapa, and Situ Pema Wangchok. From my brother Shedrup I received the transmission for *Bernakchen, Avalokiteshvara, and Vajravarahi* that he had received from Karmapa Kakyab Dorje himself.[12] From Zopa Tharchin, the *khenpo* at Benchen, I received the entire *Collected Works* of Patrul Rinpoche, as well as Khenchen Yonten Gyatso's *Refulgence of the Sun* and *Radiance of the Moon* commentaries on the *Treasury of Precious Qualities* and its overview, *Advice on the Four Methods.*

Then I did the detailed and concise approach, accomplishment, and activity recitations of Urgyen Lingpa's profound treasure, *Ocean of Dharma That Embodies All Teachings* several times, as well as Vimalamitra's *Essence of Blessings* guru sadhana. I also did many elaborate and abridged recitation practices of the *Heart Essence of the Immortal Arya,* and the profound treasure of Drugu Yangwang, *Hayagriva Liberating All Haughty Spirits.*[13]

As requested by about ten students that lived nearby, to purify my obscurations I read the precious *Kangyur* once in my hermitage. I also offered the reading transmission of Jamgön Kongtrül's *Extensive Treasury of Instructions* to some good lamas from Kargo. Then I went to Drungram Gyatrul Rinpoche's Azure Sky Castle hermitage. On the way I stayed the night in front of Blazing Rock at Gatod where I wrote a Padampa guru sadhana on account of my dreams.

I stayed a long time at Azure Sky Castle hermitage, where Drungram Gyatrul took care of me with great affection. I offered him the empowerments and reading transmissions of the precious *Treasury of Spiritual Instructions* and the *Secret Mantra Treasury of the Kagyu Lineage* with the instructions. I also offered him the root text and commentary of Jamgön Kongtrül's *Extensive Treasury of Instructions* and the *Treasury of All-Pervading Knowledge,* as well as three Indian Mahamudra texts. He was so gracious as to give me the complete *Chakrasamvara of the Dakini's Hearing Lineage* empowerment from Zurmang, which he had received from the Tenth Trungpa Rinpoche, Chökyi Nyinche.

I then went to Drungram Monastery to preside at the assembly of the newly founded drupchen of Ratna Lingpa's *Secret Gathering of Avalokiteshvara.* Drungram Gyatrul told me, "Most treasure revealers don't live very long, but you must live your life to the end so you can really benefit the doc-

trine and all beings extensively." He repeatedly gave me long-life empowerments and samadhi blessings, and kept making specific prayers, aspirations,
and entrustments for profound treasure transmissions to appear to me. He
also gave me and my consort extensive gifts of clothes, ornaments, and other
goods.

Then lots of sorrow suddenly arose in my life, as my mother passed away,
and, not long afterward Lama Ösel, the Dharma lord Mipham Rinpoche's
lifelong attendant and close disciple, also passed away. Then my sister Kalga's
husband, who kept the Dilgo household, died. I invited Rabjam Rinpoche to
our home, where he spent a long time doing the ritual of sending my mother's consciousness to a pure realm and also performed the cremation of Lama
Ösel's remains. Gyaltsap Chöktrul also came, and as an initial Dharma connection I requested him for the long-life empowerment of Mindroling Terchen's *Embodiment of the Innermost Essence* long-life practice. He said that he
wanted both Sangye Nyenpa and me to give him a long-life empowerment,
which we did. We also visited Palpung Situ Rinpoche at his hermitage.

During the water-sheep year, 1943, when I was thirty-three years old, Lhamo
and I had another daughter, and Khyentse Chökyi Lodro called her Dechen
Wangmo. While I stayed in retreat at Mipham Rinpoche's Tashi Palbar Ling
cabin, I wrote an empowerment ritual and sadhana for the peaceful Manjushri connected with the four classes of tantra. During the second month of the
wood-monkey year, 1944, I went to Palpung together with Sangye Nyenpa,
where I met Situ Pema Wangchok, Gyalsey Jamgön Chöktrul, and Nenang
Pawo Rinpoche, who had come to Kham.[14]

7. Teachings with Khyentse Chökyi Lodro

NEXT I WENT to Dzongsar to study with the omniscient Jamgön Chökyi Lodro. He gave the long-life empowerment of the rediscovered treasure *Combined Sadhana of the Three Roots*, the explanation of the *Condensed Perfection of Wisdom* based on Mipham Rinpoche's commentary, the great *pandita* Vimalamitra's commentary on *Chanting the Names of Manjushri, Hevajra* according to the Sakya tradition, the major empowerment of the Khon tradition, and the major empowerment of the protector Gur. On the fourteenth day of the third Tibetan month, corresponding to April, he gave the elaborate *Kalachakra* empowerment according to the Buton school, Mipham Rinpoche's guidance on the *Six-Union Kalachakra*, the *Sixth Paldey* combined with the unusual blessing of *Naro Kechari* from the Tsar tradition, the reading transmission of Khyentse Wangpo's *Profound Instructions on the Secret Path*, Mipham Rinpoche's commentary on the last medical tantra explaining the physician's diagnosis by pulse and urine analysis, Jetsun Trakpa Gyaltsen's *Hundred Water Tormas* liturgy, the empowerment and reading transmission of the red and white *Amitayus* from Khyentse Wangpo's pure vision of *Mitra's Heart Essence*, and the major *Tantra System Manjushri* empowerment.[1]

On the tenth day of the seventh Tibetan month, corresponding to August, we did a hundred thousand feast offerings according to the *Combined Sadhana of the Three Roots* in front of the Crystal Lotus Cave, a sacred place at Dzamnang, along with all the students of the Khamche Monastic College. While there, Khyentse Chökyi Lodro said, "Bring me a rock shaped either like a dog or a fox head." I found one just like it, and as I offered it to him, he said, "Bury it at the foot of the sacred place." He then turned to Chokden, his ritual master, and said, "Keep chanting the petition-offering to Dhumavati."[2] I wondered if he was having a vision.

At the Mind Expanse Cave on top of the sacred place we did a feast offering according to Jamgön's profound *Secret Essence of Chakrasamvara* treasure. Then we circumambulated the top, where we made offerings to the Singu Turquoise Lake. At the White Tiger's Nest in Rongmey we did a feast offering according to the *Combined Sadhana of the Three Roots.* Khyentse Chökyi Lodro stayed there and gave the retreatants the elaborate *Vajrakilaya* empowerment from the Khon tradition, compiled by both the Lord of Secrets Taranatha and Jamgön Kongtrül. I heard that my precious master had completed the recitation of this practice earlier, so my devotion, joy, and trust became stronger than usual. He also let me give the retreatants the root and torma empowerments of the *Secret Gathering of the Dakinis.* Then we went to the hill behind Dzongsar and stayed at Trakar Tashitil, from where Chökyi Lodro Rinpoche returned to his residence.

I received detailed teachings on the root text and commentary of the *Wish-Fulfilling Treasury,* as well as a cycle of Mipham Rinpoche's writings, which Chökyi Lodro Rinpoche gave to Kyungtrul Pemala, me, and a few others. He told me, "A long time ago I had a vision that Dzongsar Monastery was one of the sacred places of Yamantaka. You should write a guidebook about this sacred place," and he gave me a silk scarf, so according to his command, I wrote the guidebook. At the main gate of the Dzongsar temple my supreme master put up a sign saying that I was the authentic Khyentse mind emanation.

My precious master also took me as his attendant to identify the self-arisen images, the meditation cave, and so forth. On top of the Dzongsar temple was a shrine for which my master had previously performed the Holy Site Consecration, which he replenished. There he made me wear Guru Padmasambhava's robes with the previous Khyentse Wangpo's hat, and while holding one of Khyentse Wangpo's meteoric-iron-dagger treasures that had been the ritual object of the Roaring Lion Guru, he let me chant the *Awesome Command.*[3] Meanwhile a strong wind whipped up, and Chökyi Lodro said that he had a vision of the evil demon from Trayap with his retinue, whom my master subdued with the samaya mudra, after which the demons offered their life essences, saying HAM SHANG TRI.

The next day I offered him an acrostic decree to the gods and demons. I also wrote the *Heart Essence of Manjushri* and called it my mind treasure, so my master told me to give him the reading transmission on an auspicious day. The following day he said that he dreamed about Mipham Rinpoche that night.

Meanwhile the Queen of Nangchen Yudronma and her son came to visit Dzongsar, along with Tsage Trakpa Chöktrul and some others, so I met them. They asked for the omniscient Jigmey Lingpa's *Tantra System Vajrakilaya* empowerment, which I offered. I also gave them the empowerment for the *Five Visions* sadhana with the completion stage practice, which was a pure vision of the omniscient Khyentse Wangpo; the empowerment for Garab Dorje's guru sadhana; and the empowerment for Sakya Pandita's secret guru-yoga practice.

The omniscient Khyentse Wangpo's wax treasure box contained a yellow scroll that I decoded and wrote down as the *Fortress Ravine of Nectar Medicine*. While I offered the empowerment to my master in his bedroom, he said that he had a vision of Vimalamitra seated in the space above.

The medicine lady Dorje Kyungtsunma from Jomo Kharak in Tsang had offered Jamgön Khyentse Wangpo a meteoric-iron dagger.[4] I decoded the *dakini* script that I saw appearing on the surface and wrote it down as the sadhana, empowerment, activity, and feast offering of Guru Drakpo with the lower part of his body in the shape of a dagger.[5]

There was also a Tara statue made of metal with symbolic writing on the back; my master wrote down the symbolic writing and gave it to me, and I decoded it and wrote it down as the outer, inner, and secret sadhanas of Green Tara. I then offered him the empowerments in succession, along with the empowerments and instructions for the guru sadhana of the omniscient Jigmey Lingpa and the *Heart Essence of the Self-Born Lotus* that combines the Three Roots into one, with the instructions.[6] He gave me confidence by saying, "Both the words and meaning of your mind treasures are incomparable nowadays." For each empowerment and reading transmission I offered, he always gave me a present.

Then we went to the Dzamnang Crystal Lotus Cave again, where we did a drupchen according to the *Ocean of Dharma That Embodies All Teachings*, combined with the blessed-medicine practice. There were about twenty of us altogether, including my precious master Chökyi Lodro and Katok Situ. We also did the fire puja, the torma-exorcism, and the consecration ceremony. Palpung Situ Rinpoche, Ongen, and other lamas came to receive the accomplishment, and we chanted the *Lamp Prayer* together. Khyentse Chökyi Lodro also concealed some sacred medicine in tantric space, and as there was an earth treasure in the back of Trikar Tashitil, my master specifically asked me to register it at that time, but I never had the good fortune to obtain it.

To illustrate the greatness of the place, my master told us some stories: "In the past, when Khyentse Vajradhara opened the Crystal Lotus Mountain treasure land, Karmapa Tekchok Dorje and Situ Pema Kunzang came, which created the auspicious coincidence prophesied for the *Avalokiteshvara Resting in the Nature of Mind* treasure, and right now it is a most auspicious omen.[7] Here at Crystal Cave there are 725 naturally appearing deities, and when the temple was constructed, Khyentse Wangpo indicated everything himself, down to the location where the main beams were placed. He demanded the finest materials.

"Inside the main image of Guru Padmasambhava is the root text of Chokgyur Lingpa's *Heart Practice Dispelling All Obstacles,* of which Khyentse Wangpo was the main doctrine holder among ten. He used his inheritance of Guru Padmasambhava's undergarment with an image of the Guru painted with Tsogyal's blood as the wisdom being.[8] The statue had to be finished on the tenth day of the monkey month, but the smith casting the deity had made the head a little crooked, and when the consecration was performed, Khyentse Wangpo focused his attention on it so that the head became straight."

Putting me on an even higher seat than before, my master authorized me as a great treasure revealer and gave me a mandala, together with the body, speech, and mind representations. I asked my master to write a long-life prayer containing his beautiful ordination, bodhisattva, and tantric names, and he was happy to do so.

The treasure revealer Drime Lingpa's son Tulku Pema Thukjei Wangchuk,[9] his brother Yonten, and the Derge Princess Yudrön sponsored a group feast practice of the *Eight Commands: Union of the Sugatas* combined with the blessed-medicine practice, which was conducted by Katok Situ Chöktrul, Markham Gyalsey Tulku, Tulku Samten Lodro who was the senior *khenpo* from Derge Gonchen, and the tantric teacher and chant master from Katok, and attended by the rest of the monastic community. The revered On Lama Tsewang Dorje and his students performed the *Heart Essence of the Immortal Arya* long-life practice, and the vajra master from Dzongsar Monastery and the other participants did the *Dorje Tsampa* recitation according to the Khon *Kilaya* tradition.[10] They performed the concluding peaceful and increasing fire pujas and the sacred medicine sadhana for the benefit of beings, with the dissolution into the five elements and so forth done in great detail. I was fortunate to be among the participants.

Minling Khen Rinpoche came to visit and received the profound instructions of the *Heart Essence of Chetsun* from my master. He stayed for a long time and paid me a special visit. He spoke gently and insistently, saying, "I have always had a great wish to receive profound treasure empowerments and transmissions from a reliable authentic lineage. But now Khyentse Chökyi Lodro has told me that he believes you to be a modern treasure revealer, so I would like to receive your treasure teachings."

Then my master gave the *Sutra, Illusion, and Mind* from the *Nyingma Kahma*, *Vishuddha*, the two *Dongtruk* cycles, *Vajrakilaya* according to the Khon and the Rog traditions, *Vajrakilaya* according to Rongzom's tradition, the *Medicine Buddhas*, *White Umbrella*, the white and black wrathful *Vajra Subjugator*, *Lekden* according to scripture and tantra, *Palden Lhamo, Vaisravana*, and others.[11] In this way he gave the successive empowerments and reading transmissions for each of the major texts, old manuscripts, sadhanas, mandalas, and so forth, giving whatever was contained in the *Nyingma Kahma* in great detail.

After finishing the empowerment for the protector Lekden, he told us, "When Lord Khyentse Wangpo gave the empowerments and reading transmissions of the *Nyingma Kahma* in full detail to Gyatrul Dongnak Tenzin from Peyul, he came to the restricted torma empowerment of the tantric protector Lekden. While giving this empowerment, a dark blue wrathful deity like the actual Supreme Heruka, so overwhelming that it was unbearable to behold, appeared from Khyentse Wangpo's mouth and at the door of the lama's residence a raven's cry suddenly sounded. Gyatrul Rinpoche taught and propagated the empowerments and transmissions of the kahma extensively and had the entire cycle of the kahma teachings printed. He started a sadhana ceremony for the kahma that vastly benefited the continuity of the teachings. Now, during this Lekden empowerment, I also had an actual vision of Lekden, which is probably an auspicious coincidence showing that you will benefit the continuity of the kahma teachings."

Then he gave two of the root volumes of the *Heart Essence of the Great Expanse* cycle; the authorization of the inner *dakini* practice of *Twenty-one Taras*, which is one of Khyentse Wangpo's rediscovered treasures; the reading transmission for the treasure text *Purifying the Lower Realms through the Peaceful and Wrathful Deities*, which unifies the Three Roots; the *Tantra System Vajrakilaya*; the major *Essence of Liberation* empowerment; *White Tara*

from Atisha's tradition; and *Abhirati Vajrasattva*.[12] He gave the reading transmission for Dodup Jigmey Thinley Özer's empowerment outline of the
Heart Essence of the Great Expanse; the bodhisattva vow; the bodhisattva
vow according to the *Middle Way* from the *Treasury of Precious Qualities* root
text; Lerab Lingpa's extensive, intermediate, and abridged *Eliminating Inauspiciousness;* and the elaborate, unelaborate, very unelaborate, and extremely
unelaborate empowerments of the *Heart Essence of Vima*.[13] All these teachings he gave in full detail to Katok Situ Chöktrul, Sangye Nyentrul, Kyungtrul Pema Wangchen's son Pemala, and others.

When Khyentse Chökyi Lodro received the lord Khyentse Wangpo's two
root volumes of the *Heart Essence of the Great Expanse,* which were prints
from Derge Gonchen Library, the guardian of the teaching known as Great
Sage appeared in a flash of lightning.[14] Khyentse Chökyi Lodro used these
texts for his own practice and also joyfully gave the empowerments and reading transmissions from these *Heart Essence* volumes. On the tenth day of the
seventh month, when he performed the *Embodiment of the Master's Secrets,*
I had the privilege of receiving its essential one-page torma empowerment
composed by the omniscient Khyentse Wangpo.[15]

When my master gave the exegetical transmission of the *Treasury of All-
Pervading Knowledge* root text, which he had received from the learned Lama
Trapel, to Chagmey Sangye Tulku, I had the privilege of receiving it as well.
Then, to Katok Khenchen Nuden and Chaktsa Tulku from Dralak my master
gave the reading transmission of the *Heart Essence of Vima* treasure's root text
and Tsongkhapa's *Gradual Path,* which he had received from Menyak Kunzang Sonam's student Apal, and so I too received it. I also offered them the
Guru's Innermost Essence through Patrul Rinpoche's tradition that my master
said he wanted to receive.

As a ceremony for my master's long life, we did a seven-day practice of both
the detailed and concise *Sixfold White King-Spirit Ransom Rite,* along with
the elaborate *King-Spirit Ransom* from Mipham Rinpoche's *Ransom Ritual*
text. Throughout the winter the revered master stayed in retreat, doing the
recitations of the *Secret Gathering of the Dakinis* root text, the *Vajra Dakini
Long-Life Practice,* and the *Lotus Dakini Magnetizing Practice.* I stayed in the
room where Khyentse Wangpo had manifested enlightenment in the primordial ground, reciting guru yoga.

RECEIVING THE *TREASURY OF PRECIOUS TERMAS*

On the twenty-first day of the wood-bird year, 1945, we performed the *Heart Practice Dispelling All Obstacles* drupchen as a commemoration service for Lord Khyentse Wangpo, and Khyentse Chökyi Lodro said he would start the *Treasury of Precious Termas* afterward. Shechen Rabjam, Markham Gyalsey Tulku, Kyungsey Pemala, Dzongsar Khenpo Khyenrab Senge, and others were among the participants.

On a Thursday that was a very good day astrologically, during a break in the drupchen, Rinpoche gave the *Heart Practice of the Dharmakaya Master* empowerment, making a little beginning of the maturing and liberating *Treasury of Precious Termas*. For the liberating empowerment of the drupchen, he gave the extensive, intermediate, and abridged *Heart Practice Dispelling All Obstacles* with the auspicious long-life empowerment in full detail. He gave me the name Pema Garwang Dongnak Lingpa, and to eliminate obstacles, the Shechen participants with Shechen Rabjam presiding, chanted the *Ocean of Accomplishment* in great detail for two days, with a melody and different types of incense for each of the Dharma protectors.

Meanwhile, since the Katok tulkus needed to receive the empowerments, they requested the revered master to come and give the *Treasury of Precious Termas* at Katok. But that evening when he went out to the toilet, he fell down and got a little ill. He said, "In the past, after receiving the entire *Nyingma Kahma*, Gyatrul Dongnak Tenzin from Peyul wanted to start an annual sadhana ceremony for which he invited Lord Khyentse Wangpo. Lord Khyentse wanted to go to Peyul but said that if he went, he wouldn't be able to return. He stepped on a thorn near his apartment and got sick, which prevented him from going, so this became his residence. Yesterday during the *Ocean of Accomplishment*, when Lekden was invoked into the displayed, thangka of the nine great protectors, I felt that he actually dissolved into it, so I will give the empowerments in my residence here."

Khyentse Chökyi Lodro accepted more than a hundred important ordained Dharma teachers for the empowerments, such as Katok Situ, Moktsa, the revered On, Yonge Migyur Tulku, Dortrak Tulku, Shechen Rabjam, Ontrul, Barchung Tulku, Pewar Tulku, Dzongsar Gangna Tulku, a *khenpo* who was Gatod Ngawang Lekpa's nephew, Trayap Khenpo Lodro, and others. The teachings of the great *Treasury of Precious Termas* have appeared all over Kham, Central Tibet, and India without interruption down to the present day. Due to the kindness of the two Jamgöns, who are of the nature of the Second Buddha, the maturing and liberating current of explanation of the kahma and terma of the Nyingma school, which is amazing and worthy to be called the sun and moon among the four great schools, has been set forth.

Regarding the style of explanation for the general assembly and the private explanation for close disciples, the humble regent of the Lotus-Born Guru carried on the tradition of his former incarnation like yesterday's sun shining today, with the complete series of empowerments, instructions, and reading transmissions. My master's father, Lord Rigzin Gyurmey Tsewang Gyatso, who was an emanation of the great translator Vairotsana, had been prophesied as the doctrine holder of the supreme tertöns Khyentse and Kongtrül's profound treasures. He was their chief heart son and actually saw the original treasure text of the *Ocean of Dharma That Embodies All Teachings* and the yellow scroll of the *Magical Net of the Three Roots*.[16] For a long time he stayed at Mindroling Monastery, source of the Nyingma teachings, where he studied with Trichen Sangye Kunga, Jetsun Dechen Chödrön, and others, learning the maturing and liberating instructions of the kahma and terma with the practices according to our own tradition of Minling Terchen and his brother.[17] He had perfected the signs of approach and accomplishment of the Three Roots and was specifically told to continue Jamgön Tennyi Lingpa's profound treasures, of which he received the complete empowerments, instructions, and reading transmissions from Peyul Karma Yangsi.[18]

Khyentse Chökyi Lodro received this root lineage and most of the profound Khyentse and Kongtrül treasures from his father. He received the complete treasure teachings of Minling Terchen through the lineage of his father, who had received them from Jamyang Khyentse Wangpo. He received the entire *Northern Treasures* from Shechen Gyaltsap, who had received them through Khyentse Wangpo's short lineage, and received the *Five Cycles of Essential Sadhanas* and the *Heart Essence of the Great Siddha* mainly from the doctrine holder Katok Situ Pandita and three or four other times through an authentic lineage.[19]

Most of the empowerment substances were from revealed treasures, and when he had time, Chökyi Lodro would also do the self-empowerment. For each empowerment he would give all the students the empowerment substances at least once. All the sacred substances, for example the seven-rebirth pills and nectar medicine, had a special significance, such as having been accomplished by the precious master's former incarnation and so forth.

Chökyi Lodro said that the commentary on the *Eight Sadhana Teachings* tantra, the root tantra of the *Assemblage of Peaceful Sugatas,* and the tantra of the *Eight Wrathful Heruka Sadhanas* were all included in Khyentse Wangpo's short lineage.[20] The root text of the profound completion stage instructions of the *Heart Essence of the Immortal Lake-Born* treasure, the root text of the extensive, intermediate, and abridged *Heart Essence of the Immortal Arya* empowerments, and many of Khyentse Wangpo's rediscovered treasures such as the peaceful and wrathful *Rishi Lokitra* were not included in any of Khyentse's other teaching series.

On the tenth day of the sixth month, corresponding to July, he gave the major *Embodiment of the Master's Secrets* empowerment based on the Tratsang manual, and the single transmission lineage of *Avalokiteshvara Resting in the Nature of Mind* that Nyakla Thupten Gyaltsen received directly from Lord Khyentse Wangpo like a unified stream.[21] After that he gave *Resting in the Nature of Mind* from the Fifth Dalai Lama's *Sealed Visions;* the *Embodiment of the Families of the Three Kayas,* which is the major empowerment of Chokling Tertön's *Lotus Sprout* testament and which Katok Situ Chökyi Gyatso had received from Khyentse Wangpo in person; the complete treasure root text of Jamgön Kongtrül Rinpoche's profound treasure *Embodiment of Realization of the Three Roots;* and the complete treasure texts, empowerments, and instructions of the *Secret Essence of Chakrasamvara* and *Secret Essence of Vajravarahi* and so forth.[22] All these belonged to a lineage with an unusual entrustment: Kongtrül Lodro Thaye had told Chökyi Lodro's father that he was an emanation of Vairotsana and that their mind streams were identical, so he should continue these profound treasures.

Then he gave the empowerment of the *Life-Force of Ekajati* that he received from Tersey Pema Wangchuk, Jamgön's concealed treasures of the biographies of Guru Padmasambhava and Vairotsana that he received from the learned Lama Trapel, Drugu Yangwang's treasure of the *Hayagriva Liberating All Haughty Spirits* tantra that he received from Katok Situ, the entrustment of the blue-green wrathful protector Lekden from the *Embodiment of Realization* scripture according to the Tsangsho manual with Petrin's ritual arrangement, and Situ Rinpoche's revised edition of the Katokpa Dharma lord Kadampa Deshek's *Fulfillment of the Dharma Protectress Palden Lhamo* sealed blessing empowerment.[23] At that time the revered master Dharmamati usually taught additional instructions from the general oral lineage of the past vidyadharas.

He said that whenever the teaching is transmitted, the visualization should take place while hearing the words, thus mingling sound and object. He said that for the reading transmissions it was acceptable to hear the sound in general, but after giving the instructions, he said, "If the students do a visualization session, the transmission really takes place." For most of the important completion stage instructions I pretended to do a session, and I was fortunate that he especially focused his attention on me for most of the empowerment entrustments.

A funny story occurred during the empowerments. I was seated near Rabjam Rinpoche; next to me was Chokling Rinpoche and then Katok Situ and Sherab Senge, Situ Rinpoche's tutor.[24] Katok Situ was quite young at the time and was sometimes scolded or cuffed by Sherab Senge as a disciplinary measure. Sherab Senge was a very strict tutor. He wanted to keep an account of all the teachings and empowerments that he and Situ Rinpoche received, in order to have them for future reference. Chokling Rinpoche was often fidgeting and looking for something to do throughout the long hours of the empowerments, so he told Sherab Senge that he would be happy to do his writing for him. Sherab Senge was very pleased and gave all his writing books to Chokling Rinpoche.

As the hours progressed I noticed that Chokling Rinpoche was doing a nice job of journaling the rituals and empowerments. For example, during the *Mara-Taming Kilaya* empowerment he wrote that Katok Situ Rinpoche wore a black hat and described in detail the rest of the costume for the dance of that empowerment. He also described the ritual of the *zor* torma in a very fine narrative style.[25] He even wrote down how I wore the black hat and costume during the *Secret Gathering of the Dakinis* empowerment, which has a ritual in the activity dakini section. Actually Chokling Rinpoche was sitting next to me because he was always getting into trouble, arguing with the high lamas, and rustling about. Since I was older and calmer, Khyentse Chökyi Lodro had asked me to keep an eye on him. He said that Chokling Rinpoche might even try to fight with Situ Rinpoche, who was also young and mischievous.

During the *Secret Gathering of the Dakinis* empowerment, when they threw out the ritual cakes in the activity dakini section, all the lamas went outside and stood on the veranda, and there was dancing and loud ritual music. Since

I wasn't trained in the actual dancing, Shechen Ontrul danced and I played the cymbals. Khyentse Chökyi Lodro had a pet monkey who was tied to a pole outside on the veranda. When the monkey heard the music of the drums and crashing cymbals and thigh-bone trumpets, he climbed way up to the top of the pole and started to shake wildly and swing back and forth. He was also making funny faces by pulling his brow up with his fingers. Later, when Chokling Rinpoche was writing about the important and auspicious events of the day, I said to him, "Why don't you put down that the monkey did quite a wondrous dance?"

"Should I really write that also?" Chokling Rinpoche asked.

"Of course," I replied. "You are writing everything. If you miss that, it would be a great omission." So he wrote down almost the exact words I had said.

Of the many parts of the narrative that Chokling Rinpoche was recording, one part was finished, and so he gave it to Sherab Senge, who thanked Chokling Rinpoche by saying, "Thank you so much. I am old now, and I have wind disease, so it would be very difficult to do this writing myself; I am very grateful." As he was reading it over, I could see when he got to the part about the monkey. His brow furrowed, and he read it again. He then looked over at Chokling Rinpoche, who had again drifted off somewhere else, and said, "You need a good scolding! All of you young high lamas are like this! Do you think this is a part of Khyentse Chökyi Lodro's life story? Why ever did you put that dancing monkey business in here?" Sherab Senge was shaking his fist, and Chokling Rinpoche was very afraid. Sherab Senge was getting madder and madder and said, "Even Katok Situ Rinpoche is like this now. He acts like a monkey just like you." Situ Rinpoche was of course the incarnation of Sherab Senge's root teacher.

Chokling Rinpoche at first was speechless, but finally he said, "Hey, Tulku Salga told me to write that in the book."[26]

"Yeah, now you want to blame it on poor Tulku Salga, who is always so gentle and well behaved," said Sherab Senge, berating him. "I thought you were trying to help me! But instead you ruined this, and it has all been for nothing."

Chokling Rinpoche turned to me and said, "Now come on. You told me to write that didn't you?" But Sherab Senge interrupted him, "Don't lie now, and leave him alone! Thank heavens Tulku Salga is very compassionate and gentle. As for the rest of you..." Then he cuffed Chokling Rinpoche and wouldn't speak to him for several days.

Chokling Rinpoche wasn't too pleased with me and said, "See, now these sons of aristocratic families show their true colors. You told the lie, and I got the beating. Yet you still keep quiet!"

Chokling Rinpoche was a lot of fun to tease. One time he and I were having a lesson in poetry with Sherab Senge. For practice we had to actually compose poetry. Chokling Rinpoche was using other poets for inspiration, and one day he said to me, "Tulku Salga, it seems that the poems just pour out of you without your even thinking about them. For me it is more difficult." I replied that I thought that I just had more practice and experience writing poetry, and not to worry. But again after a few days he asked me about it, and again he pleaded, "Please, tell me how you do this." So I told him, "Sarasvati comes on the very tip of my pen; she tells me everything, and I just write it down."

"Do you swear that is the truth?" he asked, but I didn't say anything.

At lunch with the other lamas, Chokling Rinpoche was talking about his difficulty in composing poetry and that I had told him that Sarasvati came to sit on the tip of my pen and told me what to write. He wanted to know if the other lamas thought this was true. Khyentse Chökyi Lodro said that of course it was true. Then I became very afraid and told Chokling Rinpoche that I had only been joking.[27] Khyentse Chökyi Lodro found the whole thing very amusing.

Sometimes when I teased Chokling Rinpoche, he would get so infuriated that he wouldn't talk to me for the rest of the day. But he was such a wonderful person and so flexible, and eventually he would come up to me and say, "No, you are Khyentse and I am Chokling, so we must remain friends."

Unlike most monasteries, Dzongsar was a very busy place. There were always high lamas coming and going. According to the rank of the visiting lama, it was traditional to have elaborate welcoming ceremonies with incense, music, and twenty-one or one hundred riders on horseback. The first time I went to Dzongsar, I was still single, and Khyentse Chökyi Lodro received me quite elaborately. When I visited Dzongsar the second time with my wife, Lhamo, an old lama from Dangtok Monastery said, "Last year he was received in such a grand way. I wonder how he will be received this year." But I was received in an even more grandiose manner than the year before, so they said Khyentse Chökyi Lodro was very pleased that I took a consort.

Before that, when I had been to Dangtok Monastery to see Ato Tulku's family, I used to be received quite well, but without any instruments. Later, after I had taken a consort, when I went from Benchen Monastery to Dangtok Monastery they used to play the instruments upon my arrival. Many people used to say that since I was Jamyang Khyentse Wangpo's tulku, I would benefit the doctrine more with a wife. Still many people didn't like the fact that I got married, though they never said anything bad. Whenever I returned to Dzongsar, it was always a great event for me and I looked forward to it. I knew that Khyentse Chökyi Lodrö would be waiting for me at the door of his residence with incense and the ceremonial white offering scarf. I prostrated to him three times whenever we met in this way, and he prostrated to me.

When I first visited Dzongsar, only Katok Situ came to stay, but gradually more and more lamas came. After Situ Rinpoche came, the reincarnation of Shechen Gyaltsap and other tulkus from Shechen came one by one. In the summer Khyentse Chökyi Lodrö liked very much to go to a particular beautiful field near Dzongsar for picnics. Sometimes he would stay for a week or even a month. One time we all went on a picnic and returned about eight days later.

I really felt that Khyentse Chökyi Lodrö could see other realms besides the human realm, and for that reason he acted differently than other people and was even afraid sometimes. Once we were staying in a tent in the lower meadow of Dzongsar Monastery. There was a little bit of rain, and Khyentse Chökyi Lodrö mentioned that he was afraid of Shukten, the Geluk protector. I thought that this might have some special significance, so I made no reply. While I was wondering what he might have meant, Khyentse Chökyi Lodrö repeated, "I'm really worried. Could you visualize yourself as Guru Rinpoche to help us?" Since it was a request from my spiritual master, I chanted some Guru Rinpoche mantras and visualized myself as Guru Rinpoche. After a while Khyentse Chökyi Lodrö said, "That's good. I feel better now, I'm sure everything will be all right."

Sometimes he acted like a small child. From his bedroom, the toilet was about ten meters down an unlit hallway. It was a dark passageway. I used to stay in a room right outside his bedroom with the general secretary of the monastery. There was also another room connected to his bedroom where his personal attendant Samten stayed. At night, especially if he had a stomach problem, Khyentse Chökyi Lodrö would have to use the bathroom at the end of that dark hallway. On those nights he would call out to me, "Hey, Tulku Salga, I need to go to the bathroom!" and he would wake us all up to help him. I told him many times that there was nothing to be afraid of, yet he was still afraid. I believe this is because he could see things that ordinary people couldn't see.

He was also afraid of rats, and even a harmless little rabbitlike creature. He used to say that he was afraid of devils and ghosts. Even when I and his attendant Tashi Namgyal and his secretary Tsewang Paljor were all sleeping nearby, he still claimed to be afraid. At the monastery the windows were made out of thick handmade paper. These were the outside windows, and on some of them the paper was torn. His ritual master, Chokden, mentioned that mice must have eaten through the paper. That night Khyentse Chökyi Lodro appeared to be very worried. He told me, "I would feel a lot more comfortable if someone could repair those windows; otherwise I will be up all night worrying." According to his wish, they repaired the windows for him, but even after they had finished, he told me that he was still worried that one of the rodents would get in and bite him on the nose. I thought that this was very childlike and finally chuckled a bit. All of a sudden Khyentse Chökyi Lodro looked at me and said, "No, I'm telling the truth; it's not a joke." So I said, "Please don't worry. You are a grown man. Rodents sometimes bite a small child, but they certainly will not bite you, a grown man." Then Khyentse Chökyi Lodro said, "Do you really think they know that I'm a grown man?" and I reassured him again, asking him not to worry.

He used to sleep near the building where the empowerments were performed, and I always stayed in his quarters when I stayed at Dzongsar. I usually took my meals with him, so we could talk. Sometimes during the night I would go to my own quarters, which the general secretary had arranged for me, but often I would stay in the passageway outside Khyentse Chökyi Lodro's room. He often didn't want me to leave his presence, and if someone came for an audience, they had to get to the point straight away so that our conversation could be resumed. When there were many people who had audiences with him, I would go to the room next door, where Jamyang Khyentse Wangpo had passed away. I would practice there until he was free again, and then we would resume our conversations.

As I mentioned earlier, Khyentse Chökyi Lodro had a pet monkey, and someone once informed him that it would be a good idea to remove its tail, as it would no longer be able to be so mischievous. So one day, Khyentse Chökyi Lodro rather abruptly said, "We should cut off the monkey's tail right now." Tashi Namgyal held the monkey and I held the tail and Khyentse Chökyi Lodro cut off his tail with a kitchen knife. Afterward I thought that Khyentse Chökyi Lodro might change his expression somehow—that perhaps he would be sad or feel compassion for the monkey, but to my surprise he remained perfectly relaxed and normal.

When other lamas visited Dzongsar—like the Karmapa, Katok Situ, or Shechen Gyaltsap—it was a great affair. All of Khyentse Chökyi Lodro's monks and attendants would be happy, as the great and wealthy lamas would give many gifts on their departure. Since they also brought their own attendants with them, there was relatively little extra work for the monks and attendants to do. However when I came, as I wasn't wealthy, I had relatively few gifts to give, and sometimes there was more work for the monks and students at the monastery, as I often brought writings and texts to work on.

Khyentse Chökyi Lodro liked the students from the monastic college at Dzongsar very much; he didn't favor the ordinary monks from the monastery in the same way. Being a monk can be just like an ordinary job, going to do village rituals for money and so forth. The students from the college, on the other hand, studied very hard. So these students managed to visit Khyentse Chökyi Lodro's place rather easily, but when I stayed there, I heard that they used to say, "Oh! That long-haired Tulku Salga is here; that's the end of our visiting time."

Meanwhile Minling Khenchen Ngawang Khyentse Norbu came and received the detailed and concise empowerments of the rediscovered *Secret Gathering of the Dakinis* treasure with the empowerment and instructions for the *Dakinis of the Four Classes*. To most of the students Chökyi Lodro gave the long-life empowerment for the *Embodiment of the Innermost Essence* long-life practice. In his room he gave Nyang's treasure of the *Four-Armed Mahakala*, a long-life empowerment of the *White Life Protector*, and instructions based on the *Embodiment of the Innermost Essence* treasure root text, which I also received.[28]

Minling Khenchen Rinpoche said to me, "You should offer an empowerment connection of one of your most profound treasure teachings, whatever comes to mind." When I asked Khyentse Chökyi Lodro about it, he said,

"There is a great need to continuously teach the former Khyentse Vajradhara's ocean of maturing and liberating orally transmitted and revealed treasure teachings, and you should give it in the empowerment room of my apartment." So based on the treasure root text, I offered the nine-vehicle empowerment of the *Heart Essence of Manjushri*, and the empowerment of the five-family female deity Sarasvati to the omniscient Jamyang Chökyi Lodro, Khenchen Khyentse Norbu, Shechen Rabjam, On Tsewang Dorje, Katok Situ Chöktrul, Moktsa Tulku, Katok Ontrul, Shechen Ontrul, Gyaltsap's kind ritual master and a great practitioner Lama Jamyang Losel, my vajra brother Lama Chokden, and some others. The next day my master said to give Minling Khenchen the instructions based on the daily practice, which I did.

On the tenth day of the seventh month, headed by the Shechen lamas and monks with Rabjam Rinpoche presiding, we performed the *Embodiment of the Master's Secrets* feast offering from the Mindroling tradition, with chanting, music, libation offering, and dances. Rabjam Rinpoche made elaborate offerings and gave a lot of feast substances and gifts. It was Khyentse Chökyi Lodro's custom to do an elaborate *Embodiment of the Master's Secrets* feast offering in either the earlier or later seventh month;[29] he said that he seemed to have visions of Guru Rinpoche during that time.

When all the maturing and liberating teachings were completed, we did a drupchen of Minling Terchen's *Heart Practice of Vajrasattva* with the ritual for making pills that liberate through taste. The Third Shechen Ontrul was the chant master and performed it according to the Shechen tradition. During breaks in the drupchen, my precious master explained the *Gradual Path of the Wisdom Essence* commentary.[30] He said that Khyentse and Kongtrül would usually give detailed teachings during the feast offering of the drupchens. We concluded with an elaborate longevity ceremony, and Rinpoche gave the *Secret Essence of Vajrasattva* empowerment from the *New Treasures of Chokgyur Lingpa* to the entire gathering of faithful ones, both distinguished and common, and distributed the liberation-through-taste pills to everyone present.[31]

Meanwhile a vulture had landed on the roof of the lama's residence, and to dispel obstacles we did Yakchar's elaborate *Tara Ransom Ritual* and *Averting the Call of the Dakinis* with the longevity ceremony from the *Secret Gathering of the Dakinis*. To a small gathering my precious master gave the empowerments and oral transmissions of the three volumes from the *Treasury of*

Precious Termas that have a seal of secrecy, which he himself had received from Gyaltsap Vajradhara.

To a group of disciples headed by Terchen Rolpei Dorje Chöktrul from Zurmang Monastery, Rinpoche gave the detailed empowerments and oral transmissions from the *Heart Essence of the Luminous Three Roots,* a mind treasure of the revered Lord Khyentse Wangpo for which I compiled the empowerment ritual and wrote a guidance manual. When I previously had made a connection with the *Vajrakilaya* practice from the *Heart Essence of the Luminous Three Roots,* a nine-syllable *Kilaya* approach mantra and a fourteen-syllable accomplishment mantra had manifested in my awareness as a contin-uation of the decoding of a *Kilaya* treasure that had been put off by Khyentse Wangpo. I didn't write anything down at the time, so now Chökyi Lodro Rinpoche said to write them down. As Shedrup and my consort Lhamo and the children had arrived, I requested the essential self-empowerment for the *Heart Essence of the Immortal Arya,* as well as the empowerment and instruc-tions for the *Lotus Dakini* of the *Secret Gathering of the Dakinis.*

After the temple of the Khamche Monastic College was expanded, a large statue of Maitreya was built according to the former Khyentse's plans, and underneath it Khyentse Chökyi Lodro said to bury an authentic destructive charm against recurrent enemies, family deaths, and misfortune. I recited the *Secret Assembly Longevity Practice* for a few days and offered the essential empowerment. My master was so kind as to bestow the omniscient Khyentse Wangpo's root text of Asanga's short lineage of the *Five Treatises of Lord Mai-treya,* along with the explanation of the Mahasiddha Luhipa's short lineage of the *Chakrasamvara Root Tantra.*[32] I also had the privilege of receiving the root and branch empowerments with the reading transmissions and instruc-tions of the *Tsotrak* treasure teachings that my master specifically received from Roldor Chöktrul.

When the empowerments and teachings were finished, Roldor Rinpoche gave my revered master and me the symbols of enlightened body, speech, and mind. Along with that he asked my precious master to compose a commen-tary on the *Vajrapani Tantra* and asked me to compose a medium-length com-mentary on the *Oral Instructions in the Gradual Path of the Wisdom Essence.* And he said, "You should maintain and spread the *Tsotrak* treasure teach-ings. It would be worthwhile to come to Zurmang Monastery and give the *Sutra, Illusion, and Mind* empowerments that Trungpa Rinpoche asked you to give before but that you haven't given yet." He even gave me a few liturgical arrangements and told me to practice the *Dugtrak Bumthangma* transmission and use the fermented blessed medicine from Mindroling, which I did.

I offered him the *Supreme Heruka* empowerment from the *Heart Essence of the Great Expanse,* the empowerment for the specific practice of the *Four Heruka Families,* as well as the reading transmission of all the available prints at Derge Gonchen of Mipham Rinpoche's *Collected Works.* I also had the privilege of receiving the empowerment and reading transmission of Lingkar Pema Zheypa's profound mantra treasure of the *Chandali Mother of Life* set of teachings, and he told me, "I gave you the empowerment because the treasure revealer said that you are one of the doctrine holders."

Once at Crystal Lotus Cave, where the *Three Classes of the Great Perfection* was revealed, Khyentse Chökyi Lodro performed the drupchen of the *Dharma Ocean that Embodies All Teachings.* His attendant Samten was always forgetting things. It seemed like he was always going up to Rinpoche to confess about something that he had forgotten. For this drupchen they needed representations of the four great kings,[33] and they needed pictures of Amrita Kundali for the inside and Hayagriva for the outside of the door. It didn't surprise me that Samten had left all these pictures back at Dzongsar. Crystal Lotus Cave was in the middle of nowhere, so there was no hope of borrowing these images or making them.

Whenever the attendants made mistakes, they would come to me first and ask me to tell Khyentse Chökyi Lodro. In this way they had a much better chance of avoiding any kind of punishment. I was a little concerned that this could be an inauspicious way for the drupchen to begin. Right before the ceremony, I discreetly remarked that the pictures of the protectors had been forgotten. So Khyentse Chökyi Lodro said to the two ritual masters, "All right, then just paint two HUNG syllables with good ink on the door; that will do." They tried to find ink, but they couldn't find any. Finally Khyentse Chökyi Lodro yelled at them to just write the syllables with a piece of charcoal from the fireplace, which they did. Later on they did manage to find some good ink and painted the letter properly.

Khyentse Chökyi Lodro was originally from Katok, which is a very rugged place, and the people there are quite tough. When the monks there would make even a small mistake, it was typical for them to receive five lashes with a leather strap. It happened that Katok Situ and his general secretary were also attending this drupchen. At the end of the first day, the general secretary went to Khyentse Chökyi Lodro and said, "It seems that lamas and monks just do whatever they want here. In Katok they would have had to suffer the lashes. Because the Dilgo son is here, even Hayagriva's picture can be substituted with a little charcoal and the letter HUNG."

When I planned to return home for a while the omniscient master got very sad and even shed tears, so I also felt very sad. I asked him about my life span and he gave me a composition written in verse that said, "Do the recitation of various general and specific Three Roots long-life practices and perform many hundreds of thousands of feast offerings to the Three Roots. You will have a few obstacles to your life, and especially your forty-ninth year will be very harsh. If you get through that, you will live until you are seventy-three." In addition to that he said, "If the outer, inner, and secret omens are not mistaken, you could possibly become eighty. Generally speaking the revered Lama Khyentse Wangpo showed signs of becoming 108 years old, and though it seemed like he was meant to live long, he only made it into his early seventies. After him a Khyentse reincarnation will manifest who will definitely live long."

He gave me a very good quality statue of Sakya Pandita that was his personal practice support, and as a speech support he gave me about twenty volumes of the most necessary teachings from the *Treasury of Precious Termas* and the most important teachings from Khyentse Wangpo's profound treasure teachings.[34] As a mind support he gave me a Mahayana vajra and bell that he said had actually belonged to Kadampa Deshek. He also gave me the blessed horse-headed, *dzikshim* dagger that was Khyentse Wangpo's practice support for *Hayagriva Liberating All Haughty Spirits,* my master's decorated small hand drum that he had used throughout his life, his own vidyadhara hat that he had worn while giving the *Treasury of Precious Termas,* a cloak and the rest of a set of clothes, nonsectarian sacred substances of whatever was in his relic box, very valuable yellow scrolls of Sanskrit manuscripts, a lot of sacred medicine that liberates through taste, and other things, as well as a list of the offerings and an auspicious long-life prayer.[35] Then he also gave me a large, beautiful metal mandala plate with a heap of various gems that the previous Khyentse Wangpo had used; the omniscient Khyentse's profound *Five Cycles of Essential Sadhanas* treasure that contained the empowerment rituals, liturgies, and guidebooks; and a publication about the appropriate way to render service to the Khyentse treasures. Then he said, "There is a great need for your treasures; you must decode them and not neglect those who are linked

to this present time. You must come back next year! If I don't act like you, I'm
not sure if I will live very long."[36] He gave my consort a three-eyed *zi* stone
that had been revealed by Khyentse Wangpo and told her not to cause any
breaches of samaya. After he gave extensive presents to my brother and two
daughters, we left my unsurpassed master's residence.

During our journey we visited places sacred to Arya Tara and went to Lhundrupteng palace in Derge, where I did a ceremony mainly for the great queen
and Prince Thupten and performed the *Mamo Ransom Offering of the Hearing Lineage* and other rituals. On the way we incidentally stopped to take a
bath at the hot springs above Marong Drugutil. In the Den region we visited Panchen Smritijana's reliquary while we attended the lama dances on
the tenth day.

I stayed at the Secret Mantra Awareness Palace retreat center of Benchen
Monastery. For the newly constructed temple I prepared vases for eliminating
misfortune and for the earth lords and nagas, and auspicious treasure vases
from hidden treasures of the New and Old schools, as well as many other
things. I performed the *Majestic Command,* constructed symbolic abodes for
the local guardians and Palden Lhamo, and did the *Raksha Thotreng* subjugation for spirits causing recurrent obstacles.[37] As a stability ceremony for
Nyentrul Rinpoche's newly built temple, we performed an elaborate *Profound Sevenfold Kilaya* drupchen with Ladro Norbu Tulku and forty students,
while combining the higher and lower rites.[38]

During the early summer of the fire-dog year, 1946, I received the reading
transmission for the *Collected Works* of the Jonang Jetsun, the savior Lord of
Secrets Taranatha, from Karma Tseten, who was a personal student of the
tokden from Zurmang Namgyaltse called Tersey Rigzin Tsewang Norbu and
of Karma Khenchen Ratna and Trungpa Rinpoche Chökyi Nyinche.[39] From
Benchen Khenpo Zopa Tharchin I received the reading transmission for
Patrul Rinpoche's entire *Collected Works,* as well as Khenchen Yonten Gyatso's
Refulgence of the Sun and *Radiance of the Moon* commentaries on the *Treasury
of Precious Qualities,* which he had received from the great *khenpo* himself.

In late autumn I went to Zurmang Monastery, where I offered the complete empowerments and reading transmissions for the *Magical Display of
the Peaceful and Wrathful Ones,* the *United Assembly* connected to the nine
gradual vehicles, the *Mind Class,* the *Space Class,* and the *Seventeen Tantras of the Instruction Class* from the *Nyingma Kahma* to most of the sangha

community, headed by Terchen Roldor Chöktrul, Trungpa Rinpoche Karma Chökyi Gyatso, Garwang Chöktrul from Zurmang Namgyaltse, Ladro Norbu Chöktrul, Khenchen Khyenrab from Do Monastery, the Zurmang Dutsitil khenpo, and the vajra master.[40]

I received the *Kilaya* empowerment from the Khon tradition with the liberating empowerment of the higher and lower rites according to Jamgön Kongtrül's manual, which was Garwang Rinpoche's wish, as well as Roldor Chöktrul's elaborate main and branch empowerments of *Chakrasamvara of the Dakini's Hearing Lineage* from the Zur tradition and the *All-Embodying One* empowerment from the Karma Kagyu tradition.[41]

At the holy site where the *Heart Practice Dispelling All Obstacles* was revealed above Trungpa's Khargenma residence, they asked me to perform the *Holy Site Consecration* and the *Majestic Command* in full detail, which I did. I also requested to see the *Heart Practice Dispelling All Obstacles* thangka, which had been the practice support of both the great treasure revealers Chokling and Khyentse Wangpo while they performed the drupchen of the combined *Heart Sadhanas* at Lhundrupteng in Derge.[42]

Next we went to Fox Cave at the former Trungpa's retreat center Vajra Garuda Fortress, where I offered the Trungpa Tulku the *King's Sovereignty* empowerment from the *Northern Treasures*.[43] From there we went to Roldor Rinpoche's Tramo Nang retreat center, where Roldor Rinpoche said he wanted to establish an annual sadhana ceremony of both Nyang's *Black Lady of Wrath* and the *Secret Gathering of the Dakinis* and needed the empowerments and oral transmissions,[44] so accordingly I offered Roldor Rinpoche, Trungpa Tulku, and the retreatants that lived there both the *dakini* empowerments and oral transmissions.

Stopping at Ladro Monastery along the way, we went to the Gyamgyal Crystal Lotus Mountain, a pacifying holy site of the vajra family and one of the twenty-five important sacred places in Dokham. There we went to the Infant Milk Lake in front of Dothi Gangkar, where I made offerings to the local deities and performed the feast offering of *Dharmakaya Master Amitayus* from the *Heart Practice Dispelling All Obstacles* for a few days and even wrote a guidebook to the sacred place. There were many pilgrims at the light blue lake, and as the waves were stirred by the wind, a vivid pattern of a peaceful mandala complete with doors appeared on the lake, along with other auspicious signs. I also saw the Black Lake at Gyam and performed a feast offering. That night in a dream, I saw a text of the *Nine Deities of Infinite Life* in Jamyang Khyentse Wangpo's handwriting. This appeared to me as a mind treasure, *Pema's Heart Essence of Longevity,* which I wrote down.[45]

Next I went to the Ösel Ling retreat center of Mindrol Norbu Ling, the monastic seat of the great Chokling tertön, situated in front of Tsikey Norbu Punsum, where I met Tersey Tulku.[46] I requested the detailed empowerments and reading transmissions of the peaceful *Profound Sevenfold Magical Display of Purified Metal* with the wrathful *Shaken from Its Depth,* a Chokling treasure.[47] I also requested the empowerments and reading transmissions for the specific sadhanas of the *Heart Practice of the Sambhogakaya Lama Akshobya, Vairochana, Shakyamuni,* and the *Medicine Buddha* according to Tersey Tsewang Trakpa's liturgical method, as well as the *Dharmakaya Master* empowerment and an empowerment that Tersey Tulku said he had received directly from Jamgön Kongtrül.

Then I went to Mindrol Norbu Ling, where I met the Chokling Tulku and offered him the most profound longevity blessings from the *Heart Essence of the Immortal Arya.* I got a close look at Terchen Chokling's possessions, empowerment articles, and representation of Guru Rinpoche. In front of Terchen Chokling's precious remains I made offerings along with the *Seven-Chapter Supplication* and the *Clearing the Obstacles of the Path* supplication and performed the feast offering of the *Heart Practice Dispelling All Obstacles* in full detail.

After the great tertön Chokgyur Lingpa had passed away, the omniscient Khyentse Wangpo divided his terma objects among the tertön's consort, sons, and daughters. The share that he said belonged to the tertön's daughter Konchok Paldron was a sheet of yellow parchment of the female deities from the *Eight Sadhana Teachings* inside a silver tube. Tersey Tulku told me to decode whatever it contained and gave it to me along with a pure white undergarment of Ratna Shri Tara. It contained a collection of outer, inner, and secret sadhanas of the nine heruka consorts from the *Eight Sadhana Teachings* and of Dutro Mamo, the guardian of the teachings, which I wrote down and asked him to examine. Tersey Tulku said, "None of the Khyentse choktruls were able to see it, but now you have seen it accurately! I feel so relieved!" and was delighted.[48]

He then gave me a good quality *Heart Practice Dispelling All Obstacles* thangka done in the Central Tibetan style, which had been Tsewang Norbu's practice support.[49] He asked me to offer it to Chökyi Lodro Rinpoche on his behalf and told me to ask Khyentse Chökyi Lodro to decode the *Six Bardo Completion Stage* from the *Lotus Sprout Embodiment of the Families.*[50]

I continued on to Sera Kyidudey Monastery and to Shongnak Monastery, a branch monastery of Shechen, where I offered a long-life empowerment to Tulku Atsang, his consort, and his son. Then I went to Drungram Monastery to see my brother Shedrup, my consort, and my daughters who had gone there ahead of me.

I met Gyatrul Rinpoche and told him everything that happened lately in great detail. I crossed the river in Gonto in a boat via the south and met the cheerful countenance of Khenpo Khyenrab at the Ontod Monastic College. Then I went to Lhundrupteng in Derge where I met Situ Pema Wangchok, Peyul Karma Yangsi, Dzogchen Kongtrül, Driter Ösel Dorje, and the Derge prince, queen, and ministers. Together with the Derge queen and prince, I received Choje Lingpa's pure-vision empowerment of the *Mahasiddha's Longevity Practice* 108 times from Situ Rinpoche.[51]

Then I returned to Dzongsar Tashi Lhatse, second only to glorious Nalanda, where I had the fortune to meet the cheerful countenance of Chökyi Lodro. My precious master's younger brother, Chimey Rinpoche, cared for me with great affection, giving me the long-life practice of the senior Serpa Tertön as well as a *Hayagriva* empowerment. I decoded the *Secret Gathering of the Dakinis,* with the great ransom offering and the guardian of the teachings.

My master wrote his autobiography as I had previously requested and insisted that I write mine too, together with the history of my treasures. He published the general and specific fourfold cycle of the *Heart Practice* that was not included in Chokgyur Lingpa's treasury of teachings, the treasure root empowerment texts for the *Profound Sevenfold Cycle* and so forth, notes on the commentary and whatever the two Jamgöns had written on it, two volumes of Chokgyur Lingpa's own writings that Tersey Tulku had, and the thirteen-deity empowerment of the *Wish-Fulfilling Guru* from the *Heart Practice of the Wish-Fulfilling Essence Manual of Oral Instruction.*[52]

For Katok Mipham Chöktrul, Gyaltse Troga's son Ladro Norbu, and others, I chanted the complete empowerments and reading transmissions of the *Wishing Vase* sadhanas, and from the *Treasury of Precious Termas* I gave the empowerments and reading transmissions for the three volumes with the seal of secrecy. To Muksang Kalek Tulku Kunzang Rangdrol and others,

I gave the reading transmission for the five volumes of Tsele Natsok Rang-drol's *Collected Works*.

I had the privilege of receiving explanation and guidance on the *Hidden Meaning of Path and Result* from Chökyi Lodro, when he taught it in accordance with the request of the Khamche Monastic College's teaching assistant.[53] First Khyentse Chökyi Lodro told me that I didn't need to receive the *Path and Result* or its commentaries, and I said that was fine. Actually I had given him the transmission and teaching of a commentary by Konchok Lhundrup on *Path and Result*. I didn't ask him again, but when the teachings started, he told me it was better that I received it, and I said I would do whatever he said. He would alternate the *Path and Result* and the *Compendium of Sadhanas*. Sometimes he would teach the *Path and Result* for five days and then again give three or five transmissions of the *Compendium of Sadhanas*, together with the commentaries. So I received the complete oral instructions from Khyentse Chökyi Lodro.[54] The general instructions of the *Path and Result* are contained in the *Treasury of Spiritual Instructions* which I had already received from Shechen Gyaltsap when he gave the *Treasury of Spiritual Instructions*, so I received it twice.

My master said, "The profound *Three Classes of the Great Perfection* treasure has been a single transmission lineage with a strict seal of secrecy from the Terchen until now, and though I feel that from the present fifth transmission onward, the seal may be loosened up a little, it is up to you." During the empowerments and reading transmissions of the *Three Classes of the Great Perfection*, Katok Khenchen Nuden, Tertön Drimey's son Tulku Pema Thukjei Wangchuk, Tersey Dechen Namgyal's son Drimey Tulku, and others also came.

When my revered master was receiving the *Stirring the Depths Hundred-Petaled Lotus* empowerment from the kahma from Tulku Pema Thukjei Wangchuk, I incidentally received it as well. When Terchen Drimey Pema Lingpa passed away he departed for the Copper-Colored Mountain.[55] My revered master had his special guru-sadhana testament for after death, and I had the privilege of receiving the empowerment and reading transmission for that as well.

While Khenpo Nuden was staying at Crystal Lotus Cave, my precious master wrote a teaching on the profound key points of the path of skillful means, about how to enhance realization on the path by relying on a lotus-endowed mudra for the vajra long-life practice. Khenpo Nuden and Chökyi

Dilgo Khyentse in his thirties. Shechen Archives. Photographer unknown.

Lodro sent lots of letters back and forth to exchange their views. We performed over a hundred thousand feast offerings of the *Secret Gathering of the
Dakinis,* and when my master received the *Profound Quintessence* empowerment from Khenpo Nuden, I had the privilege of receiving it as well.[56]

My master sent me a letter written in verse telling me to decode the most
important treasures from the *Secret Gathering of Dakinis Tantra,* mainly the
ransom offering ritual, and gave me a good quality Indian vajra and bell. As
requested by the Khamche *khenpo,* he was kind enough to give detailed teaching on the *Hidden Meaning of Path and Result.*

Menyak Khenpo Damchoe gave teachings on the *Golden Key* for twenty days,
and I received that too. The *Path and Result* has a lot of teachings on the third
empowerment, which he elaborately explained, and Khyentse Chökyi Lodro
praised the teachings on the third empowerment a lot. Menyak Damchoe
had a lot of faith in Khyentse Chökyi Lodro, and when he left, he mentioned

Khyentse Chökyi Lodro. Shechen Archives. Photographer unknown.

that maybe Khyentse Chökyi Lodro was thinking about taking a consort. Later, during a meal Khyentse Chökyi Lodro told me that because he praised the teachings about the third empowerment a lot, Menyak Damchoe had thought that he wanted to take a consort, and he had been right.

So that winter, as an auspicious connection to carry his life span to the end, expand the fortune of the doctrine and beings, and pacify the foreign invasion, Khyentse Chökyi Lodro took Tsering Chödrön as his consort. She was the daughter of the Lakar family and had been prophesied as an emanation of the queen of dakinis, White Crystal Vajra Lake Queen.

When Khyentse Chökyi Lodro got married, my wife Lhamo and two daughters were also there and all held ceremonial scarves. On the twenty-fifth day I had the fortune to offer the couple a longevity ceremony by means of the *Queen of Great Bliss dakini* liturgy, and I offered all the Three Root empowerments and transmissions for my own treasure entitled *Pema's Heart Essence of Longevity*. Mipham Rinpoche's tulku, my brother Shedrup,

Chokden, and Tashi Namgyal all attended. On the roof of Dzongsar Monastery, Ngakpa Tashi Palden from Rekong and I installed a golden victory banner filled with mantras of the *Heart Practice Dispelling All Obstacles*, while reciting the *Placing the White Umbrella Banner* liturgy that had been consecrated at the holy site of the *Heart Practice*.

Khandro Tsering Chödrön had never been to Dzongsar; she was with her sister Tselu and my nephew Jamga. When she arrived, she was a nun with shaved head, so Khyentse Chökyi Lodro gave her refuge and told her to grow her hair. She stayed for a month and then went back home. At New Year's she returned.

Upon his taking a consort, many people were surprised, but when Khyentse Chökyi Lodro was younger, he had gone to Lakar to give the *Gathering of the Vidyadharas* empowerment to Yakze Tertön.[57] While there he met the two young Lakar daughters, Tselu and Tsering Chödrön, who were seven or eight years old at the time. Yakze Tertön told him that it was a very auspicious connection and that the daughters could prolong his life. Khyentse Chökyi Lodro was very embarrassed and wouldn't talk to the tertön for several days.

There was no criticism from any of the monks at the monastery or the monastic college; only Gelek Khyentse scolded him a little. When Gangna Tulku offered a long-life ceremony, he said that taking a consort was the best way to prolong Khyentse Chökyi Lodro's life. Zhabdrung Dampa was extremely surprised that Khyentse Chökyi Lodro had given back his *pratimoksha* vows, and said that since Khyentse Chökyi Lodro was as realized as Saraha, he could even give *Vinaya* vows though he had a consort, and he further said that Chökyi Lodro was a great master.

Khyentse Chökyi Lodro said that having a consort might not be good for the monastery, and was thinking of building a house at Crystal Lotus Cave and moving there; but the Dzongsar monks headed by Gangna Tulku asked him to stay at the monastery.

Khyentse Chökyi Lodro then went all over Derge, Nangchen, Dzongsar, and so forth, and everywhere they rejoiced and offered him long-life ceremonies. Palpung Situ didn't like mantrikas, but he said it was the right thing to do for Khyentse Chökyi Lodro's activities and offered a mandala and a long-life ceremony. Khenpo Shenga had once said that if Shechen Gyaltsap

Khandro Tsering Chödrön. Shechen Archives. Photographer unknown.

would become a tertön, he would become Guru Rinpoche's representative, but Shechen Gyaltsap didn't get married; so Khenpo Shenga was very happy when Khyentse Chökyi Lodro got married. Dzogchen Monastery had a good connection with the Lakar family. Since Khyentse Chökyi Lodro married a daughter from the Lakar family, they didn't say anything.

Once Khyentse Chökyi Lodro and his consort found some termas at a sacred spot on a hill near Dzongsar; I wasn't there at the time, but it seemed like he often found terma objects at that place. Many times in the very early morning, after doing his prayers and just before sunrise, when his attendants came, they would notice that Khyentse Chökyi Lodro had something special. For instance, one day Tsewang Paljor, the general secretary, came in the early morning. As soon as he had passed through the doorway, Khyentse Chökyi Lodro said, "Hey, look on the windowsill—something is there. That's my share."[58] When Tsewang Paljor went over and looked, he found a small vajra that looked very unique. When the attendant picked it up, Khyentse Chökyi

Lodro became like a small boy who had found a favorite lost toy. He was excited and wanted to have it right away.

Often the dakas, dakinis, and Dharma protectors offer this kind of treasure to the *tertön*. Once I walked into my precious master's room early in the morning, and he said, "Didn't you receive some sort of treasure box last night?" I became slightly fearful and wondered what he could possibly be referring to. After considering everything, I replied, "No." He then explained, "Last night I had a vision in which Ekajati offered a treasure. I thought she had offered it to you!" But she hadn't.

My master gave the *Embodiment of the Master's Realization* empowerment in full,[59] and to benefit religion and politics in Derge, we performed the ritual for making sacred medicine based on the *Profound Essence of Vishuddha from the Hearing Lineage* at the Tashi Lhatse cottage, south of Trori Ziltrom. While my precious master presided over the ceremony, I had the fortune to be among the participants and he was kind enough to arrange the liturgical methods of the sadhanas. The revered master said he had a good dream about doing the *Most Profound Vidyadhara Long-Life Practice* recitation from *Pema's Heart Essence of Longevity*.

Sponsored by the manager of the Jago home, we performed a sacred medicine ritual combined with a drupchen based on the *Supreme Heruka Assembly* from the *Heart Essence of the Great Expanse* at Manigenko, east of Ziltrom. Altogether there were over a hundred participants: me, Gyalrong Namtrul, the lamas and tulkus from Yakze Washul, and others. At Lhari Palace I did the detailed wind horse practice of my own *Gesar* treasure.[60] After requesting the liberating empowerment connected to the four classes of tantra, I moved from my master's place,[61] and together with the Derge king and the Jago minister, we went to Ziltrom to practice the *Holy Site Consecration* from the *Combined Sadhana of the Three Roots*, and *Employing the Local Deities*. My precious master was so kind as to perform the accomplishment of the treasure vases, mandalas, and so forth, and he donated the offering utensils and other things of the earlier and later Jamgöns for the consecration.[62]

Sponsored by the Khardo manager Chimey Gonpo, in back of Marong Drugutil and west of Ziltrom, we performed an intensive *Abhirati Vajrasattva* drupchen with about twenty monks from Zang Go. We also performed the *Holy Site Consecration* and *Employing the Local Deities* there, after which I returned home.

At Benchen Monastery I performed the usual mantra offering for a gilded copper statue of Guru Padmasambhava an arrow's length in height, and in particular I prepared the mandala and practice materials for the principal deity and retinue of the entire Wealth God mandala. At home I performed the *Heart Practice Dispelling All Obstacles* and performed the extensive *Peaceful Lama* higher activity based on the *Wealth God Eminent Being*,[63] as well as the protection, exorcism, slaying, and suppression based on the *Destroying Demons* lower activity.

I was about thirty years old the first time I went to Zurmang Dutsitil, where I performed the *Dharmakaya Master Long-Life Practice* from the *Heart Practice Dispelling All Obstacles* and completed many treasure vases for enriching the earth and eliminating misfortune. To Zurmang Garwang Rinpoche, Roldor Tulku, Trungpa Rinpoche, Tsikey Chokling Tulku, and disciples of the previous Trungpa Rinpoche, such as the retreat master, the *khenpo*, and many others I offered Sangye Lingpa's major *Embodiment of the Master's Realization* practice empowerment and the reading transmission for Jamgön Khyentse Wangpo's entire *Collected Works*.

At Roldor Rinpoche's Tramo hermitage I offered the empowerments and reading transmissions of Chokling's *Three Classes of the Great Perfection* to the Roldor and Trungpa Tulku and some retreatants, and from Roldor Chöktrul I received the reading transmission of Terchen Roldor's *Collected Works*. I wrote a commentary on Terchen Roldor's revealed treasure of the *Vajrapani Tantra* and read the transmission.

I first saw electricity when I was in Lhasa and thought it was very useful for houses. In Kham everyone had electric flashlights, but I didn't like them. The Chinese had given a jeep to Jago Topden from Derge, who was an official. The Jago family had a lot of faith in Dzogchen Kushab Gemang, and once when Kushab Gemang went to visit them, he said he had to go to Trangu to take out a treasure teaching. The Jago family said they would take him in the jeep, and I asked if I could come; that was the first time I saw a car. They said it was fine, and there were four of us in the jeep: Kushab Gemang, one of his monks, me, and the Jago family's driver.

We left by jeep at three o'clock in the morning from Lhari Phodrang; when we arrived at Traglhagon it was dawn. Kushab Gemang took out a treasure there without anything special happening; then he said he wanted to go to

Trangu to take out another treasure. I said I would stay at Peri Monastery. He asked me why I didn't want to come, and I said that since there were many disciples of Khyentse Rinpoche at Trangu, if I went there I would have to visit everywhere, so I preferred to stay where I was.

I stayed upstairs in Nyarak Monastery with Kushab Gemang's monk. So Kushab Gemang left for Trangu, which was not very far from Traglhagon. The monk said he wanted to go see a Nyingma monastery nearby, the name of which I forget, and we went there together. They were constructing a new temple, and there were many carpenters and painters at work. We went to see the protector temple, which was a Tsemar temple with a beautiful new image of Tsemar. The monk who was beating the drum had seen me at Dzongsar and asked if I was the Dilgo Tulku, so I said yes. He asked me where I had come from, and I said I had come as an attendant of Kushab Gemang. Then he took me to the guesthouse of the monastery, where the caretaker brought us food and tea. They asked why I didn't stay there since I was the Dilgo Tulku and this was a Nyingma monastery. I said that I was waiting for Kushab Gemang to return from Trangu where he had gone to take out a treasure, and after having some tea, we went back to the place where Kushab Gemang had left us. He came back at eight o'clock in the morning.

The Peri family heard that Kushab Gemang was there and invited us to come and eat at their home; I didn't want to go and asked to be excused. They kept asking me, but I didn't want to go, so Kushab Gemang went and ate there. When they came back, they gave me thirty-two silver coins. Then we left in the car and arrived at Lhari Phodrang around noon. At that time there was already a direct road; the Chinese had made a road from Manigenko up to Derge Gonchen. Kushab Gemang stayed at the Jago residence home at that time. Before we got back to the Jago residence, Kushab Gemang also took out a treasure at Trakri Yangkar. At that time Lama Dole, who was an attendant of Khandro Tsering Chödrön, was in retreat in Trakri Yangkar, and he and some monks came to get blessings from Kushab Gemang and myself. When we came to Lakar, the treasurer and Tselu had gone to Dzongsar, so we didn't stop there. When we returned to the Jago residence, Kushab Gemang had three round stones.

Khyentse Chökyi Lodro didn't reveal any treasures before crowds, but he might have revealed a few material treasures. When Khyentse Chökyi Lodro stayed in Katok, he was thirteen years old. His teacher was Katok Situ's tutor,

Thupten Rigzin Gyatso. At that time the Lingtsang king and queen came and asked him for a Dharma connection, so he gave them the "Gangloma."[64] When they met him, they thought of the previous Khyentse Rinpoche and started to cry; soon after, they invited him to Lingtsang, and he went there.

Around the same time, Katok Situ Rinpoche went to Trangkog and to Tralak; at that time Khyentse Chökyi Lodro was the chief lama next to him. On the way back Katok Situ spent the night at Yilung Lhatso, which was a very nice place, so he toured the area and had a look. Khyentse Chökyi Lodro also wanted to look around, but as he was very small, the Katok monks told him to stay behind and study. But he got up on his horse anyway, and when he caught up with the others, Katok Situ didn't scold him but showed him the lake and the mountains. Years later, when the Jago family wanted to do a drupchen in Manigenko, I went to Yilung Lhatso on the way and stayed there a day.

Khyentse Chökyi Lodro said that when the Communist regime ended, we should go and build a house at Yilung Lhatso and stay there. A very nice wooden house was built but has since been destroyed. The Panchen Lama was going to build a house on the same land; he already had the required signatures. On the mountain above was a cave from where one could see the lake; the previous Luden Gyatso did a lot of retreat there. The previous Deshung Tulku wanted to do a one-year retreat and asked Khyentse Chökyi Lodro about it, but was told that it would be better to serve the Sakya Gongma. Khyentse Chökyi Lodro also said the *mamos* would deceive Deshung Tulku if he were to do retreat.[65]

Kalu Rinpoche stayed one year in that same cave without any attendants. He told me it went very well; he was completely alone without any distractions. The Lhari family used to send him food. He wanted to stay there many years, but his relatives told him not to. I first met Kalu Rinpoche when the Tsadra Rinchen Trak retreat in Palpung finished. I didn't know him then; they used to call him Rata Kalu. When coming out of retreat, his father brought him a light-colored horse with a gold ornament and brocade on its head.

When Situ Rinpoche offered a *Victorious Thousandfold Offering*, Kalu Rinpoche attended. Khyentse Chökyi Lodro gave the Shangpa teachings for the Karma Taktsang retreat center and stayed there for about fifteen days. He also took some reading transmissions from Kalu Rinpoche. Kalu Rinpoche composed his own biography supplication where he mentions that he had a vision of Jamgön Kongtrül, and a disciple of Kalu Rinpoche gave it to

Khyentse Chökyi Lodro. One day when they were talking together, Khyentse Chökyi Lodro asked Kalu Rinpoche if he had had a vision of Jamgön Kongtrül, and Kalu Rinpoche got a little embarrassed. We got to know each other quite well in Lhasa, where we often visited each other.[66]

When Sakya Gongma went to China, Khyentse Chökyi Lodro went into retreat. At that time I stayed at the Crystal Lotus Cave and did retreat on the *Supreme Heruka Assembly*. It is a very blessed place, but I got quite sick. There was a Guru Rinpoche statue directly in front of me, and when I looked at it, my heart would start pounding. All this seemed to be due to the blessings of the place, and after a month I got better and felt fine. I spent a day at Gyaltsap Rinpoche's former cabin at the Shechen Hermitage, which is a lovely place.

Though I never met her, there was a woman named Yudron who lived at Peyul where we used to stop for tea.[67] Whenever anyone used to go on that road at night, they were quite scared of evil spirits. She was very fat and used to wear a *chuba*. She had about five or six dogs that she took care of; she used to stay and sleep with the dogs. There was no sign of dog feces or anything like that. The dogs were always barking at people. Two of the dogs were called Gyaruma and Uguma, and when they would bark, she would say, "Gyaruma, Uguma, sit," and they would be quiet. When people who came by wanted to make tea, she said that she would slowly make it, but that she didn't have any flint stones to make the fire. She never retired but would talk on and on.

Whenever Katok Situ, Khyentse Chökyi Lodro, or Khenpo Ngaga traveled they used to pass her place, and she would say, "Rinpoche, Rinpoche, please come here and talk to me. I am old and can't hear well." So they used to go and talk to her. The first time Khyentse Chökyi Lodro passed by on his way to Katok, she said, "Oh, you are the Jamyang Khyentse Tulku and are staying at Dzongsar, aren't you?" It appeared she could tell just by looking. When asked how she knew, she would just say that she had been on the main road and heard it; but nobody, including Katok Situ and Khyentse Chökyi Lodro, had ever seen her get up in seventy or eighty years.

Once someone from Katok had seen her walking around. She told him it wasn't good that he had seen her walking, and asked if he had anything to give her. He gave her a bag with tsampa, and she thanked him and said it would be OK. Then he went to Katok and asked the lama there if he would be harmed because he had seen Yudrön walking around. The lama asked if she had harmed him, and he said he gave her a bag with tsampa. The lama then gave him a protection against untimely death, so though he did get very sick, he got better after a month.

The Long-Life Temple at Dzongsar contained a lot of gold images, and when Khyentse Chökyi Lodro needed to restore them, he sent someone to Yudrön to ask for help, and she sent some urine which all turned into gold. Then one day she offered her conch-shell *mala* to the Derge king and said good-bye. Seven days later she died. Rakong Sotra, who was the governor of Horpa, offered her skull to Khyentse Chökyi Lodro and told him many stories about her; she was very unusual.

Speaking of unusual happenings, when Khyentse Chökyi Lodro gave the *Compendium of Sadhanas* empowerments to about one hundred monks in Dzongsar, Tsewang Paljor was sitting behind Katok Situ and saw some gold pellets the size of sesame seeds on the floor. He thought they were coming from Khyentse Chökyi Lodro's table but later saw that they were falling, like a rain of gold, from the hangings above Khyentse Chökyi Lodro's throne. He gathered the gold up and used it to guild a statue. The first time I myself gave the *Compendium of Sadhanas* was to Khyentse Chökyi Lodro's reincarnation, the Khyentse Yangsi, but no gold fell from the sky. The first time I gave the *Three Classes of the Great Perfection*, it was to Trungpa Rinpoche and Rolpai Dorje in Zurmang, and the second time I gave it was to the Khyentse Yangsi.

On the way to Rekong there was an emanation of Avalokiteshvara, a tulku of Patrul Rinpoche, who lived in Amdo; he was a very remarkable person. He would give food to any beggar who came, provided they performed the preliminary practices.[68] He would supply them with food for their entire stay. The monastery was full of hundreds of such beggars, all performing the preliminary practices.

I stayed at Rekong Monastery for about one year. While there I gave the *Treasury of Precious Termas* for the first time. At the place where Shabkar Tsogdruk Rangdrol used to stay, there was a large stone with a tree behind it. Shabkar often used to sit there and sing songs, and the local people graciously offered me to sit upon the stone as well. When I gave teachings there, many rainbows appeared, and snowflakes fell from the sky like flowers, which led people to believe that I was Shabkar's reincarnation.

From Rekong I traveled to the Machen Pomra Mountain, where there was a sacred place that needed to be opened up. Chokgyur Lingpa and Jamyang

Dilgo Khyentse at Rekong. Shechen Archives. Photographer unknown.

Khyentse Wangpo had been supposed to open it up, but they had been unable to get there. Fortunately I was able to open it. That night, in a dream, I saw Chokgyur Lingpa in the form of a *tertön*. He told me that it was wonderful that I had been able to open the entrance to this sacred place, and that it was of greater merit than to offer a piece of gold the size of a sheep's head. Upon my departure back to Derge, a great number of mantrikas and a vast crowd gathered to bid me farewell.

Khyentse Chökyi Lodro was very pleased when we met again. "You must have many termas to benefit others," he said. He explained that in a dream he had seen clouds in the forms of the eight auspicious symbols and many other shapes, including many buddhas and bodhisattvas; and a lot of rain fell to benefit beings. "You must spread your spiritual treasures," he told me. Khyentse Chökyi Lodro was then preparing to go on pilgrimage in Central Tibet. I asked him to give me advice about whether or not I should stay in lifelong retreat. "It is not necessary for you to stay in retreat," he replied. "Little by little I will check on what you should do."

That summer for the first time I gave the *Treasury of Spiritual Instructions* to Drungram Gyatrul at Ngonmo Hermitage. One of Troga Rinpoche's broth-

Left: Dilgo Khyentse's brother Sangye Nyenpa Rinpoche.
Photographer unknown.
Right: Dilgo Khyentse in his forties. Shechen Archives. Photographer unknown.

ers, a good monk, lived in Dzongsar, and at Khyentse Chökyi Lodro's request, I gave him the *Wishing Vase* empowerments, which are like an abridged *Treasury of Precious Termas*. I got the pictures necessary for the empowerments from the previous Khyentse Rinpoche, and I also gave the *Sealed Teachings of the Treasury of Precious Termas*. I gave that another time in Zurmang, once in Mindroling, and now, so this was the fourth time.

The Gyalrong Khandro was very fat and used to wear robes with a raw-silk shawl.[69] She used to joke a lot with Tsering Chödrön. One time the Gyalrong Khandro gave Khyentse Chökyi Lodro a long-life empowerment that I received as well. During the invocation the Gyalrong Khandro would sing a tune, and because she was quite old, her voice would tremble. Tsering Chödrön was laughing, so the Gyalrong Khandro said, "If you take an empowerment from me like that, will you really get it?" She was very special; her long-life empowerment benefited me a lot, and she did a lot of ceremonies for Khyentse Chökyi Lodro. She was someone who had returned from death and said she would go to the Copper-Colored Mountain pure land. When she was sick, Khyentse Chökyi Lodro brought her many precious pills. After swallowing them, she would take them out of her chest and say they didn't help.

One time in Jagen Shingtok she was performing a feast offering with Khyentse Chökyi Lodro and Khandro Tsering Chödrön. During the ceremony Gyalrong Khandro had a vision and got up. She walked straight to a place where a treasure was but had difficulty reaching it as she was so fat, so she asked Khandro Tsering Chödrön to help her. When she got up to the spot, she removed some small rocks and earth, and found a ritual dagger in the rock. When they took it out of the rock, it was still warm. Gyalrong Khandro told Khandro Tsering Chödrön to give it to Khyentse Chökyi Lodro. It is now in Gangtok, and I have a copy of the sadhana and empowerment related to this dagger, in which Vajrakilaya is multicolored and surrounded by the ten wrathful deities.

In the summer I used to enjoy stopping at Zikok when traveling from Denkok to Dzongsar. To get there, one has to cross a very high pass called Goser La. Nearby is a small plain where Jamyang Khyentse took out the *Quintessential Kilaya of the Hearing Lineage* treasure. Between the Shri Singha Monastic College and Dzogchen Monastery there are several very nice meadows full of flowers, surrounded by many solitary retreat places, such as Tsering Jong and the Yamantaka cave where Patrul Rinpoche wrote *The Words of My Perfect Teacher*. When looking down from there, Dzogchen Monastery looks like an offering place.

When Khenpo Shenga was in Shri Singha Monastic College, Khenchen Zhabdrung Dampa came to receive teachings on the thirteen great commentaries from him. Between Dzogchen Monastery and Shri Singha there is a shallow stream that has many frogs which make a lot of noise at night. Dogs used to go there and eat the frogs. Zhabdrung Dampa's attendant didn't know what was causing the noise, and he said to Zhabdrung Dampa that one really had to have good practice at Dzogchen Monastery because there were so many evil spirits. Zhabdrung Dampa asked him why, and he told him about the noises. So Zhabdrung Dampa told him it was just the frogs. Later he went to check on it and found it was true.

While I was in Dzongsar, Sakya Gongma came, and as he could rarely visit, he was given a very elaborate welcome. As the rumor had spread that Sakya Gongma was coming to give teachings, there were many monks who gathered. Besides all the local monks, the whole Dzongsar mountaintop was filled with Khyentse Chökyi Lodro's disciples wearing yellow robes. A hundred laypeople went ahead to receive him, followed by a hundred monks; Khyentse Chökyi Lodro, Dangtok Tulku, Nyarak Tulku, Pewar Tulku, and I rode horses and wore golden hats. First Sakya Gongma was received at Tashi Barthang in a tent where everyone offered ceremonial scarves. According to the Shechen and Dzogchen tradition, we circled around him with our hats off and then put them on again. When he arrived at the Summit Palace, Khyentse Chökyi Lodro's residence, the Mipham Tulku and ten monks did the dance of the offering goddesses.

On Sakya Gongma's son's birthday—he was six or seven years old—Khyentse Chökyi Lodro, I, and several others did a long-life ceremony, and Gangna Tulku and ten others did an *Amitayus* ceremony. The monks from the monastic college offered a longevity ceremony, and after that the Khamche Monastic College had a ceremonial debate. Sakya Gongma had a very good voice for chanting, and as I had a good voice too, when offering the longevity ceremony for Khyentse Chökyi Lodro, Sakya Gongma asked me to chant the *Ocean of Mirror-like Wisdom* with a strong voice.

The Summit Palace was very beautiful, and Sakya Gongma stayed there for about a year. Khyentse Chökyi Lodro used to go see him and have meals with him every day. When he gave the *Path and Result* teachings and the *Compendium of Sadhanas,* the teachings were held in the temple, and in the evening he would return to the Summit Palace.

Not only did my precious teacher tell Sakya Gongma that I was an incarnation of Jamyang Khyentse Wangpo, but he said that I was a great tertön as well. He also told him that he should ask me for my long-life mind treasure in order to prolong his life. So Sakya Gongma asked me for it, and one day I offered him the long-life empowerment.

When the news went around that Sakya Gongma was at Dzongsar, more and more people came to see him every day. Whenever Khyentse Chökyi Lodro requested any teachings from Sakya Gongma, he often used to call Gangna Tulku and me. Otherwise we wouldn't dare to request anything. Finally Sakya Gongma went to China, though his wife stayed on at Dzongsar.

At the Infant Milk Lake in front of the Gyamgyal Crystal Lotus Mountain I did the *Red Amitayus Long-Life Practice.* From there I went to the Black Lake in Gyam and performed the feast offering of the *Embodiment of the Three*

Roots. Then I went to see Tersey Tulku at the Ösel Ling retreat center which belonged to Chokling's Tsikey Norling Monastery and requested him for the specific empowerments of Tersey Tsewang Trakpa's teaching on *Resting in the Nature of Mind* from the *Heart Practice's Sambhogakaya Master Stirring the Depths of the Lower Realms,* the *Meaningful Lasso, Lotus Crest,* and *Vajra Heart.*[70] In front of the precious representation containing Chokgyur Lingpa's remains, I did a hundred feast offerings of the *Heart Practice Dispelling All Obstacles.*

From there I went to Karma Monastery and saw the Shakyamuni statue there.[71] In the apartment of the great sage Karmapa I got a close look at the frescos of Saraha, the images of the successive Karmapas that had actually spoken, and many other special body, speech, and mind representations. I also made elaborate offerings in the temple of the Karmapa lineage and the Secret Mantra Palace. I met Tulku Rinchen Nyingpo and, in the great protector temple, saw the magnificent metal sculpture of Chakrasamvara in union. This had been Gyalwang Chötrak Gyatso's practice support, and on special occasions, white essence would come down from the deity's place of union. I also saw the extraordinary metal sculptures of Mahakala and Palden Lhamo, and obtained a small but complete yellow scroll from the lap of Palden Lhamo, which was labeled *Nyak Kilaya.*[72]

Then I went home and stayed in retreat at a hermitage, and during breaks between my sessions I wrote down the *Nyak Kilaya* teachings. When I was done, I went to Dzongsar to show it to my master's Dharma eyes, and after he had purposely received the empowerment and reading transmission, he said, "The omniscient Khyentse Wangpo had a profound treasure transmission of the nine-headed eighteen-armed Vajrakilaya, and this seems to be part of it." He kindly wrote the liturgical methods for the sadhana, the daily practice, the torma-exorcism, and the empowerment.

In the ninth month, corresponding to October, Khyentse Chökyi Lodro said that he was leaving on pilgrimage. The Chinese were not the only reason he left; he must have known that his life was near its end. As Khandro Tsering Chödrön and her sister had never been to Lhasa before, they asked him to go to Lhasa. So I returned home and stayed in retreat.

8. Visions and Rediscovered Treasures

This chapter contains excerpts from the author's terma writings,
including an oral story about revealed treasures and visions.

DURING THIS TIME of the five degenerations even ordinary people endowed with karma and emotions like me have by chance written a few
things which are now viewed as mind treasures; even so, my all-pervading,
glorious protector Lama Manjushri Pema Yeshe Dorje told me, "It is very
important to have a clear and detailed history of your termas, so put it in writing!" Reflecting on his words, I will start to write it down.

There are two kinds of terma: treasures which are taken from the earth and
treasures which arise in the mind. Padmasambhava hid the earth treasures
in mountains, rocks, lakes, and so on. He then entrusted various protectors,
gods, nagas, local deities, and so forth, to guard these treasures until, according to his predictions, the time came to deliver them to the tertön. When the
right time comes, the tertön can extract these treasures from their place of
concealment.

Mind treasures arise in the following way: In many instances, after bestow-
ing an empowerment or giving a teaching, Padmasambhava made the prayer,
"In the future, may this treasure arise in the mind of such and such tertön."
While doing so, he would focus his prayers and blessings on the tertön, usually an incarnation of one of his disciples. When, due to Guru Rinpoche's
blessings, the time comes, both the words and the meaning of the treasure
arise clearly in the tertön's mind. The tertön can then write these down without having to think. Most of my own treasures are mind treasures. As I was
traveling to various places, it occurred to me several times that there were
some earth treasures to be taken out, but they didn't come into my hands.

Yellow scrolls are written in *dakini* language on palm leaves. There are many types of *dakini* script; Terdak Lingpa's script, however, is all in Tibetan. In the past, all the sign language was in cursive script with the *o* vowels in printed script; Yeshe Tsogyal's script was like that. The terma texts sometimes have sign script which is for remembering things, not only for the tertön. A tertön can read his own sign script; hardly anyone else can read it. It is not possible to learn the sign script; it can only be known by remembering one's past life and whatever teachings one had at that time. When seeing the yellow scrolls, the tertön remembers his past lives. One symbol can contain a hundred thousand words; in fact the past king of Bhutan said that in one sign there could be a whole volume. Once when Chokgyur Lingpa found a terma, there was no sign script, but when he and Jamyang Khyentse Wangpo were doing a medicine sadhana, they soaked the yellow scroll in a sacred medicine skull and after seven days all the symbols appeared on the parchment. Shangpa Namkai Chimey, a Sakya khenpo who was there, said that Chokgyur Lingpa and Khyentse Wangpo were unmistaken and real tertöns.

When I was in my twenties, I had many yellow scrolls but I didn't care so much about them, and they were lost. When I went to Karma Monastery, there was a statue of the four-armed protector Mahakala, which was the practice support of the Seventh Karmapa. It was kept in a sandalwood box and only shown to special people. I asked to see it and discovered a yellow scroll with *dakini* script in its arms, which I took and gave to Khyentse Chökyi Lodro. From this scroll I wrote down the *Nyak Kilaya*.

One time in Kham I read the *Seven-Chapter Supplication* transmission to some faithful disciples. Reading the short history that is interspersed between each prayer made me remember the time when Padmasambhava was teaching in Samye. I then wrote down the *Heart Essence of the Self-Born Lotus*.

Regarding the *Heart Practice of the Three Roots*, once when I was reading the "Delightful Sun and Moon Cloud of Profound Secret Experience," a spontaneous vajra song, which takes the three channels as the path, at the beginning of Jamgön Khyentse Wangpo's *Garland of Vajra Songs*, I felt a strong wish to have a sadhana corresponding to that song. Though I looked through the *Treasury of Precious Termas* and other texts, I didn't find anything like it.

Then when I was twenty-one years old, I think it was the iron-horse year, 1930, I was doing retreat near a cave called White Rock, which was known as the cave of the lord of siddhas Padampa Sangye. Below the cave was a dense forest of medicinal plants and turquoise juniper trees where I was staying alone in the Victorious Tamer of *Mara* Grove Hermitage. One time at dawn, as I was engaged in my practice, within a dream state mixed with luminosity, a wondrous vision arose; my body appeared with the three channels and the five chakras, and within the chakras was the bodily mandala as explained in the *Heart Practice* text, sparkling clear and without obscuration. I felt joyful thinking that my deluded experience was similar to the song that had so impressed me earlier, but the writing of a sadhana and so forth was postponed. At the time all I did was write a similar song and frequently supplicate.

Later, when I was thirty-six years old, not long after having had the fortune of receiving the entire maturing and liberating *Treasury of Precious Termas* at my unsurpassed teacher's residence in Dzongsar, I chanted the reading transmission of Guru Rinpoche's *Seven-Chapter Supplication* to some faithful ones. In the course of giving the transmission, I read the annotations regarding the history of Guru Rinpoche's answers to the prince's questions. And as I thought of him with intense longing, Guru Rinpoche's forms of various sizes, great and small, showered down and dissolved into me. In my awareness, the Abbot, Guru, Dharma King, and ministers at what I think was the Arya Palo Temple at Samye Monastery kept arising clearly without obscuration. Due to that, I decoded the *Three Root Guru Sadhana* and offered it to my master; shortly afterward he received the empowerment and reading transmission.

Later, when performing a tenth-day feast offering in his Auspicious Celestial Grove residence, Chökyi Lodro said, "I feel that this is compatible with the wording used in old termas and has great blessings." I also felt confident about it, and though I wrote down a few pieces of the practice, a daily sadhana and so forth, it disappeared with the passage of time.

Later on, in Nepal, while making a connection to the sacred place of Yanglesho, I remembered what had happened and suddenly felt like writing the rest of it down. As Trulshik Rinpoche had insistently requested me to do so, I finally did. Though I didn't remember the incomparable word-pattern, the significance is the same, and so I think it is acceptable.

Regarding the *Ultimate Spontaneous Vajra Heart Song,* while I, the fortunate, aimless yogi Mangala, was roaming about in free countries, I accidentally went to the celestial Tashi Ding Mountain in the hidden holy land of Sikkim.[1] I had a mixed feeling of joy and sadness like a dense cloud, and my feelings of bliss and sorrow continued like a hailstorm. Singing a song of supplication, while mentally focusing on my master with intense longing and mingling my mind with his, I had a direct vision of the self-existing awareness Longchen Heruka, who also conferred a symbolic empowerment. Through his blessing, I also discovered the essence of this text and decoded it in a state of confidence. As one embodiment emanates innumerable magical displays, I also saw the joyful countenance of my master Jamgön Chökyi Lodro, and while awakening to the nonconceptual expanse of realization, I kept receiving his comforting compassionate blessings:

> Oh son, watch the illusory spectacle!
> All birth and death is projected by delusion;
> Not existing in reality, I am beyond coming or going.
> Let your fixation on distinction embrace the expanse!
> As your old father Lodro wanders through many pure lands,
> You, noble being, always act for the welfare of others.
> We, father and son, are not apart, but are one in the intrinsic nature.

> Don't follow illusory sense objects;
> Overpower the mirage of pleasure and pain with the view of one taste.
> Help the doctrine and beings through pure interdependence,
> And see the dualistic experience of non-duality as a reflection of the
>   moon in water.

> Endeavor in protective rituals against obstacles at the right time;
> With pure outer, inner, and secret links,
> Freedom will naturally be attained, so use them directly.
> Overcome all contradictions at all times.

> According to the secret teachings, it is very important not to place
>   your hopes elsewhere;
> Gain control over the magical display of the essences with the hook
>   of vital energy, and
> Keep the hidden secrets like the content of your heart.
> You may experience the relief of sixteen joys;
> Feeling at ease, bind them like a paint brush.

> The queen of space, Ekajati, will support you and
> Rahula will help you in whatever way.

Decode the definitive scriptures, infallible in time,
According to their meaning, and establish them with the *dharmakaya* seal.

SAMAYA GYA GYA GYA.

Regarding *Pema's Heart Essence of Longevity*, around the wood-pig year in the twentieth century, 1935, I was on pilgrimage at the Crystal Lotus Mountain at Gyamgyal, a pacifying *vajra*-family place and one of the twenty-five sacred places in Dokham. Crystal Lotus Mountain is a permanent glacier in the natural form of the glorious heruka, with a white lake in the shape of a long-life vase for immutable long-life practice in front of it, called the Infant Milk Lake. When I arrived there for that purpose, I performed the *Dharmakaya Master Amitayus* feast offering from the *Heart Essence Dispelling All Obstacles*. During the feast offering, a square mandala with four gates and all the higher and lower designs appeared on the surface of the white lake in blue-green patterns, visible to everyone, while the *Pema's Heart Essence of Longevity* sadhana clearly dawned in my mind. That night I dreamed that I was reading a commentary on the *Jetari Amitayus Sutra* written by the former Khyentse, and the next day, when I was reading Lord Taranatha's commentary on the *Amitayus Sutra*, I gained certainty that it mingled as one stream of blessing with the nine-deity *Amitayus* of Jetari's tradition.

The following year, on my way to see my venerable master Chökyi Lodro Rinpoche at Dzongsar, I stayed one day at Dzamthang in front of the Crystal Lotus Cave. That night I dreamed that a large juniper tree which had sprouted from Guru Rinpoche's staff was growing above the boulder in front of the sacred place. When I reached this tree, a woman, who I thought was Tsogyal, gave me a yellow scroll. When I looked at it, the complete cycle of teachings for *Pema's Heart Essence of Longevity* manifested in my awareness: the *Immutable Long-Life Tantra* with the outer practice of the nine-deity *nirmanakaya* Amitayus; the inner practice of the seventeen-deity *sambhogakaya* Amitayus; the secret practice of the five-deity *dakini* Mandarava combined with the six yogas' completion stage; the innermost vidyadhara long-life practice based on the Guru Padmasambhava and his retinue; the *Hayagriva* long-life practice for dispelling obstacles; and the practice of the Goddess Chandali, guardian of the teaching. All of this I wrote down and also practiced a bit myself. I also offered my master the empowerment and reading transmission; he perfected the practice, and the signs were good.

Though such a long-life practice had earlier manifested in my awareness due to reading a sheet of the former Khyentse's writings on the Indian text of Jetari's long-life practice, at the time I didn't write it down. My master said, "What you have written and the meaning of the words are one, so it is perfect," and he taught the ritual arrangement of the empowerment, the inner practice, and so forth. I also gave the empowerment to the Sixteenth Karmapa, Minling Khenchen and Chung Rinpoche, Trulshik Rinpoche, the son of Sakya Gongma of Puntsök Palace, Sangye Nyenpa, and others. I did the recitation practice myself and felt that it was auspicious. When I offered the Dalai Lama the empowerment for the combined outer, inner, and secret practices, he was very pleased, and I respectfully offered him the history of the teaching.

In Jamyang Khyentse's pure vision practice, the *Heart Essence of the Five Heruka Brothers,* the land where he goes is extremely vast and flat, like India, with meadows and lakes decorated with various flowers. It is a delightful place, where he rides a tortoise, symbolizing that he is an emanation of Manjushri. Zhalu Chöktrul Lösel Tenkyong rides a white lion, symbolizing that he is an emanation of Kalachakra, and within the glorious Sakya tradition, his kindness was the greatest. The Dzogchen practitioner Shenpen Thaye rides an elephant, symbolizing that he is an emanation of our kind Buddha. Terchen Chokgyur Lingpa rides a strong Indian tiger, symbolizing that he is an emanation of the knower of the three times from Uddiyana. Jamgön Kongtrül rides a blue dragon, symbolizing that he is an emanation of the great translator Vairotsana. These three have been extremely benevolent toward the teachings of the kahma and terma of the Nyingma school. They are all in heruka dress and surrounded by many dakas and dakinis adorned with silks and bone ornaments, playing small hand drums and bells, and holding various attributes, and the whole group is singing vajra songs and performing dances. Jamyang Khyentse said that he experienced this extremely delightful vision for a long time and was struck with wonder.

When I read the history of the omniscient Khyentse Wangpo's pure-vision treasure entitled *Five Visions,* I kept thinking how extremely profound and vast the meaning of the words of the guru sadhanas were. And so, when I was thirty-six years old, I was staying at Karpo Nang in Padampa Sangye's cave, and on the very auspicious day of the twenty-fifth day of the first month, corresponding to February, I performed a very elaborate feast offering according to the *Heart Essence of the Immortal Arya*. In conjunction with the four joys, the four modes of emptiness, and the four visions, I wrote a supplication to the five powerful yogis that appear in the *Five Visions*. When I chanted this supplication a few times, the river suddenly swelled, and I felt that it was an auspicious coincidence.

Later, when I was forty-seven, soon after completing the anniversary offering ceremony for Khyentse Wangpo at Dzongsar Tashi Lhatse, I saw a thangka of the *Five Visions* displayed in his bedroom. In the room where the Dharma lord Khyentse Wangpo passed away I did a guru-yoga supplication, and while I was there, I saw a manual of the actual writings of the omniscient master called the *Heart Essence of the Heruka Assembly* with what seemed to be a list of symbols from Chokgyur Lingpa decoding the *Vishuddha Union of Buddhas*. Due to that I wrote, in vajra lines, the *Heart Essence of the Glorious Heruka Brothers* of the outer *Five Visions* guru sadhanas with the completion stage of the *Magical Net* gradual path, the *Kalachakra Six Unions*, the *Chakrasamvara Five Stages*, the *Five Hung Trolo*, and the *Manjushri Great Perfection*.

When I showed it to my master, he said, "When I saw that thangka during the anniversary ceremony yesterday, I also wanted to write something similar, but I ignored it and didn't write anything. What you wrote is very good!" He immediately wanted to receive the empowerment. When I offered it, Katok Situ also came, so offering the empowerment became an appropriate occasion.

Later I gradually wrote the inner practice of the specific *Hundred Peaceful and Wrathful Deities, Kalachakra, Red Chakrasamvara, Trolo,* and the *Manjushri Five Families* sadhanas, and the secret practice of the *Eight Sadhana Teachings* combined into one empowerment. Though my master received the complete maturing and liberating empowerments, at present only the *Manjushri Five Families* sadhana exists as a text, and in that I pretend to combine the outer, inner, and secret meaning into one ritual arrangement. Though for the inner practice I had to write each of the visualizations one after the other, as it was a long time ago, it is not very vivid in my mind now.

For the secret practice of the *Eight Sadhana Teachings,* in the autumn of the wood-monkey year, 1944, I had the fortune to be among the participants when Lord Manjushri Dharmamati went to the Crystal Lotus Cave in Dzamnang and performed the drupchen of the *Twenty-one Mandala Clusters of the Gathering of the Transmitted Precepts* with the sacred medicine sadhana. During that time—I'm not sure if it was a dream or a meditative experience—the main deities and retinue of the *Eight Sadhana Teachings* all naturally appeared in the cave. Remembering that, the vivid presence of the Nine Glorious Ones with Chemchok in the center appeared firm, and I wanted to write it down.

The sovereign of all treasure revealers and siddhas Chokgyur Lingpa once revealed a five-inch-long and two-inch-wide parchment inside a natural copper box from the Yubal Rock sky treasury in Dokham. When he passed away, Jamyang Khyentse Wangpo gave this scroll to the great tertön's daughter, the wisdom *dakini* Ratna Shri Dipam Tara.[2] When I had the fortune to actually see it, through the compassion and activity of the great master from Uddiyana, knower of the three times, and his consort, who never fail to act when the time is right, I received a special blessing. The great tertön Chokgyur Lingpa was the natural wisdom form of Nub Namkai Nyingpo, chief holder of the profound secret teachings. His heart son Wangchok Dorje's reincarnation Tersey Tulku gave me a crystal that came from the celestial Kailash site and some white writing paper as an auspicious object and entreated me to decode the yellow scroll. Supplicating in front of the precious reliquary in the Chokgyur Mindrol Norbu Ling temple, the supreme vidyadhara revealed himself in the form of Guru Mahasukha, and having blessed me, Pema Garwang Ösel Dongnak Lingpa, humble servant of the lotus-born master, I decoded the *sadhanas* of the nine heruka consorts from the *Eight Sadhana Teachings*. May I and all infinite beings be relieved in the supreme vidyadhara abode of the supreme secret path.

Regarding the *Guru Drakpo* cycle, through a pure vision in a dream, the all-pervading lord of the mandala Pema Yeshe Dorje knew that Kharak Dorje Kyungtsunma had personally offered the supreme treasure revealer Jamgön Khyentse Wangpo a meteoric-iron dagger. Relying on the indicative script appearing on the dagger's surface, I decoded it; may this cause the omniscient siddha Jamgön Dharmamati to be victorious over the obstacles of the four *maras*, so that his aspirations and activities will be all-pervasive like space.

When I had the fortune to bring forth the profound secret known as *Nyak Vajrasattva*, I offered it to the all-pervading Vajrasattva in person, Chökyi Lodro Rinpoche, who was delighted and told me to give him the initial maturing and liberating empowerment. When I respectfully offered it in my unsurpassed master's Auspicious Celestial Grove residence, he told me that it was necessary to write a liturgical arrangement for the empowerment and *sadhana* that was easy to follow, but due to the bad times that damaged the teachings and inflicted suffering upon everyone in Tibet, I left it for the time being.

The lord who has mastered the profound and secret essential yoga of uniting space and awareness endeavored in the recitation practice and kept encouraging me time and again. I was also requested by Lama Ratna Rasmi and his son, diligent practitioners with unshakable faith in the supreme vehicle of luminosity; by Jigmey Kesang, a mantrika from Rekong who later came to Bhutan and served as my secretary and passed away in the seventies; by Trulshik Rinpoche, the supreme adornment of the doctrine of true secrets; and by many other great beings.

As they all wanted to receive the maturing and liberating empowerment and encouraged me, saying they needed the ritual arrangement, the fortunate vidyadhara Pema Garwang Dechen Ösel Lingpa,[3] who freely enjoys the blessings of the infinite treasuries of the kahma and terma teachings from the Nyingma school, composed the single text in the southern Puntsoling, where it was written down by the intelligent practitioner Urgyen Shenpen. May it be the cause of all beings as infinite as space to enjoy whatever is wished in the great bliss of Vajrasattva's wisdom display of the three secrets. MANGALAM. May it be virtuous!

In the east of the unsurpassed Karma Temple, the glorious wisdom protector with his host of haughty spirits actually appeared to the fortunate, worthy, and virtuous yogi, Heruka Pawo Longchen Namkai Ösel Pema Dongnak Lingpa.[4] As the wisdom dakini showed the secret code from the second Great Blazing Heruka's Sitavana Charnel Ground, I decoded the *Nyak Kilaya;* may it be the cause for being able to practice the tradition of the profound path without obstacles. MANGALAM.

9. Visiting Lhasa and Life in Exile

KHYENTSE CHÖKYI LODRO had already left, and the Chinese were starting to make trouble in Kham, so when I was forty-six, I went to Lhasa
on pilgrimage. On the way I visited the place where Chokgyur Lingpa had
lived and then continued on to Lhasa and all the pilgrimage places of Central Tibet. While in Lhasa I used to stay at the house of a relative of Chogye
Trichen Rinpoche known as Rasa Gyagen, whom I knew from Kham. By
the time I arrived in Lhasa, my precious master Khyentse Chökyi Lodro had
already left for Sikkim.

While Sangye Nyenpa and I visited Tsurphu, which was the seat of the
Karmapa, our sister, who had stayed behind in Lhasa, died. Shortly afterward, during our visit to Tsurphu in the sheep year, 1955, my brother Shedrup
also died.

While in Lhasa I decided to visit Mindroling. I left Lhamo and Chimey
behind with the luggage and said we would send someone to pick them up.
In Central Tibet the land doesn't really have nice plains. Near Mindroling
we came to a place with a large plain and a big tree where I sat to rest for a
while; across from it there was a rich family's house. At that time I was on
foot and asked my attendant to go buy some tea. He came back with tea and
tsampa in a yellow paper bag. So we had some tsampa, and an old lady came
and gave us more, which we put it in a cotton bag, and then headed on to see
Mindroling. While going up to Chung Rinpoche's house, we didn't see anyone. When we got there, his secretary, who was very fat and had a white spot
of hair on his head, came and asked who I was, and I told him I was Dilgo
Khyentse. Chung Rinpoche came to the door and invited me in. I asked them
to send someone for the others, so they sent some horses to get Lhamo,
Chimey, and the luggage. I stayed there for about one month, during which

Dilgo Khyentse with Khandro Lhamo and their two daughters.
Photographer unknown.

time I gave the sealed teachings from the *Treasury of Precious Termas* and did
some ceremonies.

I didn't have any attendant to take care of the shrine, so they appointed a
monk to be the ritual master and we became quite close. One day he asked
me to go see his old mother to do the consciousness transference for her, but
as we were busy doing rituals, we never got around to going. One day I asked
why his mother didn't come to see us, and he laughed. He gave me a hand-
kerchief and some money from his mother and asked for blessings for her.
It turned out that she was the old woman who had brought us the tsampa.
She had not known that I was a high lama, so now she was too embarrassed
to come see me. I, on the other hand, said I didn't think his mother was bad
at all, but rather that she was an emanation of the protectress Dutro Lhamo,
and he laughed.

The discipline in Mindroling was very strict. I never attended the daily
ceremonies but used to watch them from the corridor. The monks weren't
allowed to call anyone, so they would snap their fingers instead. There were
two big doors where the two disciplinarians would sit, and when they had
left, the monks couldn't go out. The monks were very relaxed in the temple,
without any agitation. Chung Rinpoche had returned from China and gave

Dilgo Khyentse in India. Shechen Archives.
Photographer unknown.

all the monks red and yellow brocade coats and performed a hundred thousand feast offerings.

The first time I met Dudjom Rinpoche was in Lhasa at the Copper-Colored Mountain Palace. I had seen him before in the Jokhang but didn't know it was him. He was very happy to see me and said, "I am very grateful to the Chinese; due to them I have met Khyentse Chökyi Lodro Rinpoche, and now I have met you." He used to wear a Bhutanese *chuba*, like he wore in India, and when he went out, he would wear a Western hat.

I requested him for his treasure teachings and said that I didn't dare to ask for all of them, but would like to have a teaching for which I had the fortunate karma, so he gave me the *Trolo* empowerment and reading transmission. He asked me for my long-life mind treasure, so in kind I gave him the empowerment.

At that time we were both preparing to go to India. Dudjom Rinpoche said that I could stay at his place in India as he had a big house there. Since he had two sons in China who used to write to him in Calcutta, the rumor spread that he was a Chinese spy. Later I heard that after giving the *Hundred Thousand Nyingma Tantras* transmission in Tso Pema, he was arrested on his way back to Darjeeling and put in jail in Siliguri.

A new Guru Rinpoche statue had been installed in the Jokhang, and I was asked to perform a feast offering there. While doing the feast offering, I caught whiff of some very nice incense. After some time, some officials wearing fine brocade came in, and one of them was holding the incense I had smelled. I thought they must be government officials. Then someone with a white face, wearing glasses, came, and I realized that it was the Dalai Lama. He was looking at the Guru Rinpoche and Maitreya statues, and offered a scarf to the Guru Rinpoche statue. When he came near my table, we were told that since we were doing a feast offering, we didn't need to get up for the Dalai Lama. The Dalai Lama asked where I was from and what my name was, so I introduced myself. He then asked what we were reciting, and I told him the *Embodiment of the Three Jewels*.[1] He said to do good prayers and offered a ceremonial scarf to the Maitreya statue. Then he went to the Jowo and stayed for about an hour. He had a very nice voice and did the seven-branch offering and other prayers.

Not long after this, Sakya Gongma was going to see the Dalai Lama and asked if I wanted to go along. We went to the Norbu Lingka, and Sakya Gongma went in first. The Dalai Lama was sitting on a low throne. There were not many attendants, and one attendant was standing up; we gave him the ceremonial scarves. Sakya Gongma did three prostrations and asked for blessings. Then I did three prostrations, and when I asked for his blessings, the Dalai Lama asked if I wasn't the one who had been doing the feast offering in the Jokhang. I told him that indeed I was. Then Sakya Gongma sat down, and I didn't dare to stay, so I left.

I used to go to the Ngapo's house about three or four times a month to do ceremonies.[2] He said that if we wanted to visit the Dalai Lama, he could arrange a meeting and that we should write down the names of those who wanted to come. Sangye Nyenpa had only seen the Dalai Lama once at Derge Gonchen, so the next day we went to the Norbu Lingka at nine in the morning, and the attendant saw us in. There were about ten or fifteen of us, including my nephew Ato Tulku.[3]

When we went inside, the Dalai Lama recognized me right away and told me to sit down; he gave me tea and rice. I introduced Sangye Nyenpa as a Kagyu tulku. The Dalai Lama asked him if his monastery had been destroyed in Kham. Sangye Nyenpa told the Dalai Lama that when he left, it was still standing, but he had since heard that it had been destroyed. The Dalai Lama asked where he was going now, and he said to Tsurphu, and then he offered many dedication offerings to the Dalai Lama in one heap. After that I didn't see the Dalai Lama again until I went to India.

Later Sangye Nyenpa met the Dalai Lama again in Varanasi. The Dalai Lama asked Sangye Nyenpa where his tall brother with the long hair was. Sangye Nyenpa told him that I was in Gangtok. The Dalai Lama replied that was fine and asked if I had been harmed by the Chinese. Sangye Nyenpa assured him that I had not, and then the Dalai Lama said he would meet me later.

Later during a big meeting in Dharamsala with the Karmapa, all the different schools had to offer mandalas. At that time the Dalai Lama was doing a feast offering but we didn't have to attend, so I went to see Mrs. Bedi. Sakya Gongma and Dudjom Rinpoche called me to say that the next day the Nyingma, Kagyu, and Sakya had to offer a long-life ceremony to the Dalai Lama and give an elaborate teaching with the mandala offering. I said that all the abbots of the four schools would be there, and so I didn't think I would do a good job, but Dudjom Rinpoche said it would be fine. Sakya Gongma added that it would be very kind if I would do it, so I said I would. Dudjom Rinpoche said that I should visualize Manjushri in my heart center and Sarasvati on my tongue, and he would pray that night, so I agreed and thanked him.

The next day I offered the mandala, and when the Dalai Lama took the conch shell offered as part of the eight auspicious symbols, thunder rumbled across the sky. The Dalai Lama's minister said that this was a very auspicious sign for the spreading of the Secret Mantra. The next day I was going to Tso Pema and went to ask for the Dalai Lama's blessing; he then said to me, "That was an auspicious coincidence yesterday with the thunder, wasn't it?" I must have lost some weight as the Dalai Lama asked me if I had encountered any trouble on the way. He said that I didn't look like I did when he saw me in Lhasa but that I had become very thin and looked quite old.

When I went to see him again, I asked for a long-life empowerment. A few officials received it as well. The Dalai Lama was sitting on four piled-up cushions;

my seat had four cushions as well, and there was no table between us. The
Dalai Lama said he couldn't speak as well as I could without preparation; I
felt rather embarrassed and said that whatever he said was fine.

After the mandala offering they sat me between the Dalai Lama's tutors,
Ling Rinpoche and Trichang Rinpoche. Ling Rinpoche thanked me for giving such a good speech, and Trichang Rinpoche joked, "Well, the Nyingmapas really made some speech, didn't they!"

Joking I said, "Did the Nyingmapas make a lion roar to the learned ones
from Ganden?"

"Yes, very good," he said.

When they were together, Trichang Rinpoche used to make jokes, and
Ling Rinpoche used to laugh a lot. Trichang Rinpoche said he had to give
teachings on *Khecari* in the Children's Home and asked me to come for lunch
before that.[4] I thanked him but wasn't able to accept his invitation. At that
time I had a very small place, so he said I could stay at his house. We both
had a good laugh when I replied that I didn't dare to stay in his house as I was
afraid that Shukten would hit me.[5]

When I went to Bhutan, I asked to meet His Majesty and was granted an audience. I also asked for an audience with the Queen Mother and got to meet
her. When I first met her, she seemed to like me a lot. She gave me fruits and
sweets. When we left Tibet, we had no horses to ride on, so my two young
daughters had come using walking sticks, and when I told the Queen Mother
of Bhutan about this, she felt so sorry for them that she sent them each a brocade jacket.

When my younger daughter died, the Queen Mother felt very sorry and
worried. When she came to Kalimpong, she asked me to come and see her
at the palace there. She asked me how my daughter had passed away. I told
her that she was at school in Mussoorie and had gotten a serious infection,
and that fortunately I had been able to see her in the hospital in Lucknow just
before she died. She told me not to worry and to do the right ceremonies for
her passing away and gave me three thousand rupees. Apparently the Karmapa told her to have a Guru Rinpoche thangka painted for purifying my
daughter's obscurations. She gave me ten pieces of brocade for the thangka
and said that if I needed anything to let her know. The Royal Grandmother
also treated me very well when I went to Bhutan.

Part Two

Recollections

10. My Life with Khyentse Rinpoche

KHANDRO LHAMO

Khandro Lhamo was Dilgo Khyentse's wife. She married him when she was nineteen. She passed away in March 2003 at the age of ninety-two.

I USED TO LIVE at home with my mother. One day, when I was nineteen years old, she sent me to the field to do some work, and on my way I met several lamas, including a *khenpo* who was very respected by my family. He told me that he had to take me somewhere, but I answered that my mother had asked me to work in the fields and that I didn't have time. He insisted however, saying that he would send a monk to do the work. So they took me on a long journey to Rinpoche's retreat place. The Chinese have since cut all the trees down, but at that time there was dense forest, and I was very afraid of the wild animals and that my mother would scold me.

I had heard that the Dilgo family had a son who was a tulku and very tall, but I had never met him before, so I was a bit intimidated. When I arrived, he was in his twenties. His complexion had become very dark, and he was so ill that it looked like he was going to die. Later I jokingly scolded Shedrup and the other lamas for not having told me that I was to be Rinpoche's consort, so I could have prepared myself, taken a bath, and put on nice clothes. They actually brought me there wearing old working clothes. They laughed and said they didn't tell me because they didn't want me to think about it and have a chance to refuse.

After my arrival Rinpoche's health improved, and one day he was walking around, wearing a robe of raw white silk. This was his usual attire, but when he went somewhere, he used to put on red robes. He then asked me to come and eat with him. He used to not eat meat, but because many lamas told him that he should for his health, he did so later on. However Rinpoche would never eat meat from animals that had been killed, only from animals that had died naturally.

Previously Rinpoche had said he didn't care whether he would die or not, but he didn't want to upset his mother by giving up his monk's vows and getting married. Later, in order to prolong his life and increase his activities, many lamas, including Khyentse Chökyi Lodro, and even his mother asked Rinpoche to marry me. I heard that there were some predictions that Rinpoche should marry me so that his activities would become very vast, but I'm not sure who made them, and most of these predictions seem to have been lost. One prediction that our former treasurer told me said something like this:

> In order to prolong his life,
> The young practitioner with an A on his forehead
> From the very virtuous family of the Sa home[1]
> Should join with the girl from the wood-tiger year.

Rinpoche was doing a three-year retreat in a small wooden cabin at a place called Karpuk, White Grove. He spent most of his time here and would only make brief visits to his home occasionally. His brother, who was called Apo Shedrup, was also staying at Karpuk in a small cabin of his own. I stayed in another small house. The common kitchen was a little bit further down. We had two servants, so there were five of us altogether. Rinpoche's retreat hut was a very simple hut with a wooden box to sit in.

Rinpoche always used to ask for books, mostly volumes from the *Treasury of Precious Termas*, so I used to carry books back and forth. There were so many books that they didn't fit in his room and were kept in another room. When Rinpoche first got the *Treasury of Precious Termas*, the cloth around the books was white, but because he used them so much, the color completely changed. In fact, Rinpoche's small room was so stacked with books that there was no place for a shrine. So a shrine was made out on a small veranda, though lots of books were stacked there as well. I planted many flowers out there, which Rinpoche liked a lot. Once, when we were receiving the reading transmission for the *Kangyur*, there wasn't enough room for the lama giving the transmission to sit inside, so they arranged a place for him to sit outside on the veranda among my flowers.

At night Rinpoche would never lie down; he would sleep sitting up straight in a wooden box. In the evening, after supper, he would start his session and would not speak until lunchtime the next day. After his early morning breakfast he would do practice until noon, without breaking his session. At lunchtime his brother would call me, and I would have lunch with Rinpoche and talk a little; then he would start another session and not see anyone till evening.

In front of Rinpoche's retreat cabin was a big tree. At night when I went out to go to the toilet in the forest, it looked like there was a fire burning underneath that tree. One time I told Shedrup about it, but he didn't respond. Sometimes it seemed like there were small fires burning everywhere, and sometimes it seemed like the fire was burning inside the retreat house. When I asked Rinpoche about it, he said that it was the protector Rahula, and not to go there.

One time Rinpoche was sitting on a rock somewhere near the river at Karpuk. A servant girl had gone to get cheese and milk from some herdsmen nearby. When she went to bring some to Rinpoche, he had already departed, but she saw a clear footprint on the rock where he had been sitting and claimed that it was Rinpoche's. I was told that it hadn't been there before. Rinpoche's servant Pema Shepa said that once, during a pilgrimage together, Rinpoche and Khyentse Chökyi Lodro both left their footprints in a rock. Rinpoche had been wearing boots that I had repaired. There was a hole in the boot which I had patched that could be clearly seen in the footprint. Our attendant Goka saw it as well, but Rinpoche said it wasn't his.

After six months I sent a message to my father asking him or my sister to come; so my father came and brought me nice clothes and a lot of delicious food. He told me to stay there and listen to whatever Rinpoche said.

When Rinpoche had finished his three-year retreat at Karpuk, he went to Jeykundo to see the Panchen Lama who had stopped there on his way to Central Tibet. Rinpoche wrote the Panchen Lama a letter to say that it was very good that he had returned from China, but that he should do a lot of ceremonies, such as a *Vajrakilaya* drupchen and so forth, otherwise he wouldn't be able to go to Central Tibet. Wondering what to do, the Panchen Lama consulted his treasurer, who said, "There is a lot of this kind of gossip. Why should you listen to such talk from that long-haired lama?" So they didn't do the ceremonies, and the Panchen Lama sent Rinpoche's letter back with a cermonial scarf, a gift of twenty-five cups, and a letter saying, "I cannot accomplish the ceremonies you told me to do now; please think of me." After a few days the Panchen Lama left for Central Tibet with great fanfare and a lot of Chinese soldiers. I dreamed that as the Panchen Lama was leaving, Rinpoche sent him a ceremonial scarf, which was returned. Again Rinpoche sent the scarf to the Panchen Lama, but again it came back. Then the Panchen Lama left. The next morning I told Rinpoche about the dream; Rinpoche said that it meant that the Panchen Lama wouldn't be able to go to Tibet. Sure enough, when the Panchen Lama arrived in Nakchuka, he wasn't able to continue and had to return to Jeykundo, where he passed away.

From Jeykundo we went to Benchen Monastery for about six months. While Rinpoche did retreat, I used to cook and serve him; I also had a nun and some monks to help me. In the tenth month, as I was very pregnant, we went to Zhangu. The lama dances of the tenth-day festival were about to take place, and I asked Rinpoche if we could stay to watch. Rinpoche said that he didn't have time as he had to go see Jampa Tulku's wife, who was very sick. So we headed to the Dilgo house.

One early morning while visiting my parents, a vulture came inside the house. My sister gave it some meat, which it carried off into the sky. She thought that this was a sign that I would give birth and the child would die, so she was quite worried. That evening I gave birth. After a few days I went back to Dilgo, where we stayed for a while before returning to Karpuk.

Later we went to Denkok, and then Rinpoche traveled a lot in Derge. There were many devotees who were rich herdsmen and requested Rinpoche to visit them. One of Rinpoche's nephews owned a celebrated gun and often went hunting with it. One day when Rinpoche was visiting them, Rinpoche's sister told him, "This gun has killed so many animals; please bless it." Rinpoche took the gun and said, "Is this your famous gun?" and then blew on it. After that it never fired again, so the man stopped killing. Afterward, whenever Khyentse Rinpoche visited their house, they hid all their guns.

Rinpoche's nephew had a huge dog that had killed many of the neighbors' goats, but since the Dilgo family was quite influential, no one dared to beat the dog. So another time when Rinpoche was visiting for tea, they explained that the dog killed a lot of sheep and goats, causing great hardship for the poor people of the area. So they asked Rinpoche if he knew what they should do about it. At that moment Khyentse Rinpoche was eating a ball of tsampa. He blew on it and threw it to the dog, which ate it up. After that the dog no longer bit or killed any animals, which made the people in the area very happy.

One summer we went to the top of a mountain near Tsamkhang Traktsa where we pitched tents, and Rinpoche did retreat. Rinpoche made offerings of hundreds of thousands of flowers. He asked our daughter Chimey and her friend Ösel Drolma, to take the herdsmen's kids and gather flowers. He told me to offer butter lamps, and I offered about ten thousand.

After that Rinpoche went home for a while, and then he went to Dzongsar to receive empowerments and transmissions from Khyentse Chökyi Lodro. Rinpoche stayed there for about a year, receiving the *Treasury of Precious Termas*. As our younger daughter was still very small, I didn't go along, though I did visit him once.

My younger daughter Dechen Wangmo was a very special child. She was born near Tsamkhang Traktsa. It was nighttime, but after her birth there was a very bright light, like daylight. I wondered what it could be. A hard rain came down, and then it stayed light till two or three in the morning. When they told Rinpoche about this special light, he didn't pay much attention to it; he said not to bother him with it. Her mind was very special; she was so virtuous and devoted to the Dharma, and all the servants were very fond of her. She loved to practice. My elder daughter Chimey was quite different.

Once during our pilgrimage in Central Tibet, Dechen Wangmo saw the eyes of a Guru Rinpoche statue move in a small temple near Mindroling. She was very frightened. When we spent a night at Dorje Trak, she asked me not to go to sleep because she was afraid that a girl would come. I wondered what she was so afraid of, but later I heard that not far from Dorje Trak a girl had died near a well and was reborn as a ghost. So it seemed that Dechen Wangmo could see such things. She could also see deities and would describe them, though we couldn't see anything.

Of course I was very sad when she died in Lucknow while only in her twenties,[2] though all the lamas, and especially the Karmapa, told me that since she was a *dakini,* she had gone to the *dakini's* pure land; she just wasn't able to have a long life. Rinpoche had told her to do at least a short retreat, but she hadn't been able to. She was very good at calligraphy and had copied the *Confession that Churns the Depths of Hell,* which I still have.

When we went to visit Gothi, Rinpoche's nephew Konchok, who was Ani Tsega's father, accompanied us, and while Rinpoche was eating tsampa, he gave Konchok some of his tsampa. As he was about to eat it, Konchok noticed that there was a very clear syllable A in it. So he didn't eat it, but kept it as a special blessing.

One of Khyentse Rinpoche's main teachers was Drungram Gyatrul Rinpoche, who lived his entire life in a cave near Ngoma Nangsum. I had never met him before, but one time I accompanied Rinpoche to Drungram Monastery, where we stayed near his cave. His cave was in the middle of a large rock outcropping shaped like a vajra and surrounded by meadows. Five or six hundred of his disciples lived in the surrounding caves and practiced the *Guru Rinpoche sadhana*. So many people circumambulated the rock that the earth was worn away down to waist level.

When I met him, his hair hadn't turned gray yet, so he must have been in his fifties. He would eat only once a week and almost never slept. He had only one servant, and his hair was short. During the day Rinpoche would go for teachings. Throughout the month that we spent there, Drungram Gyatrul never saw anyone else but Khyentse Rinpoche and me, and he exchanged many transmissions and empowerments with Rinpoche.

Khyentse Rinpoche received most of his empowerments, transmissions, and teachings from Khyentse Chökyi Lodro. Often when Rinpoche would go to Dzongsar to receive teachings from Khyentse Chökyi Lodro, I would stay at my father's place near Dzongsar, but I still received some teachings from Chökyi Lodro.

I didn't do retreat with Rinpoche in Kham but instead stayed at Sakar Monastery where I studied medicine with Shedrup. I practiced medicine for twenty-five years and benefited many people. Then we had to escape the Chinese, and in India I wasn't able to practice much medicine.

As I am very afraid to die, I tried to practice and pray most of the time. From the time I came to live with Rinpoche, I have done a couple months of retreat a year.. When Rinpoche would travel, I would stay home in retreat. Giving birth to my daughters didn't interfere with my practice. I tried to help the sangha, had temples and statues built, and tried to practice as much as I could.

When Rinpoche went to stay at Rekong, I didn't go, but he took our daughter Chimey and servant Tsepa. On his way to Rekong, he went to visit some nomads, and they offered him butter, yogurt, cheese, and other provisions, as is customary when a lama visits. Suddenly Rinpoche got up and said, "Let's go see what happened to our pack horses." Upon reaching his camp, the first thing he did was to inquire about the horses and was told that the animals were grazing in a pasture nearby. Not satisfied, he sent a few people to check on the horses, but when they reached the pasture, they found no trace of the horses. Apparently they had been stolen by some bandits from Golok, so Rinpoche requested the help of the nomads, who provided new horses and provisions.

Meanwhile many strange things happened in the bandits' tribe. The young boy of the chieftain was attacked by a band of great ravens, and when a woman who had churned milk to make butter wanted to empty her churn, blood poured out of it instead of whey. This and many other ominous signs appeared, such that the bandits got really scared and drove Rinpoche's horses all the way to Rekong. When the bandits met Rinpoche, they begged him to take the horses back. Rinpoche told them he did not need them anymore, and that they may as well have them, but the bandits wouldn't listen; they left all the horses at the monastery's door and ran away.

Among his few attendants, Rinpoche had brought along a monk named Achoe who could read well and fast; he had therefore been employed in Rinpoche's family home to read scriptures. He was very devoted to Rinpoche, but was rather short-tempered. Rinpoche used to scold him a lot with the hope of improving his bad character, but Achoe couldn't stand being scolded all the time and decided to run away. He left a note for Rinpoche with a piece of yellow silk with which he had intended to make himself a monastic robe.

Achoe wandered throughout Amdo, begging for food. A family who lived in black tents made of yak hair in a remote nomadic area offered to provide him with food and clothing if he would recite the daily prayers in their home. Several other families were grouped on a vast pasture, so that a few dozen tents were pitched here and there on a secluded plateau. Winter came, and soon the whole area was covered with snow.

One day the landlady saw a lonely rider coming from afar. It was snowing, and the man was covered by a large coat of white felt, like people often wore when rain or snow fell. But a large pom-pom of red wool and a tiny small bell hung from the horse's neck, something that only a lama's horse would have. The lady immediately called, "Achoe, come quickly, a lama appears to be coming." But Achoe, who was reading his prayers inside the warm tent and didn't feel like going out into the cold, didn't heed her call. Although there were many tents and people around, the unknown lama rode straight to Achoe's tent, jumped down from his horse, entered the tent, and told Achoe, "Get up, and let's go!" Achoe was totally dumbfounded: the lama was no other than Khyentse Rinpoche. There was absolutely no way except by sheer clairvoyance that Khyentse Rinpoche could have found him in this desolate area, where even his hosts did not know his real name or story.

After Rinpoche and Achoe had joined the rest of their party, Achoe asked his companions what had happened. "That morning," they said, "Rinpoche suddenly told us to stop and wait by the small trail we were following and then rode off alone through the countryside." One of the attendants, voicing everyone's curiosity, asked Rinpoche who had told him where Achoe was. Khyentse Rinpoche simply grumbled, "Who do you think could have told me about him?" and continued on his way. The attendant explained to Achoe that nobody had said anything, and that since everything was covered with snow and nobody was outside, no one could have shown Rinpoche the way anyway.

Then Rinpoche said they should leave. Achoe thought that since his master had such supernatural knowledge, he didn't dare to ask anything else, and he left with Rinpoche.

Once at the monastery called Karma Monastery, the seat of the first eight Karmapas, there was a very precious *dharmaphala* temple, which contained an image of Palden Lhamo and the protector Bernakchen in union. When the door of the room was opened, Khyentse Rinpoche saw Mahakala as if in reality and was given a yellow scroll—many people saw the scroll emerging from Palden Lhamo's sleeve. The scroll contained the *dakini* script for the *Kilaya* cycle according to Nyak Jnana Kumara's tradition, which is one of Khyentse Rinpoche's main spiritual treasures.

Another time, Rinpoche went to Crystal Lotus Mountain, where he had a vision of Guru Padmasambhava in the form of Amitayus, the Buddha of eternal life, and received the mind treasure of *Pema's Heart Essence of Longevity.* He received many termas in similar ways.

One day Rinpoche went to Khampagar, Khamtrul Rinpoche's monastery in Lhatok, while I stayed at home. A few days after Rinpoche had left, the Chi-

nese came and asked where Rinpoche was, which made me quite nervous
as they seemed rather suspicious. I told them that Rinpoche had gone to see
his brother at Benchen. They asked where that was and told me to tell Rinpoche that he should come to a meeting, and if he did, both of us would be
paid very well. I told them I would give him their message. A few days later
they came again and repeated that I must tell Rinpoche to come very soon.
They said that since he was very learned, his qualities shouldn't be wasted,
and that I absolutely must get him to go to the meeting. They also said that
one of our daughters should go to school in Chamdo and the other one in
China.

The Chinese made me go to Chokor Monastery, a Geluk monastery near
Sakar. When I arrived, there was a large gathering of people who had been
arrested by the Chinese. The Chinese again inquired about Rinpoche, so I
told them that he had probably gone to the monastery over the mountain. I
told them I'd send a messenger to ask him to come quickly. They asked me
how long it would take, and I answered it would take about fifteen days. They
wouldn't let me go and kept me there for about a week. Then I went back
home to look after the household. We had many servants and they had to be
paid.

About two weeks later the Chinese came again, asking where Rinpoche
was and how much longer it would be before he would be back. I said that
there was a lot of snow on the mountains, so it was difficult to move now, but
as soon as the snow melted, he would come. They were quite insistent and
asked why I didn't go get him. I explained that I couldn't go in the snow, but
in about twenty days, when the snow melted, I would send a messenger.

About twenty-five days later the Chinese came again. So I told them that
the snow had only just melted, and I would now go get him. After a few days,
a Chinese man came and again asked for Rinpoche. He said that since this
was the third time, if I didn't go to get Rinpoche immediately, I would be in
trouble. I told him not to worry, and said I would go.

I prepared some tsampa and got some good shoes. I asked one of the servants to get some horses from the mountain, but they only got seven or eight.
The next morning I got up at four and left. I left all my things behind because
the Chinese had many spies and I had to be very careful. I only took some
tsampa to eat along the way. After some time we arrived at Ato Tulku's. They
had already heard that Dilgo Khyentse Rinpoche had left and asked us where
we were going. I told them that we were going to Benchen to see the sacred

Khandro Lhamo, 1987.
Photograph by Matthieu Ricard.

dances. They replied that if we wanted to go to Pemako, we could go with
them. Otherwise we might have trouble on the way.

Our party had run out of feed for the horses, so a few kind villagers gave us
some. After feeding the horses, we continued and came to a fork in the road:
down was the way to Ato Tulku's place, and up was the way to Benchen. As
night fell, we hid and saw a lot of movement from the Chinese along the road,
so we fled to Benchen. We stayed there for two or three days, and Nyenpa Rinpoche gave us servants, horses, and a lot of food. From there they escorted us
to Khampagar where Rinpoche was staying with Khamtrul Rinpoche, giving
empowerments and teachings, and taking it easy. I told him that we had to
leave right away, as the Chinese were on our heels. If we didn't leave immediately, then it would be too dangerous to leave. I also told him that since the
Chinese military was everywhere, we couldn't go on the normal road with
horses and mules, as we would surely be caught. So Rinpoche agreed to leave
and stopped the teachings.

The people from Khampagar gave us yaks and provisions, and escorted
us up to the Sitsa residence in Chamdo, as the Sitsa family were patrons of
Khampagar. By then the Chinese who had chased us from our village had

Khandro Lhamo at her nunnery in Bhutan with daughter Chimey.
Photograph by Babeth Van Loo.

already arrived in Chamdo, but Sitsa Wangdu and his wife had Chinese ranks[3] and helped us a lot; in fact they sent us to Lhasa in a Chinese truck. The road was very rough, and I got quite sick.

When we arrived in Lhasa, we went to the residence of the Jago family, where we stayed for a while and had some food. Then we went to the house of one of Rinpoche's patrons and stayed there.

While in Central Tibet, Rinpoche, our two daughters, and I did the large outer pilgrimage of the Central Tibetan holy places and visited Samye, Yamalung, and Tradruk. We had two servants and two horses, and took along tsampa and other things to eat. After the pilgrimage Rinpoche stayed in Lhasa for a while, doing many ceremonies for people who had died from cholera. Though, for fear that he would become ill, they requested him not to visit the houses where there was cholera, Rinpoche never listened.

On the way to Tsurphu, Rinpoche stayed at Pawo Rinpoche's monastery for a while, and in Tsurphu he built a stupa. When Rinpoche returned to Lhasa, the Ngapo invited him to visit the Tara temple in Tradruk, which has a self-arisen Tara, to do a hundred thousand feast offerings. So Rinpoche went on another pilgrimage, visiting Samye, Yamalung, Samye Chimphu, Tradruk, Tsering Jong, Yarlung Sheltrak, and so forth. I, however, stayed in Lhasa with my daughters who were doing a hundred thousand prostrations.

Rinpoche used to sleep in a tent, and among the various places he visited were some Milarepa caves. He did elaborate feast offerings at all the sacred places. Then on the way back he stayed in Mindroling for a month.

One day while I was in Lhasa, some Chinese came to see me. I wasn't sure whether they had come from the Ngapo, so I offered them some fruit. They asked, "Sangyum Kusho, what are you doing here?"[4] I said that I was just visiting. They asked what my daughters were doing, and I said that they were doing prostrations. Then they asked me if I missed my home, and when I said that I did, they asked me why. I said that I had no money and was thinking of going back. So they asked if I was going, and I said I was. They asked where Rinpoche was and when he was going back home. I said that Rinpoche was at Samye Chimphu and would go as soon as he returned. When they asked why we had come to Lhasa, I told them that we were just on pilgrimage. They asked whether Communism had already been established in Kham when we left there, and I answered that I didn't know as I hadn't heard anything while in Lhasa.

They asked if it was our custom to eat red and white sweets, and I said that it was. They explained that red and white sweets were just like Communism. I asked what the purpose of Communism was, and they said that it was very good, just like sweets, and showed different sweets out of their pockets. I said that if it was like those sweets, I thought I might like it. Then they asked if I would do any shopping before going home, and I said I would.

I told the Chinese that Rinpoche had been invited to Lhasa by Ngapo. I had sent two or three messages to Jeykundo, asking them to come, but nobody had come yet. I knew that by now the Chinese would have taken our possessions and livestock back in Kham, but pretended I didn't. I was afraid they would arrest us. They said they didn't know why nobody had come to meet us, but said to be ready to go back to Jeykundo on the fifteenth, and that we would go by car. They said that if we went with them, we would get Chinese ranks, and Rinpoche would be paid a thousand yuan, while I would be paid five hundred. So I thanked them very much and said we would be ready to go.

Everyone that had come from Kham to Lhasa was being arrested and taken back. Some would jump in the water, but most of them were tied in trucks and forced to leave. So I sent a message to Rinpoche at the Ngapo's place that the Chinese were going to take us back, and Rinpoche soon returned to Lhasa. Shedrup, who was with Rinpoche, was very sick. I said that on the fifteenth the Chinese were going to take us back home, and asked what we should do. I explained that most Khampas had already been taken back and were forced to leave their children behind, so they were very sad.

Rinpoche wanted to go to Tsurphu, so he went to see the Ngapo to ask him for advice. The Ngapo, who had a lot of power at that time, really helped us a lot; he wrote a letter to the Chinese officials, saying that Rinpoche had nothing to do with the rebelling Khampas and was just a Dharma practitioner. He also talked to the Chinese officials on our behalf. Rinpoche asked if it was all right to go to Tsurphu, and the Ngapo said that it was; so we went to Tsurphu and stayed there over the winter. The Karmapa was still there, and the Dalai Lama hadn't left Lhasa yet, but in the second month of the pig year, corresponding to March of 1959, the Karmapa left. The Dalai Lama was also leaving; so we too had to escape.

We had many horses grazing near Tsurphu, but the Chinese stole them all. I thought we would then have to escape on foot, so I said I would go to buy some horses. I borrowed a horse from Tsurphu and rode to Lhasa. Central Tibetans were selling horses from the Khampas that had been arrested, and I bought twelve. Then I asked some people going to Tsurphu to help me go with the horses at night. Day broke, and as we crossed the bridge to Tsurphu, it became light, and I sent our horses to graze with those of Nyenpa Rinpoche and the Rada family.

When I saw him, I told Rinpoche that I had bought horses. The Dalai Lama had already fled, and one night the Karmapa did too. So the next night I went to Pawo Rinpoche's to buy a few strong pack animals. Pawo Rinpoche gave me a very good horse, and though I had brought lots of money, he refused payment.

I got back to Tsurphu but was very afraid that the Chinese would arrest us and wanted to leave right away. Ato Tulku's family had a lot of yaks and horses. They had left all their saddles at Tsurphu, so I took some to saddle our horses and yaks. We didn't dare stay at Tsurphu that night because they said the Chinese were arriving, and that evening we left and headed up the mountain high above Tsurphu. So that is how we started our escape and managed to flee up to Bumthang.

Using my wits, I managed to keep Rinpoche out of Chinese hands. A lot of people from Derge were caught in the mountains and taken down along with their sheep and goats. The day after we left, we had to cross a pass called Drula, and Nyenpa Rinpoche said that the Chinese were already guarding it, so we left everything—carpets, clothes, mandalas, books, statues, and so on—in Lhalung and fled. We crossed the mountain pass at night and saw a lot of Central Tibetans escaping as well. Then we came to a mountain pass called Dora, and, as we were very tired, we rested there for the night. It was extremely cold. Rinpoche sat on a rock with Nyenpa Rinpoche and me on either side of him. All the yaks were saddled, but we had nothing to feed them. It was so cold that the next morning some of the horses and yaks were just lying there dead.

A lot of soldiers from Khampa guerrilla forces had been killed, but those that were left were trying to escape. They had rustled some yaks from the Tibetans, and because they had no food, they killed some of these yaks to eat. I sent Rigzin Dorje, who was a Khampa guerrilla leader, to ask them to leave us some yaks so that Rinpoche could use them. The next day we put our things on the yaks. By that time there were many of us: the Benchen group, the Rada family, the Drongpa family, the Nyawe family, and some people from Gojo. When we arrived at the top of the mountain, we saw that the yaks we had left behind had also been killed and eaten.

When we finally reached the border with Bhutan, we had nothing left to eat; only a tiny bit of tsampa and some butter and dried meat. For twelve days we were blocked by the Bhutanese border guards, before the Bhutanese government let us through. When they did let us pass—along with many of Rinpoche's disciples who were with us—the government gave everyone food, horses, and so many other things that we couldn't take it all. From there we went to Kalimpong, where Dudjom Rinpoche was building a place called the Copper-Colored Mountain, and although it wasn't yet complete, that is where we stayed for about two months. We then moved to Gomchen Dratsang in the Kalimpong market. Eventually we moved to Darjeeling, and later Rinpoche went back to Bhutan.

11. My Grandfather, My Guru
SHECHEN RABJAM

Shechen Rabjam's mother is Dilgo Khyentse's daughter Chimey Wangmo [born Dronkar]. Dilgo Khyentse showed particular affection for his grandson from an early age and personally oversaw his education and spiritual development. Shechen Rabjam is the abbot of Shechen Tennyi Dargyeling in Bodhnath, Nepal as well as in Kham.

ONCE WHILE DILGO Khyentse Rinpoche was on pilgrimage in Central Tibet, his party was camping in a field. It was quite late and dark, and all of a sudden a lady came into the tent. She took a meteoric-iron dagger out of her dress and said, "This must be yours—I found it," and left. Khandro tried to follow her to give her some tea, but there was no trace of her; she must have been a Dharma protectress.

Khyentse Rinpoche never returned home from his pilgrimage. Instead, he left Tibet for Bhutan shortly after the Karmapa did; he was forty-nine years old at the time. When he arrived in Bhutan, he heard on the radio that Khyentse Chökyi Lodro had passed away in Sikkim. On his way to Sikkim, he lost most of his belongings in Siliguri. While in Sikkim, he performed the fire ceremony of Khyentse Chökyi Lodro's cremation and constructed the stupa. He remained in Kalimpong and Sikkim for a long time. In Rumtek he received the *Secret Mantra Treasury of the Kagyu Lineage* and the *Treasury of Spiritual Instructions* from the Karmapa.

My grandmother was a resourceful woman, and completely devoted to Dilgo Khyentse Rinpoche. Once they were traveling by train in India during the sixties; at that time Rinpoche couldn't afford the reserved compartment and used the public unreserved compartment, which was completely packed. So Khandro put their bedding on the floor for Rinpoche to sit on. When Khandro looked around, she saw an older Indian man and sat on his lap. The man felt a bit uncomfortable and moved over a little, so Khandro managed to get a small space next to him. That man was chewing dried tobacco and was teasing Khandro with it by putting it near her nose to smell. But she just blew on it so all the tobacco flew around in the compartment and got everyone sneezing. Then he took some more tobacco and rolled it out on his hand, preparing to chew it. She moved very near him, so he moved a little further, afraid she would blow it again, and as she moved further and further, he also moved further and further, until she managed to get a seat for Rinpoche.

Khyentse Rinpoche and the Sixteenth Karmapa were very close, not only as spiritual teacher and disciple, but also as friends. They were both from Denkok. They would spend long hours together talking about the lives of masters, the history of religion, and so forth. Sometimes they would talk from morning until evening. They enjoyed each other's company a lot; the Karmapa would tease Rinpoche, and Rinpoche would, in turn, crack lots of jokes. Sometimes after Khyentse Rinpoche had returned to his room in the evening, the Karmapa would join him there to continue talking. One night they were talking about ghosts; I was quite young and got very scared. I used to sleep next to Khyentse Rinpoche, and one day when I was about eight or nine years old, I woke up, and the Karmapa was already in Khyentse Rinpoche's room talking. Since I was still in bed, I didn't dare to get up but had to lie there pretending to sleep.

Apparently, during one of these talks before I was born, Khyentse Rinpoche and the Karmapa were discussing the fact that the Chinese had now occupied the whole of Tibet and that most masters had been killed during the Cultural Revolution. At that time there was no direct communication, and there was no reliable news coming out of Tibet. Khyentse Rinpoche therefore asked the Karmapa, "What do you think happened to my masters Shechen Kongtrül, Shechen Rabjam, and the tulku of Shechen Gyaltsap Rinpoche?" The Karmapa said that they had most likely all died. So Khyentse Rinpoche requested, "You have recognized so many incarnations, please tell me where they are reborn." The Karmapa answered him, "You don't have to look for them; they are looking for you."

Sometime after that conversation, Khyentse Rinpoche went on foot for a pilgrimage to Namo Buddha. Namo Buddha, in Nepal, is a day's walk from Kathmandu, and it is the site where, in a previous birth, the Buddha Shakyamuni had given his body to a starving tigress and her cubs. That day, Rinpoche was feeling very happy because this is said to be the place where the Buddha first conceived the most precious *bodhichitta,* the altruistic thought to achieve Buddhahood for the sake of others and the determination to do anything to achieve this goal, but he also felt sad because such a great bodhisattva had given up his life.

The night he returned to Kathmandu, near the Bodhnath Stupa, he had a dream in which he was climbing a lofty mountain. At the summit was a small temple. He entered, and inside he saw, seated side by side, his own former teachers, the three main lamas of Shechen monastery—Shechen Gyaltsap, Shechen Rabjam, and Shechen Kongtrül—who had all perished in Chinese prisons in the early sixties. Khyentse Rinpoche prostrated himself before them, and, singing in sorrowful verse, asked them how they had suffered in the hands of the Chinese. With one voice they replied, also in verse, "For us birth and death are like dreams or illusions. The absolute state knows neither increase nor decline." Khyentse Rinpoche expressed his wish to join them soon in the buddhafields, since he saw little point in remaining in a world where the teachings were vanishing fast and most teachers were but spurious impostors. At this point, Shechen Kongtrül, gazing at Khyentse Rinpoche with a piercing stare, said, "You must toil to benefit beings and perpetuate the teachings until your last breath. Merging into one, the three of us will come to you as a single incarnation, a helper to fulfill your aims." Finally they all dissolved into one, who dissolved into Khyentse Rinpoche.

When Rinpoche woke up, he wrote down these verses, which indicated that the three of them would be born into his family. He later told the Sixteenth Karmapa about this dream and gave him the songs. The Karmapa said that the incarnation was his daughter Chimey Wangmo's son who was the reincarnation of all three lamas of Shechen in one. The late Neten Chokling Rinpoche, Orgyen Topgyal's father, was there at the time, and since there were three tulkus within one, he suggested giving me the name of the highest ranking of the three, which was Shechen Rabjam, the main abbot of Shechen Monastery. Khyentse Rinpoche thought that he would have rather chosen Shechen Gyaltsap. Since Gyaltsap Rinpoche had been his closest root teacher and because he himself had also been recognized as Shechen Rabjam, Khyentse Rinpoche really wanted to call me Shechen Gyaltsap.

Dilgo Khyentse with Rabjam Rinpoche, Khandro Lhamo, and
daughter Chimey. Photograph by Lodro Thaye.

When Orgyen Topgyal told me this story, I didn't really believe it, but after
Khyentse Rinpoche passed away, when searching through all his documents,
I found a brocade cloth containing papers with his own handwriting relating
this dream of his three masters. So I had to believe it.

When I was born in Chandigarh, in 1967, my mother, who is Khyentse Rinpoche's elder daughter, was working as a nurse in a refugee camp. In those
days, due to the extreme hardship met by Tibetan refugees, many of their
children were given up for adoption to Western families. As soon as Khyentse Rinpoche, who was in Bhutan at the time, received the letter saying that
I had been born, he sent word to my mother telling her not to give me up for
adoption.

Soon after, Rinpoche came to see me in Chandigarh with his attendant
Ngodup; I was still a small baby, crying a lot, and even peed on Ngödrup's
lap. From then on, Khyentse Rinpoche kept me with him and raised me with
unfathomable kindness.

I then spent some time in Phunstöling with my grandmother, Khandro
Lhamo. When I could just say a few words, she made me repeat the Manju-

Dilgo Khyentse with Rabjam Rinpoche in Tashi Jong, 1973.
Photographer unknown.

shri mantra a hundred thousand times by repeating each syllable of the mantra herself. One day Ngodup was sent to get me. Grandmother said that we were having steamed dumplings that day. I always used to share a plate with my grandmother, but on that day I insisted on having my own plate, even though I actually set it aside and ate off of my grandmother's plate anyway. Grandmother asked why I didn't eat from my own plate, and I explained that an important guest would be arriving and I wanted to keep the plate for him. Sure enough Ngodup arrived after lunch, so I gave him the plate.

Then we all went to Rumtek, the Karmapa's seat. My grandmother thought that because it was so difficult to raise a tulku, it would be better to not give me such a big name as Shechen Rabjam. She argued that if I was a genuine tulku, I would naturally benefit beings and that otherwise it would be very embarrassing to bear such a name as Shechen Rabjam. But the Karmapa insisted that I should be recognized as Shechen Rabjam and promised, in the name of the Three Jewels, that I would benefit the Buddha's teachings. Upon hearing those words, my grandmother stopped complaining. The Karmapa did a very elaborate enthronement in Rumtek with celebration dances of goddesses and an opera, and even the Karmapa's general secretary

Dilgo Khyentse with Khamtrul Rinpoche in Tashi Jong, 1973.
Photograph by Lynn Weinberger.

participated in the dances, which were followed by a three-day picnic. I was
five years old, and from then on I stayed with Khyentse Rinpoche.

When Khyentse Rinpoche was staying in Paro Kyechu, Bhutan, giving the
Four Parts of the Heart Essence, I used to sit next to his throne. At one point
in the empowerment he asked the students, "Who are you, and what do you
want?" The students are then supposed to say, "I am the fortunate son so-
and-so. . ." But I yelled, "I am the big-headed son." Khyentse Rinpoche burst
into laughter and had to stop the empowerment for about ten minutes as he
couldn't stop laughing. It was the nickname he used to call me. During that
time Khyentse Rinpoche taught me the alphabet and made me repeat mantras, so in this way I began my studies in Paro Kyechu.

When Khyentse Rinpoche was doing a drupchen for the Queen Mother
of Bhutan, he would ask someone to put me on his lap every time they
came to the protector chants, so from then on I started doing drupchens;
I didn't have to force myself to memorize the protector chants as I heard
them every day on Khyentse Rinpoche's lap, and so memorized them that
way. To entertain me and keep me from getting bored, Rinpoche used to

Shechen Rabjam Rinpoche.
Photograph by Matthieu Ricard.

make images of different people with tsampa dough. He would also draw for me; he was very good at it, and once drew a beautiful flower with a bee flying around it.

Another time, while he was giving the *Treasury of Precious Termas* in Dechen Chöling in Thimphu, I was sitting next to Rinpoche, and whenever he had the torma for the obstructing spirits thrown at the beginning of an empowerment, he would take a piece of it and give it to me, so I could play with it. Around that time the tenth-day festival was performed in Thimphu, and we all went to see the lama dances. I had a knack for imitating, so at night Rinpoche used to make me imitate the dances. I was quite good at it, so he even let me imitate one of the dances in front of the Queen Mother.

Whenever I asked Rinpoche to do something, he always did it. My friend Samdrup stayed with me as my playmate from the time of receiving the *Treasury of Precious Termas* in Dechen Chöling. One time we were in Kalimpong at Gomchen Dratsang, and while Samdrup and I were playing, we went inside a storeroom with lots of tables and chairs. I piled up lots of tables saying I was building a monastery, making a house out of the piled-up tables.

Then I invited Rinpoche to come and sit in the table temple, so he sat there and did his protector prayers for forty-five minutes.

Rinpoche was once invited by the Sikkimese king to perform a *Vajrakilaya* drupchen as there was some trouble in Sikkim at the time. Khyentse Chökyi Lodro had given them lots of predictions to do ceremonies for the stability of the country, but they never performed the averting rituals that he had advised them to do. Rinpoche said that by now it was a bit late to do anything about it, but he performed the drupchen anyway. At that time I met Tulku Pema Wangyal, who came to see Rinpoche late at night and asked for divinations about his father, Kangyur Rinpoche, who was quite ill. Rinpoche then went to Darjeeling, but when we arrived, Kangyur Rinpoche had already passed away.

Rinpoche and Khandro often used to joke during lunchtime. Khandro used to say, "Sukhavati is so nice and peaceful," and Rinpoche would say, "The Copper-Colored Mountain is much better." Khandro said it was too noisy in the Copper-Colored Mountain, with lots of stuff happening, and thought Sukhavati was more peaceful. Then they asked me what I thought, and where I wanted to go. So I took Khandro's side and said, "I'd like to go to Sukhavati; it seems much nicer."

A little bit later I had a dream that the three of us were flying. There was a man with a feather on his head looking like an American Indian, who was our guide. I could see a red rock with a dark cloud very far away; there was a rice field, flat and empty. The guide with the feather said, "This is your place; you cannot go any farther. There is no more continuing with Khyentse Rinpoche; this is your place." I felt very sad in the dream, and since that dream, I never took Khandro's side again.

Until Khyentse Rinpoche passed away, I used to do my morning and evening prayers with him. In the morning we did *Chanting the Names of Manjushri* and in the evening we did the protector chants. So I learnt most of them by heart, but there were maybe a hundred points where I made mistakes. When I chanted them by heart in front of Rinpoche, he knew exactly where I would make mistakes, and just before reaching the passage where I was about to go wrong, he would raise his voice to guide me to say it right. Later Rinpoche wrote all the sentences where I made mistakes in a small notebook—he had actually memorized all the mistakes I made!

When I was about eight years old, Rinpoche told me to request the Karmapa for some mind teachings. So the Karmapa gave me a teaching on investigating the three phases—mind at rest, mind stirring, and awareness—and said to tell him everything I experienced. So every day I used to tell him that my mind felt like a rock, a mountain, a tree, or things like that, and Khyentse Rinpoche and the Karmapa would have a good chuckle at my expense. The Karmapa said to keep looking. He was very kind to me. One day when we said good-bye, I was wearing a sandalwood *mala,* and he said, "Oh, that's a Geluk debate *mala,*" and took it off me. He then gave me the lotus-seed *mala* that he had used during his trip in Europe. He gave Khyentse Rinpoche one of his old shirts and a monk's vest. That was the last time that I saw him.

When we returned to Bhutan, Khyentse Rinpoche did the annual ceremony at Dechen Chöling Palace, and I practiced handwriting. Every day I would sit next to Rinpoche in the ceremony and train in handwriting. One day I had a very strong feeling that my mind was completely empty and said to Khyentse Rinpoche, "I have a feeling that my mind is empty." So Rinpoche said, "That's a good tendency from past lives. Since you received mind teachings from the Karmapa, you must tell him when we see him next time." But the next time we went to Rumtek, the Karmapa had passed away, so I felt sad that I couldn't tell him. Khyentse Rinpoche and I were staying in Shamar Rinpoche's room, and one night I had a very clear dream of the Karmapa standing near the window and when I told him about my experience of empty mind, he put his hand on my head. The next day, I told Rinpoche about my dream, and he was very happy.

Of course, I heard quite a few stories about Rinpoche's life and witnessed quite a few extraordinary events with him myself, so here I will just mention a few examples to illustrate what an amazing lama my grandfather really was.

When Khamtrul Rinpoche was giving the *Vajra Garland* empowerments in Thimphu Dzong, I read something about foreknowledge and said to Rinpoche, "I want foreknowledge." It said something about doing a certain recitation and then blowing on honey and putting the honey on one's eyes; then you would see things most people usually don't see. Rinpoche said, "OK." So I got some jam, thinking it would have the same effect as honey, and asked Rinpoche to bless it. Khyentse Rinpoche said, "Ask Khamtrul Rinpoche to bless it." Since I was very young, Khamtrul Rinpoche said, "OK, put it there. I'll bless it." Later I put the blessed jam on my eyes, but nothing happened— I just got sticky eyes. After that, whenever the students had to take off the blindfold during the empowerments, he would point at me and was joking with Khyentse Rinpoche.

One time Rinpoche was doing a ransom ritual in Kyechu, and the evening that we threw the ransom offering, I was supposed to do a lama dance and so was very excited. Khandro had gone out to relieve herself in the bushes on the other side from where the offering was thrown, and at that time she heard hundreds of horsemen running toward the direction where we threw the offering, as if they were carrying it.

The late Khamtrul Rinpoche, Dongyu Nyima, was another close friend of Dilgo Khyentse's, and they used to exchange lots of teachings. After Khamtrul Rinpoche passed away, his *tokdens* and other disciples asked Khyentse Rinpoche to recognize his reincarnation;[1] Khyentse Rinpoche told them they should ask the Sixteenth Karmapa. At that time, in 1981, Khyentse Rinpoche was giving the *Kangyur* reading transmission in Bumthang and would do his practice and then not speak until eleven in the morning, but one day early in the morning he dictated to his scribe, Tulku Kunga, where Khamtrul Rinpoche could be found, with the direction, the names of the parents, and the place of birth, and then he told him not to show the letter to anyone.

After the *Kangyur* reading transmission was finished, we went to Punakha for the annual drupchen sponsored by the Queen Mother, and while there we heard that the Sixteenth Karmapa had passed away in the United States. As soon as we finished the drupchen, we went to Rumtek for the ceremonies, as the Karmapa's body had been brought to Rumtek. After a few days Khyentse Rinpoche asked the Karmapa's secretary whether the Karmapa had left a letter about Khamtrul Rinpoche's reincarnation. The secretary replied that the Karmapa had left some letters about reincarnations before leaving for the United States and that one of them must have been about Khamtrul Rinpoche. Sure enough, the Karmapa's letter described the very same details as

Khyentse Rinpoche's. The only difference was that in Khyentse Rinpoche's letter the parents' names were in Sanskrit while in the Karmapa's letter the names were in Tibetan. Both these letters were carved into the rock near Khamtrul Rinpoche's monastery, Tashi Jong, in India.

I heard that one time, when Khyentse Rinpoche was traveling on the train with Orgyen Topgyal and Yonten, they were carrying a lot of luggage, including a stove, supplies, and so forth inside huge Indian-style bedrolls. One of the bedrolls was so heavy that Orgyen Topgyal couldn't get the bundle up on the luggage rack. Seeing this, Khyentse Rinpoche laughed and teasingly saying, "You're useless," took the bedding with one hand, and effortlessly put it up. Orgyen Topgyal now thinks it was a miracle.

Once when Dzongsar Khyentse was studying in India, he neglected to do his dharmapala prayers in the evening for some days. After a few days he received a letter from Rinpoche in Nepal saying, "Don't forget to do your dharmapala prayers."

When Dzongsar Khyentse was enthroned in Sikkim, the Dzongsar household didn't have much money. After giving the *Treasury of Precious Termas* empowerments to Dzongsar Khyentse, Khyentse Rinpoche put aside all the offerings received during the empowerments. Dzongsar Khyentse's old secretary had just retired, and the new one was Tashi Namgyal, so Khyentse Rinpoche gave all the offerings to Tashi Namgyal and didn't keep one penny for himself. The Dzongsar household used it to pay for Dzongsar Khyentse's studies at the Sakya College.

After giving the *New Treasures of Chokgyur Lingpa* in Nepal, Rinpoche was going to Nagi Gonpa, Tulku Urgyen's hermitage, to give the protector empowerments for the *New Treasures* to the tulku. There was no road at that time, so Chökyi Nyima arranged an army helicopter to take us up. When we got in, there was a dark cloud above Nagi Gonpa, so the pilot said, "Maybe we will have to wait forty minutes in the helicopter until the clouds clear up." I was sitting in front, and Rinpoche in the back. After some time Rinpoche tapped me on the shoulder from the back and asked, "Who are those girls?" I didn't see anything, so I said, "There is nobody here, and we are in the helicopter." So Rinpoche said, "Oh, I must have seen Tseringma and her sisters."

When Khyentse Rinpoche gave the *Treasury of Spiritual Instructions* empowerments to Trulshik Rinpoche and his monks in Solukhumbu, in 1977, he stayed there six months and many amazing things happened. For example, one of the tormas that was on the shrine emitted flames for all to see, which amazed many people, though it is said that when master and disciple come together with an excellent connection, wondrous things can happen due to the devotion of the student and the compassion of the master. During that time, while giving the *Gesar* empowerment, and specifically while exhorting the deities to action, there was very loud thunder, even though the sky was perfectly clear. And during the *Mahakala* empowerment, which is always accompanied by a drum, the large drum in the protector's temple was beating all by itself. There was no one playing it, but everyone heard it beating. Trulshik Rinpoche is very detailed in all these things, and he had the three tormas taken to his main bedroom while the monks were playing the instruments and still keeps those tormas there. Trulshik Rinpoche never lets anyone in that room except his close personal attendants. I used to sleep at Khyentse Rinpoche's feet in that room, and one early morning I woke up while Rinpoche was doing his meditation session, sitting up. There was a lady sitting in front of him with her hair covering her face, so I couldn't see who she was. She was holding a cup. I thought it was so strange for a lady to be there, since no one was allowed in that room. I wondered how she could have gotten in. Then I went back to sleep again. Later I asked Rinpoche about it, saying, "I saw this lady sitting in front of you. Who was she?" Rinpoche just said, "You must have seen Dutro Lhamo," who was one of Trulshik Rinpoche's main protectors.

Trulshik Rinpoche always took very good care of his mother and was always worried about her health and so forth. She could barely walk, but he had a strong monk carry her down to receive the *Treasury of Spiritual Instructions* every day. One day when she was not so well, Khyentse Rinpoche was in Bodhnath giving the *New Treasures of Chokgyur Lingpa*. Trulshik Rinpoche asked Khyentse Rinpoche to do a divination, so Rinpoche did a mirror divination and set the mirror before him, blessed some rice, and threw it on the mirror. There was one monk from Dabzang Rinpoche's monastery who could see images in mirrors. In the mirror he saw an iron pillar with the number 94 above it. Then he actually saw Trulshik Rinpoche's mother in the mirror, sitting in a wooden meditation box like she used to sit in. So

Rinpoche sent a reply to Trulshik Rinpoche that she would live to be ninety-four years old.

Khyentse Rinpoche added quite a few things to the *Root Volumes of the Heart Essence* about how to give the empowerments; without those instructions it would be difficult to give the empowerments. Yudrön, Rigdzin Dorje's wife, told Rinpoche that some narrow-minded people didn't like the way he did it; they felt that he wasn't entitled to do such things. Then Rinpoche told us the following story:

At Paro Taktsang in the monkey month of the monkey year, 1980, Rinpoche had a vision of Jigmey Lingpa. In the vision he had a book tied up in his hair, and was wearing a white robe and a red-and-white-striped shawl. In the vision, Jigmey Lingpa put his hand on Khyentse Rinpoche's head, and Rinpoche recited the prayer called *Ocean of Accomplishment*. Jigmey Lingpa told him, "In the future, you will be the holder of the *Heart Essence* tradition. You may do whatever you think best for this tradition."

Following this, Rinpoche also prophesied that four great stupas, each filled with one hundred thousand small clay stupas, should be built in four particular places in Bhutan for the peace of the country. Simultaneously, he advised that a hundred thousand butter lamps and the same number of feast offerings should be offered at some of the holy places in Bhutan, Bumthang Kurje, and Paro Taktsang. This was soon accomplished by the royal family. Rinpoche also said that the stupa containing the relics of Palgyi Senge—a disciple who with Yeshe Tsogyal had accompanied Guru Padmasambhava when he gave the *Vajrakilaya* empowerment in Taktsang, miraculously displaying the mandala in space—should be restored at Taktsang.

Once when Rinpoche was in Nepal, he suddenly decided to go back to Bhutan. When he reached Puntsoling, he called Menyak Tulku and asked him to check on the large Guru Rinpoche statue at Paro Kyechu temple, which had been built in 1966 under the patronage of the Queen Mother for the benefit of all beings and to ensure peace in Bhutan. It turned out that mice had made a hole in the back of the statue and were destroying the mantras and precious relics that had been put inside the statue. Khyentse Rinpoche then traveled all the way to Paro to have it repaired and do the consecration again. The lamas who were doing the ceremonies at Kyechu joked, "Why didn't Guru Rinpoche give *us* a sign about the mice instead of making Khyentse Rinpoche travel all the way from Nepal?"

It is a local custom in Bhutan that when you go to see a lama, you bring the local liquor to offer. One time we were traveling from Bumthang Kurje to Thimphu and stopped in Tongsar. That night Rinpoche stayed in the Tongsar Palace while the other tulkus and I stayed in the Tongsar guesthouse. Though we were not supposed to drink alcohol, that night we secretly drank some of the local beer that was always around in abundance, and the next day I had a little headache, since we were not used to drinking it. No one knew we had been drinking. As usual we went to see Rinpoche to get a blessing in his room, and while I was sitting in the corner with my hands on my head, Rinpoche asked, "What happened?" So I said, "I have a headache," and Rinpoche said, "You drank too much beer last night."

I secretly learned how to drive when I was about fifteen years old, and I didn't dare tell Rinpoche about it. At one time in Puntsoling, the Drikung Kyabgon[2] had asked Rinpoche to give the *Treasury of Spiritual Instructions*, but since he was a higher lama than Dilgo Khyentse, Rinpoche said he wanted to pay the Drikung Kyabgon a visit before he came to see Rinpoche. Rinpoche prepared his ceremonial scarf and offering and came out of his room, but his usual driver Bandu wasn't expecting Rinpoche to want to go anywhere and had gone off, so there was no driver. Then Rinpoche said, "You know how to drive quite well now, so you can drive me." I was so happy as it was my first time to drive Rinpoche, and he said it felt very comfortable when I was driving, since I drive very carefully.

One of my friends, a monk called Dennis, never had any money, but one day he got some from a friend and used it to build a retreat house at Thupten Choling, Trulshik Rinpoche's monastery in Solukhumbu, in the mountains of Nepal. But Dennis never stayed in retreat and was usually running around in Kathmandu. One day Khyentse Rinpoche said to him, "Your house is in retreat, but you're not!" So Dennis thought he should do retreat and left to do a three-year retreat at his new retreat house.

After one year he got fed up of staying in his room and planned to end his retreat, since he had a strong habit of going around to all the lamas to gossip and joke. So he made arrangements for coming out of retreat and did the feast offering and so forth. Then he received the first letter he had ever gotten in his life from Khyentse Rinpoche, saying, "I am very happy you are doing retreat and hope you will continue." So he then felt obliged to continue, and in the end, he completed the three years he had promised to do.

One time Rinpoche was traveling by plane to Europe, and Orgyen Topgyal was sitting next to him. It was Orgyen Topgyal's first trip abroad. When the meal was served, Orgyen Topgyal prepared the tea for Rinpoche and offered it to him. Rinpoche drank the whole cup, but there was a little bit left, and as Tibetans usually take the remnants of a lama's food or drink as a blessing, Orgyen Topgyal drank it. It burned his mouth so badly that he felt like smoke was coming out of his ears. Instead of putting milk in the tea, he had put the liquid-mustard packet in Rinpoche's tea! He said, "Rinpoche, I am so sorry! I put chili in your tea." But Rinpoche said, "Oh, I thought Western tea must just taste like that."

Another time, when Rinpoche was in France, he met a student of Tulku Pema Wangyal's who was a doctor and said he was an expert at Chinese medicine. Since Rinpoche had a knee problem, that doctor, who was a bit proud, said his moxa treatment would be helpful and started putting moxa on Rinpoche's knee. While holding the burning moxa on Rinpoche's knee, he chatted with Tulku Pema Wangyal. All of a sudden we smelled the scent of burning flesh, and when we looked, he had burned Rinpoche's knee! He was waiting for Rinpoche to say, "Ouch!" But Rinpoche thought the pain was the treatment, so he didn't say anything, and for almost a month, we had to treat Rinpoche's infected knee.

In 1985, Khyentse Rinpoche returned to Tibet for the first time. His party went as an official delegation from Bhutan, so there was a very big reception at the Chengdu airport. Khyentse Rinpoche's program had not been discussed with the Chinese government, but the Chinese had already created an itinerary. Rinpoche really wanted to go to Kham, but that wasn't included on the itinerary. He was treated as a VIP, but they didn't want to listen to what he wanted to do. Tulku Pema Wangyal had to argue a lot with an important official from Beijing to let Khyentse Rinpoche go to Kham; they said he first had to go to Lhasa. So he went to Lhasa first.

In Lhasa a man from Amdo called Amdo Lungtok came to see Rinpoche. We had no idea what was going on in Lhasa since at that time communication didn't really exist. Amdo Lungtok said that he had built a huge Guru Padmasambhava statue in the Jokhang and the next day the consecration was supposed to take place, but he couldn't find any Nyingma lama to perform it. There had been a prediction to build a Guru Padmasambhava statue in the

Jokhang, but due to sectarianism over the centuries, it hadn't been built. So Khyentse Rinpoche did the consecration for the huge statue that filled an entire story, which was extremely auspicious. A monk called Lama Dawa who used to serve as Khyentse Rinpoche's chant master in Tibet in the past, happened to be in Lhasa as well, so he served as the chant master, which was very good. Khyentse Rinpoche had arrived in Lhasa in official Chinese cars, and no one in Lhasa knew who he was. They thought he was a pro-Chinese lama who had criticized the Dalai Lama, so they didn't want to approach him. Eventually word got out that Rinpoche was one of the Dalai Lama's teachers, and when it did, a huge crowd gathered and he could barely get out of the Jokhang.

During his second visit to Tibet, in 1988, Rinpoche went to Wutai Shan and visited the central peak.[3] The Chinese officials took Rinpoche up the back way in a small jeep, all the way to the top. I, however, climbed up the stairs on the front side. Just before reaching the top, I came across some mantrikas doing a fire puja. I asked where they were from, and they said they were from Rekong. I told them that I was from India and was with Khyentse Rinpoche. "Oh," they said. Ten meters higher up Rinpoche had arrived in the jeep, and we made some offerings to the Manjushri statue. Many years later a boy from Rekong came to see me in Nepal, and explained that his father was one of those mantrikas doing the fire puja. Apparently he had been one of Khyentse Rinpoche's disciples from when he gave the *Treasury of Precious Termas* in Rekong forty years earlier. When he saw me, it didn't occur to him right away that I was with Dilgo Khyentse; but after the fire puja he went up, however Rinpoche was already gone. Sadly he started crying and searched everywhere in all the hotels at Wutai Shan but never found us. He had waited his whole life to see Rinpoche again, and they had only been ten meters apart, but he had missed him.

During Khyentse Rinpoche's second visit to Tibet, he had a Khampa attendant supplied by the Chinese officials. He became very devoted to Rinpoche and later became his disciple. One time he had to go to Dartsedo for an important job. He used to pray to Rinpoche along the way. When he got to Dartsedo, they asked when he had arrived, and so he said, "Just now." They said that wasn't possible as the road had been closed for the past five days. He had actually driven there that day, without noticing any roadblocks or obstacles, and he believed it was due to Rinpoche's blessings.

One time in Nepal there was a very dirty and funky-looking monk who came to see Rinpoche. We neglected him and had him wait in a corner in order to let other more important people see Rinpoche first. After a while, when I tried to go inside, Rinpoche's door was closed, so I asked what was going on. The attendant said, "Rinpoche is receiving teachings from that old monk." The monk was a Sherpa who had been to Tibet and got some teachings that Rinpoche had not received, so Rinpoche wanted to receive them from that monk.

It seems that Khyentse Rinpoche's clairvoyance was unimpeded. Once, for instance, Trulshik Rinpoche was coming to visit him in Bhutan. While approaching the Queen Mother's beautiful palace, Dechen Chöling, Trulshik Rinpoche, who is a most perfect abbot in terms of monastic discipline, remembered a verse from the monastic code that says, "How can we like the king's palace?" A few moments later, while Trulshik Rinpoche was offering prostrations to Khyentse Rinpoche who was staying upstairs in the palace, he heard Khyentse Rinpoche say, "Oh, you the good monk keep on saying, 'How can one like the king's palace?' but nevertheless you do come to the king's palace, don't you?"

What perhaps surprised me most about this was not so much the fact that Khyentse Rinpoche had read Trulshik Rinpoche's thoughts, but that when Trulshik Rinpoche told me about it, he was hardly impressed, because for him it was totally obvious and he took it for granted that Khyentse Rinpoche knew clearly each and every thought of others. So, this wonderful incident also taught me about the degree of pure vision and faith that a great master like Trulshik Rinpoche had in his spiritual teacher.

Another time, when the Queen Mother had completed the Eight Sadhana Teachings temple in Kurje, Khyentse Rinpoche invited Trulshik Rinpoche to come to Bhutan. During the consecration, Khyentse Rinpoche was sitting on the throne wearing the Guru Rinpoche hat, and Trulshik Rinpoche was sitting to his left wearing the *pandita* hat. His Majesty the King of Bhutan was sitting to Khyentse Rinpoche's right wearing his yellow outer robe. The Queen Mother was very devoted to Khyentse Rinpoche and praying to him, and some of the ministers were doing prostrations and circumambulating the mandala and so forth. I felt that even when Guru Rinpoche was consecrating Samye with King Trisong Detsen and Khenpo Shantarakshita, the whole environment was not superior to this. I really felt like Khyentse

Rinpoche was Padmasambhava, so I started to learn how to see him as Guru Rinpoche.

One day Khyentse Rinpoche said to His Majesty, "They are doing the renovation of Samye Monastery in Tibet, and as an auspicious connection it would be good to make a donation." His Majesty offered a million rupees for the restoration.

After Rinpoche gave Shechen Gyaltsap's *Collected Works* in Nepal in the winter of 1990, we did a long-life ceremony for him. While I was making the offering, I had a strong feeling that Rinpoche would not live much longer; I burst into tears and ran out of the room crying and rushed down the stairs. On the stairs I ran into Ani Jinba, who asked, "What happened? Did Rinpoche say anything?" That was the last major set of teachings Rinpoche gave in Nepal.

As I have mentioned, my first perception of Khyentse Rinpoche was that of a wonderfully loving grandfather and an exceptionally good human being. Then, as I grew up, I began to perceive him as my spiritual master and gradually developed an unwavering faith in him. I always had total and overwhelming confidence in him, which was never challenged by ordinary thoughts. Even now, nearly twenty years after his passing away, he is constantly present in my thoughts, and I dream of him every few nights.

One time before the Khyentse Yangsi was recognized, I dreamed of Khyentse Rinpoche very clearly and told him that it was such a shock that he passed away so suddenly. Rinpoche said, "I was trying to tell you, but you always ignored my messages." So I asked him where he would be reborn, and Rinpoche said, "Don't worry. I will give you clear indications."

Another dream of mine was after my sister died. I was in Tibet, and when I heard she had died, I came back right away; I was very upset. I got in to Bangkok and planned to fly to Paro, Bhutan, the next day. That night I had a very clear dream of Rinpoche holding my sister's hand and saying, "I will take care of her. You don't have to worry." So the next morning I no longer felt that I had lost her.

Long after Yangsi Rinpoche was born, while I was on the way to Bodh Gaya, I had another dream about Khyentse Rinpoche. In the dream, I went into a room and saw him sitting there, and I said, "How can it be you? You are not with us anymore!" Rinpoche replied, "No, you are wrong. I am always with you." So I told him—still in the dream—that I had had a bad dream, and

I told him the story of Rinpoche passing away and looking for the Yangsi. I touched Rinpoche's feet, and was crying, clinging to him. I woke up with tears in my eyes, and the dream was so clear that I wasn't sure if it was a dream or if real life was a dream. So I really feel that even though Rinpoche is physically not here anymore, his blessings are still with us.

During a retreat I was doing in 1999 in Satsam Chorten, outside Paro, I felt very depressed. Yangsi Rinpoche had already been enthroned, and I felt very worried about all my responsibilities. Besides that, a rumor had spread throughout Bhutan that I—a monk—had a secret girlfriend, so I got really depressed.

During my retreat I used to listen to a series of teachings that Khyentse Rinpoche had given on *Vajrakilaya* in 1980, also in Satsam Chorten. I had never listened to those tapes before. One day the tape I was listening to started with Rinpoche saying, "In the future, when you do a *Vajrakilaya* retreat, this will be useful for you." Then Rinpoche laughed and said, "When people criticize you, saying you have a girlfriend and drink alcohol, don't worry. All sound is Vajrakilaya's mantra, so don't feel upset." It was almost like he was there that day and was talking to me—he knew all those years ago that that very day I was going to listen to that very tape!

These are indeed just a few anecdotes that are like drops of water taken from the oceanlike life story of Khyentse Rinpoche. Since he did not write his secret autobiography, which would have related all his spiritual experiences, dreams, and visions, we can only guess what they might have been from the few stories that he occasionally told to some close disciples. Khyentse Rinpoche himself once told us that after he found the secret autobiography of his teacher Khyentse Chökyi Lodro, he realized that he had been present on some occasions when his master had incredible visions of the Buddha and Guru Padmasambhava. But Khyentse Rinpoche added, "Yet, nothing in his outer behavior indicated anything about the deep and powerful vision that my teacher was experiencing at that moment." Therefore I have no doubt that Khyentse Rinpoche's visionary experiences must have been numerous and extraordinary. But above all, Khyentse Rinpoche was a constant example of what human and spiritual perfection can be, a constant and unforgiving reminder of what flawless spiritual practice should be, and a constant inspiration for humbly trying to follow in his footsteps. He has been and remains the most powerful presence in my life, and I have no other goals but to fulfill his vision.

Khyentse Rinpoche gave the empowerments and transmissions of the *Trea-sury of Precious Termas* five times: at Rekong in Amdo; in Kham; in Sikkim for the reincarnation of Khyentse Chökyi Lodro; in Bhutan; and in Clement Town, where Mindroling Monastery is. He gave the empowerments and transmissions of the *Treasury of Spiritual Instructions* four times: to Drungram Gyatrul in Kham, at Tashi Jong in India, at Solukhumbu in Nepal, and at Puntsoling in Bhutan. He gave the *Secret Mantra Treasury of the Kagyu Lineage* twice: once in Kham to Khyentse Chökyi Lodro and once in Bhutan to Khamtrul Rinpoche. He gave the *Compendium of Sadhanas* several times, one of which was to Dzongsar Khyentse in Bhutan. He gave the reading transmission of the *Kangyur* three times: once in his hermitage in Kham, once in Nepal, and once in Bhutan. The *New Treasures of Chokgyur Lingpa* he gave twice: in Tsurphu and in Nepal. He gave the *Nyingma Kahma* three times. He gave the *Three Classes of the Great Perfection* several times: to Trungpa Rinpoche in Zurmang and to Dzongsar Khyentse.

12. Visions in Exile
Tenga Rinpoche

Tenga Rinpoche was born in 1932 in Kham and was one of the main lamas in Benchen Monastery. In 1959, after the Chinese invasion, he escaped from Tibet with the Dilgo party. He eventually settled in Rumtek Monastery, Sikkim, the main seat of the Sixteenth Karmapa. There he served the Karmapa for seventeen years, acting as his vajra master for nine. Since 1976 Tenga Rinpoche has lived in Swayambhu, Nepal, where he founded the second Benchen Monastery as well as a retreat center in Pharping.

IN 1959, after the Dalai Lama had left Tibet, I was fortunate to escape in the company of Khyentse Rinpoche and his brother Nyenpa Rinpoche. The following year, all four schools of Tibetan Buddhism came together in Dharamsala to offer long-life ceremonies to His Holiness the Dalai Lama. The first to offer the long-life ceremony was the Geluk, and the teaching offered along with the mandala was given by Trichang Rinpoche. All the heads of the other three schools—the Sakya, Nyingma, and Kagyu; namely Sakya Gongma, Dudjom Rinpoche, and the Karmapa—asked Dilgo Khyentse if he could give the elaborate explanation that traditionally accompanies the mandala offering.

This is usually a piece of great scholarship which people prepare for several weeks and learn by heart. Everyone was a bit worried that, with only one day's notice, Khyentse Rinpoche would not be able to prepare such a complex speech in such a short time and would discredit the Nyingma tradition. A learned Geluk *geshe* even felt a bit sorry, and, that evening, brought Khyentse Rinpoche a text in which the explanation of the mandala of the universe was described in great detail.[1] He did not find Khyentse Rinpoche studying books, but engaged in a friendly conversation with visitors. Khyentse Rinpoche affably thanked the *geshe* for his kindness, put the text by his pillow, and continued his conversation without seeming to be worried at all. He did not actually open the book that evening.

The next morning when the time came to speak in front of His Holiness the Dalai Lama and the whole assembly of lamas from the four schools of Tibetan Buddhism, speaking for over an hour in an unimpeded flow like a river, Khyentse Rinpoche gave a most detailed and profound explanation of the universe according to the *Kalachakra Tantra,* in which he mentioned an immense number of quotes, which he obviously seemed to know by heart. At the end of the discourse, he finally approached the throne of His Holiness and offered the mandala plate into His Holiness's hands. Then he offered the eight auspicious substances, and when offering the conch, a loud thunder crash resounded. This was considered to be a most auspicious event.

Everyone was amazed at Khyentse Rinpoche's erudition and spoke about his speech for years to come. Afterward I asked him, "Did you study the *Kalachakra* a lot in the past?" He answered, "I didn't study it much; I read the *Kalachakra* commentary by Mipham Rinpoche maybe once or twice; that's all."

"It is amazing that you could give such a speech even though you only studied it once or twice," I said.

"I'll tell you something," Rinpoche replied. "According to Mipham Rinpoche, the area near our Dilgo home, which was called Gothi, was in the shape of the Shambhala pure land; that is why he decided to stay there. My father had a retreat house built for him and provided him with food and all necessities. Later Mipham Rinpoche also passed away there. When I was young, I wanted to do retreat near this hermitage, so I did so with my brother Shedrup and remained in the area for twelve or thirteen years. At that time I also did a *Kalachakra* recitation retreat, and one day I had a vision of the *Kalachakra* mandala as vast as space, emanating multicolored light rays to all sentient beings in the three worlds and eliminating their sufferings, and then emanating light rays to all the buddhafields and gathering their wisdom and activities into light that drew back into Kalachakra. Then Kalachakra became smaller and smaller, and absorbed into an orange syllable DHI which entered my throat and then dissolved into my heart. Since then, due to Kalachakra's blessings and Mipham Rinpoche's wisdom blessings, whatever teachings I give just vividly appear in my mind."

The Dalai Lama and Dilgo Khyentse in Dharamsala.
Photograph by Matthieu Ricard.

In Kham, Khyentse Rinpoche used to come to Benchen to visit his brother Nyenpa Rinpoche for long stretches of time. I used to go see him a lot, and sometimes he would give empowerments. It is true that while giving them he never needed any texts; he knew everything by heart, so I felt that he really was Manjushri and Vimalamitra in person. I told him that I felt great devotion and that he had such great wisdom that I really believed he was Vimalamitra. I think that when Khyentse Rinpoche stayed in retreat near Mipham Rinpoche's hermitage, his wisdom channels unfolded and his speech chakra was liberated.

One morning when Khyentse Rinpoche was doing a short retreat in Sikkim, he had a vision of an old yogi with a white beard and tied-up hair wearing white robes and holding a rosary. When Khyentse Rinpoche asked the old yogi where he came from, the yogi gave him something and said, "This is your share." When Rinpoche looked at it, he found a dagger made of meteoric iron. Rinpoche showed this ritual dagger to me when he returned from his retreat. Some earth treasures are offered to tertöns in this way, while others are taken from rocks or lakes. The yogi was apparently the local deity of Tashi Ding, Sikkim.

Another time, when Khyentse Rinpoche returned from Bodh Gaya, he gave me a small, flat, black rock and told me it was a dharmapala life-stone, a support for Dharma guardians that had great blessings, and he told me to always keep it. When I asked him where the rock came from, he said, "I've been to Bodh Gaya to do prayers. I also went to the Sitavana Charnel Ground where I performed the protector practice and did many prayers. Usually I always practice the protector Maning, but while I was in Sitavana, in a dream I had a vision of the protector Lekden, who promised to spread the Buddhist doctrine, extend the life of the doctrine holders, and appease the sufferings of all beings. I took this rock from the very place where I had this vision."

While Rinpoche was staying in the Durpin Monastery in Kalimpong, I attended most of the empowerments and teachings he gave, such as the *Four Parts of the Heart Essence,* and the *Root Volumes of the Heart Essence.* One time the King of Bhutan invited Rinpoche to visit Bhutan to revive the Buddhist teachings. So Rinpoche went to Bhutan and gave teachings on the *Jewel Ornament of Liberation.*[2] Later I met him in Rumtek and told him, "I heard that you gave a lot of teachings on the *Jewel Ornament of Liberation* in Bhutan. Is that true?"

"I did," Rinpoche answered. "There was a reason for this. When I was staying in Durpin Monastery, one night I had a vision of Longchenpa in a dream and shortly afterward I had another vision of Karmapa Dusum Khyenpa, who told me, 'If you proclaim the teachings like a dragon, it will benefit the doctrine and beings in a vast way.' A few weeks later the king of Bhutan invited me, and therefore I thought that teaching the *Jewel Ornament of Liberation* would greatly benefit Bhutan."

When Khyentse Rinpoche gave the *Treasury of Precious Termas* in Sikkim, I had already received the complete cycle in Kham, and so I only attended a few empowerments. Whenever I visited him, I had a lot of questions and he had a lot to say, so we used to spend a good deal of time talking together.

One day when I came early, Rinpoche was doing the *Heart Essence of the Immortal Arya* recitation practice. When I spoke to him a few days later, I asked, "Rinpoche, you never used to do the *Heart Essence of the Immortal Arya* before, but now you seem to be doing the recitation practice. Why is that?"

Rinpoche replied, "I used to do it occasionally, however I never did the recitation retreat. But a few months ago I had a dream of the Mahasiddha Thangtong Gyalpo who told me, 'If you do the *Heart Essence of the Immortal Arya* recitation retreat properly, you will live to be more than eighty years old.' That's why I am doing the practice now."

Later, when I was offering the reading transmission of the *Tengyur* at Shechen Monastery in Nepal,[3] Rinpoche called me one day and said, "Starting tomorrow, would you mind interrupting the reading transmissions for three days, as I would like to give the *Kalachakra* empowerment?"

"That's fine," I replied.

"You should do the empowerment preparations, and I will give the empowerment," Rinpoche said.

"That's fine," I again replied.

"There is a reason for me to give the *Kalachakra*," he said. And when I asked him what that was, he explained, "Last night I had a vision of my root teacher Jamyang Khyentse Chökyi Lodro, who told me, 'You have given the *Kalachakra* empowerment from Atisha's tradition many times, but you also have the Buton tradition and you must spread that now.'"

The young Dzongsar Khyentse tulku was there attending the transmissions, so Rinpoche said, "I have the special Buton *Kalachakra* transmission and must pass it on to my spiritual son, Jamyang Khyenste's tulku, and everyone else can receive it too."

So he gave the *Kalachakra* empowerment. As it is customary to wear the bone ornaments during the ceremony, Rinpoche gave the empowerment with his chest bare and wearing bone ornaments. When he prayed to Jamyang Khyentse Chökyi Lodro at the beginning of the ceremony, he shed tears.

In the eighties Rinpoche went to do a week's retreat in Maratika. Upon his return he gave me a *mala* as a support for my long life and said, "This time I received great blessings in Maratika." When I asked him about it, he said, "In a dream I had a vision of Amitayus the size of Mount Meru, wearing green silks and holding a long-life arrow. I received long-life blessings that dispelled the obstacles to my life."

13. Rainbow Body and the Pure Lands
TSIKEY CHOKLING RINPOCHE

Born in 1953, the second son of Tulku Urgyen Rinpoche, Tsikey Chokling Rinpoche was recognized by the Sixteenth Karmapa as the fourth reincarnation of the great tertön Chokgyur Lingpa. Like his illustrious predecessor, Tsikey Chokling is a tertön and lay practitioner with a wife and four children. His eldest son has been recognized by the Dalai Lama as an important Taklung Kagyu tulku, while his youngest son was recognized by Trulshik Rinpoche as the reincarnation of Dilgo Khyentse Rinpoche.

O NE OF THE MORE extraordinary features among the infinite qualities of the great tertön Dilgo Khyentse, whose learning, discipline, and nobility, as well as his teaching, debate, and composition, were matchless, was that he was extremely concerned about all the lineages of Tibetan Buddhism—he received teachings from countless masters of all four schools and then spread them. In general the whole day, whether he was having a meal or not, he was always ready to give whoever came to see him—lamas, students, high or low, from whatever lineage or tradition—whatever teachings they needed right that moment.

Most lamas are only concerned with their own tradition and lineage, but Khyentse Rinpoche was quite the opposite. He was truly nonsectarian. He had true pure vision toward all the lineages of the entire doctrine. Just as Khyentse Wangpo had about one hundred different learned and accomplished teachers, Dilgo Khyentse Rinpoche too had a vast number of teachers. Very often, though he would already have received certain empowerments and transmissions according to several lineages, if he would meet someone with the same transmission but through another lineage, he wanted to receive it again.

He would often invite lamas from other traditions and schools in order to spread their lineages, especially when certain lineages were in danger of declining. As soon as he saw that a certain lineage was in danger of decline, he would do everything to revive it. For instance, he invited Taklung Zhabdrung Rinpoche to give empowerments from the Taklung Kagyu lineage, a branch of the Kagyu school. He then received the Taklung Kagyu empowerments for many days.

Concerned that Khyentse Chökyi Lodro's Sakya lineage would decline, he invited Pewar Tulku, who had personally received the *Path and Result* from Chökyi Lodro, to give some Sakya empowerments. According to the Sakya tradition, there can only be twenty-five participants in an empowerment. One day Pewar Rinpoche was about to give a major *Hevajra* empowerment, and Trulshik Rinpoche, Dzongsar Khyentse, and Sengtrak Rinpoche were already inside. We were doing the *United Assembly* drupchen downstairs in the temple. During the break, Rinpoche called me and said to go up for the empowerment; I said that I was afraid to break the precepts as I wasn't able to do the *Hevajra* recitation, but he answered, "Trulshik Rinpoche and Dzongsar Khyentse are taking the empowerment, so it is better that you take it." So I went and took it; we were twenty-five in all and received *Hevajra* according to the Sakya tradition, where all the empowerment substances are given one by one to each student. Another day Pewar Rinpoche gave a *Khechari* empowerment through Chökyi Lodro's lineage, which Rinpoche told me I must also take; it too was with twenty-five participants only.

All the great masters of the four schools received transmissions from Khyentse Rinpoche, such as Sakya Gongma, the Sixteenth Karmapa, Penor Rinpoche, the Drikung Kyabgon, Khamtrul Rinpoche, Apo Rinpoche, and so forth. He also became one of the gurus of the highest lama in Tibet, the Fourteenth Dalai Lama Tenzin Gyatso, to whom he offered the major empowerments of the *Nyingma Kahma* and many other transmissions. Khyentse Rinpoche went to Penor Rinpoche's monastery in South India three times, where in 1979 he gave the *Four Parts of the Heart Essence,* the *Root Volumes of the Heart Essence,* and the *Seven Treasuries;* in 1984 he gave the *Nyingma Kahma;* and in 1986 he gave the *Collected Works* of Mipham Rinpoche. Whatever teachings lacked an empowerment ritual or *sadhana,* he would just compose it.

Not only did Khyentse Rinpoche give the *Treasury of Precious Termas,* the *Treasury of Spiritual Instructions,* the *Heart Essence of the Great Expanse,* the

New Treasures of Chokgyur Lingpa, the *Nyingma Kahma,* the *Four Parts of the Heart Essence,* the *Heart Essence of Chetsun,* the *Luminous Heart Essence of the Three Roots,* the *Six Volumes of Jatson,* and other transmissions many times, he also personally sponsored having all those books printed.

One time the Sixteenth Karmapa invited Dilgo Khyentse to Rumtek to give the *Four Parts of the Heart Essence* to the four main tulkus there; I had the privilege to be among the thirteen participants. The Rumtek monks were worried that everyone would become Nyingma. They used to joke with me about the *rishi,* lion, and elephant postures during the empowerments and said they resembled Hindu practices.[1]

One might perceive Dilgo Khyentse as merely a human of flesh and blood, but he was actually inseparable from Manjushri, Guru Rinpoche, and the twenty-five disciples. Nonetheless he never mentioned any of his accomplishments and was extremely humble. He used to say that he didn't know anything. It seems impossible that masters with such perfect knowledge and realization could ever appear nowadays.

When I visualize Khyentse Rinpoche surrounded by the twenty-five disciples and pray to him, due to his blessings, I can easily explain any teachings, whether sutra or tantra. If we have true faith both while in the master's presence and when apart from him, we truly can receive such blessings.

I am just ordinary, nothing special, but since the Karmapa recognized me, they say I am a Chokling reincarnation. People without pure vision call me fat Chokling. When I do divinations, they are usually accurate and I also have some spiritual powers. Sometimes I appear to be crazy, but it doesn't matter, since all the masters, from Vajradhara down to the Sixteenth Karmapa, and from Samantabhadra down to Khyentse Rinpoche were also mad.

Because I am a tulku of Chokgyur Lingpa, Rinpoche was always extremely kind to me. We have been connected for many lives, as previously Khyentse Rinpoche was born as King Trisong Detsen and Chokling as one of his sons. Khyentse Rinpoche had great pure vision toward me because I am supposed to be the reincarnation of King Trisong Detsen's son.

Whenever he would leave for Bhutan, I would see him off at the airport and feel sad and cry. He would then say, "Don't be sad. We'll meet again soon." He would often call me up to his room and tell me stories of his visions that he never told anyone else. One day he said, "Today I saw a really great spectacle," and when I asked him about it, he said, "Last night I had a vision of the

Copper-Colored Mountain pure land, with Guru Rinpoche and the twenty-five disciples as vivid as if they were actually present." Then he added, "Don't tell anyone. I'm only telling you about it!"

I used to throw the tormas during the drupchens and do special ceremonies for Rinpoche, and he said it helped him a lot. Rinpoche recomposed the *Chokyong Gongdu* and many other parts of the *New Treasures of Chokgyur Lingpa*, so I feel very grateful for that. There is no doubt that Rinpoche had a lot of visions of his *yidam* deities, but he was always very humble and, when asked about such things, used to say, "Why don't you ask the Karmapa or the Dalai Lama? I don't know anything."

The reason masters don't often talk about their inner visions is that it can shorten their life span, however once, during a *Mindroling Vajrasattva* drupchen we were doing in Bodhnath, Rinpoche called me up while he was having lunch and told me that the previous night he had an actual vision of the *Mindroling Vajrasattva* mandala, with Guru Rinpoche and the twenty-five disciples, Garab Dorje, the eight vidyadharas, as well as many dakas, dakinis, and dharmapalas, all appearing very vividly as if they were actually there. He asked me if I'd seen it too, but I told him that I hadn't. Then he told me to do a divination about it, but I said, "That's really great. No need to do a divination!" So he was very happy.

Once he told me that while he was doing retreat at Satsam Chorten in Bhutan, doing recitation of the *Three Roots of the Heart Essence,* Guru Rinpoche and Yeshe Tsogyal appeared as if they were actually there and gave many predictions. He asked me to do a divination about the predictions, so I asked whether the predictions were about the future and so forth, but Rinpoche said they were about him. At that time his retreat house became filled with rainbows and was completely luminous and transparent, which made him think that he was attaining rainbow body. Later it again appeared as solid.

Another time he told me that one day when he was doing retreat in Paro Taktsang, he was looking down from Taktsang and saw the mountain below filled with a hundred thousand dakinis, the main one being Machik Labdrön. When I asked if the dakinis gave him any predictions, he said, "I didn't ask for any predictions. The dakinis are all within one's own mind; the twenty-four special places are within one's own mind. All outer things are fabricated, so why ask?"

14. The Life of a Carefree Yogi
BY ORGYEN TOPGYAL RINPOCHE

Orgyen Topgyal Rinpoche is the eldest son of the Third Neten Chokling. He received many transmissions from Khyentse Chökyi Lodro. His root guru was Dilgo Khyentse Rinpoche, whom he often served as close attendant. After his father's death, he assumed responsibility for completing the Neten Monastery at Bir, in India, as well as overseeing the upbringing of his father's reincarnation.

DILGO KHYENTSE RINPOCHE was a tertön, and from an early age he often had visions of Guru Rinpoche and had termas transmitted to him. Rinpoche stayed in retreat in a small hermitage in Denkok where he did the preliminary practices. He studied the four mind changings by memorizing each corresponding section from both *The Words of My Perfect Teacher* and the *Treasury of Precious Qualities*. He was very determined, and his brother often told him to relax a little, but he wouldn't. His father said, "Either my son will become a great lama or all this will be useless; there is no other alternative. Let him do whatever he wants." His father passed away soon after. As none of his sons had married and were unable to look after the estate, the husband of Rinpoche's sister Kalga was placed in charge of the family affairs.

While staying in a cave, Khyentse Rinpoche practiced the yoga of the subtle channels and energies from the *Heart Essence*. By doing the inner heat practice known as *tummo* he obtained a lot of inner warmth. Although the climate there was very cold, he wore only a white cloth, day and night; his seat was a bearskin. Outside the cave there was thick ice, but inside the cave it was warm. Every night when he recited the prayers to the Dharma protectors, the protector Rahula would come. One night there was a great wind, raging like fire—it was Rahula. He did not enter the cave, but dissolved into a big juniper tree nearby. Later, the tree shriveled up and then grew again, but not like before—the wood was riddled with eyes. This was quite similar to what happened at Longchenpa's cave in Central Tibet, Gangri Thokar, where Rahula had also dissolved into a juniper tree.

Later, Rinpoche built a small wooden hut with one small window. When he looked out, there were often wolves passing by with wide-open mouths; sometimes they rubbed themselves against the hut. There were also many deer and wild sheep, and sometimes leopards. Once a month his mother came and stayed to talk for an hour. He never talked to anyone apart from his parents. His elder brother Shedrup was his helper during the retreat. Shedrup was a disciple of Mipham Rinpoche and had great devotion to him, and sometimes used to tell stories about Mipham Rinpoche. In the area it became known that when in need of rain, one simply had to request Dilgo Khyentse. Rinpoche would take a stone from outside his hut and put it at the spring; it would then rain soon after. Also it was said that the wild animals there would never harm one another. While in retreat, wild birds would often come and sit on his head, shoulders, and knees.

Sometimes Rinpoche stayed at Sakar Monastery, a Sakya monastery that belonged to the Dilgo family. The Dilgo family had a room there in which Khyentse Rinpoche would stay in retreat. When looking out the window, he could see vast fields; in the early mornings he could see thousands of birds flying up over the fields and landing again, singing and making merry. Rinpoche said it was a most delightful place. The region's mountains were filled with caves where Rinpoche spent many years in retreat, moving from one cave to another. Sometimes he stayed under the overhang of huge trees, and sometimes, during summer, in a tent on uninhabited alpine meadows among abundant flowers. Rinpoche had two daughters, and often in the summertime he sent his daughters and servants to collect thousands of flowers which he then used as daily offerings in his tent. In another tent he would offer large numbers of butter lamps.

Rinpoche often went to do healing ceremonies and bestow empowerments in the private quarters of the King of Derge and in the homes of the ministers. Dedicated to practice as he was, Rinpoche only visited his mother's home occasionally.

Every year Khyentse Rinpoche went to receive many teachings from Khyentse Chökyi Lodro. One day, Khyentse Chökyi Lodro was invited to Amdo, but could not go. He said that there was no difference between himself and Dilgo Khyentse, so he sent Dilgo Khyentse, who was then forty years old, in his place, to give the empowerments and reading transmissions of the *Treasury of Precious Termas* to a few thousand mantrikas.

In Amdo there was a huge monastery belonging to the Geluk tradition where Dilgo Khyentse was invited by a most learned and accomplished master named Lobsang Dorje. Khyentse Rinpoche offered him the empowerments for the Three Roots and received in return the empowerments and explanations of the *Guhyasamaja, Yamantaka,* and *Chakrasamvara* tantras, as well as the reading transmissions of many other tantras. Dilgo Khyentse regarded Lobsang Dorje as the most important of his root gurus in the Geluk tradition, while Lobsang Dorje dreamed that Dilgo Khyentse was a tulku of Jamyang Khyentse Wangpo, as well as of Rechung Dorje Trakpa. There were many tulkus of Jamyang Khyentse, but both Dilgo Khyentse and Khyentse Chökyi Lodro regarded Lobsang Dorje as being the reincarnation of Jamyang Khyentse within the Geluk tradition.

After the Chinese Communists started making trouble in Derge, Dilgo Khyentse headed toward Lhasa. Having been invited previously, Rinpoche and some of his attendants went to see Khamtrul Rinpoche at Khampagar. There Rinpoche offered several empowerments including the wrathful form of Manjushri known as Yamantaka. Then he went to Kela, the seat of Chokgyur Lingpa, where he received some empowerments from Tersey Tulku, and also offered some empowerments in return. Tersey Tulku said, "In my former life as Wangchok Dorje, the son of Chokgyur Lingpa, I disobeyed the command of Jamyang Khyentse Wangpo on three occasions. That unfortunate circumstance may be the reason why I have never been able to meet Khyentse Chökyi Lodro in this life. Now that I have met you, Dilgo Khyentse, I will regard you as my Jamyang Khyentse and make supplications to you."

Chokgyur Lingpa's daughter Konchok Paldron inherited a yellow parchment terma of her father's. When she passed away, it was given to her grandson, Tulku Urgyen, who subsequently gave it to his uncle Tersey Tulku. As Tersey Tulku had never been able to decode and write it down, he asked Dilgo Khyentse to decode it. Dilgo Khyentse replied, "I'll try."

They both then went to the temple containing the enshrined remains of Chokgyur Lingpa and locked the doors. First they performed a feast offering and then soaked the yellow parchment in nectar water. Upon looking at it, the text wasn't yet clear enough. After making many supplications to Guru Rinpoche and Chokgyur Lingpa, they again looked and found the text beginning to manifest. At some point, Khyentse Rinpoche asked for some paper, pen, and ink. He was given about forty folios of blank paper, and within a few hours, Khyentse Rinpoche filled them all up, writing effortlessly without pause, as if reading from the yellow parchment. He thus wrote a series of *sadhanas* focused upon the consorts of the eight herukas. Later on he commented, "There were three possible versions for this text—extensive, medium, and condensed. In accord with the amount of paper I was given, I wrote the medium-length version."

In the Jokhang in Lhasa, Rinpoche made lavish offerings, including a hundred thousand mandala offerings according to the *Heart Essence* tradition. One day during this time the Fourteenth Dalai Lama arrived at the Jokhang. He saw Dilgo Khyentse, asked where he was from, and they chatted. That, Rinpoche said, was the first time he met the Dalai Lama, and those were the first words they exchanged. During this time Rinpoche offered some brocade Dharma robes belonging to his brother Nyenpa Rinpoche to the Jowo statue, with an aspiration prayer that Rinpoche had written. Later on in 1973, some Nepalese traders put the same robes up for sale in Kathmandu, and they came back into Rinpoche's possession.

While Rinpoche was in Lhasa, everyone from Kham offered a huge gold-plated lion throne to the Dalai Lama, and Dilgo Khyentse and Shechen Kongtrül presided over the offering ceremony. During the ceremony, Shechen Kongtrül said, "This golden throne is amazing, but I don't think he will be able to sit on it for long!" However, he was very happy and said, "Today I have met Avalokiteshvara." More than a hundred major lamas and dignitaries from Kham came to participate in the ceremony. It is the tradition that at the end of the ceremony, the Tibetan government gives each important person a special long white ceremonial scarf as an expression of official appreciation, but after giving out fifty, they ran out. While Rinpoche was in Lhasa, Khyentse Chökyi Lodrö sent a telegram from Sikkim, his last words to Dilgo Khyentse: "Write an excellent arrangement for the *Three Classes of the Great Perfection* empowerments!"

Dilgo Khyentse went from Lhasa to Tsurphu where he met the Sixteenth Karmapa, offered empowerments, and performed many healing ceremonies. While there both his brother Shedrup and his sister passed away. Fighting also broke out back in Lhasa, instigated by guerrilla groups from Kham. That was the beginning of a lot of clashes and unrest. An important minister in the Tibetan government, Ngapo Ngawang Jigmey, who was close to Dilgo Khyentse, told Rinpoche that it might be best if he went to India.

Rinpoche left for Bhutan with his brother Nyenpa Rinpoche not long after the Karmapa had left. While traveling through Bhutan, he stayed under a tree below Simtokha Dzong, near Thimphu, for two days, and no one recognized him. An old Bhutanese lady gave him a big basket with rice. Later he told me, "The rice the old lady gave me under the tree when I came as a refugee from Tibet was a greater kindness than one hundred thousand rupees given by a benefactor nowadays!"

While in Bhutan, Rinpoche heard over the radio that Khyentse Chökyi Lodrö had passed away in Sikkim. So he proceeded to Sikkim via Kalimpong with his attendant and on the way lost some of his belongings. Rinpoche didn't have much money at this time and had difficulties in meeting the expenses. He saw Khyentse Chökyi Lodrö's body and remained there for a few weeks; then he went back to Kalimpong.

Later he decided to go on pilgrimage to all the major sacred places in India. Rinpoche had brought a gold-colored hat from Kham, and when he heard the train was passing over the Ganges, he took the hat off and tossed it into the river through the train window. Rinpoche visited the pilgrimage places of Bodh Gaya, Varanasi, and so forth. After having traveled to all the sacred places, as Khyentse Chökyi Lodrö had gone to Kushalnagar before returning to Sikkim where he passed away, Dilgo Khyentse said, "For the time being I will not go to Kushalnagar." Later, after the Dalai Lama gave the *Kalachakra* empowerment to a huge gathering in Bodh Gaya in 1985 however, Rinpoche did visit Kushalnagar.

On the way back from the pilgrimage, Rinpoche went through Nepal visiting all the major sacred places there and then went to Kalimpong and Sikkim to perform the funeral ceremonies for Khyentse Chökyi Lodrö. After many hassles Rinpoche finally obtained the necessary visa and arrived in Sikkim. There he completed the preparations for the body in Gangtok, and then went to Tashi Ding with many of Khyentse Chökyi Lodrö's disciples and presided over the funeral ceremonies. He also carried out most of the duties involved with enshrining the remains in a stupa. Rinpoche himself had the wish to remain in Sikkim for a while longer to take care of Chökyi Lodro's temple and disciples, but the officials wouldn't grant him any extension to his visa.

Dilgo Khyentse had a dream in which he understood that by staying in Bhutan there would be immense benefit for the Buddhadharma and all beings. Loppön Sonam Zangpo and the senior Bhutanese Queen Mother Puntsök Chödrön assisted Rinpoche and made him principal teacher at Simtokha Dzong, together with another important Nyingma teacher, Khenpo Tsondru. During the daytime he would teach in the school, while in the evening and on weekends he would give numerous teachings, including some of the major scriptures of Buddhist philosophy, to many people.

One night he had a good dream and wrote a petition to Mahadeva, which is now included in his *Collected Works*. A few days later Queen Mother Puntsök Chödrön sent for him. When he arrived, she told him, "Queen Kesang Chödrön Wangchuk, the wife of the present king, wants to come and see you. If she can connect with you and gain greater confidence in the Dharma, it will help Buddhism in Bhutan in the future. Can she come and see you?" Rinpoche replied, "I am a refugee, a man who has lost his homeland. When staying here in this country, anyone, high or low, can come to see me." The Queen Mother passed that message on to Her Majesty the Queen.

Two weeks later Queen Kesang Chödrön sent her servant to see Dilgo Khyentse Rinpoche to let him know that she would be coming to visit. When she arrived, she was accompanied by the crown prince, the present King of Bhutan, who at that time was but a small child, wearing a yellow brocade gown. Dilgo Khyentse Rinpoche thought this was very auspicious. At their meeting Queen Kesang Chödrön explained to Rinpoche some problems she was facing. After a few days she came back and received Rongzom Pandita's *Lotus Dakini* empowerment, and Rinpoche told her, "Do this practice, and your troubles will be over."

Rinpoche taught at the school in Bhutan for about a year and then went to India once more and, on the way, remained for some time in Kalimpong. During this time Rinpoche's youngest daughter fell seriously ill at her school in Mussoorie and was taken to the hospital in Lucknow. Having heard of her illness, Rinpoche, accompanied by his attendant Yonten, traveled for a few days by car and train and finally reached Lucknow. They had no idea in which hospital Rinpoche's daughter was, and Yonten just spoke a few words of Hindi.

Dilgo Khyentse with Dzongsar Khyentse. Photograph by Matthieu Ricard.

From the railway station, they went on a rickshaw tricycle and managed to ask the cyclist to take them to a hospital. Miraculously, they found the right hospital just before midnight. Khyentse Rinpoche just had enough time to give a few last words of spiritual advice to his daughter. Half an hour later she passed away. Before passing, she had asked Khyentse Rinpoche, as her last wish, to build a statue of Guru Padmasambhava, but without the mustache with which Guru Rinpoche is usually represented. The large Guru Padmasambhava statue that Khyentse Rinpoche later built at Shechen Monastery in Nepal was made without a mustache, in fulfillment of his daughter's wish.

Rinpoche took his daughter's body to Varanasi to be cremated. He then returned to Sikkim and visited the Karmapa at Rumtek. The Karmapa said, "Whenever someone linked to me passes away, I always see them once while they are in the bardo state. Your daughter is not in a bad state, such as the lower realms; she is liberated." After that Rinpoche wasn't sad anymore.

Soon after, Rinpoche received both the *Secret Mantra Treasury of the Kagyu Lineage* and the *Treasury of Spiritual Instructions* from the Karmapa. In Kalimpong, Rinpoche regularly visited Dudjom Rinpoche, with whom he was very close. He also visited Kangyur Rinpoche from who he received the *Hundred*

Dilgo Khyentse with Tulku Chökyi Nyima, Tulku Urgyen, Tulku Pema
Wangyal, and Rabjam Rinpoche at Nagi Gonpa, Nepal.
Photograph by Matthieu Ricard.

Thousand Nyingma Tantras and all the Dharma treasures of Taksham Samten Lingpa.

Once when Rinpoche was staying at Bodh Gaya with Khyentse Chökyi
Lodro's servant, Tashi Namgyal, Trinley Norbu, the son of Dudjom Rinpoche, arrived with his entourage. Tashi Namgyal later told me that one
evening Dilgo Khyentse said that he believed that Trinley Norbu's son was
probably the reincarnation of Khyentse Chökyi Lodro.[1] Several years later
Sakya Gongma also recognized this boy as the reincarnation of Khyentse
Chökyi Lodro. After the recognition by Sakya Gongma, Rinpoche traveled
back to Sikkim to perform the enthronement ceremony. In order to welcome the tulku, Rinpoche went to Tashi Trak in Sikkim where he met the
tulku arriving via Bhutan. Carrying the young tulku, who is known as Dzongsar Khyentse, on his lap, they arrived at Gangtok. On an auspicious day, the
enthronement ceremony took place in the king's palace, and Dilgo Khyentse
gave an explanation of the five perfections that lasted more than four hours.

Soon after having recognized and enthroned the tulku, Rinpoche gave
him the complete empowerments and reading transmissions for the *Treasury of Precious Termas* at Enchey Monastery. After he had finished the

Dilgo Khyentse with Dudjom Rinpoche in Dordogne.
Photograph by Matthieu Ricard.

transmissions, my family and I arrived in Sikkim. He told me, "I have passed on the *Treasury of Precious Termas* in extensive detail just for the sake of the tulku of Dzongsar Khyentse." This transmission seems to have been much more detailed than the version Rinpoche transmitted in Clement Town.

Having given the empowerments and reading transmissions, Rinpoche presided over the drupchen of the *Secret Gathering of the Dakinis,* including the preparation of sacred medicine, in the presence of the enshrined remains of Khyentse Chökyi Lodro in the temple of the king's palace. I was fortunate enough to participate in that assembly. At that time, Khyentse Chökyi Lodro's reincarnation was very young, and he could often be seen during the drupchen wearing a hat from his past life while being carried around by his servant Tashi Namgyal. I remember seeing that Dilgo Khyentse and other old disciples of Khyentse Chökyi Lodro shed tears when seeing the young tulku and remembering their guru.

Later, during a feast offering, Khandro Tsering Chödrön sang the feast song and Rinpoche said, "I have never heard anything more beautiful than this." In the presence of Chökyi Lodro's enshrined remains Dilgo Khyentse gave some important empowerments and reading transmissions. Rabjam Rinpoche was also there; he was very young at that time. Before giving it to anyone else, Rinpoche first gave water from the vase and the other empowerment substances to Khyentse Chökyi Lodro's reincarnation, so Rabjam Rinpoche interjected, "Our big Rinpoche! First give to me!" Even if Rabjam Rinpoche got nectar or pills of longevity three times, he still said, "Give me more! Give me more!"

After the empowerments Rinpoche visited several places in India. When Rinpoche arrived back in Bhutan, Her Majesty Ashe Kesang Chödrön had built Rinpoche a house at Paro Kyechu and offered him a jeep as well. Under the patronage of Her Majesty Ashe Kesang, Rinpoche then began to make a statue of Guru Rinpoche that is unmatched in this world. There are now four statues in the new Guru Temple at Kyechu: Guru Rinpoche, Avalokiteshvara, Guru Horsok Averting War, and Kurukulle. Dilgo Khyentse personally designed them, filled them with mantras, and performed the consecration. In my opinion it will be difficult to find statues with more blessings in this world. He also designed the paintings in the temple hall, depicting the eight herukas, which were painted by Bumtrak Kyilkhor Rinpoche, an outstanding artist and hermit.

The house in Paro was Rinpoche's first residence after fleeing Tibet, and he slowly developed a stronger link to the country of Bhutan. One day he was sitting in a room at Dechen Chöling Palace talking with Her Majesty Ashe Kesang. Suddenly His Majesty the King appeared from a room in the back and asked some questions, "Why do you have long hair and keep a woman? Are you a tertön?"

"I have a few teachings that look like termas, but I'm not sure whether they are authentic or just illusion," Rinpoche replied. "But when I showed them to my root gurus, they deemed them to be genuine Dharma treasures, so it seems like I am a tertön."

"If you are a tertön, you must be able to read yellow parchment. Can you?"

"If I have the karmic connection, I am able to read some yellow parchment; but others I can't," Rinpoche explained.

"In my box of blessed articles I have a few yellow parchments," the King said. "One day I'll show them to you; then we'll see if you can read them!"

Later, Rinpoche many times performed the drupchen of *Chakrasamvara Pema Vajra,* a rediscovered treasure of Jamyang Khyentse Wangpo, at Punakha Dzong, and at Bumthang he did the drupchen of the *Eight Sad-*

hana Teachings. In both places he erected new shrines and temples with many statues. Sometimes during these drupchens the king would also come, and I heard that these ceremonies were extremely dignified and had great blessings, but I didn't have the fortune to attend them personally.

One day while my father and I were staying in a guesthouse in Gangtok, we received a letter from Dilgo Khyentse at the king's palace temple. The letter was about a vision Rinpoche had recently had. He wrote that after he had completed giving the *Kangyur* reading transmission in Nepal, he went to Namo Buddha. That night he had a dream mixed with a pure vision in which he went to the top of a large mountain. On the summit he met Shechen Gyaltsap, Shechen Rabjam, and Shechen Kongtrül, each sitting on a chair. When he saw them he knew that they had experienced immense trials and had already passed away in prison under the Chinese occupation; but today, beholding them as if in actuality, he asked them questions in verse.

In this song he declared, "The Buddhadharma has faded, you have been killed by the Chinese Communists, and beings' happiness is destroyed!" Headed by Shechen Gyaltsap, who was very impressive, they replied in unison, "Serve sentient beings and the Buddhadharma! By doing so, there will be immense benefit! Our combined blessings will take birth in your bloodline as a *nirmanakaya* to serve the Dharma and all beings, like the sun rising at dawn. The Buddhadharma will now slowly flourish! Don't worry, and don't be timid!" My father and I read the letter several times and then gave it back. I was too young to think of making a copy, and I am not sure whether the letter still exists.

The reincarnation of Shechen Rabjam was enthroned at Rumtek Monastery by the Karmapa and Dilgo Khyentse, as well as many others lamas. Trangu Rinpoche gave a talk on the five perfections and Khenpo Chötrak gave an extensive exposition on mandala. The ceremony was lavish like they used to have in old Tibet; it was the largest and most impressive ceremony I have ever seen. After that there was a thanksgiving feast and banquet, lasting for three days. At the end of the year Dilgo Khyentse gave the *Treasury of Precious Termas* once more for the benefit of Shechen Rabjam at Dechen Chöling in Bhutan. That is why I believe that both the Dzongsar Khyentse and Shechen Rabjam tulkus will spread the *Treasury of Precious Termas* empowerments and reading transmission in the future.

At the age of sixty-one—an age generally considered to be full of obsta-cles—Dilgo Khyentse spent the year in retreat, practicing the *Secret Assem-bly Longevity Practice*, the spiritual treasure focused on longevity revealed by Ratna Lingpa. One night he dreamed several times that he lost his front teeth. Rinpoche thought, "This is a bad sign; losing my front teeth is an omen that there is some danger for either Rabjam Rinpoche or the crown prince, but it is more likely for the prince." He told his attendant to prepare for a *Vajrakilaya* exorcism ritual, and for a few days he did the ceremony and many petitions to the Dharma protectors. Not long after that the crown prince was in a car accident in which nearly everyone in the car died, but the crown prince escaped unharmed.

No matter where Rinpoche stayed, he would always give his disciples empow-erments and reading transmissions day and night. Rinpoche often stayed at Tashi Chodzong, the largest *dzong* in Bhutan, to perform ceremonies, and during that time no one could casually walk inside.[2] Therefore, after finishing his lunch, Rinpoche was sometimes seen sitting on a chair outside the com-pound giving teachings to nuns and lay practitioners. After a few days the minister in charge saw Rinpoche sitting outside and then changed the rules so that Rinpoche's disciples were allowed inside to receive teachings. Dilgo Khyentse also gave a lot of teachings in his quarters at the Dechen Chöling Royal Palace. Rinpoche once told me, "I have given many empowerments in Bhutan and consumed a lot of donations. Probably more than a hundred thou-sand people have received the *Thangtong Gyalpo* longevity empowerment."

Rinpoche's favorite place in Bhutan was Paro. He often performed drup-chen ceremonies in the temple there. Each year, for twenty-six consecutive years, he performed the extensive version of the *Supreme Heruka Assembly* drupchen, which lasts day and night for nine days, and sometimes he would also put on a costume and participate in the tantric dances. Once the young Dzongsar Khyentse tulku joked, "Now I will dance Dilgo Khyentse's style, just sitting down without moving the legs!" Dilgo Khyentse was unable to use his legs at that time, so the young tulku thought that Rinpoche's style was to dance with the arms while sitting down.

One day the young tulku had to go to the toilet and urinated standing up. His tutor scolded him saying, "You cannot do that standing! You are a lama!"

"The big Rinpoche also does it standing!" the boy replied. Dilgo Khyentse always treated the reincarnation of Dzongsar Khyentse with great love and respect. Later, even though he was so old and heavy of body that he almost couldn't bow down in front of the precious Buddha Shakyamuni statue in Bodh Gaya, whenever he met the tulku of Khyentse Chökyi Lodro, he always prostrated himself to the ground immediately.

One time during a visit to Nepal, he went by helicopter to Namo Buddha, where he performed an extensive ceremony of bodhisattva aspirations and told the detailed story of that former life of the Buddha. During the ceremony Rinpoche said, "This is a very special place. It was very fortunate to come here today, but it will be more difficult to come back in the future." After that it seems he had only one more opportunity to return there.

Rinpoche also went to Tashi Jong several times, where, in 1973, he gave the empowerments and reading transmissions for the *Treasury of Spiritual Instructions* as well as many other teachings. The reincarnations of both Sangye Nyenpa and Dzongsar Khyentse were present on that occasion. The previous Khamtrul Rinpoche and the entire community of Tashi Jong were very close to Rinpoche. In Darjeeling, Dilgo Khyentse visited the seat of Kangyur Rinpoche many times and gave many teachings, chiefly the *Nyingma Kahma* and the complete treasures of Jatson Nyingpo, but also many other empowerments and reading transmissions.

Rinpoche also came to visit us in Bir about five times in all. In 1973 he performed the funeral ceremonies for my father, the Third Chokgyur Lingpa, Pema Gyurmey. He also visited all the monasteries in Bir, consecrated them, and gave empowerments. He did healing ceremonies and gave people personal advice. It is due to his kindness that the people in Bir chant ten million Mani and Vajra Guru mantras every year. He was offered a piece of land to build a house there but never built it. He gave the land to Dzongsar Khyentse, who built the Dzongsar Institute there instead.

During the mid-seventies Rinpoche had more than two hundred monks come from Bhutan to chant a hundred thousand "Aspirations of Samantabhadra" at Bodh Gaya. The chanting continued from six in the morning until nine at night. Rinpoche did the morning and evening sessions in his tent and the daytime chants under the bodhi tree. After lunch he would give a commentary on the "Aspirations of Samantabhadra." He was in an exceptionally good mood during that time. After the last session in the evening, he would again give teachings to his disciples. The following year he had a hundred thousand *Confessions of Bodhisattva Downfalls* chanted; this chant is also known as the *Sutra of the Three Heaps.* He had previously offered several hundred thousand butter lamps at Bodh Gaya, and every day, during these two chants, he again presented innumerable lamp offerings.

In 1978, Rinpoche was invited to Mindroling Monastery in Clement Town, India, where he gave the empowerments for the *Treasury of Precious Termas* to forty or fifty tulkus and about seven hundred monks, nuns, and laypeople. It took more than four months. The reading transmissions were given by Dodrupchen Rinpoche. At that time I was working as the shrine master with several other helpers, and I became very familiar with Rinpoche's daily conduct.

He would rise at three in the morning. As soon as he got up, he would hold the vase breath once, but for a very long time, probably almost half an hour, for it was noticeable when he finally exhaled. Then he ate many sacred substances and medicines, pills of longevity and the like. He would also set out in front of him some pills for Shechen Rabjam and his close attendants to eat. When beginning his daily chants, he would start with the *Heart Essence of the Immortal Arya* and *Mindroling Vajrasattva,* reciting a few thousand of each and using a different *mala* for each *sadhana.* Then he would chant the *Vajra Armor,* after which he would go to the large shrine hall.

During the transmission of the *Treasury of Precious Termas,* he chanted the *Combined Sadhana of the Three Roots,* which is a rediscovered treasure of Jamyang Khyentse Wangpo, and then the *Seven-Chapter Supplication* and other daily practices. In total, Rinpoche's morning prayers filled one large volume of texts. By the time he finished, it would be dawn.

Rinpoche then had breakfast and soon after began the preparations for the empowerments. For each empowerment he would recite three hundred or more of the main mantra and more than one hundred for the vase recitation. After finishing all the preparations for the empowerments of that particular day, he would take lunch. The empowerments would start at one in the afternoon and continue to half past six, seven, or sometimes eight at night. In the evening after the empowerments, he would perform a feast ceremony as a conclusion and also chant many aspirations.

After going back to his room, he had dinner and then chanted an extensive petition to the guardians of the Dharma. After the petition Rinpoche would give at least one hour of teachings. Remember, this went on for not just one or two days but for many months on end. When I think about this, it seems impossible for any human being to emulate him. Nonetheless he always found time to joke and play around in between.

During this time he performed in great detail the commemoration of Khenpo Bodhisattva, Padmasambhava, and the Dharma King Trisong Detsen, [Abbot, Guru, and King] as well as the arrival of Buddhism in Tibet. He also performed an extensive ceremony on the anniversary of Longchenpa; during this ceremony the renowned Nyingma Khenpo Tsondrü gave a speech in front of all the lamas and participants of the empowerments. While reaching the passage on Maitreya, he collapsed and passed away right then and there.

While in Clement Town, Dilgo Khyentse received two letters from the Dalai Lama in Dharamsala asking for empowerments and teachings. So Rinpoche went there and offered a few empowerments in the Dalai Lama's private quarters. When he returned, Rinpoche said that to offer one hour of teachings to His Holiness the Dalai Lama was more profitable for the Buddhadharma than to offer months of empowerments to a thousand monks and tulkus.

Back in Clement Town, he completed the transmissions for the *Treasury of Precious Termas* with a drupchen of the *Eight Sadhana Teachings,* including the consecration of sacred medicine. At the thanksgiving ceremony at the end of the empowerments, Dzongnor Rinpoche presented a lavish offering. Everyone else presented white scarves, made offerings, and paid their respects. During this time Rinpoche read the handwriting on each and every envelope from the donors, saying, "They have made this offering to me, so I must read it."

Rinpoche visited Penor Rinpoche's Namdroling Monastery in Mysore three times. He gave the transmissions for the *Four Parts of the Heart Essence,* the *Root Volumes of the Heart Essence,* the *Seven Treasuries,* and the *Trilogy of Natural Ease* of Longchenpa, the *Nyingma Kahma,* Mipham Rinpoche's twenty-six volumes of *Collected Works,* Patrul Rinpoche's six-volume *Collected Works,* and numerous other empowerments and reading transmissions. Penor Rinpoche showed him great respect, and Dilgo Khyentse also received some empowerments from Penor Rinpoche in return. In 1986, after the completion of the reading transmission of Mipham Rinpoche's *Collected Works,* at the end of the *Supreme Heruka* drupchen, Penor Rinpoche cried loudly when he was reciting the *Lamp Prayer* in front of Khyentse Rinpoche.

Dilgo Khyentse also made several trips to the United States and Europe. His chief destination on his first trip to Europe was France, at the invitation of Tulku Pema Wangyal, but he also visited England, Denmark, Norway, Sweden, and Switzerland, before continuing to the United States and Canada at the invitation of Chogyam Trungpa Rinpoche. Dilgo Khyentse also went to Southeast Asia several times and thus had seen most of this world.

At the Eiffel Tower in Paris he said, "The effort to build such a structure is quite useless. In Tibet we would only take such trouble for something like a stupa or a temple that would be of benefit to the teachings or beings." He also went to the United Nations in New York. An interpreter informed Rinpoche, "This is where all the countries of the world meet to discuss important matters!" But Rinpoche thought to himself, "Whether they meet or not, they probably don't discuss even one word in accordance with the Dharma—this is pointless!" He then chanted a prayer for the propagation of the Dharma written by Jamgön Kongtrül called the *Infallible Refuge* three times.

When traveling for extended periods in the West, he never interrupted the feast ceremonies on the tenth and twenty-fifth days of the Tibetan month, but he did break the extensive ceremony of fulfillment and mending on the twenty-ninth. In apology he composed a new fulfillment and mending ceremony in poetry, which is now in his *Collected Works*. He wrote many other works while traveling in the West.

Judging from his words, it seems that he never really enjoyed these travels. Once, after a visit to the West for a few months, I went to Delhi to welcome him back to Asia. The previous Khamtrul Rinpoche was also there, and they talked a lot about the countries abroad. "What did you do over there in the Western countries?" I asked.

"I couldn't do anything important, neither religious nor political," Rinpoche responded. And then he added, "I gave Karma Thinley the reading transmission for the *Treasury of All-Pervading Knowledge,* and I met Trungpa Rinpoche. That was very good."[3]

"Are there any good practitioners in the West?" I asked.

"All of Trungpa Rinpoche's students came to offer their understanding, one by one, and I met a few who seemed to have recognized intrinsic awareness," Rinpoche replied. "Trungpa has many students, and they are very disciplined. They chant the *Supplication to the Kagyu Lineage* and the petition to the guardians of the Dharma in English. When meditating, they remain in the posture of Vairochana for a long time. Some may know how to meditate; some just pretend. Some of Tulku Pema Wangyal's retreatants are also genuine practitioners."

"Did you enjoy the West?" I asked.

"Not at all! There were no Buddhist shrines to visit, no temples, no gatherings of the ordained sangha, and no exposition and study of the Dharma of scripture and realization. Compared to the West, India and Nepal are much better; arriving in Delhi is like arriving in my homeland."

Nonetheless Rinpoche went back to the West many times. Once I also went as his attendant. In France, due to the kindness of Tulku Pema Wangyal, a three-year retreat center was started and later another one as well. In both these places Rinpoche gave many empowerments, reading transmissions, and oral instructions, and the retreatants behaved very well.

Rinpoche also gave teachings at Sogyal Rinpoche's and Chimey Rinpoche's Dharma centers in England. One day he did a feast offering at Sogyal Rinpoche's center, and while singing the "Leymon Tendrel" feast song, many of the students danced during the song, modern style. We all laughed, but Rinpoche himself didn't flinch. Afterward he commented, "Today there was something to experience while abroad! In the past the yogis, once their experience blazed up, would traverse freely through solid walls. Maybe that happens these days too!"

On another trip to the United States, Trungpa Rinpoche came with hundreds of students to welcome Dilgo Khyentse in the airport near Boulder; the cars all carried flags right and left. Rinpoche stayed at Marpa House and gave a few empowerments and reading transmissions. The main ceremony during his stay was the enthronement of Trungpa Rinpoche as King of Shambhala, which was done with great pomp and grandeur at Dorje Dzong. Trungpa in return gave Dilgo Khyentse the rank and emblems of a general of Shambhala. Each of his attendants also got an official rank in the Shambhala army. When we returned to his room, Khyentse Rinpoche said, "Attach my emblem to the cloth wrapper of my daily chant book." After a few days it disappeared.

Sakya Gongma of Puntsok Palace then came to Boulder to see Dilgo Khyentse and was offered a few empowerments and reading transmissions. They showed deep mutual respect for each other. Khyentse Rinpoche also went up to Rocky Mountain Dharma Center, traveling by helicopter, where Trungpa Rinpoche and all his attendants were in army uniform. At Rocky Mountain

Dharma Center, Rinpoche performed several ceremonies. The result of all these visits was that Rinpoche has a great number of disciples in Western countries, and many of them have stayed in retreat for three or more years.

Among Dilgo Khyentse Rinpoche's great services were performing the funeral and cremation ceremonies for Khyentse Chökyi Lodro, the Eighth Khamtrul Dongyu Nyima, the Third Chokgyur Lingpa Pema Gyurmey, Kangyur Longchen Yeshe Dorje, and the Eleventh Zurmang Trungpa Chökyi Gyamtso. The Second Dzongsar Khyentse Thupten Chökyi Gyamtso, as well as the Fourth Neten Chokling Gyurmey Dorje, and the Ninth Khamtrul Shedrup Nyima were chiefly recognized by the Sixteenth Karmapa and Sakya Gongma, but the decisive word, enthronement, and reinstatement in their seats were all arranged by Dilgo Khyentse. In Kham, Central Tibet, Nepal, and India, he also recognized and enthroned many tulkus.

Tulku Pema Wangyal, the best attendant among all of Rinpoche's disciples, accompanied him on all his journeys back to Tibet, as well as to the countries abroad where he also functioned as interpreter. Tulku Pema Wangyal and his own disciples helped vastly in sponsoring Rinpoche's monastery in Nepal, and they also looked after the expenses involved in Dilgo Khyentse Rinpoche's plan to build a temple in Bodh Gaya. Rinpoche's unfinished projects include building a stupa in each of the eight major pilgrimage sites: Bodh Gaya, Rajgir, Sarnath, Shravasti, Lumbini, Vaishali, Kushalnagar, and Sankisa. The last time Rinpoche went on pilgrimage, he visited some of the sites and performed preliminary consecration ceremonies. The stupa in Bodh Gaya was built by Rinpoche when he was still alive, and he made the *tsatsas* for it, the small clay images that are used to fill it. The stupas at Rajgir, Vaishali, and Sarnath have now also been completed.

Trulshik Rinpoche and Dilgo Khyentse treated each other mutually as master and disciple, with immense respect. As soon as Dilgo Khyentse would see Trulshik Rinpoche, he would immediately prostrate, and on merely hearing Trulshik's name, he would make the gesture of homage with his right hand, though I never saw him join his palms. If Trulshik came into the presence of Dilgo Khyentse unannounced and we didn't all rise and pay respects, Dilgo Khyentse would display displeasure. Whenever one of us arrived in Nepal while Trulshik Rinpoche was in the Kathmandu Valley,

Dilgo Khyentse's first question was always, "Have you gone to pay respects to Trulshik Rinpoche?" Trulshik Rinpoche always made incredibly generous offerings to Dilgo Khyentse, with countless precious things such as old and valuable statues. I heard that once he even offered Thangtong Gyalpo's personal drinking cup.

Dilgo Khyentse visited many monasteries in Nepal, and in 1977 he went by helicopter to Solukhumbu. There he gave the empowerments and reading transmissions for the *Treasury of Spiritual Instructions,* as well as many other teachings, at Trulshik Rinpoche's seat, Thupten Choling Monastery. I didn't have the fortune to accompany him, but later I asked him what it was like there, and he responded, "I found it to be extremely nice. The monastery is not large, but the body, speech, and mind representations on the shrine are excellent, and the numerous implements for empowerments are old and very precious. There are many disciples, including pure monks and nuns, and all are genuine practitioners. They live on alms, but the monastic household is prosperous, so at any occasion, even for minor empowerments or *sadhana* gatherings, they would present lavish feast offerings, including hundreds of butter lamps, tormas, and so forth."

I was surprised to hear that once when the cook didn't prepare good food for Dilgo Khyentse, Trulshik Rinpoche slapped him. Trulshik Rinpoche is an extremely gentle and humble person, always disciplined and careful. In fact I can't believe that he has ever gotten angry, so he must have slapped the cook because his devotion to his guru was so strong.

When Dilgo Khyentse conceived of the project to build a monastery in Nepal, Dabzang Rinpoche was asked to try and acquire a piece of land, but it seems that the land he got was only of average quality. Later on, Tulku Pema Wangyal and I managed to buy, with the help of some donations, a property that was in the possession of Dzongnor Rinpoche. Satisfied with the property, Rinpoche accepted to build there, so Trulshik Rinpoche went with his congregation of monks to perform the *Auspicious Restoring the Vow Ceremony* on the site. The building was then commenced but involved great difficulties causing various delays due to surveying issues.

During the construction, I went to Tibet and brought back some sacred substances from Dzongsar. In order to increase the blessed substances and thus bring benefit to numerous beings, I requested and sponsored Rinpoche to perform a drupchen for sacred medicine according to *Heart Practice Dis-*

pelling All Obstacles. Since no structure was yet complete, the ceremony was performed in a tent on the future temple's building site. This drupchen was most enjoyable. Rinpoche participated in the ceremonies from morning to night, and he wore completely new clothing of excellent quality every day.

Several tents had been erected on the site to house the assembly, shrine, and so forth. One night some of the silver articles disappeared from the shrine. On the same shrine, behind a curtain, sat the blessed body representation of Guru Rinpoche called a *kutsab* or "regent" of Padmasambhava and other priceless articles, including several antique statues. Fortunately none of these were taken, and some of the missing silver implements were found tossed outside the tent door. It was probably due to Rinpoche's blessings that the important shrine objects remained safe. I joked that the thief must have been a bodhisattva.

It is traditional to chant the *Summoning of Prosperity of Lama Norlha* once during the *Heart Practice Dispelling All Obstacles* drupchen. On the chosen day, there was a big rain and windstorm which made it quite difficult to stay in the tents, but Rinpoche said, "The rain today is a most auspicious sign; in the future you will become very wealthy!" That was definitely true; since then I have never been exactly poor.

We had brought all our monks from Bir with dancing gear, and they performed the elaborate version of the sacred dances. Rinpoche said, "Since this drupchen was the first here at my new seat, and it was both most extensive and completed without obstacles, in the future many drupchens can be performed here without obstacles."

During the drupchen, Dilgo Khyentse put on a costume looking like that of Padmasambhava, wore the authentic crown of Chokgyur Lingpa, and allowed a photo to be taken; copies of this photo have spread throughout the world. Rinpoche later said, "To let that photo be taken was the biggest mistake in my life. Now everyone comes by with it, wanting me to bless it with a signature or a thumbprint; it's so embarrassing!"

When Rinpoche was seventy-three years old, another drupchen was held at Shechen Tennyi Dargyeling, using Rinpoche's own terma, *Pema's Heart Essence of Longevity.* Trulshik Rinpoche was invited, but due to bad weather, all the planes were grounded, so he walked on foot all the way down from Solukhumbu. The drupchen was done with immensely lavish feast ceremonies and offerings. During the increasing-activity fire puja, a foreigner came with five loads of marigolds; the shrine was covered with them, and all the lamas and monks had to wear them. Rinpoche himself also wore numerous flowers on his head, around his neck, on his arms, and so forth. Trulshik Rinpoche wore many flowers too. Rinpoche said repeatedly, "Very auspicious, very auspicious!" I believe that foreigner must have accumulated a vast stock of merit.

In those days we all worried that the monastery would take too long to finish, so one evening Rinpoche did a pacifying fire puja for the purpose of completing the building work. The next morning he told me, "You don't have to worry. The monastery will be completed, and I won't die any time soon. I will be able to stay and give some empowerments and reading transmissions. Don't worry about it at all!" After that the monastery building was soon completed. The filling of the many statues with *dharanis* and the consecration ceremonies were all supervised and carried out personally by Khyentse Rinpoche himself.

Slowly a sangha of many monks gathered, a monastic college of religious studies was started, and the tantric dances for the Grand Ceremony of the Tenth Day were commenced. Rinpoche established the tradition of performing two drupchens every year: the *Mindroling Vajrasattva* and the *United Assembly*, which have both been continued annually without break.

Rinpoche passed on a vast number of empowerments and reading transmissions at Shechen. He also invited Tenga Rinpoche to give the available reading transmissions for the *Tengyur,* which Dilgo Khyentse also personally received. Later, Taklung Zhabdrung Rinpoche was invited to give the empowerments and reading transmissions for the *Collected Works of Jedrung Jampa Jungney* and the rest of the Taklung Kagyu teachings. He also invited Taklung Tsetrul Rinpoche to give the *Openness of Realization Tantra* and other empowerments and reading transmissions of the Dorje Trak tradition of the Nyingma school. Penor Rinpoche was invited to give the complete transmission for the Kham tradition of the *Do Gongpa Dupa.*

Dilgo Khyentse, Trulshik Rinpoche, Dzongsar Khyentse, and many other lamas performed the consecration very elaborately by means of a drupchen. After that, Trulshik Rinpoche and Taklung Tsetrul Rinpoche gave ordination to hundreds of people, including some of the most important tulkus. The yearly progress of the monastery went at a magical speed. All this must be due to his blessings and the activity of Rinpoche's Dharma protectors. Rinpoche's main benefactor, His Majesty the King of Bhutan, also visited the monastery in Bodhnath once.

At Ka-Nying Shedrup Ling Monastery in Nepal, Rinpoche gave the complete empowerments and reading transmissions for the *New Treasures of Chokgyur Lingpa* and the *Four Parts of the Heart Essence*. He also explained the *Oral Instructions in the Gradual Path of the Wisdom Essence* and the *Guhyagarbha Tantra*. One day, between empowerments, a huge throne for Situ Rinpoche was made, and he was invited to perform the crown ceremony and bestow an empowerment. When Khyentse Rinpoche publicly prostrated three times, Situ Rinpoche sat straight up without responding, so many of the Nyingma followers were displeased. Dilgo Khyentse respected Situ Rinpoche immensely and said, "Jamgön Situ is my guru not just once, but life after life. After the late Karmapa, I have the greatest faith in and hope for Jamgön Situ among all the Kagyu tulkus." To illustrate this, Dilgo Khyentse once went to the seat of Situ Rinpoche, Sherab Ling, and stayed for five days talking and relaxing with him. While there he requested the crown ceremony to be performed for him in private, as well as a longevity empowerment.

Upon completing the empowerments at Ka-Nying Shedrup Ling, Dilgo Khyentse gave a talk which I, in particular, felt was meant to be taken personally. This talk was not like Rinpoche's usual ways of addressing a gathering. Instead he said, "Soon the sun of happiness will again rise in Tibet. Restore the three Dharma wheels! Spread the Buddhadharma, and make it flourish!" Sure enough, it soon became possible to visit Tibet for the first time since it was cut off from the rest of the world at the start of the Cultural Revolution.

Dilgo Khyentse went back to Tibet three times. The first time was through Hong Kong and China, and in fact the Chinese government sponsored that trip. During that journey he visited Lhasa, Mindroling, Tsering Jong, Samye, Tashi Lhunpo, Sera, Drepung, Shechen, and Dzogchen. In all these places he gave a few empowerments and reading transmissions. Everywhere he went, he made extensive aspirations and fulfilled the hopes and wishes of tens of thousands of people. Before leaving, he said to them that they would meet again and again.

Two years later he went back again and stayed at Shechen for quite some time. Day and night he gave teachings, empowerments, and reading transmissions; he also performed several drupchens. He visited Derge Gonchen and consecrated the printing press at Chodzo Chenmo, where he promised to sponsor the building of a huge statue of Buddha Shakyamuni.

Then Rinpoche went to Dzongsar Monastery where he gave empowerments and reading transmissions. The many wonderful signs that appeared during this time, the different types of rainbows in the sky and so forth, were seen in actuality by the ardent Communist escorts appointed by the Chinese government, with the result that even they gained faith in Buddhism. At Shechen Monastery Rinpoche established a monastic college of religious studies and a retreat center. Thus his activities and deeds, even in newly reopened Tibet, were amazing and extensive.

His third, and last, trip to Tibet was in 1990. It was then that he performed the consecration ceremony of the newly restored temple at Samye. At the temples in Lhasa he made formidable offerings. He also visited Reting; I wasn't there myself, but people have said that nectar came out of statues and along the frescoes, a rain of flowers fell, and rainbows and other amazing signs appeared.

Be all this as it may, what I do know is that, from the very moment Tibet was opened up and temples could be rebuilt and sacred places restored, Dilgo Khyentse put forth incredible effort to spread the Buddhadharma there once again. Rinpoche repeatedly gave all his lamas, tulkus, and lama disciples throughout Tibet, Kham, India, Nepal, and everywhere else the command to spread the Buddhadharma there to the utmost of their abilities, to build new monasteries, establish congregations of monks, and transmit teachings and empowerments. He also conferred with the Chinese government to help rebuild the monasteries at Samye, Mindroling, Dorje Trak, Tsering Jong, Shechen, Dzogchen, Katok, Peyul, Ganden, Sera, Drepung, Sakya, Nartang, and other places. He sent about half of his income to rebuild the monasteries and further the practice of Buddhism. In this way he undertook the immense responsibility of rebuilding monasteries without partiality toward the school or sect, and he did many ceremonies for the propagation of all four schools of Tibetan Buddhism. One can actually say that most of the rebuilding of the temples in Tibet, beginning with Samye, is due to his blessings.

The Dalai Lama received many transmissions from Dilgo Khyentse and invited him to Dharamsala several times. During these visits, lasting from two weeks to about a month, Rinpoche gave the Dalai Lama numerous empowerments and reading transmissions, including the *Three Roots of the Heart Essence*, the *Do Gongpa Dupa*, the three main *Eight Sadhana Teachings*, and the *Magical Display of the Peaceful and Wrathful Ones*. The teachings he transmitted to the Dalai Lama included the guidance manual for the Great Perfection known as the *Primordial Wisdom Guru,* and the following commentaries on the *Guhyagarbha Tantra*: Longchenpa's *Dispelling the Darkness of the Ten Directions,* Rongzom Pandita's *Three Jewel Commentary,* Minling Lochen Dharmashri's *Adornment of Realization of the Lord of Secrets* and *Oral Advice,* Dodub Tenpai Nyima's *Overview,* and Mipham Rinpoche's *General Meaning of the Secret Essence: Core of Luminosity.* Rinpoche also taught the *Jewel Ornament of Liberation* and several other scriptures that I don't know about.

During those periods, the Dalai Lama would offer Dilgo Khyentse something very precious each day, such as a gold coin or some silver. The Dalai Lama is the highest lama in Tibet in both religious and secular affairs, and yet he always sat lower than Dilgo Khyentse when receiving teachings, and he showed great respect and humility by prostrating to Dilgo Khyentse before the empowerments. When the Dalai Lama transmitted the *Kalachakra* empowerment in Bodh Gaya, Dilgo Khyentse also went there to receive it. Moreover, in Dharamsala Rinpoche also received the extensive empowerment for the *Eight Sadhana Teachings* of the Fifth Dalai Lama.

Of all his inspiring and numerous activities, Dilgo Khyentse's chief activity was his practice and retreats. In total he spent about twenty years in retreat. In addition, he was extremely diligent in his daily practice. He would never waste even an instant, and his hand was never without a rosary; in fact he would even continue counting mantras on his rosary while urinating. To his disciples Rinpoche always placed emphasis on personal practice as the most important thing.

His second most important activity was studying. He was extremely learned in all five sciences and was a great *pandita*. There is almost no empowerment or teaching among the eight great chariots of the practice lineage available that Rinpoche didn't receive. He had more than fifty root gurus from whom he had received transmissions. Even in his old age, he would still request teachings from anyone in possession of a tradition he had not yet received, and sometimes he would even engage in new studies. He was often heard to say, "I am not learned myself, but I like the fact that other people are called learned."

His third activity of importance was acting for the welfare of others by giving teachings, building temples, printing books, and so forth. He gave empowerments and reading transmissions throughout his entire life to whoever requested them. If people would come to request a teaching, he would even get out of bed in order to teach them. We, the attendants, would then get angry at the people who came so late at night, but Rinpoche would say, "This is my duty; I'll teach them!"

There has almost never been a single day that he didn't give several empowerments or taught the tantras or oral instructions several times. Even for the benefit of just two people, he would explain the *Guhyagarbha Tantra* or the *Primordial Wisdom Guru* in detail; even for the sake of one humble nun, he would give the reading transmission for an entire volume. When in strict retreat, in which he wouldn't utter a single ordinary word day or night, he would still continue to teach two or three times a day. Dilgo Khyentse never got tired or bored no matter how many hours would pass discussing the Dharma, but when the conversation turned to mundane topics or politics, he would nod off while others continued the discussion.

There is no doubt that Dilgo Khyentse's main benefit to others was teaching. There is no greater benefit or merit to achieve than expounding the Dharma. When there is no one left to teach, only then will Buddhism disappear from this world.

Rinpoche accepted the responsibilities of building of five monasteries, both designing and supervising the construction. One cannot count the representations of body, speech, and mind that he had made. His primary task was to propagate representations of enlightened speech, as he probably arranged for the printing of more than one thousand different texts. He also made many large offerings, such as feast offerings on the tenth and twenty-fifth days of the lunar month. No matter where he went, he would make offerings in temples without partiality as to school or sect. Besides expenses for food and clothing, I never saw him waste any money on ordinary things; all his funds went to Dharma purposes. Even the richest and most important people in this world never seem to spend their funds in such a generous and precious way.

Rinpoche treated everyone alike: if a king or minister would invite him, he would go to their house; and if poor people invited him, he also went. When driving somewhere, he would even chant the Mani or the names of the Buddha so that the cattle along the road could hear. When someone came to see him, whether high or low, he never made them wait but let them see him right away. Though he treated everyone equally, in his heart he knew their exact inner feelings. Nor did it matter whether someone had faith in him or not. He often said, "Whoever comes to see me, whether a dignitary or a beggar, they come out of the hope of getting some benefit, so don't stop them from seeing me; I will do my best to help them!" Later on, due to his age and health, his attendants stopped the flow of visitors, but he wasn't pleased about it.

Dilgo Khyentse would never utter a single word about the qualities of his accomplishment, neither have I ever seen mention of it in his writings. Over the years I spent a lot of time with him, and there is no doubt that his clair-voyance of perceiving the minds of other people was completely unimpeded; there was nothing outside of his knowledge. This is a 100 percent true: what-ever you had done, whether good or evil, it was impossible to keep it secret or hide it from him. Someone, like me, who does mostly bad things, got more and more scared the longer I spent with him. Rinpoche would never tell peo-ple if they did something wrong, nor would he scold them; though he knew everything that was going on, he simply remained undisturbed.

It wasn't like you could simply befriend Rinpoche, becoming a close acquaintance. Unlike normal companionship which gets easier and smoother as time passes, and you never have to feel embarrassed, with him one would feel more and more afraid as the years went by; finally one became almost paralyzed with fear. No one ever knew what he was thinking or really felt; no one knew whether he was displeased or happy with someone. He would always listen to people and agree, and yet just follow his own wisdom in any matter of importance. Sometimes, however, if his wish was not carried out, or if we tried to obstruct his wish or persuade him in some other direction, then obstacles would arise as a consequence, or the particular task at hand would turn out unsuccessful.

Before he had trouble walking, Rinpoche would do circumambulations; in Kalimpong he even walked to the town a few times. He used to walk from Trulshik Rinpoche's place by foot. Later it hurt if he just walked a little, so Rinpoche would also just sit where he had slept. He said that he had a leg problem, but all the doctors in the world said he was just overweight and that his legs were underused.

Over the years I noticed that his manners and behavior changed. When I was young, after rising in the morning he would immediately wash and tidy his hair, dress elegantly in his Dharma robes, often made of brocade, and then sit down to say his daily chants. But in 1980 Rinpoche stayed four months in retreat at Puntsoling, after which he dressed simpler and simpler. I believe there was a prophesy that Khyentse Chökyi Lodro was supposed to go naked and wear bone ornaments, like a heruka, in the latter part of his life, and as an auspicious coincidence for that, our Khyentse Rinpoche would most of the time go topless and wear two small bone ornaments about which he said, "These are my yogi attire."

When people took photos or filmed him, he still wouldn't wear anything from the waist up. Once when some dignitaries were visiting, Shechen Rabjam tried to cover Rinpoche's chest with a shirt, but Rinpoche just took it off again. During his last visits to Tibet, tens of thousands of people were waiting along the roads to welcome him, with monks forming the traditional clerical procession and hundreds of horsemen in formal attire; still Rinpoche went by the procession with a naked chest. He also visited Dzogchen, Shechen, Peyul, and Katok monasteries with his chest naked, despite the high altitude and cold weather, and when we asked him to put on a shirt or a shawl, he replied, "Unless you keep quiet, I will also drop my skirt!"

Dilgo Khyentse always wore a necklace with *zi* stones and other ornaments. One or two of these ornaments were from Guru Rinpoche and Yeshe Tsogyal, termas revealed by Jamyang Khyentse Wangpo, while some of the gemstones were blessed by Mipham Rinpoche. There were also some beads from the rosaries of his root gurus. Earlier Rinpoche wore a long necklace of pearls, saying it was good against sickness, but later he stopped wearing it. On his hands he wore two rings of pure gold, one with a vajra and one with a bell, which he never took off. He also wore a diamond ring given to him by the Queen Mother of Bhutan. He said, "This is the most eminent gemstone and so the best ornament; it also helps against sickness."

If going somewhere, even for a couple of days, Rinpoche always seemed to need to bring along at least twenty or thirty volumes of books, as well as a ritual dagger and several statues. In a small gold box he carried around his neck was a Manjushri painted on a piece of Mipham Rinpoche's skull, as well as other special relics. Later he also kept the tiny Indian bronze statue of Manjushri that Mipham Rinpoche had kept as the support for his own sadhana practice. This precious statue had recently been offered to Rinpoche in Kham. Rinpoche never cut his nails either. In fact, he once said, "Cutting one's nails harms the Vajrayana precepts."

No matter how busy Rinpoche was, every day he would chant an entire volume of daily practices. Inside this volume there were also many photos; at the top were pictures of his gurus, then his disciples and benefactors or people who had passed away and those who had requested his protection. At night he would again recite an extensive petition to the dharmapalas. While he was healing from an eye operation in France, he couldn't read; he had one of his attendants read aloud from his chant book while Rinpoche would recite from memory.

Although Rinpoche was a great tertön, the auspicious link for earth treasures was not established to a strong degree. There are five volumes of his termas, and the lineage for the empowerments, reading transmissions, and instructions is extant today. Some of Rinpoche's Dharma treasures were lost in Tibet during the Cultural Revolution. His most important treasures are *Nyak Kilaya* and *Pema's Heart Essence of Longevity,* which is on the Buddha Amitayus. He never showed any fondness for prophesies.

In 1990 Rinpoche went to Bodh Gaya, where he had some trouble in his neck. After a few days, the Dalai Lama arrived and received some empowerments. Rinpoche's disciples did many healing ceremonies, and Rinpoche got slightly better. The Dalai Lama invited him to Dharamsala, so he went there right after Bodh Gaya. While offering empowerments to the Dalai Lama at Dharamsala, Rinpoche's illness came back twice, at night. Then Rinpoche returned to Nepal where he celebrated the Tibetan New Year. In the New Year he intended to travel back to Tibet, but due to his health, this plan was cancelled and instead he went to do retreat in His Majesty's cottage in Paro Satsam Chorten.

One night Rinpoche fell down on the way to the toilet. He then had to have a small operation on his leg for a complication that developed due to the fall; but even during his stay in the hospital, he still remained in strict retreat, not talking or seeing visitors. After he had recovered, I went to Bhutan to see him and found that his appearance and behavior were unlike his earlier majestic presence. Nonetheless he still continued to give empowerments and reading transmissions.

When I saw him the last time, he gave me some special transmissions he had never passed on before. He ended his retreat and performed a fire puja and a ceremony with a hundred thousand feast offerings. He then went to

Thimphu where he consecrated the Great Stupa and stayed for a couple of days at the nunnery at Sisinang. After that he went to Kalimpong where he gave the Queen Mother's mother, who was then over ninety years old, some longevity empowerments. The Queen Mother arranged a helicopter so that Rinpoche could go directly to Kalimpong. Afterward he went by helicopter from Kalimpong to Hashimara, as he insisted on going to Puntsoling so that he could see and give last spiritual advice to his old servant Druptop, who had kept his house in Puntsoling for nearly twenty years. Rinpoche then went by car to Paro, where he presided over the twenty-sixth annual *Supreme Heruka Assembly* drupchen in the Guru Temple at Paro Kyechu.

On the evening of the first day of the drupchen ceremony, he fell seriously ill. Trulshik Rinpoche was invited from Nepal and arrived quickly. Trulshik Rinpoche performed a detailed ceremony requesting him to remain, but it was of no avail. Dilgo Khyentse also conferred the complete empowerment of longevity upon himself by placing the vase, vajra, and crystal on his own head. On the eighteenth day of the lunar month he was taken to the hospital, and during the night he passed away.

The government of Bhutan conducted an official grand offering ceremony to his remains. A great number of Rinpoche's lama disciples, headed by Minling Trichen, came to pay their respects, as did many of his other followers. After keeping his body for some months in Bhutan, it was brought to Nepal where it was welcomed by hundreds of thousands of people on the road to his monastery in Bodhnath, where all five religions of Tibet and several Nepalese Buddhist groups held ceremonies of worship. After a few months it was returned to Bhutan, where the cremation was performed at Satsam Chorten, in the presence of sixty thousand devotees, one tenth of the population of Bhutan.

15. Fleeing over the Mountains
KHENPO PEMA SHERAB

Khenpo Pema Sherab was Khyentse Rinpoche's attendant for about ten
years. He is now the main *khenpo* at the Namdroling Monastic Institute,
in Penor Rinpoche's settlement in Bylakuppe, India.

I FIRST BECAME DILGO Khyentse's attendant when I was about eighteen
years old, and stayed with him until I was about twenty-seven. Before I
became a monk, I went to Lhasa on pilgrimage. When the Chinese trouble began in Derge, Dilgo Khyentse came to Lhasa and stayed there for a
few years. One of Rinpoche's attendants from Nangchen wanted to go back
home and asked me to replace him. At that time I hadn't studied and only
knew how to read.

While in Lhasa Rinpoche performed ceremonies and consciousness trans-
ferences to benefit many beings who were sick. He went to the homes of both
high officials and poor people; if they didn't know his name, they used to call
him "the tall lama." Khyentse Rinpoche then went to all the main pilgrimage
places and did ceremonies at each one.

In 1956 he returned to Lhasa and stayed a year in Nenang Pawo Rinpoche's
monastery. His wife and two daughters were also there, as well as his treasurer, Hawa Tulku, Tulku Nguden from Bumthang, and me. He gave the
Guhyagarbha Tantra teaching over the course of four months; he had already
given the empowerment in Lhasa. In the morning he did his practice, and
after lunch he would teach the *Guhyagarbha Tantra* until about three o'clock.
After that there was time to ask questions. At that time Pawo Rinpoche was
in retreat. I don't know when they met each other, but they were very close,

and Pawo Rinpoche gave Rinpoche everything he needed. Then Rinpoche's elder brother Shedrup fell ill, and Rinpoche had to go to Lhasa.

On the way back to Lhasa Shedrup passed away. At that time there were not many cars, and we had to go by horse. Shedrup was a fully ordained monk and stayed in the state of postmortem meditation known as *tukdam* for one day; then we took the body to Nenang Monastery to do the cremation.

After presiding over the cremation, Khyentse Rinpoche went to Tsurphu. Shechen Kongtrül was in Tsurphu as well. We stayed there for about a month, and on the way down from Tsurphu to Lhasa, Rinpoche passed by Nenang Monastery and Mindroling. Then he returned to Tsurphu where Nyenpa Rinpoche was staying. Gyaltsap Rinpoche gave many empowerments, including the elaborate empowerment of Karma Lingpa's *Peaceful and Wrathful Ones.*

That summer a big stupa was built above Tsurphu monastery, accomplished by Nyenpa Rinpoche, Khyentse Rinpoche, Palpung Atrul, Ongen Tulku, Topga Rinpoche, and the vajra master, about fifteen people altogether. For three months they stayed in a tent and practiced the *Immaculate Ushnisha* and *Spotless Rays of Light* mandalas. After that they prepared another stupa near the monastery and stayed there for another month. Khenpo Karma Thinley was there too.

Then Rinpoche spent about three months giving some elaborate empowerments in Tsurphu including the *New Treasures of Chokgyur Lingpa* and the *Magical Net.* That winter he stayed in retreat at Tsurphu. In the daytime he gave elaborate teachings to about thirteen people on the *Oral Instructions in the Gradual Path of the Wisdom Essence* according to Jamgön Kongtrül's commentary. Then a practitioner from Rekong came and requested *atiyoga* teachings, so Rinpoche gave him the *Guru's Innermost Essence* teachings.

At the Great Prayer Festival in Lhasa in 1958 the Dalai Lama did prayers, and the Chinese were making a lot of trouble. Around that time Khyentse Rinpoche's sister died, and he went to Lhasa for that; it was the twenty-fourth of the first month, corresponding to February. At that time I asked to be excused for a month to do mandala offerings in front of the Jowo. Shechen Kongtrül came from Kham and he too did mandala offerings in front of the Jowo. Rinpoche and Shechen Kongtrül were very close and used to visit each other a lot. Rinpoche had been in Lhasa for two years, and he used to visit the Jowo every day and do mandala offerings. Once, sponsored by the Ngapo, he did a hundred thousand feast offerings. When Mindroling Chung Rinpoche had come to Lhasa in 1956, they had also done a hundred thousand feast offerings.

Rinpoche received the *Crystal Cave Chronicles* reading transmission from Shechen Kongtrül, whose vision was not so good.[1] About fifteen of us received it with him. In the evening he would teach the six yogas, and as it used to get dark while he was reading, he had to read with a lamp. When the patroness came in, she used to say, "Oh, it is dark. You can't see anything!" and then he would stop.

While Rinpoche was giving the *Treasury of Precious Qualities* root text and commentary to Rigzin Chimey from Dorje Trak Monastery, the situation with the Chinese became quite troublesome. Chozangla from Dorje Trak, who later became the Zhabdrung's tutor in Tso Pema and has now passed away, requested some teachings on poetry. Sometimes Rinpoche used to go to people's homes to do ceremonies. Once he did a feast offering in the Jokhang in front of the Guru Rinpoche statue, and the Dalai Lama came; that was the first time he talked with the Dalai Lama. Later Rinpoche met the Dalai Lama in the Norbu Lingka during the *Kalachakra* empowerment, which was attended by more than a hundred thousand people, including Sangye Nyenpa and Shechen Kongtrül. There were loudspeakers for everyone to hear; we used to sit on the lawn and have tea, and had a real nice time.

Rinpoche then left for Tsurphu, and not long after, war broke out in Lhasa and the situation became really dangerous. I was staying in Rigzin Dorje's mother's house, and one morning there was a lot of commotion outside. People were saying that the Chinese were against the Dalai Lama, and everywhere there were posters against the Chinese. All the shops around the Jokhang were closed. At three o'clock in the afternoon, some people came back and said that the brother of a government official had been stoned to death as he was sitting in a jeep and people had started throwing stones at his Chinese driver. I received a letter from Rinpoche asking me to come to Tsurphu. I was very afraid while going around preparing for the journey and buying a horse, but fortunately the Chinese didn't stop me on my way to Tsurphu.

When I arrived, a big crowd was receiving a long-life empowerment from the Karmapa. He performed a black-hat ceremony and gave many blessings. The Karmapa said that he was going to Bhutan on pilgrimage and he wished us well. That night around midnight he left without anybody knowing. We decided to leave as well but didn't have any horses, yaks, or anything, so we asked the Tsurphu monastic household for help. They lent Sangye Nyenpa and Dilgo Khyentse fifty horses and yaks; however they were all out grazing on the mountains and it took three days to gather them, so we were four days behind and very afraid. In the meantime, Lhasa was taken by the Chinese, and the Dalai Lama fled.

When we finally left, we didn't go through Lhasa, but took the mountain pass above Tsurphu. At one point we weren't allowed on a ferry to cross a river. The next day Rigzin Dorje arrived. He was working for the Khampa guerrilla army, so he intervened and they let us on the ferry immediately.

After that we arrived at Sakya Monastery. We didn't go into the monastery, but people came to see Rinpoche to ask for divinations and to consecrate things. Then we went over the next mountain pass and took about seven days to go around the lake. Luckily, we didn't run into any Chinese and that night we arrived in Lhalung. The yaks were very tired and couldn't move anymore, so we rested for a few days. We stored all our things in Lhalung Sungtrul's monastery. Some Tibetan soldiers arrived and said that the Chinese had won, so we really got afraid. Rinpoche's things were mostly books and statues, so we left everything there and continued at night crossing the next pass called Drula. Then we arrived in Drumtso Pemaling, where there was another big lake. There was more and more Chinese commotion, and we were very nervous. We continued a difficult journey along muddy roads and over shaky bridges. We got covered in leeches and had nothing but some tsampa to eat.

Eventually we reached the Bhutanese border, but the Bhutanese wouldn't let us in. As we had to stay at the border, in Bhutanese territory, for over a month, some of us went back to Lhalung to get more tsampa, as well some books, statues, and precious relic boxes. The Lhalung Monastery gave us five yaks to carry everything. It took three days to go and come back. Ponlop Rinpoche had left a lot of things at Lhalung, and I also met Khenpo Karthar there, who said that some Chinese were giving Tibetan clothes of monks, laypeople, and women to Chinese people. At a small village some people who were grinding roasted barley said we could reach the border by the following evening. So we spent the night there, and it was very cold. The next morning we continued. At one point my companion got completely freaked out thinking that the Chinese were coming toward us. We hid among the rocks, but when we looked, it wasn't the Chinese but cattle from the villagers; all the people had fled.

That afternoon a man told us that the next village was deserted except for about ten Chinese soldiers. As any Tibetan caught passing through there would be killed, he told us to go at night. I asked him to take some of the books, among which was Dilgo Khyentse's *Amitayus* long-life practice and a lot of other mind treasures, and gave him a lot of money. He came back at midnight and showed us a way around the village. Below the village was a river we had to cross by bridge; it was freezing cold and snowing. I was terrified of being shot by the Chinese. It continued snowing for about three days and nights, and we couldn't light a fire to make tea as the Chinese would see the smoke. There was nowhere to rest comfortably, just rocks among which we would hide during the day. When the moon came up, we would continue on our journey. One time I fell asleep, and when I woke up, it was already light. I was terrified. Before reaching the pass, which was just before the Bhutanese border, many yaks died, and it was snowing so hard that we couldn't even see their corpses. We didn't see a single Tibetan; everyone had already fled. We huddled under a tree, made some tea, and spent the night.

The next morning we finally arrived at the border. The Bhutanese had let Rinpoche into Bhutan the day before, so we were allowed through as well. The Bhutanese were very kind and gave us tsampa and rice. An old lady gave us each some soup. I had about five kilos of tsampa, which I loaded onto a horse. Yeshe Tsepa, Karma Tsultrim, Rigzin Dorje, Yudrön, and Chökyi Lodro's attendant Katsela were all with us. One day as we were about to have lunch, I discovered that all my tsampa was gone; apparently someone had eaten it all. We spent a day in Bumthang where the Tongsar monks gave each of us a measure of tsampa, and the Bhutanese laypeople gave us rice and food.

The Karmapa stayed briefly at Tashi Choling in Bumthang before heading on to Sikkim. Rinpoche was with his brother Sangye Nyenpa and their relatives Traga, Sotop, Chimey Yungdrung, his mother, and one of his sisters. Tenga Rinpoche was with us too. There were about thirty of us altogether. We went through Bumthang, and in one village a family sponsored the performance of a hundred thousand feast offerings in Tharpaling, so Rinpoche went there for a week. We were told that we couldn't stay in Bumthang, so many people went down to Ha, where it was very hot. We ourselves went to Wangdu Podrang. Every day more people came to the border fleeing the Chinese. We slowly proceeded and stayed at Tongsar Dzong for a few days, where Khyentse Rinpoche gave a *Kalachakra* empowerment to the monks. From there we continued and arrived below Simtokha, where we stayed for two days.

As we had no tents and had to stay outside, Rinpoche came down with a cold at Thimphu, which was the first time he had gotten sick on the journey. One man from Gojo had a radio, and we heard on the Indian news from Delhi that Khyentse Chökyi Lodro had passed away in Sikkim. In Thimphu there was a small market where some Tibetans were selling things like soap, matches, and cheese. Besides that there was nothing, just a little temple. There were so many leeches that Karma Tsultrim had trouble walking. When we arrived at Kyabja Dzong, as Nyenpa Rinpoche was also a bit sick, we rested for two weeks. The Bhutanese kindly gave us tsampa and rice, so we didn't need to buy anything. It was raining a lot, and one night a family put us up for the night; they even gave Rinpoche a mattress to sleep on. There were many thieves about, and that night some things were stolen.

We went on through heavy forests with endless rain, mud, and leeches everywhere. When night fell, we arrived at a village called Dala. We were all completely soaked from the rain; at that time Rinpoche was very thin. We were covered with insect bites and bleeding all over.

As we continued toward Puntsoling, we met Rinpoche's niece Yanga and her husband Thupga; that was the first time we had seen them since parting ways in Tibet. Rinpoche said he would go to Kalimpong where Dudjom Rinpoche had bought a house. They had met back in Lhasa, where Dudjom Rinpoche had given Rinpoche a *Trolo* empowerment, and Rinpoche had given Dudjom Rinpoche the empowerment for his long-life mind treasure. At that time Dudjom Rinpoche had told Rinpoche he could stay in his house. So Rinpoche left for Kalimpong without anybody knowing.

We didn't have visas, and so it took a day to arrange that; and we couldn't get rations as we didn't have the right papers. Rinpoche was invited to stay at the Copper-Colored Mountain in Kalimpong. I was very surprised to see all the cars and trains, and it smelled bad everywhere. I got very sick; but Rinpoche stayed healthy. We arrived at the Copper-Colored Mountain Monastery at night; Rinpoche was again soaked from the rain.

At that time the Copper-Colored Mountain was very small; Dilgo Khyentse stayed in the office, and the attendants stayed next door. Taklung Tsetrul Rinpoche came and requested the *Guhyagarbha Tantra*, which took about a month. Eventually Rinpoche rented a house in the market where he stayed for a few months. Then Rinpoche was invited to stay at Durtro Lhakang, where he resided until he gave the *Treasury of Precious Termas* in Sikkim.

Once Rinpoche had obtained the proper permits, he went to Gangtok to see Dzongsar Khyentse's remains in the palace, and that winter he performed the cremation. At that time the Karmapa was giving the *Treasury of Spiritual Instructions* in Rumtek. Then Rinpoche gave the *Four Parts of the Heart Essence* and the *Root Volumes of the Heart Essence* in Durtro Lhakhang.

In 1963 Dudjom Rinpoche gave the *Treasury of Precious Termas* in Kalimpong. When Rinpoche was invited to Nyimalung in Bumthang by Gelong Pema Dorje, I asked if I could stay to receive the *Treasury of Precious Termas* from Dudjom Rinpoche. Meanwhile Trungpa Rinpoche had gone to the West and had left his monk Yonten there without work, so Yonten asked Rinpoche's wife if he could be Rinpoche's attendant. When I came back, she told me that they didn't need so many attendants, so I left for Baxaul.

Then Rinpoche went to Bhutan. The Royal Grandmother was staying in Thimphu. They wouldn't let Rinpoche go to Nyimalung, and Gelong Pema Dorje, who had invited Rinpoche, was sick and couldn't travel. It was said that there were evil spirits at Dechen Podrang, so Rinpoche was asked to do retreat there, and he stayed in retreat for one year.

I stayed at Baxaul, in India, and that summer I went to Bhutan. I had to walk most of the way to Sisinang. There Bhutanese put me up and gave me food. The next day I arrived at Simtokha Dzong where Rinpoche was staying; Khenpo Tsondru was there too. I stayed there for six months, during which Rinpoche gave the *Sublime Light of Excellent Discourse* to about 250 people— there were 125 students, 100 laypeople, and 25 monks. Khenpo Tsondru gave teachings to the monks, and Loppön Pemala gave teachings to the laypeople. Besides that Rinpoche didn't have much to do. There was a lama called Je Khenpo Simpuk Lama who was a descendant of Dorje Lingpa; Rinpoche had received a lot of teachings from him when he was staying at Mindroling. He in turn invited Rinpoche to Thimphu where they arranged a throne, and Rinpoche spent a day there giving teachings. Then Norbu Wangchuk came and asked for the *Four Parts of the Heart Essence,* the *Primordial Wisdom Guru,* the *Tantra System Kilaya,* and so forth, which took about six months.

That winter there was some trouble with the Chinese. So Rinpoche went back to Darjeeling where he stayed in Gyaluk Monastery. Upon hearing that his brother Sangye Nyenpa had passed away, Rinpoche tried to go to Sikkim, but the government hadn't issued him a travel visa, and we were stopped at the border. They held us for four hours while they went through every piece of luggage, and I lost all my things. Next Rinpoche tried to go back to

Bhutan, but once again the Indians stopped him, so he went back to Darjeeling instead where he stayed for another year. I, however, wasn't granted a visa and had to stay behind.

In Darjeeling, Rinpoche received the *Hundred Thousand Nyingma Tantras* from Kangyur Rinpoche. Dilgo Khyentse and Kangyur Rinpoche gave each other a lot of teachings and transmissions. Later the Bhutanese Royal Grandmother gave Rinpoche a Bhutanese passport so the Indians couldn't stop him anymore. When Rinpoche had arrived in Simtokha, his daughters were sent to school in Mussoorie. At that time Rinpoche composed a very beautiful poem for his youngest daughter about death and impermanence, clearly mentioning that she would die. It was about thirty pages that I wrote out; I should have taken it with me, as it appears to have gotten lost. Rinpoche's daughter died in 1963. I really don't remember much more.

16. Blessing Bhutan
QUEEN MOTHER KESANG CHÖDRÖN WANGCHUK
AND LOPPÖN PEMALA

Queen Mother Kesang Chödrön Wangchuk is the wife of the previous king of Bhutan and the mother of the present King Jigmey Senge Wangchuk. She was a devoted disciple of Dilgo Khyentse, and with his guidance, she and her mother, Mayum Choying Wangmo, sponsored the annual sacred drupchens performed by Dilgo Khyentse in the Paro Kyechu temple, the Punakha Dzong Chakrasamvara temple, and the Bumthang Kurje temple. She also sponsored the building of many beautiful temples and holy images in Bhutan.

Loppön Pemala is a lama from Nyimalung Monastery in Bumthang, and is a great scholar and historian. He was a close disciple of Dilgo Khyentse and received all the teachings that Rinpoche gave in Bhutan.

AFTER THE CHINESE Communists invaded Tibet, Dilgo Khyentse with his wife, daughters, elder brother Nyenpa Rinpoche, and a group of refugees escaped the oppression in the second month of the female earth-pig year, 1959. Fleeing via Lhodrak, they eventually arrived at the Bhutanese border. On behalf of the Bhutanese government, Prime Minister Jigmey Palden Dorje went to the border to meet the Tibetan refugees at Jakar Dzong and offered support to the refugees in the form of tsampa, and so forth. The prime minister helped those who wanted to go to India, as well as those who wanted to stay in Bhutan.

The Prime Minister also took care of Dilgo Khyentse and his entourage, and Dilgo Khyentse told him that he was extremely grateful that he and his group of refugees were looked after so well. The Prime Minister asked Khyentse Rinpoche to stay in Bhutan, and Rinpoche answered that he would really like to stay in such a free place endowed with the Dharma, but because his elder brother Sangye Nyenpa had to follow the Karmapa to India, he had to go there as well and go wherever the Karmapa went.

During a pilgrimage to Tibet in the male earth-dog year, 1958, Bhutanese Minister Sangye Paljor had met Khyentse Rinpoche, and so later on, when Rinpoche was leaving Jakar in Bumthang, he invited him to Pangto Monastery to give his sick mother the *Supreme Heruka* empowerment from the *Heart Essence of the Great Expanse* cycle. Then Rinpoche went to Tashi Choling where he stayed in a tent for a while, at which point Ani Rigzin Chödrön invited him to Longchenpa's residence at Tharpaling and from there to Lorepa's residence at Chötrak. At Chötrak Monastery, Rinpoche performed a hundred thousand feast offerings according to the *Heart Essence of the Great Expanse* cycle, and he gave the monks and nuns participating in the feast offerings the *Self-Liberation of Clinging* empowerment. Then he gave the reading transmission of Patrul Rinpoche's *Spontaneous Vajra Song* pith instructions, and thinking of the omniscient Longchenpa, he spontaneously wrote a song of his own.

Ashe Pema Dechen, the Junior Queen Mother, sent Rinpoche a letter from Tekchog Choling saying that she would like to see him, and she asked him to pray for her. Dilgo Khyentse sent her a reply from Tharpaling. Then he received a letter from Ashe Chökyi and Dasho Urgyen Wangdu from Wangdu Choling, also requesting an audience and his prayers for them. While doing the hundred thousand feast offerings according to the *Three Roots of the Heart Essence of the Great Expanse* cycle in the temple of the eleven-headed Avalokiteshvara at Chötrak Monastery, Khyentse Rinpoche felt very happy and composed a ground, path, and fruition supplication, which he wrote on the back of Ashe Pema Dechen's letter. Then he performed the *Spontaneous Fulfillment of All Aspirations* feast offering in the old Chötrak temple and returned to Tashi Choling, where he gave the reading transmission for Khenpo Ngakchung's *Guide to the Words of My Perfect Teacher*.

From Bumthang, Rinpoche went by horse to Chokor Rabten, the Tongsar Dzong, where he was requested to give the *Kalachakra* empowerment. Then Rinpoche continued on to India via the main road from Thimphu and settled in Kalimpong. Some of his faithful students who had received teaching from him at Chötrak Monastery went to see him in Kalimpong, where for one month he gave the complete empowerments and reading transmissions of the *Heart Essence Root Volumes,* as well as the *Heart Essence of Mother and Son,* the *Heart Essence of the Dakinis,* the *Quintessence of the Dakinis,* the *Guru's Innermost Essence,* and the *Profound Quintessence* to many disciples at Durpin Monastery in Kalimpong. After that he gave the *Guhyagarbha Tantra* as well as Mipham Rinpoche's *Collected Works* to some lamas and tulkus. As the texts were not complete, he sent a message asking to borrow four volumes from Chumey Naktsang, which they did, so he was very pleased. When Dudjom Rinpoche was giving the *Treasury of Precious Termas* empowerments in the twelfth month of the iron-mouse year, 1960, at Durpin Monastery in Kalimpong, Rinpoche went there to receive the *Mindroling Vajrasattva* empowerment as a Dharma connection.

Prior to Dilgo Khyentse's arrival, my mother, Mayum Choying Wangmo Dorje, had always told me to take good care of Simtokha Dzong, as it was such a beautiful and historical *dzong.* Due to this advice, I suggested to His Majesty King Jigmey Dorje Wangchuk to make Simtokha Dzong into a Buddhist school. His Majesty agreed and told me to ask his mother who would be a good teacher to appoint. I then went to Kalimpong to give birth to my third daughter Ashe Pem Pem and to stay with my mother for a bit; the Queen Mother Puntsök Chödrön also went along with me.

When I was in Kalimpong, I asked Queen Mother Puntsök Chödrön which lama would be a good teacher for the new Buddhist college in Simtokha Dzong, so she suggested that Dilgo Khyentse Rinpoche would be the most suitable. His Majesty then told his ministers that it was very important to establish a Buddhist college and to start making the necessary arrangements to accomplish it. So the ministers started organizing the college and the necessary books on disciplines such as grammar, poetry, and spelling, and had more than a hundred copies of the root texts and commentaries of *The Way of the Bodhisattva* and other texts printed.

Later, during the first month of the iron-bull year, 1961, several lamas from the central congregation of monks in Thimphu were sent to Kalimpong to invite Dilgo Khyentse to become the principal of the monastic college. He accepted the post and left Kalimpong for Bhutan on the twenty-fifth of the first month. After arriving in the Bhutanese capital of Thimphu, while Simtokha Dzong was still being prepared, Rinpoche first started the college at

Wangdutse for over a hundred intelligent young monks and laymen. Later the college moved to Simtokha Dzong, where the students also added Sanskrit to their studies.

The monastic college was founded to prevent the degeneration of the Buddhist doctrine in Bhutan. So spiritual teachers were invited from India to restore the teachings that had been corrupted and spread those that had not. Altogether there were over a hundred students from different monasteries and communities, who were told to endeavor in studying culture and tantra. Once they had learned the traditional science of grammar and spelling, they could leave, but if they also wanted to study philosophy, they were welcome to continue their studies. After having learned traditional science and philosophy they had the option of staying on to study the four tantras.

The books that were made available were a hundred copies each of the *Lamp of Speech Grammar* root text and its commentary, the grammar root text and its *Sublime Light of Excellent Discourse* commentary, Situpa's detailed commentary, the root poetry text and commentary, the *Letter to a Friend* root text and commentary, the *Thirty-seven Practices of a Bodhisattva* root text and commentary, and *The Way of the Bodhisattva* root text and commentaries.

Khyentse Rinpoche taught at the college until the winter of 1962 when he had to go to India as his brother Sangye Nyenpa had passed away in Rumtek and his youngest daughter was seriously ill in the hospital in Lucknow. Khyentse Rinpoche arrived just in time to see his daughter before she passed away. He took her body to Varanasi to be cremated and then went to Rumtek for the funeral ceremonies of his elder brother. Some years later, while Khyentse Rinpoche was in Dharamsala with His Holiness the Dalai Lama, a man from Kham brought the Dalai Lama a piece of the self-arisen Avalokiteshvara statue from the Potala that had been rescued during the Cultural Revolution. Khyentse Rinpoche received a part of it and used it to build an Avalokiteshvara statue at Paro Kyechu in memory of his daughter. After leaving for India that winter, Khyentse Rinpoche didn't return to Bhutan for a few years.

In 1965 Nyimalung Monastery's vajra master Jamyang Yeshe Senge and chant master Tsering Dondrup discussed with Queen Mother Puntsök Chödrön their wish of inviting Khyentse Rinpoche to become the principal at Nyimalung Monastery. Queen Mother Puntsök Chödrön then invited Khyentse Rinpoche to come from Darjeeling to Nyimalung, and when Rinpoche arrived at Dechen Chöling in Thimphu, he gave Tertön Sangye Lingpa's

Embodiment of the Master's Realization empowerments and transmissions to Jamyang Yeshe Senge and many fortunate lamas and students, both monks and laypeople.

There was a lot of turmoil in Bhutan at that time. In 1964 Prime Minister Jigmey Palden Dorje had been assassinated in Puntsoling, so Khyentse Rinpoche came to see me in Kalimpong to offer his condolences. There had previously been a civil war between East and West Bhutan, and at that time the subjugation rituals for spirits causing recurrent obstacles had not been performed properly. The Dharma King Urgyen Wangchuk had asked the Fifteenth Karmapa Kakyab Dorje for advice, and he had sent his heart son Tertön Zilnon Namkai Dorje from Tsurphu to Bumthang to give empowerments and transmissions. He started by giving teaching on *The Way of the Bodhisattva* and then turned the Dharma wheel of the inconceivably profound maturing and liberating teachings. To avert the influence of spirits causing recurrent obstacles for the king's son, Zilnon Namkai Dorje appointed four monks to do a *Raksha Thotreng* recitation retreat, to last three years and three months until they completed the signs. For this retreat, he gave the transmissions, taught all the rituals, and also performed a *Vajrakilaya* drupchen.

The Je Khenpo Simpuk Lama, who was from the lineage of Dorje Lingpa and was a student of both Khyentse Rinpoche and Bomta Khenpo, had a book of prophecies by Guru Padmasambhava that had been revealed by Tertön Drukdra Dorje about the birth of His Majesty. Guru Rinpoche gave thirteen prophecies and described the birth of the present king. The king was born in the wood-sheep year, 1955, in Wang Drong, which is now Dechen Chöling Palace. It said that the one born in the wood-sheep year would greatly benefit the Dharma, but due to a negative spirit, the one born in the iron-dragon year, 1940, would try to harm the glorious Drukpa Kagyu teachings, so many ceremonies should be done and treasures should be revealed in Bumthang Chumey. If the demon succeeded there would be a sea of blood in Bhutan, but if the demon failed there would be many years of peace.

While Khyentse Rinpoche was staying in Thimphu, I sent him the book of prophecies and asked if this prophecy concerned the crown prince. Khyentse Rinpoche said that indeed it did concern the crown prince and that he would do all the averting rituals in Queen Mother Puntsök Chödrön's place at Dechen Chöling. So I sent a reply, saying, "If it really concerns my son, please come to Paro and perform the ceremonies in Paro Taktsang or the Jowo Temple in Paro Kyechu." Loppön Nyabchi then asked Khyentse Rinpoche whether it would be good to have a Vajrakilaya drupchen performed to avert the obstacles. Khyentse Rinpoche answered that *Vajrakilaya* was very special, but there was nothing better than the *Supreme Heruka* from the *Heart Essence of the Great Expanse,* since all the deities are included in Chemchok Heruka. So in the ninth month of the wood-snake year, 1965, on Divine Descent Day, he started the first *Supreme Heruka Assembly* ceremony from the *Heart Essence of the Great Expanse* cycle in the Jowo Temple at Paro Kyechu, for the stability of the country.[1]

Because of this, instead of going to Nyimalung, Khyentse Rinpoche went to Kyechu in November 1965, and because of Tertön Drukdra Dorje's prophesies about the birth of His Majesty and the rituals to be performed, Khyentse Rinpoche did the drupchen of Jigmey Lingpa's *Supreme Heruka Assembly* in the Jowo temple at Paro Kyechu. During the drupchen he bestowed the empowerment on crown prince Jigmey Senge Wangchuk, who was then ten years old. I said to Rinpoche, "I wish you would always stay here," and Rinpoche said he would like to. So I sent a message to His Majesty asking if Khyentse Rinpoche could stay in Paro instead of going to Nyimalung. "Yes, it is more important that he stays there," the king replied. This is how Bhutan came to be blessed with the presence of Dilgo Khyentse Rinpoche.

In 1965 Queen Mother Puntsök Chödrön invited some Nyingma lamas to the Karpandi Temple in Puntsoling; the party consisted of Dudjom Rinpoche as the main lama, with Chatral Rinpoche, Dilgo Khyentse, Bomta Khenpo, and others. They performed the *Gathering of the Vidyadharas* drupchen, and while they were in the midst of the drupchen, I arrived. Because I thought that Dilgo Khyentse was the only one responsible for the drupchen, without bowing to the other lamas, I went straight up to his throne, touched it with my head, and respectfully bowed down. Khyentse Rinpoche said that he felt a little embarrassed, but since I had complete trust in him, he felt fully responsible for my well-being.

During that time Khyentse Rinpoche was requested to give a speech on the five perfections as a thanksgiving offering. He asked his attendant Ngodup to get the *Gathering of the Vidyadharas* text from his table, and during this speech, leaning on Ngodup who was holding the text in front of him, Khyentse Rinpoche would occasionally turn the pages. What Khyentse Rinpoche was saying had nothing to do with the text he was pretending to read, so in the evening when Ngodup asked him about it, Rinpoche said, "This old man doesn't need to refer to books to give a lecture on the subject, but in front of Dudjom Rinpoche, Chatral Rinpoche, and Bomta Khenpo, it would look like I was showing off."

In 1966 Khyentse Rinpoche advised me to a build a new temple with a large Padmasambhava statue in the form of Guru Nangsi Zilnon, the Glorious Subjugator of All that Appears and Exists, for the stability of the country and the doctrine in general. So my mother, Choying Wangmo, and I had a one-story-tall statue made. In the New Year, the construction of the Guru Temple to the left of the Jowo Temple in Kyechu was started. Khyentse Rinpoche also oversaw the making of one hundred thousand six-inch clay images, as well as one hundred thousand printed pictures each of Chemchok Heruka, the Bodhisattva Kshitigarbha for the sake of the wealth in the country, Vajrakilaya, Vajrasattva, and the Eight Manifestations of Guru Rinpoche, as well as one hundred thousand two-inch clay statues of Guru Horsok Averting War and one hundred thousand four-inch-tall clay statues of Guru Nangsi Zilnon. For six months Khyentse Rinpoche personally performed the blessing of the *dharanis* to be placed inside of the statues. He gave exact instructions on how to build the Padmasambhava statue, and it was ready in eighteen months.

During the male fire-horse year, 1966, and the male fire-sheep year, 1967, Khyentse Rinpoche gave the reading transmissions of the *Seven Treasuries* and the *Primordial Wisdom Guru* to the young Dzongsar Khyentse and other disciples at Paro Kyechu. He continued the annual performance of the *Supreme Heruka Assembly drupchen,* and in 1967 the new Guru Temple at Paro Kyechu was completed. Its main statue was the one-story-high Guru Rinpoche, with Guru Horsok Averting War, Kurukulle, and so forth on either side. The Avalokiteshvara Naturally Liberating Suffering statue was made later in memory of Khyentse Rinpoche's daughter.

The Sixteenth Karmapa performed the first consecration according to the *Heart Practice Dispelling All Obstacles* from the *New Treasures of Chokgyur Lingpa,* while His Majesty King Jigmey Dorje Wangchuk, the junior Queen Mother Ashe Pema Dechen, myself, and my family were all present. Je Khenpo Jamyang Yeshe Senge and the congregation of monks from Punakha did the second consecration according to Amitayus in 1967. Dilgo Khyentse did the third consecration at the end of 1967 according to Jigmey Lingpa's mind treasure, the *Supreme Heruka Assembly.*

Dilgo Khyentse with His Majesty the King of Bhutan at Paro.
Photograph by Matthieu Ricard.

During this consecration, Khyentse Rinpoche composed the following longevity prayer for Crown Prince Jigmey Senge Wangchuk, who was then twelve years old.

Prayer of Longevity for His Majesty the King, Jigmey Singye Wangchuk

Om Swasti Vijayantu.
Embodiment of the three omniscient ones who span all time
    and space,
Urgyen Pema, the one who is all and one,
I urge you to impart here and now,
Your enduring teachings to all deluded beings.
During this time of the five degenerations,
You promised to be the sole savior of weary beings;
Now the time has come to remember your vow,
So hasten to protect us, Maha Guru!
Emanation of the Indestructible One, whose mere sight is chastening,

Dilgo Khyentse with Queen Mother Kesang Chödrön and Loppön
Sonam Zangpo. Photograph by Matthieu Ricard.

With your power of blessing and pervasive charisma,
In the southern great land of Dharma,
Let evil be subdued, let good prevail,
Let disease, hunger, and strife be pacified,
And let the world and its beings savor the Golden Age.
Above all, let the precious teachings of the Buddha,
Be propagated and established,
And may they endure and flourish.
Let the crown prince Jigmey Senge Wangchuk,
The Dharma King Jigmey Dorje Wangchuk, father and son,
Lakshmi Dipam, the blessed Ashe Kesang,
And the ministers and subjects all come together, and
Invoke your blessing to keep this congregation ever in union.
Let wisdom grow like the waxing moon,
Subduing evil and scheming foes.
May the crown prince reign supreme in great fame,
During his noble reign as Dharma king,
And may his service toward all people

Equal that of Mey Yun Namsum.
May the outer world abound with fruits and foliage,
And the inner world teem with virtuous deeds and wholesome
    means,
And may fraternity prevail in the Sangha community.
May the era of epidemics, hunger, and strife ebb away,
And be replaced by the eternal epoch of light for men and gods.
May the spreading of evil forces lose strength,
And out of the great union of the king and ministers,
May the Golden Era of constant stability arise.
In short, like the pandits and the incarnate king and subjects,
Who diffused the light of Dharma in Tibet,
May you, the second Buddha,
Keep the light of Dharma in this land shining evermore.

Because of Khyentse Rinpoche's presence, Bhutan was filled with blessings, and everyone felt surrounded by his love and blessings at every moment.

In the male iron-dog year, 1970, Dilgo Khyentse did a year of strict retreat on the *Secret Assembly Longevity Practice* in his house at Paro Kyechu. During this retreat he gave some fortunate lamas the complete empowerments and transmissions from the *Four Parts of the Heart Essence,* two sections of the *Heart Essence Root Volumes,* the *Guhyagarbha* empowerment from the *Nyingma Kahma,* and Longchenpa's *Dispelling the Darkness of the Ten Directions.*

In the ninth month of that same year, crown prince Jigmey Senge Wangchuk, who was then fifteen years old and studying in Satsam, had gone on a trip to the southeastern border of Assam. Rinpoche was silent and did not talk to anyone for the duration of the retreat, but he would talk a little bit to his attendant Ngodup in the evening before going to sleep. One evening he dreamed that he lost two front teeth, which is considered to be a sign of an obstacle for someone's life, but that he could then put back the two teeth in place. He said that the two persons that were dearest to him, and with whom this dream might be connected, were Rabjam Rinpoche and the young crown prince of Bhutan, now the king, Jigmey Senge Wangchuk. He felt that there were no obstacles for Rabjam Rinpoche but that there were some for the young prince.

Rinpoche told Ngodup that since he could put back both teeth in place, these obstacles could be overcome. He then told Ngodup to prepare a torma for special ceremonies that he would do during the night, and at dawn to take it to the cremation ground just behind the Kyechu Temple and throw it in the southeastern direction, looking carefully at how it fell on the ground. If the tip of the torma fell facing the front direction, that would be a good sign, but if its tip fell facing back toward him, it would not be so good. He added that Ngodup should then return to the house without looking back. Rinpoche did an elaborate ceremony, and according to his instructions, at dawn, Ngodup took the torma. When he threw it, it fell auspiciously in the right direction. When Ngodup returned home, Rinpoche was silent, but at night he asked how things had gone. After Ngodup told him, he put his hand on Ngodup's shoulder and said with a warm smile, "Good, well done! We could really help the young prince."

In the meantime, as the crown prince was on his way to Assam, his attendant Karma had gone a little ahead. When he looked behind, he saw the crown prince's jeep collide head-on with a bus. The driver and one young school friend were killed, and another friend escaped with a sprained wrist. The car was completely destroyed. The crown prince himself was thrown out of the car and landed on a plot of grass in the middle of some rocks. Other than a small scrape to his head, he wasn't harmed at all. His attendant drove the crown prince back to Puntsoling in another jeep.

When they arrived at the palace, he told me that the crown prince had been in an accident. I immediately told His Majesty, who was in Thimphu at that time, and he came down to see the crown prince right away. His Majesty and everyone else were very surprised that the crown prince merely had a scrape to his head. His Majesty went to see the place of the accident and said it was a miracle that his son was still alive. He asked his son how he fell. The crown prince said he felt that he was being pulled out of the car and left on the grass. Though Khyentse Rinpoche had known all this, he had not said anything but instead performed the rituals to avert harm. When the crown prince came back, Khyentse Rinpoche performed a long-life empowerment and a *lalu* healing ceremony for him.

In the iron-pig year, 1971, both Paljor Gyaltsen and Sangye Dorje asked Rinpoche if they could sponsor the *Treasury of Precious Termas,* so that year Khyentse Rinpoche gave the *Treasury of Precious Termas* empowerments and transmissions at Dechen Chöling for all the lamas, teachers, monks, nuns, practitioners, and laypeople, in short, whoever wanted to receive it. He also performed the elaborate *Union of Sugatas drupchen* with the sacred medicine consecration, and he gave detailed teachings on the *Primordial Wisdom Guru.* After that he did a month's practice of *Tara Warding Off Invasions* as a protective ritual for the government.

While giving the *Treasury of Precious Termas,* Rinpoche used to go to the teaching hall at three in the morning to prepare the empowerments. One morning, he called his attendant Ngodup at four in the morning. When Ngodup entered the temple, Rinpoche told him to go get three thousand rupees from his room, and when he brought the money, Rinpoche did a prayer and then told him to send two men to Tsamtrak Monastery immediately and give the money to the monks there to read the *Kangyur.*

That day I left the Urgyen Palri Palace in Paro to go to Kalimpong with my son and four daughters. We had called a helicopter to come from Hashimara to take us. On the way to Paro the helicopter exploded in midair and crashed at Tsimakoti. There is no doubt that Rinpoche had the *Kangyur* read to save the lives of myself, the crown prince, and the princesses. We later were told that Khyentse Rinpoche had also personally performed a powerful exorcism ritual that morning. And thus the accident was averted.

After completing the annual drupchen in the ninth month of the pig-year, 1971, Khyentse Rinpoche left for India on the first day of the tenth month. The secretary Chötrak escorted him from Puntsoling to Siliguri. Though Rinpoche hadn't said anything, Chötrak returned with a letter from Rinpoche addressed to me, saying I should have a hundred thousand *Tara* practices done as a healing ceremony for the crown prince and that we should start that very day. They quickly gathered those who knew how to do the practice and started the ceremony in the Guru Temple, continuing the recitation throughout the night. The next day the crown prince returned for a holiday from his school abroad and went straight south to ride his father's elephants. While the elephants were running, Minister Sangye Paljor fell off an elephant and was injured, but nothing happened to the crown prince.

Previously Khyentse Rinpoche had completed a stupa the height of a man at Dechen Chöling Palace, which was then filled with *dharanis* to prevent the influence of spirits causing recurrent obstacles. The elaborate consecration had been performed by Khyentse Rinpoche presiding over fifteen practitioners reciting the *Raksha Thotreng* ceremony and accumulating one hundred thousand recitations. On May 15, 1972, His Majesty enthroned his son, Crown Prince Senge Wangchuk, as the Tongsa Ponlop in Dechen Chöling Palace, then in Tashi Chodzong and finally in Chokor Rabten Dzong in Tongsar.

On July 21, 1972, His Majesty Jigmey Dorje Wangchuk passed away suddenly in Nairobi, Kenya. His remains were brought back to the Garden Palace, his residence in Thimphu, where the Je Khenpo, the Sixteenth Karmapa, Dilgo Khyentse, and many other lamas performed the *Mindroling Vajrasattva* drupchen and did the *Peaceful and Wrathful Deities* purification rituals. Khyentse Rinpoche took care of all the necessary ceremonies, and the cremation was performed on Divine Descent Day in November 1972 at Kurje in Bumthang. After the cremation, the crown prince and the whole family returned to Thimphu. In December 1972, the prince was consecrated as the fourth king of Bhutan at Zhabdrung Rinpoche's Machen Temple in Punakha, where he received the traditional five-colored scarves from the Zhabdrung's stupa.

In 1972, Khyentse Rinpoche gave the *Compendium of Sadhanas* empowerments to Dzongsar Khyentse Chökyi Lodrö's reincarnation and many other lamas in Paro Kyechu. When Khamtrul Dongyu Nyima was giving the *Vajra Garland* empowerments in Thimphu Dzong, Khyentse Rinpoche also went to receive the complete cycle. Then Rinpoche was invited to do the *Mindroling Vajrasattva* drupchen for the passing of lord chamberlain Thinley Dorje at his residence in Mendalgang, after which he completed the remaining transmissions of the *Embodiment of Realization* empowerments that he had started earlier at Dechen Chöling for vajra master Yeshe Senge and four other teachers, along with many other Dharma brothers and sisters.

In the tenth month of the water-ox year, 1973, in Paro Kyechu Rinpoche did an elaborate three-week-long *Mahakala and Mahakali Ransom Offering for Averting War,* which was prepared in an authentic way according to Rinpoche's instructions. At that time there was once again a lot of turmoil in Bhutan, but due to the power and strength of Khyentse Rinpoche's performance of the *Eight Sadhana Teachings:* Manjushri Body, Lotus Speech, Vishuddha Mind, Nectar Quality, and Kilaya Activity, comprising the Great Glorious One; as well as *Liberating Sorcery of Mother Deities, Maledictory Fierce Mantra, Mundane Worship,* and *Mahakala* and *Shridevi,* everything was resolved, and my faith in spiritual masters became much stronger. In particular, I came to regard Dilgo Khyentse as Padmasambhava in person.

In Padmasambhava's prediction text revealed by Tertön Drukdra Dorje it said, "The one born in the male iron-dragon year, [1940], will cause obstacles for the one born in the wood-sheep year, [1955], to govern." At the age of sixteen or seventeen, crown prince Jigmey Senge Wangchuk encountered obstacles created by the secret underground movement, who were preparing to cause trouble through various means.

And also at that time, the one born in the male iron-horse year, 1930, Queen Mother Kesang Chödrön, driven by merit, came to respect the mind incarnation of Jamyang Khyentse Wangpo, the tertön endowed with the seven transmissions, the supreme Dilgo Khyentse, victory banner of the supreme doctrine, as her sole refuge. When he performed the *Supreme Heruka Assembly* drupchen and the *Mahakali* and *Mahakala* rituals to overcome war and so forth, they were always very effective, done at the right time, and expertly suited to the situation. Hence the celestial mansion of Jigmey Senge Wangchuk, and all the people living in his kingdom of medicinal valleys endowed with Dharma, began to enjoy peace and happiness.

In the fifth month of the water-ox year, 1973, Khyentse Rinpoche and his retinue did a nine-day *Vajrakilaya* exorcist rite at Tashi Chodzong in Thimphu, as a protective ritual for the government, after which the torma was thrown. In the seventh month, as requested by Khamtrul Dongyu Nyima, Khyentse Rinpoche gave the complete empowerments and teachings of the *Secret Mantra Treasury of the Kagyu Lineage,* which is one of the *Five Treasuries of Jamgön Kongtrul,* at Bumthang Kurje Monastery for the Chotse congregation and many faithful ones.

Prior to the public coronation, on an extremely auspicious Thursday, at the tiger hour, three o'clock in the morning, on the tiger day of the tiger month in the tiger year, 1974, Dilgo Khyentse bestowed the *Blazing Gem of Sovereignty* empowerment and long-life initiation on His Majesty. This empowerment was originally given by Padmasambhava to the young King Trisong Detsen in Samye at the same hour, day, and month in the tiger year, in order to protect the king and subdue all enemies and obstacles from the Bon masters. Before the enthronement Khyentse Rinpoche slept near the throne room at the *dzong* and said that early that morning he dreamed that His Majesty was a true incarnation of Tertön Pema Lingpa and that he would do great good for the Dharma.

In the first month, the miracle month, Khyentse Rinpoche headed the accumulation of one hundred thousand *Raksha Thotreng* recitations at Dechen Chöling Palace as a beneficial rite for the public enthronement and to prevent obstacles with a fixed amount of time. In Tashi Chodzong he performed the *Mahakala and Mahakali Ransom Offering for Averting War* lasting for a full month. Then, on the fifteenth of the fourth month of the wood-tiger year, 1974, Khyentse Rinpoche attended the public coronation of His Majesty the King of Bhutan.

In the eleventh month of the wood-rabbit year, 1975, Khyentse Rinpoche went abroad to benefit fortunate students and whoever encountered him, and in the fifth month of the fire-dragon year, 1976, he returned to Thimphu. In the fire-snake year, 1977, he did a strict retreat; at the request of Jigmey Gyalwai Wangchuk from Bumthang Tharpaling and Lama Karma Tsultrim Tharchin from Nubri in Nepal, he wrote a commentary on the meaning of the *Chemchok Heruka sadhanas*.

Earlier in 1966, when the crown prince was eleven years old, while staying in his cottage at the Paro Palace, he had a very vivid dream of Chakrasamvara in union with consort, colored red and surrounded by flames. He also heard the mantra HA HA very loudly. When Dilgo Khyentse and Khamtrul Rinpoche heard about this dream, they explained that he had seen the red Pema Vajra and heard Chakrasamvara's mantra. That is why my mother and I decided to build a large Chakrasamvara statue and another smaller statue of Pema Vajra in Punakha Dzong, a place sacred to Chakrasamvara.

Khyentse Rinpoche performed the ceremonies for all the life-trees, special supports, and mantras needed to fill the statues.[2] The life-tree of the main Chakrasamvara statue was made of fine white sandalwood, the *dharanis* were written in gold and covered with brocade, and the inner body, speech, mind, quality, and activity supports were all very special. This beautiful new Chakrasamvara temple was completed in 1978, and Khamtrul Rinpoche performed the first consecration with the sixty-deity *Chakrasamvara sadhana*. In 1978, the second consecration was performed by Je Khenpo Ninsey Tulku and the Punakha monks with the thirteen-deity *Chakrasamvara sadhana*, and Dilgo Khyentse performed the third consecration with the *Mindroling Vajrasattva* drupchen.

My mother Choying Wangmo asked for the *Chakrasamvara Pema Vajra* drupchen to be performed at Punakha, but a drupchen for Jamyang Khyentse

Wangpo's *Chakrasamvara Pema Vajra* had never been performed, so the liturgy had yet to be written. Thus, the *Mindroling Vajrasattva* drupchen was performed that year instead. Meanwhile Khyentse Rinpoche prepared the writings for the *Chakrasamvara Pema Vajra* drupchen, and then performed it for the first time in Punakha in 1979. He continued to hold this drupchen every year until his death.

On the fifteenth of the second month of the earth-horse year, 1978, Khyentse Rinpoche gave the complete reading transmission of the *Hundred Thousand Nyingma Tantras* in Satsam Chorten to a large gathering of tulkus, lamas, monks, nuns, and laypeople, whoever wanted to receive it. In the female earth-sheep year, 1979, Khyentse Rinpoche performed the drupchen of Tertön Ratna Lingpa's *Secret Assembly Longevity Practice* at Dechen Chöling Palace as a longevity ceremony for His Majesty. After that, as requested by the people from Khan Tali Monastery, Khyentse Rinpoche gave the preparatory and actual empowerments of the peaceful and wrathful deities of the *Magical Net*, starting on the sixteenth of the fifth month and finishing on the eleventh of the sixth month. Then he gave the complete empowerments and reading transmissions of the *Four Parts of the Heart Essence*, the reading transmission of Longchenpa's *Seven Treasuries* with the additional writings, and the reading transmissions for the *Trilogy of Natural Ease* and the *Root Volumes of the Heart Essence*. He also gave the torma empowerment for Vajrakilaya according to the Sakya tradition; the profound teaching on Avalokiteshvara's six-syllable mantra with the blessing empowerment and reading transmission; Chokling's *Tara Dispelling All Obstacles* empowerment, Longsel's *Akshobya* empowerment, Ledrel's *Tamer of All Haughty Spirits Vajrapani* empowerment, the *Dorje Draktsal* and the *Secret Essence Vajrasattva* empowerments, all from the *New Treasures of Chokgyur Lingpa*; the *Raksha Thotreng* empowerment for subjugating spirits causing recurrent obstacles; and the reading transmission of Karma Lingpa's Vajra Guru mantra benefits.

In the iron-monkey year, 1980, a Gesar temple for making petition-offerings to Dharma protectors was built behind Dechen Chöling Palace. In Tertön Drukdra Dorje's predictions it mentioned taking out a treasure as a means to avert a crisis, so I requested Khyentse Rinpoche to please reveal any treasures that there might be. He explained that certain treasures were destined to each tertön and that it wasn't possible for him to reveal these specific ones. Instead, he performed a hundred thousand feast offerings and butter lamp offerings in Bumthang Kurje, and in the sixth month he went to Paro Taktsang and performed a hundred thousand feast offerings according to the *Vidyadhara Dzutrul Tuchen sadhana* from the *New Treasures of Chokgyur Lingpa,* along with a hundred thousand butter lamp offerings, smoke offerings in the morning, and dharmapala offerings in the evening, all for fifteen days without break. Along with that he performed the *Majestic Command* to restrain gods and spirits, the *Holy Site Consecration,* and so forth.

He also said that building four stupas around Thimphu and Paro according to the *Immaculate Ushnisha* and *Spotless Rays of Light* mandalas would definitely avert a crisis. The woodblocks for the mantras of these two *kriya-yoga* tantras were at Tongsar Dzong, so they were brought to Rinpoche, who gave instructions on how to build the stupas and fill them. When the stupa construction was completed, he performed the various consecrations. He then started giving the complete empowerments and reading transmissions of the fourth volume of the *Heart Essence of the Great Expanse Root Volumes* at the sacred place of Taktsang, and he completed them at Kyechu.

When His Majesty was twenty-six years old, he expressed a deep wish to build a large image of Chemchok Heruka, and my mother had a great desire to build a Vajrakilaya image. When they conveyed their wishes to Khyentse Rinpoche, he was very pleased and said, "Very auspicious!" He told them to build a Kabgye, Gongdu, and Kilaya temple in Kurje and said that there was a mind treasure of Khyentse Chökyi Lodrö's which said that building a Kabgye, Gongdu, and Kilaya temple in Kurje would be of great benefit for Bhutan. Thus, His Majesty's and my mother's wishes were very auspicious.

Khyentse Rinpoche performed many drupchens and averting rituals for Bhutan in Kyechu, and that is why there is peace in Bhutan now. Khyentse Rinpoche performed the first consecration of the Kabgye Temple with a drupchen of Nyang Ral Nyima Özer's *Eight Commands: Union of the Sugatas* in 1990. In 1991 Khyentse Rinpoche invited Trulshik Rinpoche to come with him to perform the second drupchen at the new Kurje Temple. In April of that year Rinpoche performed the consecration of the Sixteen Arhats Temple at Kurje, while Trulshik Rinpoche gave novice and *bhikshu* ordination to many monks and nuns.

On the fifteenth of the fourth month of the iron-bird year, 1981, Rinpoche started the reading transmission of the complete *Kangyur* for the Rabde Chotse monks and many other faithful ones in front of the Kurje Temple in Bumthang. In the mornings Khyentse Rinpoche would give one blessing empowerment from the Sakya *Compendium of Sadhanas* and one of the omniscient Pema Karpo's empowerments. After that he would give the expository transmissions of Jigmey Lingpa's *Chariot of the Two Truths* and *Chariot of Omniscience*, followed by the reading transmission of one volume of the *Kangyur*. After that, Sengtrak Rinpoche would read the rest of the *Kangyur*. During that time Rinpoche also gave teachings on the advanced yogic techniques of the subtle channels and energies from the *Heart Essence of the Great Expanse* cycle with the *Eight Vidyadharas* yogic exercises to some diligent practitioners. As soon as that was finished, he performed the drupchen of Ratna Lingpa's *Secret Assembly Longevity Practice* in the Kurje Guru Temple, along with the long-life empowerment.

In the water-dog year, 1982, Rinpoche performed Pema Lingpa's *Razor of Life Vajrakilaya* drupchen in the Dechen Chöling guesthouse, and also gave the *Razor of Life* empowerment. In addition, he gave the empowerment of the higher activity of accomplishing enlightenment from his own *Nyak Kilaya* mind treasure, as well as the reading transmission of the volume containing the *sadhana* with the feast offering and the index. Many healing ceremonies, such as Ratna Lingpa's *Effigy of the Blade* ritual and Yakchar's *Green Tara Ransom Ritual*, were performed at that sacred place, and Rinpoche gave the empowerments and reading transmissions for all of these as well.

On the fourth of the sixth month of the water-pig year, 1983, Rinpoche started giving the complete *Nyingma Kahma*. Previously, the Royal Grandmother Puntsök Chödrön had invited Rinpoche from Darjeeling to stay at Nyimalung Monastery, so when Rinpoche visited Nyimalung, he performed a ritual for suppressing spirits that cause recurrent obstacles and a fire puja below the stupa behind the monastery, and he donated a large, beautifully embroidered Amitabha thangka to the monastery. In the tenth month of that year, Rinpoche went to Puntsoling and for over two months gave the complete empowerments and reading transmissions of the *Treasury of Spiritual Instructions* at the request of the Drikung Kyabgon.

In the tenth month of the wood-rat year, 1984, Rinpoche gave the complete reading transmission of Jigmey Lingpa's *Collected Works* in the garden of the palace at Paro Kyechu. At the same time, he also gave Ngari Tsultrim Zangpo's *Avalokiteshvara* blessing empowerment; the empowerment of his own mind treasure of the outer peaceful *Vajrasattva* practice; Chokling's *Lord of the Families Amitabha* empowerment from the *Heart Practice* cycle; the Kadam *Amitabha* empowerment; Longsel's *Akshobya* and *Medicine Buddha* empowerments; Choje Lingpa's *Vajrapani* and *Chandali* empowerments; the *Heart Practice Dispelling All Obstacles* torma empowerment; Chokling's *White Canopy Ushnisha* empowerment; Kyerkang's *Secret Hayagriva* practice empowerment; Chokling's *Secret Essence Vajrasattva* empowerment; Yakchar's *Green Tara* empowerments; Chokling's *Mahapratisara* empowerment; Longsel's *Pinnacle of the Victory Banner* empowerment; the *Horse Garuda* empowerment from the *Heart Essence of the Great Expanse;* Karma Lingpa's *Peaceful and Wrathful Ones* torma empowerment; Sangye Lingpa's *Sixteen Arhats* empowerment; Chokling's *Raksha Thotreng* empowerment; the *Gathering of the Vidyadharas,* the *Lion-Faced One,* and the *Great Bliss Queen dakini* empowerments from the *Heart Essence of the Great Expanse* cycle; the *Fasting Practice* blessing empowerment according to Gelongma Palmo's tradition that was composed by Jamgön Kongtrül; all the reading transmissions of Jamgön Kongtrül's commentaries on meditation instructions; the ritual for conducting the ordination ceremony; the additional prayers and auspicious wishes, and so forth. He also gave teachings on *Vajrasattva's Four Tantra Sections,* the *Notes* of the Drukpa Kagyu preliminaries, the *Abridged Notes on the Six Yogas,* and the *Meditation Stages on Dependent Origination.* Around that time Rinpoche additionally taught on Patrul Rinpoche's *Virtuous in the Beginning, Middle, and End.*

In the wood-ox year, 1985, in the garden of his house at Paro Kyechu, Rinpoche gave the empowerments and reading transmissions for the *Six Volumes of Jatson,* along with the protector entrustment. During the winter of that year, he went to the hot springs in Gelekpu, and during his one-month stay there, he recognized the reincarnation of Gyalsey Tulku, who had been born in a village in Bumthang, and sent him to Shechen Monastery in Nepal. To the Khan Tali monks in Gelekpu, he gave the complete empowerments and transmissions of Pema Lingpa's cycle of teachings and performed the *Mahakala and Mahakali Ransom Offering for Averting War.*

After that, in the fire-tiger year, 1986, as entreated by Penor Rinpoche, he went to Mysore in southern India to give the complete reading transmission of Mipham Rinpoche's *Collected Works.* He also gave the reading transmissions of Patrul Rinpoche's *Collected Works* and select works by the omniscient Longchenpa.

On other occasions during various periods at Dechen Chöling, Khyentse Rinpoche gave all the empowerments for Ratna Lingpa's *Secret Assembly Longevity Practice* cycle; all the empowerments of Pema Lingpa's *Vajrakilaya* cycle; all the empowerments and reading transmissions of the *Guru's Innermost Essence;* all the empowerments of Chokgyur Lingpa's *Raksha Thotreng* cycle; the profound empowerments and reading transmissions of the *Heart Essence of Chetsun* cycle; the expository transmissions of Longchenpa's *Dispelling the Darkness of Ignorance* and Mipham Rinpoche's *General Meaning of the Secret Essence: Core of Luminosity,* two commentaries on the *Guhyagarbha Tantra;* the instructional transmission of Adzom Drukpa's special commentary *Essence of the Perfect Path;* the instructions on Patrul Rinpoche's *Three Lines That Strike the Vital Point;* the reading transmission of Ngulchu Thogmey's commentary on *The Way of the Bodhisattva;* the reading transmission of the *Treasury of Dharmadhatu;* the reading transmission of Jamgön Kongtrül's *Treasury of All-Pervading Knowledge;* the reading transmission of Ngok Zhedang Dorje's *Like a Jewel Ornament,* which is a commentary on the *Two Segments;* the reading transmission of the brief *Chakrasamvara Root Tantra;* Ngari Pema Wangyal's commentary on the three vows with Minling Lochen Dharmashri's *Wish-Granting Grains* commentary; as well as Khenpo Karma Ngelek's *Words of Manjushri* commentary on the three vows.

From Jigmey Lingpa's *Collected Works* Rinpoche gave the *Explanation on the Embodiment of Realization* and the *Treasury of Precious Qualities* with Sokpo Tendar's commentary, followed by Patrul Rinpoche's *Questions and Answers on Meditation.* He also gave the empowerment and instructional transmission for the *Guru's Innermost Essence,* Khenpo Nuden's commentary on Lama Mipham's *Gateway to Knowledge,* Tenpai Nyima's *Notes on the Development and Completion Stages,* Dotrul's commentary on the recitation manuals of the Three Roots and the guru yoga of the *Heart Essence of the Great Expanse,* Shabkar's *Flight of the Garuda,* Khenpo Kunpal's commentary on the *The Way of the Bodhisattva,* and all the reading transmissions of the required collection of liturgical texts, and so forth.

In the fire-rabbit year, 1987, in the Wind Horse Temple of Dechen Chöling, Rinpoche gave *Gesar's Vajra Victory Banner* empowerment; Lerab Lingpa's pure-vision empowerment of *Gesar's Nine Glorious Ones* with the activity and feast offering; the complete reading transmission of Mipham

Rinpoche's *Gesar* practices; the reading transmission of Khyentse, Kongtrül, and Chokling's *Gesar Burned Offerings* composed by Tertön Sogyal; the
reading transmission of Dilgo Khyentse's own writings on the *Gesar sadhana*
cycle, burned offerings, wind horse ransom rites, wind horse prosperity-
propitiation rites, and his autobiography in verse; the reading transmission
of Do Khyentse's mind treasure on burned offerings and libation offerings
and Dudjom Rinpoche's writings on wind horse; the *Kyechog Tsulzang*
empowerment from the *Heart Practice* and the reading transmission of the
prosperity-propitiation rite; Lama Mipham's *Divine Hook Gesar* ritual for
summoning prosperity; Chagmey's ritual for pacifying phenomenal existence, and many others.

In 1987 Rinpoche also gave Gyaton Pema Wangchuk's profound *Chakrasamvara Pema Vajra* empowerment for the drupchen, with all the related reading transmissions, such as the *Chakrasamvara* lineage prayer; the *Self-Liberation
of Fixation* maturing *sadhana;* the *Self-Liberation of Great Bliss Wisdom* from
the *Chakrasamvara Heart Practice,* including the *Essence of the Two Stages;* the
essential five cycles of mind treasures with *Chakrasamvara* as the main one;
the *Light of Wisdom* self-empowerment ritual with the *Praise to Chakrasamvara;* the commentary on the *Two Stages of Chakrasamvara,* and so forth. He
also gave the reading transmission for the short dharmapala petition-offerings,
such as the four-armed Mahakala, Dhumavati, and Palden Lhamo; the reading
transmission for the *Dakini Bliss Tantra* and the *Mahamudra Storeroom* from
the omniscient Pema Karpo's *Collected Works;* the blessing empowerments
for Marpa's, Milarepa's, and Gampopa's guru yogas with the reading transmission for the *sadhanas* and feast offerings from Kongtrül Rinpoche's *Extensive
Treasury of Instructions;* the reading transmission for *Self-Liberation of Clinging,* a volume on chö practice; the expository transmission of the *Laughter of
the Dakinis;* and the *Opening the Sky Door* Chö empowerment.

Again in Dechen Chöling Rinpoche gave the elaborate, medium, and
abridged empowerments of Lerab Lingpa's *Eliminating Inauspiciousness,* with
the reading transmission for the entire volume; the reading transmission for
the rituals to build stupas according to the *Immaculate Ushnisha* and *Spotless
Rays of Light* mandalas with the ritual procedures; the empowerment for his
own *Pema's Heart Essence of Longevity* mind treasure with the instructions;
the lineage prayer with the appendix for the *Essence Practice,* with the fulfillment and the elaborate and short dharmapalas; the reading transmission of
Rinpoche's long and short guru yoga with the long and short supplication to

the succession of incarnations and the longevity supplication; the commentary on Jigmey Lingpa's feast song "Leymon Tendrel" and the *Three Kaya Guardian* supplication with its commentary.

In the male earth-dragon year, 1988, while doing the drupchen in Paro Kyechu, along with the *Gathering of the Vidyadharas* long-life empowerment from the *Heart Essence of the Great Expanse,* Rinpoche gave the preparation and main empowerment of the *Supreme Heruka Assembly.* He also gave the empowerment for the four blood-drinking herukas; the wrathful *Horse-Garuda* empowerment; the *Great Bliss Queen* empowerment with the long-life blessing; the empowerment for the secret practice of the *Lion-Faced Dakini;* the *Abhirati Vajrasattva* empowerment and the reading transmission for the volume of tenth-day liturgies; Rongzom Pandita's *Lotus Dakini* empowerment with the reading transmission for the daily practice and the abridged fire puja; the reading transmission for the *Three Roots sadhanas* from the *Heart Essence of the Great Expanse;* the commentary on the *Supreme Heruka Assembly;* the empowerments for the outer practice of Rinpoche's own *Vajrasattva* mind treasure, the inner practice of the *Three Families* and the *Peaceful and Wrathful Ones,* and the secret practice of *Vajra Vidarana;* the empowerments for the *Seven-Chapter Supplication* and the *Dispeller of All Obstacles;* the empowerment for the *Spontaneously Accomplished Treasury of Qualities;* the empowerment and reading transmission for the *Ocean of Dharma That Embodies All Teachings;* the empowerment for his own *Heart Essence of the Self-Born Lotus* mind treasure with the reading transmission for the lineage prayer, the *sadhanas,* the daily practice, and the brief feast offering of the Three Roots; the blessing empowerment of *White Tara* from Atisha's tradition; the reading transmission for Mipham Rinpoche's *White Lotus Commentary* on the "Seven-Line Prayer"; the daily *Tara* practice according to the four tantra classes; and the Third Khamtrul Kunga Tenzin's *Pure Gold Oral Instructions* on the view, meditation, and conduct of *mahamudra.*

Khyentse Rinpoche performed numerous drupchens in Bhutan: at Paro Kyechu he performed the drupchen of the *Supreme Heruka Assembly* twenty-six times, Guru Chowang's *Kilaya* drupchen twice, and his own *Nyak Kilaya* drupchen once. At Dechen Chöling he performed the drupchen of the *Secret Assembly Longevity Practice* once and Pema Lingpa's *Kilaya* drupchen once. In Paro he performed the drupchen of the *Heart Practice Dispelling All Obsta-*

cles once. In Bumthang Kurje he performed the drupchen of the *Secret Assembly Longevity Practice* once and the drupchen of the *Eight Commands: Union of the Sugatas* sixteen times. In Punakha Dzong he performed the *Mindroling Vajrasattva* drupchen once and the *Chakrasamvara Pema Vajra* drupchen thirteen times. In Thimphu Dzong Rinpoche performed the *Mahakali and Mahakala Ransom Ritual Averting War* eighteen times. Furthermore, in Paro Kyechu he performed Rolchen's torma-exorcism ritual. In Dechen Chöling he performed the *Secret Assembly Longevity Practice*, the *Raksha Thotreng*, the *Kurukulle* fire puja, and Ratna Lingpa's *Ransom Ritual* twice.

Rinpoche also performed many subjugation rituals: At Thimphu Dzong below Palden Lhamo's armor in the protector temple and below the fence in Bumthang Kurje he performed subjugating rituals aimed at the gongpo spirits; in Punakha he performed four subjugating rituals in the Chakrasamvara Temple and at the stupa at the Manjushri Temple for spirits that cause recurrent obstacles. He also performed subjugation rituals through building five stupas: four according to the *Immaculate Ushnisha* and *Spotless Rays of Light* mandalas and one according to Lang Palseng. In Bumthang Kurje he performed three subjugations underneath the holy supports of the *Eight Sadhana Teachings*, Gongdu, and Vajrakilaya; in Samtenling he performed two subjugation rituals to the right and left of His Majesty's residence for spirits that cause recurrent obstacles; in the Great Secret Dharma Wheel Temple, underneath the images, he performed three subjugations for spirits that cause recurrent obstacles; in Dechen Chöling he performed a subjugation ritual below the Wind Horse Temple, one at the fence gate of the residence, and one at the stupa along the way. At the stupa behind the Nyimalung Temple he performed one subjugation ritual for spirits that cause recurrent obstacles; at Dechen Chöling he performed Pema Lingpa's *Ritual for Averting Misfortune* after which the effigy was thrown in the water at the river junction; and in Thimphu Dzong he once performed the *Radiant Black Yamantaka* activity as a method to avert enemies and war. All these ceremonies were done with Dilgo Khyentse presiding.

Every year in Bhutan without interruption he performed the two annual drupchens; the *Secret Assembly Longevity Practice* healing ceremony; the *Raksha Thotreng* ritual for averting the influence of spirits that cause recurrent obstacles; the *Kurukulle* recitation; the *Gesar Wind Horse Ransom Ritual;* the *Lama Norlha* rites for propitiation of prosperity; the *Clearing the Obstacles of the Path* prayer; the *Spontaneous Fulfillment of All Aspirations* prayer; the *Tara* practice; the *Genyen* fire puja; and the New Year healing ceremonies for the entire royal family, and so forth, of which the dates were unfixed.

Khyentse Rinpoche often said that he loved Bhutan, and even if Tibet would become independent, he would stay in Bhutan, as it was now his home. A few years before he passed away, he wanted to build a house at Satsam Chorten. At that time I was in Kalimpong, so I had Ashe Pem Pem look for land in Satsam Chorten. When Khyentse Rinpoche went to look at the land, he chose the place where his house should be built and said he would like to have a Vajrakilaya temple built there facing Taktsang. He jokingly told Rabjam Rinpoche that by the time they would finish building the Vajrakilaya Temple, it would be right to build his memorial stupa there, but as Rabjam Rinpoche looked very upset, he said he was joking.

Before his house was finished, Khyentse Rinpoche wanted to stay one night there. A tent was put up outside where he stayed for seven days and performed a hundred thousand fire pujas. After Rinpoche passed away, I had the Kilaya Temple built with a large Vajrakilaya statue in the center, and with Yeshe Tsogyal and Guru Rinpoche statues on either side. The temple was consecrated by Trulshik Rinpoche in 1998 just before he went to Bumthang to transmit Khyentse Rinpoche's entire *Collected Works* at the Kurje Temple. When Khyentse Yangsi Rinpoche arrived in Bhutan, the new Kilaya Temple was offered to him, and that is where Khyentse Yangsi and Shechen Rabjam Rinpoche perform the annual drupchen of Khyentse Rinpoche's *Nyak Kilaya* mind treasure.

Thus, because the great masters from Tibet were forced to escape their homeland and settle in India and Nepal, Dilgo Khyentse, whose kindness can never be repaid, came to live in the medicinal valleys of Bhutan. He came to Bhutan through the power of past karma and prayers to guide fortunate students with the nectar of the sacred Dharma, to act for the welfare of the doctrine and beings. From the time he arrived at the border in 1959 until he passed away in Thimphu Hospital in 1991, Dilgo Khyentse blessed and protected Bhutan. Through his special blessings and protection for His Majesty the King of Bhutan, the royal family and all the people of Bhutan enjoy peace and happiness and are always surrounded by Khyentse Rinpoche's unceasing blessings, even today. Bhutan is very fortunate to enjoy the presence of Khyentse Rinpoche's reincarnation, Yangsi Rinpoche, who continues to bless our kingdom.

17. Building Shechen Monastery in Nepal
TRULSHIK RINPOCHE

Trulshik Rinpoche was Dilgo Khyentse's main disciple, spiritual friend, and lineage holder. The following is taken from the index he wrote for the twenty-five volumes of Khyentse Rinpoche's *Collected Works*.

THE TREASURE REVEALER Dilgo Khyentse was predicted by the knower of the three times from Uddiyana in Chokgyur Lingpa's profound *Life Drop of the Consorts* from the *Eight Commands: Union of the Sugatas* treasure:

> During the Dark Age, a vidyadhara blessed by Pema, Lhasey Chökyi Lodro's last birth as Chokgyur Lingpa, will manifest interdependent illusory acts in which method and wisdom are not dual, and this authentic path will be spread widely. At that time, through dependent arising, the great lord Manjushri will emanate as the Heruka Garwang Dongnak Lingpa, born in the iron-dog year, 1910; this fortunate noble person who assimilates everything all at once, will be taken care of by me, the master from Uddiyana. He will open the door of many profound and vast secret treasures, practicing them himself and spreading them for others. At that time this treasure will be blessed with good fortune.

He was also predicted in his own treasure, *Pema's Heart Essence of Longevity:*

> A manifestation keeping the yogic discipline, one who is of gentle character and highly intelligent, wise, self-confident, and firm in

Dilgo Khyentse with Trulshik Rinpoche in Solukhumbu, 1977.
Photograph by Marilyn Silverstone.

meditation, a vidyadhara who will help the beings of the Dark Age,
a wisdom form of the great *pandita* Vimalamitra and King Trisong
who has perfected the power of natural realization, a majestic and
powerful daka, Dharma King Dongnak Lingpa Ösel Trulpai Dorje,
will be born in the iron-dog year, 1910, endowed with the marks of
a daka, and exclusively teach this as his share.

On the fourth day of the eleventh month in the fire-dragon year, 1977,
the great tertön Dharma king came to my monastery Thupten Choling in
Solukhumbu, Nepal. As I had requested, Khyentse Rinpoche mainly gave the
Magical Display of the Peaceful and Wrathful Ones empowerments, the *Four
Parts of the Heart Essence,* the *Treasury of Spiritual Instructions,* the *Compendium of Sadhanas,* most of his earlier and later profound treasures, and many
additional transmissions, and was so kind as to stay at my monastery, very
relaxed, until the twenty-ninth of the fourth month of the following year.
One day Rinpoche's wife came to see me and said, "Rinpoche is not

Dilgo Khyentse during a drupchen at Shechen Monastery,
Nepal. Photograph by Matthieu Ricard.

interested in building new monasteries, but Shechen Rabjam Tulku is now
ten years old and it would be good to build a small monastery in Nepal so
that he might have a base. Would you be so kind as to discuss this with Rinpoche—I don't dare to!"

As she had requested, I went to see Rinpoche and made an offering with
a silk ceremonial scarf, and I proposed to Rinpoche what Khandro Lhamo
had asked me to. For a while he just stared at me, and then he said, "Lhamo
probably encouraged you to ask this. Previously the senior Queen Mother of
Bhutan also gave me some money to build a monastery, but I used it to print
the *Hundred Thousand Nyingma Tantras*. Now you have built this small monastery which the Dalai Lama has called Thupten Choling." Then, laughing,
he teased me, saying, "When I was young, I didn't make any effort to build a
monastery, but now that I'm getting old, since you've got a small monastery

Shechen Monastery, Nepal. Photograph by Matthieu Ricard.

in Nepal, I'm going to build an even larger one here, and I'll call it Shechen Tennyi Dargyeling!"

Afterward Khyentse Rinpoche built Shechen Tennyi Dargyeling near the Bodhnath stupa in Nepal, which he described as follows:

> In this age, when the supreme point of decadence has been reached, though lacking the ten qualifications of a vajra master, I was given just such a title. In this state of imposture, as the wind of sins blew favorably for me, the clouds of distracting activities swelled, and I became loaded with a burden of possessions acquired through wrong ways of living, which became heavier than my own body. I was quite sure that, unless I was to perform a deed of great merit to the best of my capacities, I would have to endure the unbearable torment of the flames of hell. This created the cause of my determination, and the fortunate condition was offered through the emanation of Shechen Rabjam, on whom the flower of my devotion had already fallen in many past lives, and who came into my descent. This is how the construction work of this monastery came to be started in 1980.

This is the second Shechen Tennyi Dargyeling, the first being the great monastery in Kham of the same name where myriad learned and accomplished beings have flourished. The site of this new monastery is in front of the great stupa, which arose from the strong compassion of the Abbot, Guru, and King for the beings of the Land of Snow; they were the blazing torch of the three ancestors and the single eye of the universe. Here is the sacred place of the charnel ground of Nyewai Tsendoha, the gathering place of the Secret Mantra vidyadharas and dakinis. It is a place that was blessed by seven generations of Buddhas, by Manjushri, the two ornaments of this world Nagarjuna and Vasubhandu, the great vajra master Padmasambhava, and by many other peerless and glorious protectors of the Dharma and sentient beings. This central valley of Nepal is also surrounded by many diamondlike holy places existing since time immemorial.

In the secret predictions from the visionary teaching of the wish-fulfilling *Heart Practice*, which was rediscovered conjointly by the undisputed great tertöns Pema Ösel Dongnak Lingpa and Chokgyur Lingpa, who were like sun and moon, one can find the following words:

In the Dark Age some *lotsawas* and *panditas* will gather in this holy place through the strength of their wisdom, and unfolding the various activities of learning and spiritual accomplishment of the Buddha's precious teachings, they will definitely benefit the doctrine.

Remembering these true vajra words, which I had seen in the omniscient Khyentse Wangpo's own handwriting, and having total confidence that this undeceiving prediction could be accomplished, I set the wheel of work in motion. For the actual realization of this work, the door of the great sky treasure was opened in an exceedingly vast way:

• by Nyenang Tenpel, Chimey, Namgyal, and their relatives, who have a broad mind for giving a pure and worthy meaning to illusory wealth;

- by the supreme Tulku Pema Wangyal, whose knowledge and good qualities are matchless, a son of the all-encompassing great Kangyur Rinpoche, the master of the Great Perfection Longchen Yeshe Dorje;
- by the foreigners Kunzang Rangdrol; the Sakya *bhikshu* Konchok Tenzin and his mother; the *bhikshuni* Ngawang Chödrön, and many others from all nations whose faith and aspirations toward the teachers and the teachings is as vast as the sky and who contributed out of devotion in all sorts of ways;
- by my consort Lhamo, who knows the heaviness of the karmic maturation from using offerings made by faithful people and for the sake of dead people, and realizing the meaninglessness of hoarding wealth, offered all her precious objects and jewels with a pure motivation;
- by the great Dharma king from the southern land of the dragon, Bhutan, His Majesty Jigmey Senge Wangchuk; the senior Royal Grandmother Puntsök Chödrön; Her Majesty the Queen Mother Kesang Chödrön; her mother Choying Zangmo; and her daughters the royal princesses, the great benefactors of the Buddhist teachings, who through their prayers established a strong connection with the enlightened Buddha Longchenpa and his successive incarnations who came to their holy land, and all of whom, with their ministers and subjects, contributed with vast offerings and in many other ways, providing cement, wood, and countless other facilities, and always extended their most kind assistance to us;
- by the virtuous Ngodup Gyatso, who established good connections by the power of his past prayers and karma and his unwavering pure intention; and by all the other workers, who disregarded all the hardships they encountered and endeavored day and night to complete their task, only having in mind to serve their teacher and the Buddhist teachings;
- by the physician Amche Kunzang, well-versed in the traditional way of building and decorating monasteries in

Tibet, who made beautiful plans for the outside of the monastery and the arrangement of the temples inside;

- by Kushab Tsechu Rinpoche, head of the Office of Religious Affairs in the government of His Majesty King Birendra of Nepal, endowed with the five glories, who facilitated all the formalities to establish the monastery and the status of its religious community in an immeasurable way;
- by the standard bearer of the Nyingma school, the supreme Tulku Dzongnor Jampa Lodro of Peyul Monastery, who provided the land.

In order to establish a perfect and auspicious connection for the thorough realization of the work, Trulshik Rinpoche, the *vajradhara* of the Nyingma school, endowed with perfect qualities and knowledge; our vajra brother Trangu Rinpoche, the great abbot of Karma Monastery; Trarik Rinpoche; Dabzang Rinpoche; Tulku Chökyi Nyima, and many other great abbots of perfectly pure discipline performed a confession ceremony of good omen. I, myself, graced by merely bearing the name of the omniscient Manjugosha, performed a *Vajrasattva* ceremony for the granting of the land and a pacifying fire puja according to my own *Nyak Kilaya* mind treasure. At the initiative of Tulku Orgyen Topgyal, a son of the great siddha Chokgyur Lingpa, a drupchen according to the *Heart Practice Dispelling All Obstacles* was performed and attended by Chokling Tulku and many others. Sacramental substances that liberate by merely tasting them were prepared, and fire pujas for accomplishing the four activities were performed. I, myself, performed the subjugation and binding under oath of the *devas* and *rakshasas*. This is how the ground was perfectly blessed and prepared.

Then the main temple, well-planned and beautiful, was erected, solid as a diamond. The roof was topped with a golden pinnacle, and on the four corners golden victory banners were placed, with a golden Dharma wheel flanked by two deer in the front, their light glimmering to all horizons. Inside, the main sacred image is the statue of the peerless Shakyamuni Buddha, our sole object of reliance for this and future lives, whose kindness has been the very compassionate sun of the Three Jewels in this degenerate age. To his right is the past Buddha Kasyapa; to his left the future Buddha Maitreya. These images, which grant liberation by sight, are fifteen feet high. Around each of these statues are smaller statues that represent the parents and son of the Buddha, his main disciples and attendants. In between the main statues are images of Vajrasattva, the sublime teacher of the Secret Mantra; Vajradhara; Kshitigarbha, who prevents the decline of the Mahayana sangha in this Dark Age; and Samantabhadra, who brought the bodhisattva's prayer to infinite perfection.

At the top of the temple pillars the seven generations of Buddhas are carved, with the Buddha Shikhinra and the eight medicine buddhas. On the panels to the right and left sides are statues of the main followers of the Buddha, headed by Ananda and Mahakashyapa, surrounded by the sixteen arhats and the main abbots who introduced the monastic lineage in Tibet: the great Khenpo Shantarakshita for the lower lineage of *Vinaya* and the Kashmiri *pandita* Shakya Shri for the upper lineage of *Vinaya;* this is an auspicious connection for spreading the Nyingma tradition, the vajra essence which stands at the summit of all the teachings of the Victorious One in the Land of Snow. In the temple one also finds a life-size statue of Terdak Lingpa, the great chariot leader of the Nyingma school. All these statues were made out of clay by the most expert artists from Bhutan, the masters Damchoe and Omtong with their students.

The frescoes on the vast walls were drawn on the basis of nine thangkas depicting the various visions that the omniscient Jamyang Khyentse Wangpo had of the teachers of the various lineages of Buddhist teachings. The former incarnations of Shechen Gyaltsap and Shechen Rabjam, two of the main disciples of Jamyang Khyentse Wangpo and Jamgön Kongtrül, as well as the Dharma protectors, are also painted in frescoes. All these were beautifully drawn by my disciple, the Tibetan artist Konchok Özer, and the master artist from Namkai Nyingpo's monastery in Lhodrak, who were assisted by the expert Bhutanese painters Loppön Dawa Dorje and Urgyen Tenzin and their students. As a symbol of the Buddha's mind, eight stupas of the *sugatas* have been carved in fragrant sandalwood. These are the sacred objects found in the main temple, which is called the Pleasant Grove where *Vidyadharas Gather.*

On the second floor is the main library, Pleasant Grove of the Nectar of Perfect Speech. The main statue on the shrine is the embodiment of wisdom, Manjushri, depicted according to the tantric tradition. He is surrounded by eight statues of the six ornaments and the two supreme ones. To the right of Manjushri is the sole eye of the doctrine in the Land of Snow, Guru Padmasambhava, in the aspect of Nangsi Zilnon, Glorious Subjugator of Appearance and Existence. He is surrounded by statues of the main teachers of the eight great chariots of the practice lineage. To the left of Manjushri is the image of Mipham Jamyang Namgyal, our own object of refuge, who is the true heir of the two omniscient ones, Rongzom Pandita and Longchen Rabjam. He is surrounded by the teachers of the ten traditions of scriptural explanation. On elegant shelves all around are volumes of the *Kangyur* and the *Tengyur,* the *Hundred Thousand Nyingma Tantras,* the *Five Treasuries,* and the *Collected Works* of Jamyang Khyentse Wangpo, Lama Mipham, and Shechen Gyaltsap, together with countless other volumes of teachings on the sutras, tantras, and religious sciences.

The third floor, the Perfect Pinnacle, is covered by the top roof, under which are all the elements and sacred objects related to the *Rain of Blessings on the Holy Places,* prepared and consecrated in a very detailed way according to the *Four Heart Sadhanas.* Inside the top temple itself are statues of the *dharmakaya* Buddha Amitabha flanked by the *sambhogakaya* Avalokiteshvara and the *nirmanakaya* Padmasambhava with his two dakinis. On the first floor, just above the main temple, are the various rooms in which many old and new sacred objects related to the Buddha's body, speech, and mind are found.

In the protector's room, the Utsala, are statues of the nine main protectors of the Mindroling tradition, as depicted in the *Ocean of Accomplishment sadhana,* with some other related protectors, as well as all the main protectors of the new and ancient traditions. There is also a casket of prosperity, called the Treasure Gem Fulfilling All Needs, with Guru Rinpoche in the form of the Supreme

Being of Perfect Display as the main statue, surrounded by all the deities of prosperity and wealth that appear in the kahma and terma of the Nyingma school.

All the statues that were newly erected on all the floors have been thoroughly filled with precious objects, as well as the collection of prayers and mantras used for this purpose in the Mindroling tradition, including the five great *dharanis* and mantras bearing the names of each particular deity. At the heart center of the largest statues, precious and ancient statues of the five metals have been offered as wisdom beings. The life-trees of the statues have been brought from various holy places, and the four main kinds of most precious and rare relics have been attached to them. Relics the size of sesame seeds from buddhas and bodhisattvas have been used as mind relics for each statue. Yellow scrolls of rediscovered treasures and original Sanskrit and Pali scriptures have been used as speech relics, and all sorts of precious relics, such as hairs, bones, and cloth from great saints have been used as body relics. The bottoms of the statues were filled with medicinal plants, earth from various holy places, precious stones, various grains, and multicolored brocades. The consecration of the mantras and *dharanis* to be put in the statues was conducted over one hundred days; they were actually placed in the statues without any mistakes and in their proper order by *bhikshus* observing a pure discipline, following the procedure described by past learned and accomplished sages of the Nyingma school. All these statues have been covered with gold, some entirely, some partially on their faces and hands, some on their ornaments and dress. White conches spiraled to the right have been set between the eyebrows of the Buddhas of the three times.

For the consecration of all these sacred objects, as there is no distance in the compassion of the victorious ones, we requested Dudjom Rinpoche Jigdral Yeshe Dorje, the embodiment of Guru Rinpoche in this decadent age, to turn his wisdom mind toward this temple and let the blessings of his adamantine mind fall upon it. We also requested Trulshik Ngawang Chökyi Lodro Rinpoche, the yogi of the great compassionate Avalokiteshvara, protector of the beings of the Land of Snow, to perform an elaborate consecration ceremony during a drupchen focused on *Avalokiteshvara:*

Embodiment of All the Tathagatas, a rediscovered treasure of the great tertön from Mindroling. For the consecration itself Trulshik Rinpoche used the text known as *Providing Abundance.* As an auspicious conclusion for the consecrations, ceremonies related to the long-life practice revealed by Garwang Dorje to the dakini Sangwa Yeshe, and the protector Mahadeva, were also used, all according to the unmistaken Mindroling tradition. This consecration was completed in the second month of the fire-hare year, 1987.

Many other teachers from all schools came and blessed this place with their wisdom. I myself performed over three hundred consecration rituals, invoking the infinity of supreme deities, and recited one hundred thousand *Essence of Causation* mantras. A virtuous sangha abiding in pure discipline has also been installed in the monastery; the sangha endeavors in contemplation, reading the scriptures, and working for the community, thus perpetuating the three activities of upholding, preserving, and propagating the precious teachings.

Regular yearly, monthly, and daily ceremonies are held here, of which the major ones are the *United Assembly* drupchen combined with the preparation of sacred medicine that liberates upon taste, an elaborate *sadhana* that is like the foundation of the *Nyingma Kahma* and encompasses the nine vehicles of the *anuyoga* tantras; the great dance festival of the tenth day, performed in connection with the *Embodiment of the Master's Secrets;* and the three main performances related to the *Vinaya*—the Buddha and Dharma blended into one—which are the *posadha* confession, the summer retreat, and its conclusion. Every year a ten-day teaching on the king of all tantras, the *Guhyagarbha,* is given, as well as one month of transmission of empowerments and reading transmissions. We also make boundless prayers to the buddhas and bodhisattvas to grant their blessings that we may be able to perform the full array of activities as performed in Shechen Monastery in Kham in the near future, such as *sadhanas* and ceremonies of the kahma and terma, the monastic college, the retreat center, and so forth.

The monthly ceremonies include the feast offerings on the tenth and twenty-fifth days of the lunar month, devoted to the peaceful and wrathful aspects of Guru Rinpoche and to the dakinis; the offerings to Lord Buddha, the eight bodhisattvas, and the sixteen arhats on the eighth, fifteenth, and thirtieth days, as well as the offering ceremonies to the Medicine Buddha and the thousand buddhas of this fortunate aeon, and the offering ritual based on the *Spontaneous Fulfillment of All Aspirations* prayer. On the twenty-ninth an elaborate offering ceremony to the nine main Dharma protectors and other related protectors is performed according to the *Ocean of Accomplishment* ritual, requesting them to fulfill their pledge and accomplish their activities.

The daily ceremonies include morning and evening prayers according to the Mindroling tradition, starting with refuge, *bodhichitta*, the seven-branch offering, and the renewal of the two bodhisattva vows, followed by the reading of the *Guhyagarbha Tantra* and the *Magical Net of Vajrasattva,* one different chapter every day. Then there is the reading of *Chanting the Names of Manjushri,* the *Epitome Sutra,* and the *Prayer of Excellent Conduct,* which were spoken by the Buddha himself. Every day one chapter of the *Explanation of the Three Vows* by Ngari Panchen Pema Wangyal, as well as the daily *Vajrakilaya sadhana* and the condensed offering ritual to the dharmapalas according to the Mindroling tradition are recited. These daily practices are sealed with dedication prayers and prayers for the flourishing of the teachings. This schedule is just an indication of the various practices and Dharma activities performed within the monastery.

Considering the needs and benefits of amassing such a heap of merit for oneself and other benefactors, it says in the *Sutra of the Ten-Spoked Wheel of the Heart,* "For those who wander in samsara there is no better way than generosity; therefore, intelligent beings who desire perfection will give with great enthusiasm." The glorious Chandrakirti said, "All beings aspire to happiness; happiness comes from prosperity, and prosperity comes from generosity. That is why Shakyamuni taught generosity first." In the *Predictions Given in Answer to the Sublime Universal Monarch* it is said, "Giving material things one accumulates merit, giving the Dharma one accumulates wisdom; these two together lead to the omniscience of enlightenment."

The omniscient Dharma king Longchen Rabjam said, "Images of the *tathagatas* are man-made emanations, permeated with the buddhas' blessings; they are worthy of offerings, and no other material object can match them, so have faith in the buddhas' images." In the *Sutra of the Perfect Miraculous Display* it says, "Some benefit beings by happily undertaking the virtuous deeds of making sacred objects, building temples, and making beautiful gardens. Some benefit beings by happily undertaking the virtuous deeds of making images; some painted, some in gold, some in silver, and some in bronze." In the *Sublime Praise* it is said, "Whoever donates earth for erecting a celestial temple like Indra's mansion will generate as much merit as Brahma and will enjoy the higher realms for aeons." Also, in the chapter on the "Body of the *Tathagata*" it is said:

You should make images of the *tathagata* with earth, stone, sand, wood, pebbles, bronze, iron, gold, silver, lapis lazuli, crystal, and incense, and paint them on cloth, wood, or walls. You should repair images with cracks and perfect those that are broken. If you do, you will never fall into the lower realms, you will not take rebirth as an evildoer, as someone holding wrong views, or with impaired faculties. Even if you have committed the five inexpiable sins, you will not fall into hell, but even if you do fall, it will not be for long. As when someone covered with filth thoroughly washes and anoints his body with fragrant essences will be purified from his foulness, one can even be purified from the five inexpiable sins. If someone who indulged in the ten unvirtuous actions develops faith in the *tathagata* and makes images of him, his sins will melt away like butter in fire, without leaving any smoke.

In the *Sublime and Wondrous Sutra* it is said:

Ananda! Not only this southern continent of Jambudvipa; not only the eastern continent of Videha; not only the western continent of Aparagodaniya; not only the northern con-

tinent of Kurava; and not only the victorious pavilion of the
mighty Indra. Even if you noble sons and daughters turn
the whole billionfold universe into the shape of the seven
emblems of royalty and offer them to the stream-winners, the
once-returners, the never-returners, and the arhats, and to all
the *bhikshus* of the sangha of the four directions, it will not be
as meritorious as making a stupa the size of a *kyuru* fruit with
a life-tree the size of a needle, surmounted by a canopy the
size of a tree leaf, with a statue the size of a barley grain, and
filled with a relic the size of a sesame seed.

These words were spoken by Lord Buddha himself and are found
in various scriptures, clearly showing the needs and boundless
merits associated with such deeds. So, may all rejoice greatly!
The moonbeams of perfect dedication as done by the buddhas
and bodhisattvas strike the white ocean of these excellent deeds.
May we follow the waves of bodhisattva activity, perfectly shown by
Manjushri and Samantabhadra, crossing the ocean of teachings and
commentaries with the sail of the nine ways of consummate learning. May we successfully fetch the wish-fulfilling gem of the flawless state and offer it on top of the victory banner of intelligence.
With the nectar of ripening and liberating the profound meaning, the precious fruits of the four vidyadhara levels beautify in the
delightful grove of the true secret supreme doctrine. May all those
connected with it reach the vajra state! This short account of the
building of Shechen Tennyi Dargyeling in Nepal was written in the
first month of the fire-rabbit year, 1987, by Dilgo Khyentrul Tashi
Paljor, so that the faithful ones can rejoice. May virtue increase!

Since Khyentse Rinpoche wrote this, Shechen Rabjam built a monastic
college at Shechen Monastery, which has produced many new Loppöns and
khenpos who have completed the nine-year study program there.[1] He completed the building of a three-year retreat center in Namo Buddha as well,
where several three-year retreats have taken place so far. Shechen Rabjam also
built an art school which offers a six-year curriculum in thangka painting.

18. Return to Kham

PEWAR TULKU

Pewar Tulku is a Sakya lama who was a close student of Khyentse Chökyi Lodro.
He is presently the most important lama in Derge Gonchen.

I FIRST MET DILGO Khyentse when we received the *Treasury of Precious
Termas* from Khyentse Chökyi Lodro in Dzongsar. In the wood-bird year,
1945, when I was thirteen years old, Khyentse Chökyi Lodro gave the empowerments and transmissions to about a hundred students. At that time Dilgo
Khyentse was thirty-six years old. The main lamas receiving the teachings
were Shechen Rabjam, Dilgo Khyentse, Katok Situ, and some other supreme
tulkus.

Some of the elaborate empowerments had both the higher activity of
accomplishing enlightenment and the lower activity of liberating enemies
and obstructers, for which there were malign tormas to be thrown and subjugations. During the elaborate empowerments, Khyentse Chökyi Lodro had
Dilgo Khyentse, who was Khyentse Wangpo's tulku, wear a special black hat
that had belonged to Khyentse Wangpo—which normally wasn't shown to
anyone—and throw the tormas. The hat was decorated with dry skulls and
peacock feathers on top, and since the doors are not very high in Tibet and
Khyentse Rinpoche was especially tall wearing the hat with the feathers, he
had to bend way down to get in and out of the temple with the tormas.

Khyentse Chökyi Lodro personally gave the vase and empowerment substances to everyone around him. My seat in the empowerments was seven
seats down from Katok Situ, so I didn't think I would receive the substances;
I didn't dare to go up. But Chökyi Lodro Rinpoche gestured to me with the

vase, so I got up and from then on received all the empowerment substances from Chökyi Lodro himself.

First all the empowerments were given, and then there was a break. Shechen Rabjam's brother had passed away, so he had to leave after receiving the empowerments; he performed the thanksgiving feast offering according to Jamyang Khyentse Wangpo's profound treasure of the *Combined Sadhana of the Three Roots*. Next to Chökyi Lodro's throne they arranged a throne for Shechen Rabjam, who was the chant master; he had a very good voice and was able to play the cymbals for a long time. After that he left to take care of his brother's funeral. I was very devoted to Shechen Rabjam, and after he had played the cymbals, I took the sweat from his hands that had collected on the cymbals as a blessing.

The reading transmission for the *Treasury of Precious Termas* was given by Khyentse Chökyi Lodro himself. One day during the transmission there was a special celebration for the Abbot, the Master, and the Dharma King; it was a day that was especially for teaching, composition, and debate. The monastery arranged special thrones for Chökyi Lodro and Dilgo Khyentse, as well as vast offerings with the four banners and so forth. At that time Dilgo Khyentse composed a few pages starting with the words "In Sanskrit. . ." that he offered to Chökyi Lodro, who said it was authentic and praised him a lot. After that Chökyi Lodro gave a special reading transmission and then there was debating. After the *Treasury of Precious Termas* was completed, we did a *Mindroling Vajrasattva* drupchen. I remember clearly that Dilgo Khyentse's brother Shedrup, an elderly lama who was much older than Dilgo Khyentse and Sangye Nyenpa, was the disciplinarian for keeping the sessions.

When I was fourteen years old, Khyentse Chökyi Lodro gave the *Treasury of Spiritual Instructions*, which I also received; Dilgo Khyentse was there and so was Shechen Gyaltsap's reincarnation. At that time my seat was very far away. In 1954 Sakya Gongma of Puntsök Palace came to Dzongsar and we received the *Path and Result*, the *Compendium of Sadhanas*, the major *Hevajra* empowerment, and many other special Sakya teachings. Dilgo Khyentse was there too attending all the teachings; I stayed there a long time receiving teachings. Khyentse Chökyi Lodro was always giving empowerments; there was never a time when he wasn't giving anything. Khyentse Chökyi Lodro and Dilgo Khyentse used to take their meals together and were always talking a lot; I used to go serve them food and tea sometimes.

In 1985, after a thirty-year absence, Khyentse Rinpoche was finally able to come back to Tibet. There he visited Lhasa, Samye, Mindroling, Sakya, and Tsurphu in Central Tibet, as well as his own monastery, Shechen, and other places in Kham. He received an extraordinary welcome by all his disciples and old friends, as well as by all the local populations. The first time Khyentse Rinpoche returned to Kham in 1985, I went to welcome him in Dartsedo, and he was very pleased to see me. When I asked him to stay in my house in Derge, he said, "Sure, we are vajra brothers, right?" From Dartsedo he went to Derge Gonchen, and though it is not a very comfortable place, he and his entire entourage all stayed in my house for many days.

While he was staying with me, he told me that in the past he had asked Khyentse Chökyi Lodro to write an autobiography, but Chökyi Lodro said, "You are much younger than me, so you should write my biography." Dilgo Khyentse felt very uneasy about this, thinking Chökyi Lodro meant that he wouldn't live much longer. Later in Dzongsar, Chökyi Lodro gave him his autobiography, quite a long text, saying, "This is what you asked for," but Dilgo Khyentse remembered what Chökyi Lodro had said before and didn't dare to accept or read it.

When I got out of prison and the monasteries had more freedom, I had the fifteen small volumes of Khyentse Chökyi Lodro's *Collected Works*, including this autobiography, carved into woodblocks. During that time a lama sent me a small text of about ten pages of Chökyi Lodro's writings. When I looked at it, I found that it was something very special: Chökyi Lodro's secret autobiography in his authentic handwriting. I showed the text to Khenpo Kunga Wangchuk upon his release from prison. He returned it soon after, and I added it to the other autobiography. Dilgo Khyentse Rinpoche asked me, "Now you have it, right?" and I said, "Yes, I do."

While he was in Derge, Khyentse Rinpoche gave the *Combined Sadhana of the Three Roots* long-life empowerment in Derge Gonchen Monastery. Next he went to Dzongsar where he gave the *Ocean of Dharma That Embodies All Teachings* and some other empowerments. Then he went to Peyul Monastery where he gave Khyentse Wangpo's profound treasure of the complete *Luminous Heart Essence of the Three Roots* empowerments for a few days. From there he went to Shechen where we did a drupchen of the *Eight Commands: Union of the Sugatas*. It was such a wonderful time; at the end we did very elaborate auspicious prayers. Rinpoche also gave the protector empowerments of the *Heart Essence of the Great Expanse* to a few people. Then he went to Dzogchen Monastery, where he gave the *Gathering of the Vidyadharas,* the *Supreme Heruka Assembly,* and the *Great Bliss Queen* empowerments from the *Heart Essence of the Great Expanse.*

After that he went down to Mount Emei in China, where he stayed for a day and gave me a few empowerments. He gave reading transmissions to me alone whenever he had time. Shechen Rabjam and the young Dzongsar Khyentse went up the mountain on pilgrimage and asked me to come, but I stayed with Rinpoche, who continued giving me reading transmissions and said, "We didn't go up there, but we finished quite a bit of transmission, didn't we?"

From there Rinpoche went to Chengdu for a few days and then to Hong Kong, where I escorted him up to the airport and felt very sad that he was leaving. He said, "Don't be sad. We'll meet again!" Then he gave me the red blanket that he used to wear over his knees, which I put in Pewar Monastery's casket of prosperity.

At the request of several monasteries, Khyentse Rinpoche had wanted to visit Kham for a second time, and through the kind patronage of His Majesty the King of Bhutan and the welcome of the Chinese government, he was able to fulfill his wish in 1988. This second journey was particularly successful, as Khyentse Rinpoche could visit and stay at all the monasteries and sacred places he wished to go to, including three months in his native region of Derge.

On his way to Kham, Khyentse Rinpoche went to Beijing to meet the Panchen Lama for the first time. The Panchen Lama received Khyentse Rinpoche with great cordiality. After this Khyentse Rinpoche drove four days from the capital of Sichuan to Kham, through the beautiful scenery of snow peaks and nomad pastures. A few miles before reaching Shechen Monastery, five hundred horsemen, monks wearing white hats as a traditional sign of welcome, and laymen dressed in fur and brocades lined the road to welcome Rinpoche. After making a large circle around Khyentse Rinpoche's motorcade, they all galloped ahead to Shechen.

Khyentse Rinpoche's party of twelve comprised his wife Khandro Lhamo; his grandson Shechen Rabjam, who is the abbot of Shechen Monastery; Dzongsar Khyentse; Namkai Nyingpo; Tulku Pema Wangyal; Lama Urgyen Shenpen; Tulku Kunga; Major Kesang Dorje from the Royal Bhutan Army; and a few other attendants.

Khyentse Rinpoche spent forty-five days in Shechen itself, fulfilling the wishes of everyone by giving many empowerments and teachings, and performing various ceremonies. Many lamas, monks, and nuns flocked from all over Kham to meet him and receive his blessings, so that the plain in front of the monastery was soon covered with white tents and hundreds of grazing horses. A ten-day ceremony devoted to Padmasambhava culminated with two days of sacred dances depicting the great tertön Guru Chowang's vision of the Copper-Colored Mountain, Guru Rinpoche's pure land.

During their stay, Shechen Rabjam and a few others visited Khyentse Rinpoche's birthplace in Denkok by the Yangtze River, in the same valley and within eyesight of where the Sixteenth Karmapa was born. There one finds many caves where Khyentse Rinpoche spent most of his early years in retreat. In some of these caves he stayed a few months, in others up to six years. This was an especially moving visit, since just to mention Khyentse Rinpoche's name to the people of that region brings tears to their eyes, and they speak of him as if he had left the place just the day before—obviously he had remained the main figure in their minds and hearts throughout their thirty years of separation and hardship.

After Shechen, Khyentse Rinpoche went to Dzogchen Monastery, near the caves where Patrul Rinpoche and many other sages had lived and taught in the past. From there he reached Derge Gonchen, the ancient capital of Kham. On the way he passed Yilung Lhatso, the Divine Lake that Captivates the Mind. The lake received its name because it is located in such a beautiful area that a princess who once passed through was so charmed by the landscape that she did not feel like going any further and so settled right there. The lake is followed by a pass, at over fifteen thousand feet, through extraordinary rocky mountains and snow peaks.

While in Derge, Rinpoche again stayed in my house; he was extremely kind. I have a small Guru Rinpoche temple with many auspicious Lama Norlha treasure vases made according to the *Heart Practice Dispelling All Obstacles*. Khyentse Rinpoche stayed with me for nearly two weeks and kept blessing the vases. I was then fifty-six years old, so he blessed me and my wife with a ceremonial scarf and gave her the *Queen of Great Bliss* empowerment.

At Derge Gonchen, Khyentse Rinpoche gave the *Quintessential Kilaya of the Hearing Lineage* and a few other empowerments. He also reconsecrated the big printing press, the largest of its kind in the world, which shelters over seventy thousand old wooden blocks that were miraculously saved from destruction during the Cultural Revolution. The press is at work again, vibrant with activity as all day long hundreds of people print by hand the precious scriptures, the volumes of the *Kangyur* and the *Tengyur,* and countless other volumes that are now available to all. In the last few years nearly twenty thousand new blocks have been carved for the sixty-three volumes of the *Treasury of Precious Termas,* the collection of the spiritual treasures that were concealed by Guru Padmasambhava for the sake of future generations. One can appreciate the magnitude of this work when one knows that a skilled craftsman can only carve one block per day.

Following this came one of the highlights of Rinpoche's visit: the journey to Dzongsar. To reach there, Khyentse Rinpoche had to be carried for three days on a palanquin and cross two mountain passes nearly sixteen thousand feet high. The first one is called Goser La, which means White Hair Pass, because it is said that one starts down in the valley with black hair and reaches the top with white hair! All the people from the villages and nomad camps enthusiastically took turns carrying Khyentse Rinpoche, thirty people at a time, while a hundred horsemen and many pilgrims on foot accompanied the party.

The first evening, upon reaching a beautiful meadow in sight of Palpung Monastery, a double rainbow shone for nearly an hour over Palpung Monastery and Tsadra Rinchen Trak, the hermitage where Jamgön Kongtrül spent most of his life and revealed many termas. The second night was spent in beautiful tents, ornate with embroidered symbols, surrounded by a medieval-style caravan of Khampa horsemen. Finally on the third morning, Khyentse Rinpoche together with the present Dzongsar Khyentse and the rest of his party, reached Dzongsar Monastery, the seat of one of his two main root teachers, Dzongsar Khyentse Chökyi Lodro. This event fulfilled the dearest dream of everyone there—a dream that we hardly dared believe would actually come true.

At noon, the very moment the two Khyentse Rinpoches, accompanied by Shechen Rabjam and many other lamas, reached the foot of Dzongsar Monastery, awaited by thousands of people, a perfectly circular rainbow brightly haloed the sun, lasting until the party entered the temple itself. While Khyentse Rinpoche remained at Dzongsar giving teachings, the younger members of his party went for numerous pilgrimages in the neighboring mountains, visiting several of Guru Rinpoche's caves and other hermitages where great sages such as Jamyang Khyentse Wangpo, Jamgön Kongtrül, Chokgyur Lingpa, and Mipham had lived for many years. Khyentse Rinpoche then returned to Derge the same way, halting one night at Palpung, which is one of the rare monasteries that suffered little destruction during the Cultural Revolution. From there Khyentse Rinpoche went to Peyul Monastery, and other tulkus of his party visited Katok, the oldest Nyingma monastery besides Samye, and a monastery which was blessed by Guru Padmasambhava himself.

While in Kham, Khyentse Rinpoche established a retreat center and a monastic college at Shechen, and he made substantial offerings to over a hundred and thirty monasteries for their restoration and the running of their retreat and teaching centers. Everywhere he gave blessings, teachings, and advice, and people would sometimes walk for days or weeks just to be able to meet him for a few moments. He saved the lives of more than three thousand animals, mainly yaks and sheep, as nomads would come before him and take an oath to spare these animals from slaughter and set them free for the rest of their lives.

The return journey passed through the incredibly beautiful plateau of Dromta, comprised of vast meadows ending in immaculate snow peaks. Rinpoche's party reached Chengdu after a four-day drive through the valleys and mountains of Kandze, Tao, Menyak, and Dartsedo, the ancient border town between Tibet and China. In his hotel in Chengdu, Rinpoche was so kind as to give me the peaceful and wrathful *Magical Net* empowerments from the *Nyingma Kahma*.

When it came time for him to depart, everyone was moved to tears and supplicated him to return many more times. Then after giving his blessing to the great metropolis of Hong Kong, Khyentse Rinpoche returned to Bhutan, where he tirelessly continued his manifold activities for all sentient beings.

In 1990 Dilgo Khyentse Rinpoche visited Tibet for the last time. First he went to Samye Monastery to consecrate the newly renovated temple. While he was there, I flew from Chengdu to Lhasa and joined him at Samye. There Rinpoche gave most of the empowerments from the *Heart Essence of the Great Expanse*, such as *Avalokiteshvara, Hayagriva,* and so forth. Rinpoche was staying in the temple itself and did the consecration according to the *Mindroling Vajrasattva;* I myself acted as the chant master. Rinpoche's wife, Khandro Lhamo, said I was the only one who could be heard chanting.

After the consecration Rinpoche and his party went to Lhasa. As it was then known that Rinpoche was one of the Dalai Lama's teachers, the people in Lhasa had incredible devotion to him, and an enormous crowd came to his hotel to get his blessings. There was so much pushing while people tried to get into the hotel that the gate collapsed.

Rinpoche then went to Tsurphu, and when he returned to Lhasa, trying to keep his whereabouts a secret, the Chinese put him up in a different hotel; but people soon found out where he was and again an enormous crowd came to see him. He then came out and blessed everyone by throwing grains and doing prayers. Then he went to Reting where he did a consecration, during which I heard that nectar came down from all the statues.[1] I had stayed behind in Lhasa and wasn't there, but everyone told me this happened. His Dharma activity was inconceivable.

19. Death and Rebirth

SHECHEN RABJAM

IN 1991, Rinpoche's health was in decline, so divinations were requested from all the great masters. Most of them expressed worries and recommended large ceremonies to be performed. Sakya Gongma advised us to conduct a most profound practice for longevity, a drupchen of Jamyang Khyentse Wangpo's mind treasure on White Tara and Avalokiteshvara known as the *Heart Essence of the Immortal Arya,* and to offer a longevity ceremony at the end of the drupchen. Accordingly, most of the tulkus and Khyentse Rinpoche's close disciples gathered and performed the drupchen. About halfway through the ceremony, Rinpoche wrote the following letter:

To all the Tulku Rinpoches:

At the initiative of the supreme Shechen Rabjam, the *Heart Essence of the Immortal Arya* drupchen is being performed in grand style. This is a most auspicious and perfect connection. Jamyang Khyentse Wangpo used to say that White Tara was the most extraordinary deity for extending life; he himself had repeated visions of White Tara. It is said that the practice of the *Heart Essence of the Immortal Arya* dispelled the obstacles for the long life of Jamgön Kongtrül, the main Dharma heir of the mind treasure *Heart Essence of the Immortal Arya,* as well as for Chokling, Khenchen Tashi Özer, Karmapa Kakyap Dorje, Jamyang Loter Wangpo, and many other masters.

The second incarnation of Jamyang Khyentse, the Vajradhara Chökyi Lodro, also had his life extended through this practice and was blessed by the deity. At Dzongsar, Jamyang Khyentse Wangpo himself did the full recitation of 108 different long-life *sadhanas* and had all the signs of accomplishment. He said that through the auspicious connections thus created, one of the Khyentse reincarnations would have a very long life. I have lived up to the age of eighty-two. I am the old man who offered you the empowerment and transmission of the *Heart Essence of the Immortal Arya*. I also have done both the full and short recitation of this *sadhana* several times. Earlier, I did not have the opportunity to perform a drupchen based on it. Today, in front of the holy place of Taktsang, with masters and disciples having pure, undefiled samaya, during this fourth month, all the five perfections have been gathered.

I continually pray, and request all of you to pray likewise, that the Dalai Lama, Trulshik Rinpoche, Dzongsar Khyentse, and all the holy beings, especially the benefactors of the Buddhadharma, led by His Majesty the King of Bhutan and the royal family, the people of Tibet and the whole world, may enjoy longevity, prosperity, and all noble qualities; and that happiness may prevail everywhere; that diseases, famines, and wars may be pacified; and that, through practicing the Dharma, both one's own aspirations as well as those of others may be fulfilled.

Khyentse Rinpoche thus meant that he had stayed the full span of his life, up to the age of eighty-one.[1] Two days later, several monks saw a rainbow directly over Khyentse Rinpoche's tent.

When Khyentse Rinpoche was in the hospital, on the tenth day Nyoshul Khenpo offered 108 statues of Longchen Rabjam and requested Khyentse Rinpoche to live long. On that day a double rainbow encircled the sun and was witnessed by everyone in Thimphu. When Khyentse Rinpoche was ill in Paro Kyechu, a rainbow had also appeared at Shechen Monastery in Nepal, but it appeared in a passage between the main temple and the Guru Temple—a place that the sun cannot reach.

According to Dabzang Rinpoche, these signs meant that the dakinis had come to invite Khyentse Rinpoche to other buddhafields and that there was no way to postpone it. The same thing had happened to the Fifteenth Karmapa Kakyap Dorje, and although many longevity ceremonies were offered, there was no way to reverse these signs. According to Rinpoche's attendant

Pema Dargye, when no one was in the room, Khyentse Rinpoche would sometimes gaze straight up into the sky for a long time in an unusual way.

Dzongsar Khyentse, Namkai Nyingpo, Chokling, Dakpo Tulku, Datang Tulku, and I offered Khyentse Rinpoche the longevity ceremony. Since Rinpoche gave the symbols of body, speech, mind, qualities, and activity back to each of the tulkus and to Ashe Pem Pem's daughter Kesang, we all had tears in our eyes. He gazed at us for a while and then wrote on his slate board, "The signs of the long-life sadhana have appeared, I shall not die for three years." We felt overjoyed, but later we knew that he only wrote this to comfort us.

When Dzongsar Khyentse was taking leave, Rinpoche put his *gao* on Dzongsar Khyentse's head and prayed for half an hour, in a most unusual way.[2] Despite his vow of silence, he spoke a few words to the young lama and recited a long wishing prayer that went in part,

> The master and the disciple will never be separated;
> May your life be long and firm like the earth.
> May circumstances always be joyful and harmonious.
> May the auspiciousness of your joy and Dharma practice prevail.

The day before Namkai Nyingpo left, Khyentse Rinpoche gave him a book of advice written by a past teacher and had him read it a few times. A few hours later, Khyentse Rinpoche took some personal, intimate advice out of his red file of special writings and gave it to Namkai Nyingpo. The day Namkai Nyingpo was leaving, Khyentse Rinpoche gestured with his hand, signifying, "Soon you will cry," and Namkai Nyingpo could see that Khyentse Rinpoche felt unusually sad. Khyentse Rinpoche put his dagger on Namkai Nyingpo's head and again repeated the long wishing prayer. On his way out, Namkai Nyingpo told Dakpo Tulku, "I think that I am going to die this year, because Khyentse Rinpoche looked at me so sadly, and as he promised that he will stay for three more years nothing should happen to him."

When Khyentse Rinpoche was performing fire pujas at the site of his new house in Bhutan at Satsam Chorten, he insisted on spending one night in the building though it was still under construction. He said, "Even if I freeze, I want to spend one night in the house." At that time, Khyentse Rinpoche wrote me some personal advice, which said in part, "You have never done

anything against my wishes. Please continue in the same way; study and practice the best you can." He also went to the retreat center where, together with
other instructions, he told the retreatants, "Even if the teacher is not present
in his physical form, pray to the absolute teacher."

On his way to Kalimpong he spent two nights at the nunnery in Sisinang and told my attendant Tsering Tenpel, "You have been serving Rinpoche
well; continue to do the same. I will not forget you." That night, Khandro
had a dream in which Khyentse Rinpoche was preparing to depart to Kham.
Khandro asked him, "How long will you be away?" and Khyentse Rinpoche replied, "One year." Khandro requested, "Please come back within
six months." Khyentse Rinpoche smiled silently and went away. When she
awoke, Khandro felt very sad.

Although everyone insisted that Khyentse Rinpoche should go to Kalimpong and back by helicopter from Paro, Khyentse Rinpoche was adamant
that on his return from Kalimpong he wanted to go to Puntsoling, to see the
old servant who had been taking care of his house there for the past twenty
years. There, he looked through all his books and gave one to Chokling Rinpoche, telling him to practice and study hard. In Puntsoling he patted my
head affectionately and gave me some more personal advice.

After the earth-breaking ritual for the drupchen in Paro Kyechu, Khyentse
Rinpoche fell ill and told Pema Dargye, "Don't be sad, but I am going to
die this year." As Pema Dargye started to cry, Khyentse Rinpoche told him,
"Don't cry. Sing a song—there is no point in being sad," and Khyentse Rinpoche himself sang a spiritual song.

Dzongsar Khyentse then arrived with two Chinese friends who had
requested an empowerment the year before. Since Khyentse Rinpoche was not
feeling well, they went back to Thimphu. However, after Khyentse Rinpoche
had moved to his house, he told Tsewang Lhundrup to call them back, as he
wanted to give them the empowerment. Tsewang Lhundrup asked Khyentse
Rinpoche to postpone the empowerment until his health improved, but Rinpoche insisted on giving the empowerment that very evening.

On the fifteenth of the eighth month, corresponding to September, Khyentse
Rinpoche took a vase and a crystal, and gave himself the self-empowerment
on his forehead, throat, and heart. I felt very uneasy, since Khyentse Rinpoche had told me once that when great masters pass away, this is how they

request the deities who dwell in their body to take leave to their pure lands.

On the sixteenth Rinpoche asked his attendant Damchoe what the date was; then he wrote on a small piece of blue paper, "On the nineteenth I will surely pass away," and left the note on the table. Around midnight, Khyentse Rinpoche gave himself a longevity blessing, rinsed his mouth with water and told Chokling Rinpoche to drink it. Then he took a long-life pill and gave it to Chokling as well. Around two in the morning he asked for pen and paper, wrote a note with red ink, gazed at me, and then gave the note to me. I immediately woke Dzongsar Khyentse up, and we tried to read the note. We were able to surmise that the note was about how long he would live, but we could not read it clearly. We hoped that it said something good, but I had the feeling that it didn't. In the morning I told Loppön Nyabchi that many things indicated that there was something amiss with Khyentse Rinpoche, and I showed him the letter.

After I went to the drupchen, Khyentse Rinpoche again told Pema Dargye, "I shall die soon. Sit next to me." During the lunch break, Pema Dargye came to me and told me what Rinpoche had said. I immediately summoned Dzongsar Khyentse, and we had a meeting with him, Chokling, and Dakpo Tulku. I told them, "We must offer the longevity ceremony right now or request Khyentse Rinpoche to live longer." Since we did not know what the best thing to do was, we decided to fax Khyentse Rinpoche's note to Trulshik Rinpoche, explaining the situation and requesting him to come the next day.

Meanwhile, in Switzerland, Namkai Nyingpo was feeling very sad and seeing bad signs in his dreams, such as all of his teeth falling out. He called Jigmey Khyentse in France, who told him that he had been having very bad dreams too. A few minutes before Namkai Nyingpo called, Dzigar Kongtrül had called Jigmey Khyentse from the United States, saying that he had been having sad dreams about Khyentse Rinpoche. Tulku Pema Wangyal also had a dream in which Khyentse Rinpoche gave him all his seals and a beautiful protection mandala, but he too had a terribly sad feeling. Dudjom Rinpoche's wife Sangyum Kusho had a dream of a huge mountain with a big monastery on its top being completely destroyed by a thunderbolt, and was told in the dream that nothing could be done.[3] She then told her intimates that this seemed to indicate that a great Nyingma lama would soon pass away.

The Dalai Lama told me that while he was giving the elaborate *Avalokiteshvara* empowerment in the Dordogne on the twenty-fourth of August, he had bad signs while making the sand mandala. Similar signs had occurred in Ladakh before one of his main teachers passed away, so the Dalai Lama felt very uneasy.

In April, Trulshik Rinpoche had dreamed that he was at Shechen Monastery in Nepal and saw Khyentse Rinpoche walking naked out through the door. Trulshik Rinpoche tried to follow him but was unable to get up from his seat. He called through the window, saying, "Rinpoche, please don't leave us. I want to come with you," but Khyentse Rinpoche could not hear him and left. Trulshik Rinpoche mentioned this dream to Khyentse Rinpoche before coming to Bhutan, but Rinpoche merely teased him in response, "Don't have such strange thoughts. It's nothing but a dream. Everyone knows that I always go around naked." After that Trulshik Rinpoche offered an elaborate longevity ceremony. That day I felt exceedingly sad and cried for a long time.

Apo Rinpoche's daughter received a letter from Khyentse Rinpoche with a lot of advice. He had closed the letter with, "We will meet again in the Copper-Colored Mountain pure land." She knew then that she would not meet Khyentse Rinpoche again in this life. Many other disciples of Khyentse Rinpoche all over the world had bad dreams, such as not being able to meet him or Rinpoche passing away in the hospital.

On the seventeenth, Trulshik Rinpoche arrived. In the morning, Khyentse Rinpoche asked us to bring his chair and put brocade on it; he sat on it for a few moments.

On the eighteenth, when His Majesty the King of Bhutan and Khyentse Rinpoche were together, Trulshik Rinpoche arrived and asked, "Do you recognize me?" Khyentse Rinpoche replied, "Of course I recognize that shining head." While Trulshik Rinpoche looked at Khyentse Rinpoche's face, Khyentse Rinpoche said, "Shouldn't I die now?" Trulshik Rinpoche immediately requested him to remain in this world.

On the nineteenth around one in the morning, Khyentse Rinpoche's condition worsened. In the morning he asked for a pearl rosary and told Tsewang Lhundrup to do the petition to the Dharma protectors, which is usually not done in the morning. Khyentse Rinpoche had once told me that, before passing away, some lamas request the Dharma protectors to continue their activities.

Before Khyentse Rinpoche left for the hospital, we all offered another longevity ceremony, at which the King of Bhutan was also present. All the tulkus and attendants confessed the faults they might have committed while serving Khyentse Rinpoche and pledged to recite a hundred thousand recitations of the Vajrasattva mantra. Khyentse Rinpoche then left for the hospital, where he passed away.

After Khyentse Rinpoche passed away, his close students turned to his most senior and accomplished disciple, Trulshik Rinpoche, to find his next incarnation. Trulshik Rinpoche had been having dreams and visions that clearly indicated the identity of the incarnation. One morning before dawn, he dreamed that twenty-five golden stupas were moving around in the Shechen Monastery courtyard in Bodhnath. Trulshik Rinpoche had only one ceremonial scarf and wanted to offer it to the main stupa but didn't know which one that was. It clearly occurred to him that these stupas contained the relics of Khyentse Rinpoche. As he was wondering which one was the main stupa, one of them stopped in front of him. A wonderful bird of an unknown species flew out of the window of the upper part of the stupa and began singing. Trulshik Rinpoche came closer and offered a white ceremonial scarf in front of the bird. All twenty-five stupas then lined up behind the first one, as if in a procession, and entered Chökyi Nyima Rinpoche's monastery Ka-Nying Shedrup Ling.

In another dream, which was more like a vision—Trulshik Rinpoche humbly said, "It was a dream, but I wasn't sleeping,"—Khyentse Rinpoche appeared to him and sang a poem revealing the year of the child's birth, the names of his parents, and the place where he could be found. Trulshik Rinpoche did not want to give too much importance to this vision, but instead of vanishing, the vision became increasingly clear and present in his mind. He kept its details secret until April 1995, when he sent me a letter.

The search was brief. Decoded, the poem had revealed that the father was his close spiritual friend Tulku Urgyen's son Tsikey Chokling Migyur Dewai Dorje and the mother was Dechen Paldron. Their son, born on Guru Padmasambhava's birthday, the tenth day of the fifth month of the bird year, June 30, 1993, was, as the verse stated, "unmistakably the incarnation of Paljor," which was one of Khyentse Rinpoche's names. The Dalai Lama later confirmed that this child was indeed Khyentse Rinpoche's reincarnation. "I have full conviction," he said, "that this young child is the true reincarnation of Dilgo Khyentse."

On December 29, 1996, a simple ceremony was held in the Maratika cave.

The Dalai Lama and the Dilgo Khyentse Yangsi in Dharamsala.
Photograph by Matthieu Ricard.

For those gathered there, some of whom had walked for days from Kathmandu or Bhutan, the sun had risen from within their hearts into the world at large. Thus the prayer that the Dalai Lama had written only days after Khyentse Rinpoche had left this world was fulfilled:

> The more helpless beings are,
> The more it is your true nature to love them;
> Therefore, to ripen and liberate all beings in this Dark Age,
> Swiftly reveal the moon-like face of your emanation!

In December 1997, the formal enthronement of the young Dilgo Khyentse Yangsi was held at Shechen monastery in Nepal. It attracted over fifteen thousand people from forty nationalities and more than a hundred eminent lamas representing all the schools of Tibetan Buddhism. Since then, the young incarnation has been studying at Shechen in Nepal and in Bhutan, and, like a flower that reveals its beauty as it blossoms, is gradually developing qualities that make one hope that he will be able to work vastly for the benefit of beings just like his predecessor.

Oral Instruction by Dilgo Khyentse

While mind is watching mind,
Though there is nothing to see, it is vividly clear;
Uncontrived, free, and at ease in that state,
Rest naturally, simply undistracted.

Whatever thought occurs from that state,
Without stopping or analyzing, watch its very nature.
Its arising doesn't obscure the absolute nature;
Whatever occurs, relax right there.

Don't follow thoughts about the past,
Don't anticipate thoughts about the future,
Directly transcend the external world;
That is called the "four parts without three."

If you maintain this recognition of thoughts,
You will feel that they do not truly begin, remain, or end.
Though you notice them, they have no effect on your true nature;
That is the bare natural state, the way it is.

If you take that empty awareness, open and carefree, as the path,
All the time, during formal practice and afterward,
You will quickly and surely acquire a confident realization
That confusion is freed by itself.

It is very helpful to mingle your mind
Inseparably with your teacher's;
By settling in equipoise within that state, developing faith and
    devotion,
You will meet the natural face of *dharmakaya.*

Especially guard the continuity of impermanence, renunciation,
And pure discipline, like your own eyes;
Never diminish your one-pointed diligence in the heart of the matter,
The essential yoga of the profound meaning.

Alternating study, reflection, and meditation,
The one will help the others;
Ultimately that is what you need to resolve,
So practice the essential meaning with tenacity.

May this delightful, sacred offering cloud
Of essential pith instructions
Cause you to gain realization
Of the definitive secret that is like space.

MANGALAM.

Dilgo Khyentse during the eighties, in India.
Photograph by Matthieu Ricard.

Notes

Foreword by Dzongsar Khyentse Rinpoche

1. The Manjushri statue that Dilgo Khyentse received during his first visit back in Kham was Lama Mipham's personal practice support.

Chapter One

1. Statements and realization, Tib. *lung rtogs;* respectively, the authoritative scriptures and the realization, through the three trainings of discipline, samadhi, and wisdom, of the precious Buddhist teachings in the minds of noble beings.

2. The ten principles of a vajra master are (1) having received the Secret Mantra empowerments and properly keeping the samayas; (2) being very peaceful and teaching ground, path, and result; (3) having studied the tantras and understood their meaning; (4) having completed the recitation practices; (5) having perfected their outer, inner, and secret signs; (6) having liberated one's being through the wisdom of realizing egolessness; (7) exclusively benefiting others through infinite activities; (8) having given up the eight worldly concerns and only being concerned with the Dharma; (9) having strong revulsion to the sufferings of existence and encouraging others to just that; (10) possessing the blessings of an authentic lineage of masters.

3. Manjushri Chökyi Lodro, one of the five reincarnations of Jamyang Khyentse Wangpo. He resided at Dzongsar Monastery, and his other names are Pema Yeshe Dorje and Dharmamati, the Sanskrit for "Chökyi Lodro."

4. "Ocean of Qualities," one of the names of the First Kongtrül, Lodro Thaye Yonten Gyatso.

5. From *The Collected Works of Jamgön Kongtrül Lodro Thaye.* The four wheels are (1) staying in a suitable place, (2) relying on spiritual friends, (3) having a high aspiration, and (4) the support of merit from previous lives.

6. Greater Tibet, Tib. *bod chen po;* consists of the three provinces of Ngari (Tib. *mnga' ris skor gsum*), the four districts of U and Tsang, (Tib. *dbus gtsang ru bzhi*), and the six ranges of Dokham (Tib. *smad mdo khams sgang drug*).

7. Tib. *smad khams* or *mdo khams;* Amdo and Kham, which comprise Eastern Tibet.

8. The winter goddess, Tib. *dgun gyi rgyal mo;* Hemantadevi, the goddess of winter.

9. Denma, Tib. *ldan ma;* literally, "endowed with something."

10. Pema Gyalpo, Tib. *gu ru pad ma rgyal po;* the Lotus King Guru, one of the eight main aspects of Guru Padmasambhava.

11. Myo, Tib. *smyos;* literally, "crazy."

12. *The Wish-Fulfilling Tree,* Tib. *dpag bsam 'khri shing;* the name of a text written by the Indian master Kshemendra, which depicts one hundred former lives of the Buddha Shakyamuni.

13. Pagsam, Tib. *dpag bsam;* meaning "wish-fulfilling."

14. *Upasaka* vows of formal refuge, Tib. *skyabs gsum 'dzin pa'i dge bsnyen;* a layperson who takes

formal refuge in the Three Jewels. Karmapa Kakyab Dorje; Kunzang Kakyab Dorje, the Fifteenth Karmapa (1871–1922).

15. Mipham Manushri; Ju Mipham Rinpoche (1846–1912), an outstanding Nyingma scholar
who was born in Dzachukha. He is usually called Mipham Rinpoche or Lama Mipham, and
his monastery was a branch of Shechen Monastery.

16. Onpo Tenga; the popular name of Gyalsey Shenpen Thaye's nephew Urgyen Tenzin Norbu
from Gemang Monastery. Shechen Gyaltsap Gyurmey Pema Namgyal was Dilgo Khyentse's
root teacher who introduced him to the nature of mind; he is also referred to as Pema Vijaya,
his Sanskrit name.

17. At the landmark of the supine tortoise with Lama Mipham's cabin at its center like an ornament in its heart, with a nearby juniper tree that Lama Mipham calls a Bodhi tree, at the head
of the turtle, who is facing west, is a hill that looks like fire (because of its reddish rocky tex-
ture); on its right is a hill that looks like wood (because it's covered with trees); on its left
is a hill that looks like iron (because of its iron-colored rocky surface); and at its tail is a hill
that looks like water (because it's surrounded by small streams).

18. OM A RA PA TSA NA DHI, Manjushri's mantra.

19. Palden Lhamo, Tib. *dpal ldan lha mo*, Skt. *Shri Devi*. A female wisdom protector. The three
ingredients used in the infant mineral-medicine are elephant bile, saffron, and bamboo
juice.

20. Khenpo Shenga (1871–1927); Khenpo Shenphen Chökyi Nangwa, Dilgo Khyentse's main
philosophy teacher, who was widely known under the name Khenpo Shenga.

21. Adzom Drukpa (1842–1924); an author and well-known, highly realized student of Khyentse Wangpo.

22. *Dzo*, Tib. *mdzo*; a cross between a yak bull and a cow. A *dri* is a female yak.

23. Sangye Nyenpa Karma Shedrup Tenpai Nyima, the full name of Dilgo Khyentse's older
brother, who was one of the main lamas of Benchen, a Kagyu monastery in Gawa, Eastern
Tibet.

24. Tib. *lam 'bras; Lamdrey*, the esoteric instructions of the Indian master Virupa within the
Sakya tradition.

25. Terma, Tib. *gter ma;* literally, "treasure." The term refers to concealed treasures of many different kinds, including texts, ritual objects, relics, and natural objects. The transmission of
the teachings through such concealed treasures, hidden mainly by Guru Rinpoche and Yeshe
Tsogyal to be discovered at the proper time by a treasure revealer for the benefit of future
disciples, is one of the two chief traditions of the Nyingma school. (The other one is the
Kahma.) It is said that this tradition will continue even long after the *Vinaya* of the Buddha
has disappeared.

26. Drugu Tokden Shakya Shri; one of the greatest yogis of the Drukpa Kagyu lineage and a disciple of the Sixth Khamtrul Rinpoche Tenpai Nyima.

27. Drupchen, Tib. *sgrub chen;* an intensive group sadhana performed over a period of seven to
ten days during which the mantra recitation is continually chanted around the clock.

28. Rabjam Rinpoche; Shechen Rabjam, the abbot of Shechen Monastery. His fifth incarnation,
Dechen Gyalpo, had just passed away, and the Sixth Rabjam incarnation that was installed
at the monastic seat, Kunzang Tenpai Nyima, was the second out of Dechen Gyalpo's three
reincarnations. The present Rabjam Rinpoche is the seventh and is called Karma Gyurmey
Chökyi Senge.

29. Shechen Kongtrül (1901–1960), also called Shechen Kongtrül Pema Drimey; one of the
main lamas at Shechen Monastery, whose full name was Shechen Kongtrül Gyurmey Kunzang Lodro Shenpen Thaye.

30. Tib. *wa le wa, hri ge wa, sa le wa;* respectively, different terms for describing vividness in
meditation.

31. The nickname he used for Khenpo Yonga.

32. The six bardos, Tib. *bar do drug;* the six intermediate states are the bardo of the place of birth (Tib. *skye gnas kyi bar do*), the bardo of dream (Tib. *rmi lam gyi bar do*), the bardo of meditation (Tib. *bsam gtan gyi bar do*), the bardo of the moment of death (Tib. *chi kha'i bar do*), the bardo of *dharmata* (Tib. *chos nyid kyi bar do*), and the bardo of becoming (Tib. *srid pa'i bar do*). Awareness-expression empowerment, Tib. *rig pa'i rtsal dbang;* the empowerment for introducing the nature of mind.

33. Ritual dagger, Tib. *phur pa;* a metal three-sided dagger used in rites of subjugation of hostile forces and associated with tantric teachings on Vajrakilaya.

34. Puntsök Palace and Drolma Palace are two families that alternate in heading the Sakya school. The present Sakya Trizin is from Drolma Palace.

35. Tib. *dgu gtor;* the name of the torma-throwing ritual done before Tibetan New Year on the twenty-ninth day of the twelfth month. Tormas are offering cakes ceremonially presented to deities or spiritual beings for diverse purposes connected with rites of service and attainment.

36. The three doctrinal centers, Tib. *chos 'khor rnams gsum;* Samye, the first monastery built in Tibet; the Lhasa Jokhang; and Tradruk.

37. The Great Prayer Festival, Tib. *smon lam chen mo;* an annual prayer festival in Lhasa performed in the first month.

38. Tib. *zhabs drung;* a main lama below the head lama.

CHAPTER TWO

1. *Yadar,* Tib. *g.yab dar;* a black silk scarf used in tantric rituals.

2. Tib. *phud kong;* an offering vessel for the first portion of a drink or food, mainly used for offerings to the protectors.

3. Tib. *sngon 'gro;* the preliminaries. The general outer preliminaries are the four mind changings: reflections on the precious human body, impermanence and death, the cause and effect of karma, and the shortcomings of samsaric existence. The special inner preliminaries are the four times one hundred thousand accumulations of the practices of refuge and *bodhichitta,* Vajrasattva recitation, mandala offering, and guru yoga. See Jamgön Kongtrül, *Torch of Certainty* (Boston: Shambhala Publications, 1977) and Patrul Rinpoche, *The Words of My Perfect Teacher* (Boston: Shambhala Publications, 1994).

4. I.e., Jamyang Khyentse Wangpo and Jamgön Kongtrül.

5. The four visions of *togal,* Tib. *snang ba bzhi;* four stages in Dzogchen practice: manifest *dharmata,* increased experience, awareness reaching fullness, and exhaustion of concepts and phenomena.

6. Tib. *bla bslu;* rites to ransom the *la,* or life energy.

7. Tib. *dge bsnyen gyi sdom pa;* precepts for a Buddhist layperson, bound by the five vows to avoid killing, stealing, lying, sexual misconduct, and intoxicating liquor.

8. Omniscient father and son; Longchen Rabjam and Jigmey Lingpa.

9. *Nyingma Kahma,* Tib. *snga 'gyur bka' ma;* the body of teachings translated chiefly during the period of Guru Rinpoche's stay in Tibet and transmitted from master to student until the present day. They were collected by Minling Terchen Terdak Lingpa and expanded by Dudjom Rinpoche, and presently consist of fifty-six volumes.

10. Nyitrak; a treasure revealer also called Rigzin Nyima Trakpa (1647–1710).

11. Kushab Gemang; Gyalse Shenphen Thaye's tulku.

12. *Sharawa,* Tib. *sha-ra-ba;* a mythical wild animal that is an emanation of a bodhisattva. It can appear in different forms, such as a unicorn or an eight-legged lion with wings, and so forth.

13. Tib. *bum chu;* the blessed water from the vase that has been used in the *sadhana* practice.

14. *The Way of the Bodhisattva,* Tib. *spyod 'jug,* San. *bodhicharyavatara;* a fundamental text on

the conduct of bodhisattvas by the great Indian scholar Shantideva (eighth century). It consists of ten chapters introducing (1) the beneficial attributes of enlightened mind, (2) repentance for sins, (3) seizing the enlightened mind, (4) vigilance with respect to enlightened mind, (5) the guarding of awareness, (6) the transcendental perfection of patience, (7) the transcendental perfection of perseverance, (8) the transcendental perfection of concentration, (9) the transcendental perfection of discriminative awareness, and (10) the dedication of merit. See Padmakara Translation Group, *The Way of the Bodhisattva*, by Shantideva (Boston: Shambhala Publications, 1997).

15. Novice ordination, Tib. *dge tshul gyi sdom pa;* the fourth month is named "Saga Dawa," and is considered a special month for practice as the Buddha's birth, enlightenment, and *paranirvana* all fall in this month.

16. Gyanak Mani; the largest field of Mani stones in the whole of Tibet, just outside Jeykundo. The stones are inscribed with entire sections from scriptures or are carved in relief with meditation deities. The original temple on this site was constructed by Gyanak Tulku in the 13th century.

17. Tib. *rgya gar shar li;* a special alloy from East India made of several metals.

18. Tib. *gcod;* literally "cutting." A system of practices based on the *Prajnaparamita* and set down by the Indian siddha Padampa Sangye and the Tibetan female teacher Machik Labdron, for the purpose of cutting through the four *maras* and ego-clinging. It is one of the eight practice lineages of Buddhism in Tibet.

19. Metsek, Tib. *sme brtsegs;* a wrathful deity.

20. *Supreme Heruka Assembly,* Tib. *dpal chen 'dus pa;* the main *yidam* deity of the *Heart Essence of the Great Expanse.*

21. Tib. *sems bskyed;* the enlightened mind, the aspiration to practice in order to free all beings and lead them to perfect enlightenment.

22. Tib. *kun gzhi'i rnam shes,* Skt. *alayavijnana;* literally, "all-ground consciousness," one of the eight collections of cognitions; consciousness as ground of all ordinary experience.

23. Brahmin Rahula started out making heaps of black pebbles for his negative actions and white pebbles for his virtuous actions. At first he had mostly large heaps of black pebbles, but slowly the white-pebble heap became the larger one.

24. Lords of the three families, Tib. *rigs gsum mgon po;* the three bodhisattvas Avalokiteshvara, Manjushri, and Vajrapani.

25. Lotus hat, Tib. *pad zha;* the type of hat worn by Padmasambhava.

26. Tib. *rgyud lugs phur pa;* a Vajrakilaya practice by Mipham Rinpoche.

27. Khon tradition, Tib. *'khon.* The Khon tradition started with Khon Konchok Gyalpo building Sakya Monastery, which was also the beginning of the Sakya school.

28. Changma Hermitage, Tib. *lcang ma ri khrod;* the hermitage of Khenpo Thupten.

29. Vase, mantra thread, and vajra, Tib. *bum pa gzungs thag rdo rje;* the little vajra connected to the vase by five-colored thread and used in the vase consecration.

30. Tib. *gso sbyong;* a ritual for monks and nuns to mend and purify broken vows.

31. Tib. *shel brag;* a famous Guru Rinpoche cave in the Yarlung Valley of Central Tibet, where the *Crystal Cave Chronicles* of Padmasambhava were revealed by Urgyen Lingpa.

32. Tib. *'dul ba;* discipline, one of the three parts of the *Tripitaka,* containing the Buddha's teachings on ethics, the discipline and moral conduct that is the foundation for all Dharma practice, both for lay and ordained people.

33. These are the different attributes a fully ordained monk must keep with him.

34. The *Eight Sadhana Teachings,* Tib. *bka' brgyad bde 'dus;* a terma in nine or thirteen volumes revealed by Nyang Ral Nyima Özer with teachings on the eight chief *yidam* deities of *mahayoga* and their corresponding tantras and *sadhanas:* Manjushri Body, Lotus Speech, Vishuddha Mind, Nectar Quality, Kilaya Activity, Liberating Sorcery of Mother Deities, Maledictory Fierce Mantra, and Mundane Worship.

CHAPTER THREE

1. Tib. *bka' gter*; respectively, the teachings transmitted orally and those revealed as treasures.

2. The three Jamgöns; the two Jamgöns (Jamyang Khyentse Wangpo and Jamgön Kongtrül) plus Mipham Rinpoche.

3. Shechen Gyaltsap Rinpoche's hermitage had a self-arisen image of Chakrasamvara in the rock, whence its name.

4. Langlab Changchub Dorje; a thirteenth-century siddha of Vajrakilaya.

5. Tib. *phur pa yang gsang spu gri*; a *Vajrakilaya* treasure revealed by Guru Chowang Chökyi Wangchuk, usually known as Guru Chowang (1212–1270), one of the five terton kings.

6. Tib. *phur pa bzhi*; (1) the dagger of primordially pure awareness (Tib. *rig pa ka dag gi phur pa*), (2) the dagger suspended by the rope of all-pervasive compassion (Tib. *khyab pa thugs rje'i dpyang thag gi phur pa*), (3) the great bliss *bodhichitta*-drop dagger (Tib. *byang sems thig le bde ba chen po'i phur pa*), and (4) the compounded substantial dagger (Tib. *'dus byas rdzas kyi phur pa*).

7. Namely, Vajrasattva and Vajrakilaya.

8. Shechen Kongtrül was the other main lama at Shechen Monastery.

9. The two *Dongtruk* empowerments, Tib. *dong sprugs gnyis*; the two empowerments for the *Narak Dongtruk*, "overturning the deepest hell," cycle of teachings from the *Nyingma Kahma*. So tradition, Tib. *so lugs*; the tradition of So Yeshe Wangchuk, one of Padmasambhava's twenty-five disciples. The *United Assembly* empowerment, Tib. *tshogs chen 'dus pa theg pa rim pa dgu'i dbang*; the major *anuyoga* empowerment of the kahma.

10. The teachings of the Great Perfection are divided into three sections, called "the three classes of the Great Perfection." The first of these is the mind class (Tib. *sems sde*). According to the mind class, all perceived phenomena are none other than the play of the nature of mind, the inexpressible, self-existing wisdom. The mind class of instructions is meant for individuals who are concerned with the workings of mind. Having recognized that all phenomena are the indescribable *dharmakaya*, the self-existing wisdom, one rests in the continuum of the empty awareness, in which there is nothing to illuminate, nothing to reject, and nothing to add. The enlightened mind is like infinite space, its potential for manifestation is like a mirror, and the limitless illusory phenomena are like reflections in the mirror. Since everything arises as the play of the enlightened mind, one does not need to obstruct the arising of thoughts, but simply remains in the natural condition of mind-as-such. The second section of the three classes is the space class (Tib. *klong sde*). According to the space class, self-existing wisdom and all phenomena emerging from its continuum never stray from the expanse of Samantabhadri: they have always been pure and liberated. The space class is meant for individuals whose minds are like the sky. Having recognized that all phenomena never leave the expanse of Samantabhadri and are primordially pure and free, one abides in the continuum of the ultimate nature, without aim, effort, or searching. There is no need to use antidotes: being empty, thoughts and perceptions vanish by themselves. Phenomena are like stars naturally arrayed as ornaments in the firmament of the absolute nature: one need not consider, unlike in the mind class, that they arise as the play of awareness. Everything is the infinite expanse of primordial liberation. According to the third, the instruction class, in the true nature of samsara and nirvana there are no obscurations to be gotten rid of and no enlightenment to be attained. Having recognized that mind-as-such is primordially pure emptiness, one practices trekcho, leaving mind and all phenomena in their natural state of pristine liberation. Then, having discovered the naturally present mandala of one's body, one practices togal and sees the very face of the naturally present luminosity, the pristine wisdom that dwells within. Without leaning either toward the cognizant aspect of the mind class or the empty aspect of the space class, one simply rests in the confident realization of primordial purity, which is inexpressible, beyond intellect, and of which phenomena are the natural radiance.

11. The *Wishing Vase*, Tib. *'dod 'jo'i bum bzang;* Terdak Lingpa's compilation of the root treasures from the *Treasury of Precious Termas*. The *Treasury of Precious Termas* was compiled by Kongtrül Lodro Thaye, based on the root treasures of Terdak Lingpa's *Wishing Vase*. (Kongtrül was long after Terdak Lingpa.) So the *Wishing Vase* is the basis for the *Treasury*.

12. The three higher empowerments; the secret empowerment (Tib. *gsang dbang*); the wisdom empowerment (Tib. *sher dbang*); and the word empowerment (Tib. *tshig dbang*). The *Profound Unsurpassable Meaning of the Great Perfection*, Tib. *rdzogs chen a ti zab don snying po;* a treasure revealed by Terdak Lingpa.

13. The bodhisattva vows are passed down within two lineages: the Vast Activity tradition (Tib. *rgya chen spyod brgyud*), the lineage first passed from Maitreya to Asanga; and the Profound Middle Way tradition (Tib. *zab mo dbu ma'i lugs*), the lineage stemming from Nagarjuna.

14. When giving empowerments, vajra masters often wear a specific hat.

15. Tibetan Dharma texts of a particular cycle are ordered according to the letters of the Tibetan alphabet.

16. Marici Goddess, Tib. *lha mo 'od zer can ma;* a consort of Hayagriva. Kurukulle, Tib. *ku ru ku le;* a female deity considered a form of Tara, whose particular function is magnetizing, whence her red color. *Arapatsa* divination; a popular divination text based on Manjushri's mantra written by Mipham Rinpoche. Mahottara, Tib. *che mchog;* Chemchok Heruka is the central figure of the *Eight Sadhana Teachings*. He is usually identical with Nectar Quality, the chief heruka of the *ratna* family. Sometimes, in the case of *Assemblage of Sugatas*, Chemchok Heruka is the heruka who embodies all the buddha families.

17. *Auspicious Offering Ceremony*, Tib. *bkra shis mchod chog;* a long offering liturgy written by Shechen Gyaltsap.

18. A *sadhana* for Dorje Trolo (Tib. *rdo rje gro lod*), one of the eight manifestations of Guru Padmasambhava, in which he is in wrathful form and rides a tigress.

19. *Seven-Point Mind Training*, Tib. *blo sbyong don bdun ma;* by Atisha.

20. Tib. *sku gsung thugs rten;* objects symbolic of enlightened body, speech, and mind—for example, statues, scriptures, and stupas, respectively—and that are given along with a mandala offering at special occasions.

21. The five sciences: philosophy, language, logic, medicine, and the arts.

22. Jamgön Chöjung; Situ Chökyi Jungney, the teacher of the Fourth Khamtrul Rinpoche Chökyi Nyima (1699–1774). The Mirror of Poetry, Tib. *snyan ngag me long*, is a text written by the seventh-century Indian brahmin master Dandi. It consists of three chapters, of which Dilgo Khyentse mainly studied and taught the middle and most important chapter.

23. Shedrung Pandita; Shechen Ontrul Thutop Namgyal, a very learned tulku who was the secretary at Shechen Monastery.

24. Perfect wheel, Tib. *kun bzang 'khor lo;* a metrical acrostic.

25. The upper lineage of *Vinaya*, Tib. *stod 'dul;* the lineage introduced to Tibet by the Kashmiri *pandita* Shakya Shri. The lower lineage was introduced by the abbot Shantarakshita.

26. This type of ring (Tib. *gri lcags*) is made from a knife with which someone has committed a murder. Wearing a ring made from the metal of such a knife is said to be a strong protection.

27. Monks are not supposed to wear rings, but Gyaltsap Rinpoche usually wore this ring as a protection.

28. Tib. *rin chen gter mdzod;* a collection of the most important revealed termas of Padmasambhava, Vimalamitra, Vairotsana, and their closest disciples, gathered by Jamgön Kongtrül Lodro Thaye with the help of Jamyang Khyentse Wangpo. It was published in sixty-three volumes by Dilgo Khyentse Rinpoche, in New Delhi, India, with the addition of several more volumes of termas and commentaries. It is one of the Five Treasuries of Jamgön Kongtrül.

29. *Treasury of Spiritual Instructions*, Tib. *gdams ngag mdod;* a collection of thirteen volumes

containing teachings of the Eight Practice Lineages, compiled by Jamgön Kongtrül Lodro Thaye. It is one of the Five Treasuries.

30. Eight great chariots of the practice lineage, Tib. *sgrub brgyud shing rta brgyad;* the eight independent schools of Buddhism that flourished in Tibet: Nyingma, Kadam, Marpa Kagyu, Shangpa Kagyu, Sakya, Jordruk, Nyendrub, and Shije and Cho.

31. *Parting from the Four Attachments,* Tib. *zhen pa bzhi bral;* four oral instructions of the Sakya school on freedom from attachment, which are given in an elaborate, medium, and abridged way. *Three Classes of the Great Perfection,* Tib. *rdzogs chen sde gsum;* a treasure revealed by Chokgyur Lingpa, known as the *Dzogchen Desum,* which contains all the three classes of Dzogchen.

32. Kshetrapala, Tib. *rgyal skyong;* a yaksha in the retinue of Six-Armed Mahakala. Yakshas are a class of semi-divine beings who are usually benevolent but sometimes harmful. Some of them are local deities and some live on Mount Meru, guarding the celestial realms. The two Jamgön Chöktruls; here referring to Khyentse Chökyi Lodro and Shechen Kongtrül.

33. The Lord of Secrets; an epithet for Vajrapani here referring to Jamgön Kongtrül.

34. The eight close sons (Tib. *nye ba'i sras brgyad*) the eight main bodhisattvas: Kshitigarbha, Akashagarbha, Avalokiteshvara, Vajrapani, Maitreya, Sarvanirvarana Viskambin, Samantabhadra, and Manjushri.

35. Skt. *nalanda;* the famous monastic university built at the birthplace of Shariputra some distance north of Bodh Gaya in Bihar. Nalanda had a long and illustrious history, and many of the greatest masters of the Mahayana lived, studied, and taught there. It was destroyed around 1200.

36. The unopened flower refers to a qualified consort, meaning that later on he should get married.

37. *Liberation with a Golden Key* (Tib. *byad grol*); a ritual to avert the harmful influence of curses.

CHAPTER FOUR

1. *Gateway to Knowledge* (Tib. *mkas-'jug*); a condensation of the *Tripitaka,* the Buddhist canonical scriptures, by Mipham Rinpoche (Hong Kong: Rangjung Yeshe Publications, 1997).

2. Small hand drum, Tib. *da ma ru;* a small hand drum used during rituals and *sadhanas,* often made of two skulls.

3. Lord Pandita; referring to Ngari Panchen Pema Wangyal.

4. Yanglesho, Tib. *yang le shod;* the sacred cave of Padmasambhava in the southern part of the Kathmandu Valley, where he is said to have practiced Vajrakilaya and Vishuddha.

5. Tib. *sgrub thabs kun btus;* a collection of *sadhanas* compiled and edited by Jamyang Khyentse Wangpo and Jamyang Loter Wangpo.

6. Dotsey, Tib. *rdo tshad;* a monetary unit.

7. *Peaceful and Wrathful Deities,* Tib. *zhi khro;* the hundred peaceful and wrathful deities. The forty-two peaceful buddhas are comprised of Samantabhadra and Samantabhadri, the five male and five female buddhas, the eight male and eight female bodhisattvas, the six *munis,* and the four male and four female gatekeepers. The fifty-eight wrathful buddhas include the five male and five female herukas, the eight *yoginis,* the eight *tramen* goddesses, the four female gatekeepers, and the twenty-eight *ishvaris.*

8. Patrul Rinpoche used to live like a mendicant. He didn't own anything and whatever was offered to him he gave away for the sake of the Dharma. Having a title was the last thing he would want, and Khenpo Thupten also lived according to those principles.

9. Self and front mandalas, Tib. *bdag mdun;* in certain *sadhanas* one visualizes oneself as the deity within the mandala and also visualizes a similar mandala with deities in front. The three beings, Tib. *sems dpa' sum brtsegs;* the samaya being, wisdom being, and samadhi being.

When doing deity practice, oneself is visualized as the samaya being; the wisdom being is the deity in the samaya being's heart center that is similar to it but with one face and two arms; and the samadhi being is the seed syllable within the wisdom being's heart center. Four aspects of approach and accomplishment, Tib. *bsnyen sgrub yan lag bzhi;* the four aspects of approach and accomplishment of the deity within the recitation of a *sadhana,* which are approach, full approach, accomplishment, and full accomplishment. Approach is like the analogy of befriending a powerful person; full approach is to mingle yourself and the deity indivisibly; accomplishment is to gain mastery over wisdom; and great accomplishment is to employ this mastery over all-encompassing activities for the welfare of others.

10. The four axioms, Tib. *gtan tshigs chen po bzhi;* the four syllogisms of *Madhyamaka:* (1) The vajra fragments (Tib. *rdo rje zegs ma*), (2) the production and cessation of the four limits (Tib. *mu bzhi skye 'gog*), (3) the supreme relativity (Tib. *rten 'brel chen po*), and (4) the singular and the multiple (Tib. *gcig dang du bral*).

11. Tib. *dam tshig;* the sacred pledges, precepts, or commitments of Vajrayana practice. Samayas essentially consist of outwardly maintaining a harmonious relationship with the vajra master and one's Dharma friends and inwardly not straying from the continuity of the practice.

12. *Shaken from Its Depth,* Tib. *zhi khro na rak dong sprugs;* a peaceful and wrathful deities *sadhana* from the kahma tradition to overturn the deepest hell.

13. Zur, Mey, and On; the three teachers Zurpoche Shakya Jungney, Zurchung Sherab Deshek Gyawo, and Drophukpa Shakya Senge, who were Nyingma Secret Mantra masters.

14. The eight auspicious symbols, Tib. *bkra shis rtags brgyad;* (1) the umbrella, (2) the paired golden fish, (3) the treasure vase, (4) the lotus, (5) the white conch shell coiling to the right, (6) the endless knot, (7) the banner of victory, and (8) the wheel of doctrine.

15. Tib. *bka' brgyud;* the lineage of teachings brought to Tibet by Marpa, and originally received from the *dharmakaya* Buddha Vajradhara by the Indian siddhas Tilopa, Saraha, and others. Transmitted by Naropa and Maitripa to the Tibetan translator Marpa, the lineage was passed on to Milarepa, Gampopa, Pagmodrupa, the Karmapa, and others. The main emphasis is on the path of means, which is the six doctrines of Naropa, and the path of liberation, which are the Mahamudra instructions of Maitripa.

16. *Balmo,* Tib. *dbal mo;* a class of female deities.

CHAPTER FIVE

1. Vijaya; the Sanskrit equivalent of Shechen Gyaltsap's name, which sometimes appears in Dilgo Khyentse's songs.

2. Tib. *rnam thar sgo gsum;* literally, "the three approaches to liberation." In this case it refers to the three Dharma robes.

3. The twelve Dzogchen masters, Tib. *rdzogs chen ston pa bcu gnyis;* (1) Kyeu Nangwa Dampa, (2) Kyeu Od Mitrugpa, (3) Jigpa Kyob, (4) Shonnu Namrol, (5) Dorje Chang, (6) Shonnu Pawo, (7) Drangsong Trospai Gyalpo, (8) Ser Od Dampa, (9) Tsewai Lodro, (10) Osung Drepo, (11) Ngondzok Gyalpo, and (12) Shakyamuni.

4. *The Two Chariots,* Tib. *shing rta gnyis;* the *Chariot of the Two Truths* (Tib. *gden gnyis shing rta*) and the *Chariot of Omniscience* (Tib. *rnam mkhyen shing rta*), both by Jigmey Lingpa.

5. The four mind changings, Tib. *blo ldog rnam bzhi;* four ways to turn one's mind toward the Dharma by reflecting on (1) how rare it is to obtain a precious human body endowed with the eight freedoms and ten advantages, (2) death and impermanence, (3) the law of cause and effect, and (4) the sufferings of samsara. For more detailed information, see *The Words of My Perfect Teacher.*

6. Tib. *spyod lam bzhi shong;* in other words, big enough for the four daily activities of standing, moving about, lying down, and sitting.

7. Tib. *rtsam pa;* roasted barley flour, which is the Tibetan staple food.

8. Milarepa (1040–1123); one of the most famous yogis and poets in Tibetan history. A lot of the Kagyu teachings passed through him, and his life story is published as Garma C. C. Chang, *Hundred Thousand Songs of Milarepa* (Boston: Shambhala Publications, 1962) and Lobsang P. Lhalungpa, *The Life of Milarepa* (New York: Penguin Books, 1992).

9. Palri, Tib. *dpal gyi ri*; refers to Palri Thekchokling, Patrul Rinpoche's hermitage.

10. Samye Chimphu, Tib. *bsam yas mchims phu*; the hermitage above Samye in Central Tibet where Guru Padmasambhava taught his twenty-five disciples.

11. I.e., the cause of being reborn in hell realms where beings drink melted copper.

12. Tib. *gtum mo*; one of the six doctrines of Naropa, a practice to develop the mystic inner heat through training the channels and energies.

13. Tib. *dbyings rig pa sgron drug*; the lights in *togal* practice. *Dzogchen* has two main sections: *trekcho*, "cutting through"; and *togal*, "direct crossing." The former emphasizes primordial purity, and the latter, spontaneous presence.

14. Tib. *cog bzhag bzhi*; the four ways of resting the awareness in the Dzogchen practice of *trekcho*.

15. Yama, Tib. *'chi bdag*, Skt. *yama*; the Lord of Death.

16. Dudjom; Jigdral Yeshe Dorje (1904–87), the reincarnation of the great treasure revealer Dudjom Lingpa, and a great modern-day master and tertön of the Nyingma lineage, who was a highly accomplished writer and poet.

17. Pure-vision treasure, Tib. *dag snang*. This particular pure vision was of five herukas riding various animals: Jamyang Khyentse Wangpo on a tortoise, Shenphen Thaye on an elephant, Zhalu Losal Tenjong on a lion, Jamgön Lodro Thaye on a dragon, and Chokling Tertön on a tiger, in five colors, appearing in the sky. Khyentse Wangpo received the seven types of transmission (Tib. *bka' babs bdun*): (1) oral tradition, or kahma (Tib. *bka' ma*), the *Tripitaka* and tantras of the Nyingma school passed on unbroken from master to disciple; (2) earth treasures (Tib. *sa gter*) revealed by the tertön; (3) rediscovered treasures (Tib. *yang gter*) revealed for the second time from a past treasure; (4) mind treasures (Tib. *dgongs gter*) revealed from the mind of the guru (or tertön); (5) hearing lineage (Tib. *snyan brgyud*) received directly from an enlightened being; (6) pure visions (Tib. *dag snang*) received in a pure experience; and (7) recollections (Tib. *rjes dran*) remembered from a former life.

18. Tib. *kye rdor mngon rtogs*; a development-stage teaching of the Hevajra *sadhana* practice.

19. During Jigmey Lingpa's time, when the *Nyingtik Tsalung*, the practice of the channels and energies according to the *Heart Essence of the Great Expanse*, flourished and was widespread, Tibet was filled with cotton-clad yogis practicing it. When the *Nyingtik Tsalung* practitioners declined and weakened, the only lineage holder left was Patrul Rinpoche.

20. Rogza Palge was Patrul Rinpoche's teacher for the yogic practices of channels and energies, and he in turn had received them from Dodup Jigmey Thinley Özer.

21. *Sutra, Illusion, and Mind*, Tib. *mdo sgyu sems gsum*; referring to three scriptures: (1) The *Do Gongpa Dupa*, the *Scripture of Embodiment of Realization* (Tib. *mdo dgongs pa 'dus pa*), the main scripture of *anuyoga*, consisting of seventy-five chapters; (2) The *Magical Net* (Tib. *rgyud sgyu 'phrul drva ba*, Skt. *mayajvala*) or the *Guhyagarbha Tantra*, which is the main *mahayoga* tantra; and (3) The *Eighteen Major Scriptures of the Mind Class* (Tib. *sems sde bco brgyad*), a set of Dzogchen tantras taught by the Indian master Shri Singha to Vairotsana and Tsang Lekdrub, which were brought to Tibet by Vairotsana and Vimalamitra. The eighteen consist of the five early translations and the thirteen later translations, of which the first five were translated by Vairotsana before his exile to Tsawarong and the remaining thirteen were later translated by Vimalamitra and Yudra Nyingpo. These are the main Nyingma Secret Mantra tantras and scriptures of the development and completion stages and the Great Perfection.

22. Yeshe Tsogyal; King Trisong Detsen's queen, who became the main consort of Padmasam-

bhava. She was the chief compiler of all the inconceivable teachings given by Padmasambhava. Her biography is available in English as Gyalwa Changchub and Namkhai Nyingpo, *Lady of the Lotus-Born: The Life and Enlightenment of Yeshe Tsogyal,* translated by the Padmakara Translation Group (Boston: Shambhala Publications, 2002).

23. Naga Jasuki, Tib. *klu nor rgyas;* one of the eight major nagas. Nagas are powerful, long-lived serpent-like beings who inhabit bodies of water and often guard great treasures. They belong half to the animal realm and half to the god realm and generally live in the form of snakes, but many can change into human form.

24. Tib. *zhi gnas,* Skt. *shamatha;* the meditative practice of calming the mind in order to rest free from the disturbance of thought.

25. *Chakrasamvara of the Hearing Lineage,* Tib. *bde mchog mkha' 'gro snyan brgyud;* an *anuttarayoga* tantra and one of the main *yidams* of the New schools.

26. Dangtok Rinpoche; a high-ranking Sakya lama who was one of Dilgo Khyentse's teachers.

27. Sakya Gongma; the title of the head of the Sakya school.

28. Gyalsey Gyurmey Dorje; the son of Adzom Drukpa who lived at Adzom Gar, Adzom Drukpa's encampment. His present incarnation was born in Bhutan and is one of the main tulkus at Shechen Tennyi Dargyeling in Nepal.

Chapter Six

1. The small Manjushri statue that was Mipham Rinpoche's practice support was inside the heart of a big Manjushri statue in Shechen Monastery. This small statue was said to have had actually spoken, and later when Dilgo Khyentse returned to Kham, it was offered to him. Dilgo Khyentse used to wear it around his neck in a golden reliquary, and now it is in the heart of the stupa containing his remains in Shechen Monastery, Nepal.

2. When important lamas come to visit, it is the custom to welcome them by horse from three distances: near the monastery, a bit further away, and quite a ways from the monastery.

3. Thread-cross ceremony, Tib. *mdos;* a tantric ritual involving structures of sticks with colored yarn and used to appease mundane spirits. Yudrön, Tib. *g.yu sgron;* Dorje Yudronma, a Dharma protectress.

4. Yellow scrolls (Tib. *shog gser*) or yellow parchments are small leaves on which earth treasures or their inventories are concealed. There are five types, symbolizing the five enlightened families. These treasures can only be decoded by the tertön who has a connection to that treasure.

5. *Vajra Club of the Lord of Secrets,* Tib. *gsang bdag rdo rje be con;* a form of Vajrapani and a practice to get rid of obstacles for samadhi, which is a treasure of Chokgyur Lingpa. This is one of the four deities that clears obstacles: (1) Tara (Tib. *rje btsun sgrol ma*), (2) Achala (Tib. *mi g.yo ba*), (3) Vajrapani (Tib. *gsang bdag rdo rje be con*), and (4) Bhurkumkuta (Tib. *smre ba brtsegs pa*).

6. Tib. *sngags pa,* Skt. *mantrika;* a Secret Mantra practitioner who relies on a consort.

7. Thangla, Tib. *gnyan chen thang lha;* Nyenchen Tanglha, an important protector of the Nyingma teachings, regarded as a bodhisattva on the eighth level. It is also the name of a mountain range.

8. Lion-Faced One, Tib. *seng gdong ma,* Skt. *singhamukha;* a wrathful *dakini* with a lion's head.

9. The four main schools in Tibet are the Geluk, Kagyu, Sakya, and Nyingma.

10. Achala, Tib. *mi g.yo ba;* literally, "the unshakable," a dark-blue wrathful deity for getting rid of obstacles to the practice of the channels and energies.

11. Ladro Norbu Tulku; known by his full name, Karma Gyurmey Tsultrim Damchoe Wangpo.

12. *Bernakchen, Avalokiteshvara, and Vajravarahi,* Tib. *nag rgyal phag;* Bernakchen (Tib. *ber nag can*) is the central Mahakala of the Karma Kagyu; Gyalwa Gyatso, "Ocean of Victorious

Ones," (Tib. *rgyal ba rgya mtsho*), is a form of Avalokiteshvara; and Vajravarahi (Tib. *phag mo*) is an important female dakini.

13. Tib. *rta mgrin dregs pa kun grol;* the chief figure in the mandala of Mundane Worship (Tib. *'jig rten mchod bstod*) among the Eight Commands (Tib. *bka' brgyad*).

14. Nenang Pawo Rinpoche (1912–1991); a Kagyu lama from Central Tibet who was one of Dilgo Khyentse's teachers and students. Later he started a center in the Dordogne in France. He was recognized by the Fifteenth Karmapa and became one of the teachers of the Sixteenth Karmapa, but returned to Nepal, where he started a new monastery in 1986 in Bodhnath, Nenang Puntsök Choling.

CHAPTER SEVEN

1. Buton (1290–1364); a fourteenth-century Tibetan scholar and historian who was an early compiler of the Buddhist canon. *Six-Union Kalachakra,* Tib. *dus 'khor sbyor drug,* Dukhor Jordruk; the Jordruk is one of the eight great chariots of the practice lineage, embodying the pith instructions for the practice of Kalachakra. *Naro Kechari,* Tib. *na ro mkha' spyod ma;* a form of Vajrayogini handed down through Naropa, which is much practiced in the Sakya tradition.

2. Tib. *dud sol ma;* Lhamo Dusolma, a Dharma protectress.

3. Roaring Lion Guru, Tib. *gu ru seng ge sgra grogs;* Guru Senge Dradrok, one of Padmasambhava's eight manifestations.

4. Dorje Kyungtsunma, Tib. *rdo rje khyung btsun ma;* one of the twelve *tenma* goddesses. She resides on Jomo Kharak, a mountain range in Tsang. Together with the five sisters of long life, she is the special protector of the *Heart Practice Dispelling All Obstacles* terma cycle, rediscovered by the great Tertön Chokgyur Dechen Lingpa (1829–70). The five sisters of long life are said to reside on Jomo Gangkar, a five-peaked snow mountain on the border of Tibet and Nepal.

5. Guru Drakpo, Tib. *gu ru drag po;* literally, "Wrathful Guru." The heart sadhana from the *Northern Treasures* cycle revealed by Rigzin Gödem.

6. *Heart Essence of the Self-Born Lotus,* Tib. *rang byung pad ma'i snying thig;* a mind treasure of Dilgo Khyentse.

7. *Avalokiteshvara Resting in the Nature of Mind,* Tib. *thugs chen sems nyid ngal gso;* a practice of Avalokiteshvara in a different form than usual, seated in the bodhisattva posture.

8. Tib. *ye shes sems dpa',* Skt. *jnanasattva;* the real deity abiding in *dharmadhatu* or the pristine-awareness aspect of a deity. Within the development-stage practice the wisdom being of a deity is usually visualized at the heart center of the main deity. In this case, the wisdom being at the heart-center of the main image is symbolized by an undergarment of Padmasambhava with an image of the guru painted on it with Yeshe Tsogyal's blood. See also chapter 4, note 9.

9. Drimey Lingpa (1700–1776), a treasure revealer also known as Tekchen Lingpa.

10. *Dorje Tsampa,* Tib. *rdorje mtshams pa;* one of the three liturgies recited during a drupchen, an intensive group sadhana. In the evening, the leader of the *Dorje Tsampa* does the black-hat dance.

11. Rongzom; referring to Rongzom Pandita Chökyi Zangpo (1012–88). Together with Longchenpa, he is regarded as a Nyingma scholar of preeminent brilliance. The medicine buddhas, Tib. *sman bla rnam bdun;* the Medicine Buddha and his entourage of seven medicine buddhas. White Umbrella, Tib. *gdugs dkar,* Skt. *sitatapatra;* a manifestation of the Buddha, who protects against all kinds of obstacles. Vajra Subjugator, Tib. *rnam 'joms,* Skt. *vajravidarana;* a wrathful deity for subjugation. Lekden, Tib. *dam can rdo rje legs ldan;* one of the main Nyingma protectors. Scripture and tantra, Tib. *mdo rgyud;* in this context, "scripture" refers to the *United Assembly* root empowerment of the nine vehicles (Tib. *mdo tshogs chen*

'dus pa) and "tantra" to *mahayoga*. Vaisravana, Tib. *rnam sras;* the god of wealth and the king of mountain deities who guards the northern quarters.

12. *The Bindu of Liberation, the Spontaneous Liberation of the Mind,* Tib. *grol thig dgongs pa rang grol;* a treasure revealed by Tertön Sherab Özer (1517–1584). *Abhirati Vajrasattva,* Tib. *rdor sems mngon dga';* a *Vajrasattva* practice from the Mindroling tradition. Abhirati is the buddhafield of Akshobya, and its name means "the realm of true joy."

13. *Eliminating Inauspiciousness,* Tib. *rten 'brel nyes sel;* a terma by Lerab Lingpa, also known as Tertön Sogyal (1856–1926), the previous Sogyal Rinpoche.

14. Great Sage, Tib. *drang srong chen po;* another name for the Dharma protector Rahula.

15. *Embodiment of the Master's Secrets,* Tib. *bla ma gsang 'dus;* a terma discovered by Guru Chowang (1212–70), who was one of the earliest and most important tertöns.

16. Khyentse Wangpo kept his treasure texts extremely secret but showed them to Khyentse Chökyi Lodro's father while giving the *Ocean of Dharma That Embodies All Teachings* empowerment.

17. Minling Terchen's brother was Minling Lochen Dharmashri (1654–1718).

18. The reincarnation of Karma Kuchen from Peyul Monastery, whose full name was Urgyen Dongnak Chökyi Nyima.

19. *Heart Essence of the Great Siddha,* Tib. *grub thob thugs thig;* the chief mind treasure of Jamyang Khyentse Wangpo, focused on the teachings of the Mahasiddha Thangtong Gyalpo. Katok Situ Pandita, also known as Katok Situ Chökyi Gyatso (1880–1925), the main lama in Katok Monastery.

20. *Tantra of the Assemblage of Peaceful Sugatas,* Tib. *bde 'dus zhi rgyud;* part of the *Eight Commands: Union of the Sugatas.*

21. A unified stream in that Khyentse Chökyi Lodro received it both from his father and from Katok Situ Rinpoche, so it was a unified lineage.

22. *The Fifth Dalai Lama's Sealed Visions,* Tib. *rgyal dbang lnga pa'i dag snang rgya can;* a terma by the Fifth Dalai Lama. *Embodiment of Realization of the Three Roots,* Tib. *rtsa gsum dgongs 'dus.*

23. *Life-Force of Ekajati,* Tib. *bka' srung sngags srung ma;* an empowerment for the Dharma protectress Ekajati. Tersey Pema Wangchuk; Tertön Drimey Lingpa's son. Kadampa Deshek (1122–92); the Nyingma master who founded Katok monastery in 1159.

24. This Chokling Rinpoche is Neten Chokling, the father of Orgyen Topgyal, Khyentse Yeshe, and Dzigar Kongtrül Rinpoches.

25. The *zor;* a ritual cake and ritual procedure, which is used for dealing with obstacles, blockages, and enemies.

26. Salga; an abbreviation of "Rabsel Dawa," one of Dilgo Khyentse's names. He was mostly called Tulku Salga, especially in the presence of Khyentse Chökyi Lodro, who out of respect was the only one called Rinpoche.

27. It is considered to be a breach of a sacred bond to lie to one's root guru, hence Dilgo Khyentse's fear when his joke reached Khyentse Chökyi Lodro's ears.

28. Nyang; Nyang Ral Nyima Özer (1124–92), the first of the five tertön kings and a reincarnation of King Trisong Detsen. Several of his revealed treasures are included in the *Treasury of Precious Termas,* among which the most well-known is the *Eight Commands: Union of the Sugatas*—a cycle of teachings focusing on the *Eight Sadhana Teachings*—and the biography of Guru Rinpoche called *Zanglingma,* now published in translation: Yeshe Tsogyal, *The Lotus-Born* (Boston: Shambhala Publications, 1993). See also chapter 2, note 34.

29. Sometimes one of the lunar months of the Tibetan calendar occurs twice in a year, and when that was the case, Jamyang Khyentse would do this ceremony during either of the earlier or later seventh months.

30. Tib. *zhal gdams lam rim ye shes snying po;* a most precious, concise, and profound teaching by Guru Padmasambhava, which condenses the entire path. Praised by Jamyang Khyentse

Wangpo as being more valuable than thirty yak-loads of scriptures, it comprises, together with a commentary by Jamgön Kongtrül, the last volume in both the *Treasury of Precious Termas* and the *New Treasures of Chokgyur Lingpa*. See Jamgön Kongtrül, *The Light of Wisdom*, vol. 1 (Boston: Shambhala Publications, 1986).

31. *Secret Essence of Vajrasattva*, Tib. *gsang thig rdor sems;* one of the cycles of the *Three Cycles of the Secret Essence,* which are termas by Chokgyur Lingpa and Jamgön Kongtrül. *New Treasures of Chokgyur Lingpa,* Tib. *mchog gling gter gsar;* the collection of termas revealed by Chokgyur Lingpa together with Jamyang Khyentse Wangpo and Jamgön Kongtrül.

32. Asanga; a great Indian master of philosophy who was a direct disciple of Maitreya.

33. The four great kings, Tib. *rgyal chen bzhi;* Dhritarashtra in the east, Virudhaka in the south, Virupaksha in the west, and Vaishravana in the north.

34. Sakya Pandita (1182–1251); one of the five Sakya forefathers and the grandson of Sachen Kunga Nyingpo. He was a 13th-century Tibetan master and scholar who exercised political power on behalf of the Mongols.

35. *Dzikshim*, Tib. *dzhi-kshim;* a precious material made of different types of metal. Relic box, Tib. *rten sgam;* a box containing relics and attributes of various lamas such as hair, bones, clothing, and so on.

36. Meaning that in order to extend his life, he might also have to take a consort, just like Dilgo Khyentse had.

37. Raksha Thotreng, Tib. *rak sha thod phreng;* one of twelve manifestations of Guru Rinpoche.

38. *Profound Sevenfold Kilaya*, Tib. *zab bdun phur ba;* one of the major *Vajrakilaya* termas revealed by Chokgyur Lingpa, the sacred dances of which are performed yearly at Rumtek Monastery in Sikkim and at Benchen Monastery in Nepal. The higher and lower rites; the higher rite of accomplishing enlightenment (Tib. *stod las byang chub sgrub pa*) and the lower rite of liberating enemies and obstructers (Tib. *smad las dgra bgegs bsgral ba*).

39. Taranatha; known by his full name Taranatha Kunga Nyingpo (1575–1635); he was the most eminent master of the Jonang tradition. *Tokden*, Tib. *rtogs ldan;* a realized person, the title of someone who has realization in Vajrayana practice. It can also refer to a yogi-monk in the Drukpa Kagyu lineage.

40. *Magical Display of the Peaceful and Wrathful Ones*, Tib. *sgyu 'phrul zhi khro;* the *mahayoga* style of the mandala of the hundred peaceful and wrathful deities. Instruction class, Tib. *man ngag gi sde;* the third of the three classes of Dzogchen arranged by Manjushrimitra and emphasizing special key points. According to the instruction class, in the true nature of samsara and nirvana there are no obscurations to be gotten rid of and no enlightenment to be acquired. To realize this allows an instant arising of the self-existing wisdom beyond intellect. In the class of pith instructions, having recognized that mind-as-such is primordially pure emptiness, one practices *trekcho,* leaving mind and all phenomena in their natural state of pristine liberation. Then, having discovered the naturally present mandala of one's body, one practices *togal* and sees the very face of the naturally present luminosity, the pristine wisdom that dwells within. Without leaning either toward the "cognizant" aspect of the mind class or the "empty" aspect of the space class, one simply rests in the confident realization of primordial purity, which is inexpressible, beyond intellect, and of which phenomena are the natural radiance.

41. *All-Embodying One*, Tib. *kun rigs rnam par snang mdzad;* a form of Vairochana, one of the buddhas from the five buddha families.

42. The combined *Heart Sadhanas;* the heart practices of *Spontaneous Fulfillment of Wishes* and *Clearing the Obstacles of the Path* combined.

43. Vajra Garuda Fortress; the meditation center above Zurmang. The Trungpa Tulku mentioned here is the Eleventh Trungpa Rinpoche, Chögyam Trungpa (1939–1987), who later moved to the West and founded the worldwide community now called Shambhala International.

44. Black Lady of Wrath, Tib. *khros ma nag mo;* Tröma Nagmo, a wrathful black form of the female Buddha Vajrayogini, according to a treasure revealed by Nyang Ral Nyima Özer.

45. *Pema's Heart Essence of Longevity,* Tib. *pad ma tshe yi snying thig;* a long-life practice revealed by Dilgo Khyentse, of which he had a vision while on pilgrimage at the glacier Dothi Gangkar. It is one of his main treasures.

46. Tersey Tulku; known by his full name Tersey Chöktrul Gyurmey Tsewang Tenpel, the reincarnation of Chokgyur Lingpa's son Wangchok Dorje. For more on Tersey Tulku see Tulku Urgyen Rinpoche, *Blazing Splendor* (Hong Kong: Rangjung Yeshe Publications, 2005) chap. 12.

47. *Profound Sevenfold Magical Display of Purified Metal,* Tib. *zab bdun sgyu 'phrul lcags byang ma;* a terma of the 108 peaceful and wrathful deities by Chokgyur Lingpa.

48. For more details about this see *Blazing Splendor* (Rangjung Yeshe Publications, 2005), pp. 281–84.

49. Tsewang Norbu; one of Chokling Tertön's sons, who was an incarnation of Yudra Nyingpo, the main disciple of the great translator Vairotsana.

50. Tib. *sku gsum rigs 'dus zab thig;* a terma of Chokgyur Lingpa.

51. Choje Lingpa (1682–1725); a tertön also known as Urgyen Rogje Lingpa. *Mahasiddha's Longevity Practice,* Tib. *grub thob tshe sgrub;* the long-life practice for the Mahasiddha Thangtong Gyalpo (1361–1485), a Tibetan siddha.

52. *Wish-Fulfilling Guru,* Tib. *gu ru yid bzhin nor bu;* a form of Padmasambhava in which he does not hold a vajra or have the trident in the crook of his arm, but his hands are in the meditation mudra, holding the *kapala* and vase of immortality. This form is also known as Guru Dewa Chenpo. *Heart Practice of the Wish-Fulfilling Essence Manual of Oral Instruction,* Tib. *thugs sgrub yid bzhin nor bu'i zhal gdams snying byang;* the basic and major text among the collection of treasures belonging to the *Heart Practice Dispelling All Obstacles.*

53. *Hidden Meaning of Path and Result,* Tib. *sbas don lam 'bras;* a commentary on the *Path and Result.*

54. Oral instructions, Tib. *slob bshad;* the secret explanation of the *Path and Result* for close disciples, emphasizing the oral instructions for meditation. General instructions, Tib. *tshogs bshad;* the explanation of *Path and Result* for the general assembly.

55. Pema Lingpa (1445–1521); was a mind emanation of the great translator Vairotsana.

56. *Profound Quintessence,* Tib. *zab mo yang thig;* part of Longchen Rabjam's *Four Parts of the Heart Essence.*

57. Lakar; the home of Khyentse Chökyi Lodrö's consort Tsering Chödrön and her sister Tselu, who is the mother of the present Sogyal Rinpoche.

58. Often for a given terma there will be several different treasure finders, each one finding a different part or section. This is the notion of "share" here.

59. *Embodiment of the Master's Realization,* Tib. *bla ma dgongs 'dus;* a cycle of treasures revealed by Tertön Sangye Lingpa (1340–96) in eighteen volumes of approximately seven hundred pages each.

60. Wind horse, Tib. *rlung rta;* a practice for success and fortune, symbolized by the horse of fortune inscribed on flags. Gesar; King of Ling and an epic Tibetan hero.

61. The four classes of tantra (Tib. *rgyud sde bzhi*); *kriya* (Tib. *bya rgyud*); *charya* (Tib. *spyod rgyud*); *yoga* (Tib. *rnal 'byor rgyud*); and *anuttarayoga* (Tib. *bla med rnal 'byor rgyud*).

62. Chökyi Lodro gave the offering utensils of the previous Jamgöns to the Derge king and Jago minister to put in the symbolic abode of the local guardians that they were consecrating.

63. Tib. *skyes mchog tshul bzang;* one of the twelve manifestations of Guru Rinpoche.

64. Tib. *Gang blo ma;* a famous praise to Manjushri that takes its name from the first few words in the Tibetan, "*gang-gi lodro. . .*"

65. *Mamo,* Tib. *ma mo;* literally, "mundane mother deities." One of the *Eight Sadhana Teachings;* a class of female divinities who manifest out of the *dharmadhatu* but appear in ways that cor-

respond to mundane appearances due to the interrelationship between the mundane world and the channels, winds, and essences within our bodies. The term can also refer to a class of semidivine beings who sometimes act as protectors of the Dharma.

66. Kalu Rinpoche (1905–1989) studied at Palpung Monastery and was appointed retreat master of the three-year retreat center there by Situ Rinpoche. After escaping to India, where many Western students came to study with him, he started the first three-year retreat center for Westerners, in France in the 1970s. Later, he established more retreat centers in the West. His tulku was discovered by Tai Situ Rinpoche in 1993.

67. This Yudrön seems to have been some sort of witch with extraordinary powers.

68. See chapter 2, note 3.

69. The Gyalrong Khandro; the sister of Gyalrong Namtrul from Gyalrong Monastery, a branch of Dzogchen Monastery.

70. Meaningful Lasso, Tib. don yod zhags pa'i rgyud, Skt. amoghapasha; a tantra focused on Avalokiteshvara that belongs to kriya.

71. Karma Monastery; the seat of the Karmapa in Eastern Tibet.

72. Tib. gnyag lugs phur ba; literally, "Vajrakilaya according to the Nyak tradition." This became Dilgo Khyentse Rinpoche's main Vajrakilaya treasure. "Nyak" refers to Jnana Kumara of Nyak, one of Padmasambhava's twenty-five disciples. He was one of the first Tibetan monks and an expert translator who received the four great rivers of transmission, referring to his transmissions from Padmasambhava, Vimalamitra, Vairotsana, and Yudra Nyingpo. In particular, he worked closely with Vimalamitra, translating the tantras of mahayoga and atiyoga. In unison with Trisong Detsen, his empowerment flower fell on Chemchok Heruka. Subsequently, he received the transmission of Nectar Medicine from Padmasambhava. He practiced in the Crystal Cave of Yarlung, where he drew water from solid rock. It is said the water still flows today.

CHAPTER EIGHT

1. Mangala; the Sanskrit word for Tashi, referring to Tashi Paljor, one of Dilgo Khyentse Rinpoche's names. He signed many of his writings with "Mangala."

2. Konchok Paldron; sometimes referred to by the Sanskrit version of her name, Ratna Shri Tara or Ratna Shri Dipam Tara. She was Tulku Urgyen's grandmother. For more on her see Blazing Splendor (Rangjung Yeshe Publications), pp. 79–85.

3. Pema Garwang Dechen Ösel Lingpa (Tib. pad-ma gar-dbang bde-chen 'od-gsal gling-pa) is one of the tertön names of Dilgo Khyentse.

4. Longchen Namkai Ösel Pema Dognak Lingpa (Tib. klong chen gnam mkhai 'od-gsal pad-ma mdo-snags gling-pa) is another one of Dilgo Khyentse's tertön names.

CHAPTER NINE

1. Tib. dkon mchog spyi 'dus; a terma cycle revealed by the great Jatson Nyingpo (1585–1656) and focused on Padmasambhava. Jatson Nyingpo transmitted this set of teachings first to Düdül Dorje (1615–72).

2. The Ngapo; Ngapo Ngawang Jigmey, an influential government official in Lhasa during the 1950s. He was one of the ministers who had signed the Seventeen-Point Agreement for the Peaceful Liberation of Tibet. It was signed and sealed in Beijing on May 23, 1951, under the People's Liberation Army's military presence.

3. The son of one of Dilgo Khyentse's sisters, who now lives in England.

4. Khechari, Tib. mkha' spyod ma; an aspect of Vajrayogini.

5. Shukten; a protector that was practiced by the Geluk a lot, until the Dalai Lama told them to give it up because of the possible harm he could do.

Chapter Ten

1. The Dilgo home is at Sakar.
2. Dilgo Khyentse Rinpoche's younger daughter died in a hospital in Lucknow, India, when Khyentse Rinpoche was living in Bhutan. The daughters had been sent to boarding schools in India. She fell ill with bile trouble, and the person in charge did not inform her family until she was taken to the hospital, where Khyentse Rinpoche was just able to see her briefly before she passed away.
3. People who cooperated with the Chinese government officials were paid and given a rank within the Communist Party.
4. Sangyum Kusho, Tib. *gsang yum sku zhabs;* literally, "Venerable Secret Consort," the respectful form of address for wives of high lamas.

Chapter Eleven

1. *Tokden;* here referring to Khamtrul Rinpoche's yogi disciples, who have a tradition of staying in lifelong retreat, have matted hair, and wear a white lower robe with a red-and-white-striped upper robe.
2. Drikung Kyabgon (Tib. *bri-gung skyabs-mgon*), born in 1946 to the Tsarong family in Lhasa, is the head of the Drikung Kagyu school. He studied at Drikung Thil, the main Drikung monastery in Central Tibet. In 1956 his parents fled to India while he was left behind at the monastery. In 1975 he was able to escape Tibet and was reunited with his family in the United States, where he studied English. In 1985 he started the Drikung Kagyu Institute in Dehra Dun, India, in the Himalayan foothills, which is now his main residence.
3. Wutai Shan; literally "five-peaked mountain," located in Shanxi Province, China, and on which Manjushri is said to reside.

Chapter Twelve

1. *Geshe;* a scholar in the Geluk school equivalent to a *khenpo* in the other schools and similar to having a doctorate in Buddhist philosophy.
2. Tib. *chos yid bzhin nor bu thar pa rin po che'i rgyan;* a text by Gampopa of which numerous translations are in print, including one by Herbert V. Guenther (Boston: Shambhala Publications, 1986).
3. *Tengyur,* Tib. *bstan 'gyur;* a collection of several hundred volumes of canonical scriptures explaining the *Kangyur.*

Chapter Thirteen

1. During these empowerments the postures for togal practice are practiced at certain parts of the empowerment.

Chapter Fourteen

1. This is the present Dzongsar Khyentse, who is also called Khyentse Norbu, a well-known writer and film director, who directed *The Cup* and *Travelers and Magicians,* and published his first book, *What Makes You Not a Buddhist,* in 2006.
2. *Dzong,* Tib. *rdzongs;* the equivalent of a monastery in Bhutan. The *dzong* are run by the government.
3. Karma Thinley Rinpoche (born 1931 in Nangchen, East Tibet) is the fourth incarnation of the Karma Thinley tulkus, who were teachers of the Karmapas. He fled Tibet in 1959 with the Karmapa's party and became abbot of the first Kagyu nunnery in India, in Tilokpur, founded

by Mrs. Bedi. In 1971, he was invited to Canada and he founded a center in Toronto. He now divides his time between his center in Toronto, his nunnery in Nepal, and his small monastery in Nangchen.

CHAPTER FIFTEEN

1. *Crystal Cave Chronicles,* Tib. *pad ma bka' thang shel brag ma;* a biography of Guru Padmasambhava said to have been discovered by Urgyen Lingpa at Yarlung's Crystal Cave, from whence it takes its name.

CHAPTER SIXTEEN

1. Divine Descent Day, Tib. *lha babs dus chen;* the twenty-second day of the ninth lunar month, when the Buddha Shakyamuni is said to have descended from the Heaven of the Thirty-Three.
2. Life-tree, Tib. *srog shing;* a special stick placed in the center of a statue to indicate the central channel.

CHAPTER SEVENTEEN

1. *Loppön,* Tib. *slob dpon,* Skt. *acharya;* here referring to the students that have completed the nine-year curriculum at a monastic college but have not yet received the *khenpo* title.

CHAPTER EIGHTEEN

1. Reting; the residence of Dromtonpa, Atisha's main disciple, near Lhasa.

CHAPTER NINETEEN

1. According to the Tibetan system, babies are one year old at birth, and if the Tibetan New Year (Losar) happens to occur right after their birth, they are considered to be two years old then, since everybody's birthday is celebrated at the New Year.
2. *Gao,* Tib. *ga 'u;* an amulet box that is used to keep precious relics.
3. This is Dudjom Rinpoche's second wife, Sangyum Kusho Rigzin Wangmo.

Glossary

Abbot (Tib. *mkhan po*)   In general, the transmitter of the monastic vows. This title is also given to a person who has attained a high degree of knowledge of Dharma and is authorized to teach it.

Accomplishment (Tib. *dngos grub*, Skt. *siddhi*)   Either supreme or common. Supreme accomplishment is the attainment of Buddhahood; common accomplishments are the miraculous powers acquired in the course of spiritual training. The attainment of these powers, which are similar in kind to those acquired by the practitioners of some non-Buddhist traditions, are not regarded as ends in themselves. When they arise, however, they are taken as signs of progress on the path and are employed for the benefit of the teachings and disciples.

Adzom Drukpa   Adzom Drukpa Natsok Rangdrol, a great siddha and author who was a student of Jamyang Khyentse Wangpo.

Aeon (Tib. *bskal pa*, Skt. *kalpa*)   World age, cosmic cycle. A great *kalpa* corresponds to a cycle of formation and destruction of a universe, and is divided into eighty intermediate *kalpas*. An intermediate *kalpa* is composed of one small *kalpa* during which life span, and so on, increases, and one small *kalpa* during which it decreases.

All-ground consciousness (Tib. *kun gzhi'i rnam shes*, Skt. *alayavijnana*)   Consciousness as the ground of all experience. According to the Mahayana, the all-ground is the fundamental and indeterminate level of the mind in which karmic imprints are stored.

Amdo   One of the provinces of Eastern Tibet.

Ananda (Skt.; Tib. *kun dga' bo*)   The son of Buddha Shakyamuni's uncle, and the Buddha's personal attendant. He could remember every word the Buddha spoke, compiled his teachings, and served as the second patriarch in the oral transmission of the Dharma.

Anuyoga (Skt.; Tib. *rjes su rnal 'byor*)   The second of the inner tantras, according to the system of nine vehicles used in the Nyingma tradition. *Anuyoga* emphasizes the completion stage of tantric practice, which consists of meditation on emptiness, as well as the subtle channels, energies, and essences of the physical body.

Appearances   *See* Perceptions.

Arhat (Skt.; Tib. *dgra bcom pa*)   Lit. "foe-destroyer." One who has vanquished the enemies of conflicting emotions and who has realized the nonexistence of the personal self, thus being forever free from the sufferings of samsara. Arhatship is the goal of the teachings of the fundamental vehicle or Hinayana.

Arya (Skt.; Tib. *'phags pa*)   Sublime or noble one; one who has transcended samsaric existence. There are four classes of sublime beings: arhats, *pratyekabuddhas,* bodhisattvas, and buddhas.

Atiyoga (Skt.; Tib. *rdzogs chen*)   A synonym of Dzogchen, the Great Perfection. The last and highest of the inner tantras, the summit of the system of nine vehicles according to the Nyingma classification.

Ato Tulku   Dilgo Khyentse's nephew, who is the son of one of Rinpoche's sisters and lives in the United Kingdom.

Auspicious Blazing Splendor Hermitage (Tib. *bkra shis dpal 'bar gling*)   Lama Mipham's hermitage in Denkok. Khyentse Rinpoche's father had a retreat house built there for Lama Mipham where Dilgo Khyentse and Sangye Nyenpa Rinpoches did retreats.

Avalokiteshvara (Skt.; Tib. *spyan ras gzigs*)   Chenrezig, the "Lord Who Sees"; the bodhisattva who embodies the speech and compassion of all buddhas, the *sambhogakaya* emanation of Buddha Amitabha, sometimes referred to as Lokeshvara, the "Lord of the World."

Awareness (Tib. *rig pa*, Skt. *vidya*)   Consciousness devoid of ignorance and dualistic fixation, when referring to the view of the Great Perfection.

Barlha Tsegyal (Tib. *bar lha rste rgyal*)   A mountain peak in Denkok which is the abode of the local deity Barlha Tsegyal.

Bedi, Freda   A British lady living in India in the sixties, who was married to an Indian and did a lot to help the Tibetan lamas when they first escaped there in 1959. She organized the Tibetan Lama School in Dalhousie where tulkus were trained to learn English. She was one of the first Western women to be ordained as a nun and named Sister Kechok Palmo by the Karmapa and started one of the first Tibetan nunneries in India, in Tilokpur, near Dharamsala. She passed away in the seventies.

Benchen Monastery (Tib. *ban chen phun tshogs dar rgyas gling*)   A Kagyu monastery in Gawa, Kham, which was the monastic seat of Dilgo Khyentse's brother, Sangye Nyenpa Rinpoche, and also the seat of Tenga Rinpoche. Tenga Rinpoche and the present Sangye Nyenpa live in Benchen Monastery in Nepal, which is in Swayambunath.

Bhikshu (Skt.; Tib. *dge slong*)   A fully ordained Buddhist monk.

Bhikshuni (Skt.; Tib. *dge long ma*)   A fully ordained Buddhist nun.

Bhumi (Skt.; Tib. *sa*)   The levels or stages of the bodhisattvas.

Bodh Gaya (Tib. *rdo rje gdan*, Skt. *vajrasana*)   Lit., "the vajra seat." The place in modern-day Bihar, India, where the Buddha Shakyamuni attained enlightenment and where all the buddhas of this aeon are to attain enlightenment.

Bodhichitta (Skt.; Tib. *byang chub kyi sems*)   Awakened state of mind. It can refer to the aspiration to attain enlightenment for the sake of all beings or, in the context of Dzogchen, the innate awareness of awakened mind.

Bodhisattva (Skt.; Tib. *byang chub sems dpa'*)   One who, through compassion, strives to attain the full enlightenment of Buddhahood for the sake of all beings. Bodhisattvas may be ordinary or noble depending on whether or not they have attained the path of seeing and are residing on one of the ten *bhumis*.

Bomta Khenpo (nineteenth–twentieth century)   Also known as Polo Khenpo; a renowned disciple of Khenpo Ngakchung. He passed away in Bhutan.

Brahma (Skt.; Tib. *tshangs pa*)   Referring, in the Buddhist tradition, to the ruler of the gods in the form realm.

Brahmin (Skt.; Tib. *bram ze*)   A member of the priestly caste of ancient India. This term often indicates hermits and spiritual practitioners. It should be noted that the

Buddha rejected the caste system and proclaimed on several occasions that the true Brahmin is not someone so designated through an accident of birth, but one who has thoroughly overcome defilement, and attained freedom.

Brahmin Rahula (Skt.; Tib. *bram ze sgra gcan 'dzin*)   Rahula. The Buddha's son in Simhaladvipa; one of the sixteen arhats, who used white and black pebbles to count his positive and negative deeds.

Buddha (Skt.; Tib. *sangs rgyas*)   The "Fully Awakened One"; a being who has removed the emotional and cognitive veils, and is endowed with all enlightened qualities of realization.

Buddha Shakyamuni (Skt.; Tib. *sangs rgyas sha kya thub pa*)   The Sage of the Sakyas; the Buddha of our time who lived around the fifth century B.C.

Buddhafield (Tib. *zhing khams*)   A sphere or dimension, manifested by a buddha or great bodhisattva, in which beings may abide and progress toward enlightenment without ever falling back into lower states of existence. Also, any place seen as the pure manifestation of spontaneous wisdom.

Chagmey Rinpoche (1613–78)   Karma Chagmey Raga Asya, a famous master and poet who was an emanation of Guru Rinpoche's disciple Chok and was Tertön Migyur Dorje's uncle. He wrote the renowned *Chagmey Retreat Manual* and *The Union of Mahamudra and Dzogchen*.

Chakrasamvara (Tib. *'khor-lo bde-mchog*)   Wheel of Supreme Bliss. The main yidam or tantra of the New Schools, belonging to Anuttara Yoga.

Changling Tulku   A holder of the *Northern Treasures*, and one of the main tulkus living at Shechen Monastery in Nepal, where he teaches at the monastic college.

Chatral Rinpoche   Chatral Sangye Dorje, a well-known Nyingma master who established several retreat centers in Nepal and mostly lives at Yanglesho in the Kathmandu Valley. He is one of the last disciples of Khenpo Ngagchung and is now in his mid-nineties.

Chimey Dronkar   Dilgo Khyentse Rinpoche's eldest daughter Chimey, who is the mother of Shechen Rabjam Rinpoche and presently lives in Bhutan. Later she was named Chimey Wangmo.

Chimey Rinpoche   One of Dilgo Khyentse's nephews who lives and teaches in England; he has several Dharma centers in Europe.

Chimey Wangmo   *See* Chimey Dronkar.

Chimphu (Tib. *chims phu*)   A hermitage of caves above Samye, where Padmasambhava and many other great masters spent years in retreat.

Cho (Tib. *gcod*)   The practice of cutting through attachment to the body and the ego, which was taught by Padampa Sangye and Machik Labdrön.

Chokling Tertön   The First Chokgyur Lingpa, who revealed the *New Treasures of Chokgyur Lingpa* together with Jamyang Khyentse Wangpo and Jamgön Kongtrül Lodro Thaye, who were his contemporaries.

Chuba (Tib. *chu-pa*)   Traditional Tibetan dress used by both men and women but in a different style with different folds.

Completion stage   *See* Development and completion.

Conqueror (Tib. *rgyal ba*, Skt. *jina*)   An epithet of the Buddha.

Copper-Colored Mountain (Tib. *zangs mdog dpal ri*)   Glorious Copper-Colored Mountain. The terrestrial pure land of Guru Rinpoche situated on the subcontinent Chamara to the southeast of the Jambu Continent. Chamara is the central island of a configuration of nine islands inhabited by savage *rakshasas*. In the middle of Chamara rises the majestic red-colored mountain. On its summit lies the magical palace Lotus Light, manifested from the natural expression of primordial wakefulness. Here resides Padmasambhava in an indestructible bodily form transcending birth and death for as long as samsara continues and through which he incessantly brings benefit to beings through magical emanations of his body, speech, and mind.

Crystal Cave (Tib. *shel brag*)   A famous Guru Rinpoche cave in the Yarlung Valley of Central Tibet, where the *Crystal Cave Chronicles* of Padmasambhava were revealed by Urgyen Lingpa.

Crystal Lotus Cave (Tib. *pad ma shel phug*)   A sacred place in Dzamnang where the *Three Classes of the Great Perfection* was revealed by Chokgyur Lingpa. It was here that Dilgo Khyentse revealed his mind treasure the *Immutable Long-Life Tantra*.

Crystal Lotus Mountain (Tib. *pad ma shel ri*)   A pacifying holy site of the vajra family among the twenty-five important sacred places in Dokham. Situated at Gyamgyal, it is the place where Dilgo Khyentse revealed his mind treasure *Pema's Heart Essence of Longevity*.

Dabzang Rinpoche   A master from Dilyak Monastery in Nangchen, who was an emanation of Gampopa. He built one of the first Tibetan monasteries in the Kathmandu Valley and was a close friend of Dilgo Khyentse. He passed away in 1992.

Dagger (Tib. *phur pa*, Skt. *kilaya*)   A short stabbing weapon with a pointed, three-edged blade used in tantric rituals. There are four types of dagger: the dagger of intrinsic awareness, the dagger of bodhichitta, the dagger of immeasurable compassion, and the physical dagger.

Daka (Skt.; Tib. *dpa' bo*)   Lit., "hero." The tantric equivalent of a bodhisattva and the male equivalent of a dakini.

Dakini (Skt.; Tib. *mkha' 'gro ma*)   Khandro, lit., "moving through space." The representation of wisdom in female form. There are several levels of dakinis: wisdom dakinis who have complete realization and worldly dakinis who possess various spiritual powers. The word is also used as a title for great female teachers and as a respectful form of address for the wives of spiritual masters.

Dakini script (Tib. *mbha' 'gro'i brda-yig*)   Symbolic script used by the dakinis which can only be read by certain treasure revealers.

Dalai Lama   The Fourteenth Dalai Lama, Tenzin Gyamtso. In Tibetan Buddhism, the successive Dalai Lamas form a lineage tracing back to 1391. They are incarnations of Avalokiteshvara, the bodhisattva of compassion, and belong to the Geluk school.

Dartsedo (Tib. *dar-rtse-mdo*)   A border town between Eastern Tibet and China.

Definitive meaning   *See* Expedient and definitive meaning.

Demon (Tib. *bdud*, Skt. *mara*)   Either a malevolent spirit or, symbolically, a negative force or obstacle on the path. The four demons (Tib. *bdud bzhi*) are of the latter kind. The demon of the aggregates refers to the five *skandhas*, as described in Buddhist teachings, which form the basis of suffering in samsara. The demon of the emotions refers to the conflicting emotions that provoke suffering. The demon of death refers not only to death itself but also to the momentary transience of all phenomena, the nature of which is suffering. The child of the gods demon refers to mental wandering and the attachment to phenomena apprehended as truly existent.

Denkok (Tib. *ldan khog*) A district in Derge where Dilgo Khyentse was born.

Derge (Tib. *sde dge*) Former kingdom in Eastern Tibet.

Derge Gonchen (Tib. *sde dge dgon chen*) Lit., "Great Monastery of Derge," but also referring to the capital of the Derge province.

Deva (Skt.; Tib. *lha*) Gods, the highest of the six classes of samsaric beings, who enjoy the temporal bliss of the heavenly state.

Development and completion (Tib. *bskyed rdzogs*) The two principal phases of tantric practice. The development stage (Tib. *bskyed rim*) involves meditation on sights, sounds, and thoughts as deities, mantras, and wisdom, respectively. The completion stage (Tib. *rdzogs rim*) refers to the dissolution of visualized forms into an experience of emptiness. It also denotes the meditation on the subtle channels, energies, and essential substances of the body. Development and completion may also refer to the first two inner tantras, *mahayoga* and *anuyoga*.

Development stage *See* Development and completion.

Dhanakosha (Skt.; Tib. *dha na ko sha*) Lit., "treasury of wealth." An island in Uddiyana, present-day western India, encircled by many sublime kinds of trees, whence its name.

Dharani (Skt.; Tib *gzungs*) A verbal formula, often quite long, blessed by a Buddha or a bodhisattva, similar to the mantras of the Vajrayana, but found in the sutra tradition. The term is also used to refer to the *siddhi* of unfailing memory.

Dharma (Skt.; Tib. *chos*) The Buddhist doctrine. In its widest sense it means all that can be known. In this text, the term is used exclusively to indicate the teachings of the Buddha. It has two aspects: the Dharma of transmission (Tib. *lung gi chos*), namely the teachings that are actually given, and the Dharma of realization (Tib. *rtogs pa'i chos*), or the states of wisdom, and so on, which are attained through the application of the teachings. Dharma can also simply mean "phenomena."

Dharma protector (Tib. *chos skyong*, Skt. *dharmapala*) Guardians of the teachings, protecting them from being diluted and their transmission from being disturbed or distorted. Protectors are sometimes emanations of buddhas or bodhisattvas, and sometimes spirits, gods, or demons that have been subjugated by a great spiritual master and bound under oath.

Dharmadhatu (Skt.; Tib. *chos dbyings*) The absolute expanse; emptiness pervaded with awareness.

Dharmakaya (Skt.; Tib. *chos sku*) The first of the three kayas, which is devoid of constructs, like space. The body of enlightened qualities. *See also* Three kayas.

Dharmapala *See* Dharma protector.

Dharmata (Skt.; Tib. *chos nyid*) The innate nature of phenomena and mind—emptiness.

Dhumavati (Skt.; Tib. *dud sol ma*) Dusolma, a protectress of the Dharma teachings.

Dilgo Khyentse (1910–91) A treasure revealer who was regarded by followers of all the four schools as one of the greatest Tibetan masters of the last century.

District-controlling temple (Tib. *ru gnon*) The geomantic temples built by King Songtsen Gampo to guard Tibet.

Do Khyentse (1800–1859) Do Khyentse Yeshe Dorje, a great master and tertön who was the mind emanation of Jigmey Lingpa.

Dokham (Tib. *mdo khams*) Eastern Tibet.

Dokhampa Tenpai Nyima (1849–1907)   The Sixth Khamtrul Rinpoche, a renowned master of the Drukpa Kagyu school, whose Khampagar Monastery is in the Lhatok area of Eastern Tibet. One of his most famous students was Shakya Shri.

Drogon Chophak Rinpoche (1235–1280)   Drogon Chögyal Phagpa, a founder of the Sakya Lineage.

Drugu Chögyal Rinpoche (born 1946)   A well-known lama from Drugu, Kham, who is an outstanding artist and lives in Tashi Jong, Khamtrul Rinpoche's community in Himachal Pradesh, India. He is the eighth incarnation of the Drugu Chögyals and is called Chögyal Yonten Gyatso.

Drugu Tokden Shakya Shri   *See* Shakya Shri.

Drungram Gyatrul   One of Dilgo Khyentse's teachers, who spent his entire life in a cave.

Drupchen (Tib. *sgrub chen*)   An intensive group sadhana performed over a period of seven to ten days during which the mantra recitation goes on round the clock.

Duality (Tib. *gnyis 'dzin* or *gzung 'dzin*)   The ordinary perception of unenlightened beings. The apprehension of phenomena in terms of subject and object, and the belief in their true existence.

Dzogchen   The highest teaching of the Nyingma. *See atiyoga.*

Dzogchen Monastery (Tib. *ru dam rdzogs chen dgon*)   Rudam Dzogchen Monastery, one of the main Nyingma monasteries in Kham, situated near Shechen Monastery in Derge.

Dzongsar (Tib. *rdzong gsar*)   Sakya monastery in Derge, which was the seat of Jamyang Khyentse Wangpo and Dzongsar Khyentse Chökyi Lodro.

Dzongsar Khyentse (born 1961)   The main reincarnation of Jamyang Khyentse Chökyi Lodro. He is the son of Trinley Norbu Rinpoche and is head of the Dzongsar Monastery in Kham and the Dzongsar Institute in Bir. He is responsible for approximately sixteen hundred monks in six monasteries and institutes across Asia. He is also the writer and director of the films *The Cup* and *Travelers and Magicians*. Also known as Khyentse Norbu.

Early Translation (Tib. *snga 'gyur*)   A synonym for the Nyingma tradition referring to the teachings translated before the great translator Rinchen Zangpo, during the reigns of the Tibetan kings Trisong Detsen and Ralpachen. *See also* Nyingma.

Effortless Fulfillment Printing Press (Tib. *lhun grub steng gi spar khang*)   An important library of woodblocks in Derge Gonchen.

Eight charnel grounds (Tib. *dur khrod brgyad*)   Places where dakas and dakinis meet, which internally correspond to the eight consciousnesses: (1) Cool Grove, Sitavana (Tib. *bsil ba tshal*), in the east; (2) Perfected in Body (Tib. *sku la rdzogs*) to the south; (3) Lotus Mound (Tib. *pad ma brtsegs*) to the west; (4) Lanka Mound (Tib. *lan ka brtsegs*) to the north; (5) Spontaneously Accomplished Mound (Tib. *lhun grub brtsegs*) to the southeast; (6) Display of Great Secret (Tib. *gsang chen rol pa*) to the southwest; (7) Pervasive Great Joy (Tib. *he chen brdal ba*) to the northwest; and (8) World Mound (Tib. *'jig rten brtsegs*) to the northeast.

Eight classes of gods and demons (Tib. *lha srin sde brgyad*)   According to the sutras, the devas, nagas, yakshas, gandharvas, asuras, garudas, kinnaras, and mahoragas, who were all able to receive and practice the Buddha's teachings. These eight classes can also refer to eight types of mundane spirits that can help or harm, but are invisible to human beings: *gings, maras, tsens,* yakshas, *rakshasas, mamos,* rahulas, and nagas.

Eight manifestations of Guru Rinpoche Padmasambhava, Loden Choksey, Shakya Senge, Senge Dradrok, Padma Gyalpo, Dorje Trolo, Nyima Özer, and Pema Gyalpo.

Eight Sadhana Teachings (Tib. *sgrub pa bka' brgyad*) The eight chief *yidam* deities of *mahayoga* and their corresponding tantras and sadhanas: Manjushri Body, Lotus Speech, Vishuddha Mind, Nectar Quality, Kilaya Activity, Liberating Sorcery of Mother Deities, Maledictory Fierce Mantra, and Mundane Worship.

Ekajati (Skt.; Tib. *ral chig ma*) Dharma protectress especially of the *atiyoga* teachings.

Empowerment (Tib. *dbang,* Skt. *abhisheka*) The authorization to practice the Vajrayana teachings, which is the indispensable entrance to tantric practice. It enables one to master one's innate vajra body, speech, and mind, and to regard forms as deities, sound as mantras, and thought as wisdom. *See also* Four empowerments.

Emptiness (Tib. *stong pa nyid,* Skt. *shunyata*) The ultimate nature of phenomena.

Enlightenment (Tib. *byang chub,* Skt. *bodhi*) Generally, the state of Buddhahood, characterized by the perfection of the accumulations of merit and wisdom, and by the removal of the two obscurations. It can also refer to the lower stages of enlightenment of an arhat or *pratyekabuddha.*

Expedient and definitive meaning (Tib. *drang don* and *nges don,* Skt. *neyartha* and *nitharta*) The expedient meaning refers to conventional teachings on the Four Noble Truths, karma, path, and result, which are designed to lead the practitioner to the definitive meaning, the insight into emptiness, suchness, and buddha nature.

Expedient meaning *See* Expedient and definitive meaning.

Feast offering (Tib. *tshogs 'khor,* Skt. *ganachakra*) A ritual offering in tantric Buddhism in which oblations of food and drink are blessed as the elixir of wisdom and offered to the *yidam* deity as well as to the mandala of one's own body in order to purify breaches of one's sacred commitments.

Fierce mantra (Tib. *drag sngags*) Type of mantra belonging to the wrathful deities that are used to dispel demonic forces which obstruct the Buddhist doctrine or the welfare of beings.

Five aggregates (Tib. *phung po lnga,* Skt. *panchaskandha*) The basic component elements of form, feeling, perception, conditioning factors, and consciousness. When they appear together, the illusion of self is produced in the ignorant mind.

Five conflicting emotions (Tib. *nyon mongs lnga*) Ignorance, desire, anger, jealousy, and pride.

Five elements (Tib. *'byung ba lnga*) Earth, water, fire, wind or air, and space as principles of solidity, liquidity, heat, movement, and space, respectively.

Five families (Tib. *rigs lnga,* Skt. *panchakula*) The five buddha families: *tathagata, vajra, ratna, padma,* and *karma.* They represent five aspects of the innate qualities of our enlightened essence. Each of them is presided over by a Buddha: Vairochana, Akshobya, Ratnasambhava, Amitabha, and Amoghasiddhi, respectively.

Five poisons (Tib. *nyon mongs lnga*) *See* five conflicting emotions.

Five sciences (Tib. *rig pa'i gnas lnga*) The five disciplines of grammar, dialectics, healing, philosophy, and arts and crafts.

Five wisdoms (Tib. *ye shes lnga,* Skt. *panchajnana*) The five wisdoms of Buddhahood corresponding to the five buddha families: mirror-like wisdom (vajra family), wisdom of equality (*ratna* family), all-discerning wisdom (*padma* family), all-accomplishing wisdom (*karma* family), and wisdom of *dharmadhatu* (*tathagata* family). They represent five distinctive functions of our enlightened essence.

Formless realms (Tib. *gzugs med khams*)   The four highest states of samsaric existence.

Four continents (Tib. *gling bzhi*)   The four continents located in the four directions around Mount Meru, constituting a universe. They are the semicircular Sublime Body in the east; the trapezoidal Land of Rose Apples in the south; the circular Bountiful Cow in the west; and the square Unpleasant Sound in the north.

Four empowerments (Tib. *dbang bzhi*, Skt. *catuhabhisheka*)   Transference of wisdom power from master to disciple, authorizing and enabling one to engage in a practice and reap its fruit. There are four levels of tantric empowerment. The first is the vase empowerment, which purifies the defilements and obscurations associated with the body, grants the blessings of the vajra body, authorizes the disciples to practice the yogas of the development stage, and enables them to attain the *nirmanakaya*. The second is the secret empowerment; this purifies the defilements and obscurations of the speech faculty, grants the blessings of vajra speech, authorizes disciples to practice the yogas of the completion stage, and enables them to attain the *sambhogakaya*. The third is the wisdom empowerment, which purifies the defilements and obscurations associated with the mind, grants the blessings of the vajra mind, authorizes disciples to practice the yogas of the path of skillful means, and enables them to attain the *dharmakaya*. The final empowerment, which is often simply referred to as the fourth initiation, is the word empowerment; this purifies the defilements of body, speech, and mind and all karmic and cognitive obscurations; it grants the blessings of primordial wisdom, authorizes disciples to engage in the practice of Dzogchen, and enables them to attain the *svabhavikakaya*. *See also* Empowerment.

Four kayas (Tib. *sku bzhi*)   The four bodies of the buddhas: the *dharmakaya, sambhogakaya, nirmanakaya,* and *svabhavikakaya*. *See also* Three kayas.

Four Noble Truths (Tib. *bden pa bzhi*)   The truths of suffering, origin, cessation, and path expounded by the Buddha Shakyamuni in his first teaching. These teachings, referred to as the first turning of the Dharma wheel, are the foundation of the Hinayana and Mahayana teachings.

Four types of right discrimination (Tib. *so so yang dag pa'i rig pa bzhi*)   The right discrimination of definitive words, meaning, phenomena, and courageous eloquence.

Four visions (Tib. *snang ba bzhi*)   The four visions of *togal*: the visionary appearance of the direct perception of reality (Tib. *chos nyid mngon sum gi snang ba*), the visionary appearance of ever-increasing contemplative experience (Tib. *nyams gong 'phel ba'i snang ba*), the visionary appearance of reaching the limit of awareness (Tib. *rig pa tshad phebs kyi snang ba*), and the visionary appearance of the cessation of clinging to reality (Tib. *chos nyid du 'dzin pa zad pa'i snang ba*).

Four wheels (Tib. *'khor lo bzhi*)   The four wheels of practice: (1) dwelling in a favorable country; (2) following a great being; (3) one's individual good aspirations; and (4) having accumulated merit formerly.

Fruition (Tib. *'bras bu*, Skt. *phala*)   The result of the path, the state of perfect enlightenment.

Ga (Tib. *sga*)   A district in the Derge province.

Gampopa (1079–1153)   The foremost disciple of Milarepa who was a highly realized, great scholar. He was the author of the *Jewel Ornament of Liberation* and was the forefather of all the Kagyu lineages.

Garab Dorje (Tib. *dga' rab rdor rje*, Skt. *prahevajra*)   The first human vidyadhara in the Dzogchen lineage. He was the incarnation of Semlhag Chen, a god who had been empowered by the buddhas. Immaculately conceived, Garab Dorje's mother was a nun, the daughter of King Dhahena Talo or Indrabhuti of Uddiyana. Garab Dorje received all the tantras, scriptures, and oral instructions of Dzogchen from Vajrasattva and Vajrapani in person. Having reached the state of complete enlightenment through the effortless Great Perfection, Garab Dorje transmitted the teachings to his retinue of exceptional beings. Manjushrimitra is regarded as his chief disciple.

Garuda (Skt.; Tib. *khyung*)   A kind of bird, in both Indian and Tibetan traditions. A creature of great size, it is able to fly immediately upon hatching. It is a symbol of primordial wisdom.

Geluk (Tib. *dge lugs*)   The Tibetan Buddhist school started by Tsongkhapa, which was a reformation of Atisha's tradition.

Gemang (Tib. *dge-mang*)   Gemang Monastery in Kham Dzachukha.

Geshe (Tib. *dge bshes*)   A learned Buddhist scholar in the Geluk tradition.

Glorious Copper-Colored Mountain   *See* Copper-Colored Mountain.

Gods   *See Deva.*

Great Perfection (Tib. *rdzogs pa chen po*, Skt. *mahasandhi*)   *See Atiyoga.*

Great Prayer Festival (Tib. *smon-lam chen-mo*)   Monlam Chenmo, a prayer festival performed on the fifteenth day of the first Tibetan month in Lhasa.

Great vehicle   *See* Mahayana.

Guru Chowang (1212–70)   One of the five tertön kings.

Guru Rinpoche   *See* Padmasambhava.

Gyalse Shenpen Thaye (born 1740)   A famous master from Dzogchen Monastery.

Gyaltsap Rinpoche   *See* Shechen Gyaltsap.

Gyalwa Drikungpa (1509–57)   Gyalwa Drikungpa Rinchen Puntsök, head of the Drikung Kagyu school.

Gyogchen Dongra (Tib. *sgyogs chen gdong ra*)   One of the nine deities who created existence (Tib. *srid pa chags pa'i lha dgu*): (1) Ode Gungyal, (2) Yarlha Shampo, (3) Nyanchen Thanglha, (4) Machen Pomra, (5) Gyogchen Dongra, (6) Gompo Lhatse, (7) Zhoglha Gyugpo, (8) Jowo Gyulgyal, (9) She'u Khara.

Habitual tendencies (Tib. *bag chags*, Skt. *vasana*)   Habitual patterns of thought, speech, or action.

Hearing lineage (Tib. *gang zag snyan rgyud*)   The lineage transmitted orally from individual to individual, in which it is necessary for the teacher to use words for the disciple to hear, rather than transmitting them mind-to-mind or through symbols.

Hell (Tib. *dmyal ba*, Skt. *naraka*)   One of the six realms, where beings experience intense suffering as a result of past actions, especially those actions related to anger, such as killing. There are eighteen different hells, comprised of the eight hot hells, the eight cold hells, and the neighboring and ephemeral hells.

Heretic (Tib. *mu stegs pa*)   Non-Buddhists, referring to teachers of non-Buddhist philosophy who adhere to the extreme views of eternalism or nihilism.

Heruka, (Skt.; Tib. *khrag 'thung*)   Lit., "blood drinker." A wrathful deity, drinker of the blood of ego-clinging.

Hinayana (Skt.; Tib. *theg dman*)   The fundamental system of Buddhist thought and practice deriving from the first turning of the Dharma wheel and centering around the teachings on the Four Noble Truths and the twelvefold chain of dependent arising.

Ignorance (Tib. *ma rig pa,* Skt. *avidya*)   In a Buddhist context, not mere nescience but mistaken apprehension. It is the incorrect understanding of, or failure to recognize, the ultimate nature of beings and phenomena, and hence the false ascription of true existence to them.

Indra (Skt.; Tib. *dbang po*)   The supreme god and king of the Heaven of the Thirty-three. Indra is regarded as a protector of the Buddhist doctrine. He resides on the summit of Mount Meru in the palace of Complete Victory and is also known as Shakra (Tib. *brgya byin*), the Ruler of the Devas.

Indrabodhi   The King of Uddiyana who found, fostered, and, for a time, protected Padmasambhava.

Innate nature   *See Dharmata.*

Inner tantras   *See* Three inner tantras.

Instruction class (Tib. *man ngag gi sde*)   The third division of *atiyoga* as arranged by Manjushrimitra.

Jamgön Kongtrül Lodro Thaye(1813–1899)   A contemporary of Khyentse Wangpo. He was also called Jamgön Chökyi Gyalpo or Guna Sagara. He compiled the *Five Treasuries,* including the *Treasury of Spiritual Instructions* and, with the help of Jamyang Khyentse Wangpo, the *Treasury of Precious Termas.*

Jamgön lamas   In this text Jamgön Kongtrül, Khyentse Wangpo, Lama Mipham, and others are often referred to by Dilgo Khyentse as "Jamgön Lama."

Jamyang Loter Wangpo (1847–1914)   A Sakya master.

Jatson Nyingpo (1585–1656)   A treasure revealer who revealed the *Embodiment of the Three Jewels.*

Jetsun Trakpa Gyaltsen (1147–1216)   Son of the great founding master of the Sakya tradition, Sachen Kunga Nyingpo (1092–1158).

Jigmey Gyalwai Myugu (1750–1825)   The chief disciple of Jigmey Lingpa; Patrul Rinpoche's root guru. His reincarnation was Kunzang Dechen Dorje.

Jigmey Lingpa (1729–98)   A treasure revealer who is considered to be the combined emanation of Vimalamitra, King Trisong Detsen, and Gyalsey Lharje. He revealed the *Heart Essence of the Great Expanse.*

Jigmey Senge Wangchuk, King   The present King of Bhutan, who is an emanation of Pema Lingpa.

Jokhang (Tib. *jo khang*)   The main temple in Lhasa built by Songtsen Gampo that housed the Shakyamuni image brought to Tibet by his wife.

Jowo (Tib. *jo bo*)   The Indian image of the Buddha Shakyamuni in *sambhogakaya* form, brought to Tibet by the Chinese queen of King Songtsen Gampo. It was originally in the Ramoche temple and is now the central figure of the Lhasa Jokhang; it is the most important image of worship in Tibet.

Kahma (Tib. *bka' ma*)   The oral lineage of the Nyingma school. The teachings translated chiefly during the period of Padmasambhava's stay in Tibet and since then transmitted from master to student until the present day. *See also* Kahma and terma and Terma.

Kahma and terma (Tib. *bka' gter*)   The kahma and terma of the Nyingma school, i.e., the orally transmitted teachings and the revealed treasure teachings, which are based on both the outer and inner tantras, with emphasis on the practice of the inner tantras of *mahayoga, anuyoga,* and *atiyoga. See also* Kahma and Terma.

Kailash   *See* Mount Kailash.

Kalachakra (Skt.; Tib. *dus kyi 'khor lo*)   Lit., "Wheel of Time," a tantra and a Vajrayana system taught by Buddha Shakyamuni himself, showing the interrelationship between the phenomenal world, the physical body, and the mind.

Kalapa (Tib. *ka la pa*)   *See* Shambhala.

Ka-Nying Shedrup Ling   The monastery founded by Tulku Urgyen at the Bodhnath stupa in Nepal; the abbot and vajra master are his sons Chökyi Nyima and Chokling Rinpoches.

Karma (Skt.; Tib. *las*)   Action, the unerring law of cause and effect according to which all experiences are the result of previous actions, and all actions are the seeds of future existential situations. Actions resulting in the experience of happiness are defined as virtuous; actions that give rise to suffering are described as unvirtuous.

Karma Chagmey   *See* Chagmey Rinpoche.

Karma Monastery (Tib. *kar ma dgon*)   The monastic seat of the Karmapa in Kham, situated in Lhatok on the road between Zurmang and Chamdo.

Kakyab Dorje   *See* Karmapa Kakyab Dorje.

Karmapa Kakyab Dorje (1871–1922)   Gyalwang Kakyab Dorje, the Fifteenth Karmapa.

Kashyapa Buddha (Skt.; Tib. *sangs rgyas 'od srung*)   The buddha that appeared right before Shakyamuni Buddha.

Katok (Tib. *ka thog*)   One of the four main Nyingma monasteries in the Derge region of Eastern Tibet; it was founded by Kadampa Deshek in 1159.

Katok Situ (1880–1925)   Katok Situ Chökyi Gyamtso, one of the main lamas of Katok Monastery in Derge. His reincarnation was called Katok Situ Chöktrul Jampa Chökyi Nyima.

Kesang Chödrön, Queen Mother   The present Queen Mother of Bhutan, the wife of the previous King of Bhutan and mother of the present King of Bhutan, Jigmey Senge Wangchuk.

Khamche Monastic College   The college belonging to Dzongsar Monastery in Derge.

Khamtrul Dongyu Nyima (1932–80)   The Eighth Khamtrul Rinpoche, who was both a student and teacher of Dilgo Khyentse. After escaping Tibet, he founded the Tashi Jong community in Northern India. He passed away in 1980, and the present Ninth Khamtrul now presides over the Khampagar Monastery in Tashi Jong.

Khamtrul Tenpai Nyima (1849–1907)   The Sixth Khamtrul Rinpoche, an important Drukpa Kagyu master who was Shakya Shri's main teacher.

Khandro Lhamo (1913–2003)   Dilgo Khyentse's wife, who married him when she was nineteen years old and he was in his early twenties. She passed away in Nepal while in her nineties, and after her cremation, left very special relics of her eyes, tongue, and heart.

Khandro Tsering Chödrön (born 1925)   Khyentse Chökyi Lodrö's spiritual consort. After Chökyi Lodrö's passing in Sikkim, she spent forty-five years at the palace where his remains were enshrined. She recently moved to the Dzongsar Labrang in

Bir, where Chökyi Lodro's reliquary was moved as well. Being Sogyal Rinpoche's aunt, she also spends time at his retreat center in France, Lerabling.

Khenchen (Tib. *mkhan chen*) A title given to a great scholar of the highest degree.

Khenchen Pema Vajra (1807–1884) An important lama in Dzogchen Monastery. His present incarnation is Tulku Kalzang, the head lama of Dzogchen Monastery in Kham.

Khenpo (Tib. *mkhan po*) A title for a person who has completed the major course of roughly ten years' studies of the traditional branches of Buddhist philosophy, logic, *Vinaya*, and so forth, and afterward has been granted the title in order to teach. This title can also refer to the abbot of a monastery or the preceptor from whom one receives ordination. *See also* Abbot.

Khenpo Bodhisattva *See* Shantarakshita.

Khenpo Ngakchung (1879–1941) Khenpo Ngawang Pelzang, a scholar from the Katok monastic college, who was considered to be an emanation of Vimalamitra and Longchenpa. He was an important reviver of the scholastic lineage of teaching the Dzogchen scriptures. He is the author of the *Guide to the Words of My Perfect Teacher.* Chatral Rinpoche is one of his last living disciples.

Khenpo Pema Sherab (born 1936) Dilgo Khyentse Rinpoche's attendant in Lhasa and India for about ten years. Now the senior teacher in the Namdroling Monastic Institute in Bylakuppe, Penor Rinpoche's settlement.

Khenpo Rigzin Özer Konchog Lodro, a *khenpo* from Dzogchen. He was a close student of Khenpo Yonga and was one of Dilgo Khyentse's teachers.

Khenpo Shenga (1871–1927) Shenpen Chökyi Nangwa, a renowned *khenpo* from Dzachukha who was one of Dilgo Khyentse's main philosophy teachers.

Khenpo Yonga (nineteenth century) Gemang Khenpo Yonten Gyamtso, one of Patrul Rinpoche's main disciples. He wrote the famous *Refulgence of the Sun* and *Radiance of the Moon* commentaries on the *Treasury of Good Qualities.* He was the teacher of Changma Khenpo Thupten, who taught Dilgo Khyentse the *Guhyagarbha Tantra.*

Khenpo Yonten Gyamtso *See* Khenpo Yonga.

Khon tradition (Tib. *'khon lugs*) The Khon branch of the Sakya lineage.

Khon Konchog Gyalpo (1034–1102) Founder of Sakya Monastery; from his time onward, it was the Khon family that continued the Sakya school.

Khyentse Chökyi Lodro (1896–1959) One of five reincarnations of Jamyang Khyentse Wangpo; also known as Jamyang Khyentse or Dharmamati. He was a great master upholding the Ri-me tradition, as well as being one of the two main root gurus of Dilgo Khyentse. His three reincarnations live presently at Bir, Northern India; in Dordogne, France; and in Delhi, India.

Kilaya (Skt.; Tib. *phurba*) The activity aspect of all the buddhas, a wrathful manifestation of Vajrasattva. Practice on this deity is related to the four daggers. *See* Dagger.

Kriya (Skt.; Tib. *bya ba*) The tantra of activity, which is the first of the three outer tantras. *Kriya* tantra emphasizes ritual cleanliness: cleanliness of the mandala and the sacred substances, together with physical cleanliness of the practitioner who practices ablutions and changes clothes three times a day, and eats specific foods.

Kunzang Dechen Dorje An emanation of Jigmey Gyalwai Myugu from Dzagyal Monastery. He was also known as Tsamtrul Rinpoche.

Jeykundo (Tib. *dkye dgu*) A major town in Eastern Tibet.

Lama (Tib. *bla ma,* Skt. *guru*)   A highly realized spiritual teacher. In colloquial language, it is sometimes used as a polite way of addressing a monk.

Lama Ösel   Choying Ösel; one of Dilgo Khyentse's teachers who had been Lama Mipham's main lifelong attendant and student.

Lama Mipham   *See* Mipham Rinpoche.

Lerab Lingpa (1856–1926)   Another name for Tertön Sogyal, a treasure revealer from the last century who emanated two reincarnations, Khenpo Jigmey Puntsök and Sogyal Rinpoche. One of his treasures is *Eliminating Inauspiciousness* (*Tendrel Nysel*).

Level (Tib. *sa*)   *See Bhumi.*

Lhakhang (Tib. *lha khang*)   Temple or shrine room.

Lhasa (Tib. *lha sa*)   The capital of Tibet, literally meaning "abode of the gods."

Longchenpa (1308–63)   Longchen Rabjam Drimey Özer, an incarnation of King Trisong Detsen's daughter Princess Pema Sal, to whom Guru Rinpoche had entrusted his own lineage of Dzogchen known as the *Heart Essence of the Dakinis.* He is regarded as the most important writer on Dzogchen teachings and is the author of the *Seven Treasuries.*

Longchen Rabjam   *See* Longchenpa.

Loppön Nyabchi   Religious secretary to the present Queen Mother Kesang Chödrön.

Loppön Pemala   The head lama from Nyimalung Monastery in Bumthang, Bhutan.

Lord of Secrets (Tib. *gsang ba'i bdag po*)   An epithet for Vajrapani, who is an emanation of Vajrasattva and the compiler of the tantric teachings.

Lords of the three families (Tib. *rigs gsum mgon po*)   The three main bodhisattvas: (1) Manjushri, (2) Avalokiteshvara, and (3) Vajrapani.

Lotsawa (Tib. *lo tsa ba,* Skt. *locchava*)   Tibetan translators of the canonical texts who usually worked closely with Indian *panditas.* The title literally means "bilingual."

Lower realms (Tib. *ngan song*)   The hell, hungry ghost, and animal realms.

Luminosity (Tib. *'od gsal,* Skt. *prabhasvara*)   The clarity or cognizant aspect of the mind, referring to being free from the darkness of unknowing and endowed with the ability to cognize.

Machik Labdrön (1055–1153)   The female master and incarnation of Yeshe Tsogyal who was a student of Padampa Sangye and propagated the *cho* teachings of cutting through ego-clinging.

Madhyamaka   A Mahayana Buddhist tradition taught by Nagarjuna and Ashvagosha. Madhyamaka represents the middle way between eternalism and nihilism. The Indian Madhyamaka schools were divided into Svatantrika, Prasangika, and Yogachara Madhyamaka.

Mahamudra (Skt.; Tib. *phyag rgya chen po*)   Lit., "Great Seal." This refers to the seal of the absolute nature of all phenomena. It is the most direct practice for realizing one's buddha nature. This system of teachings is the basic view of Vajrayana practice according to the New schools of Kagyu, Geluk, and Sakya.

Mahayana (Skt.; Tib. *theg pa chen po*)   The Great Vehicle. The characteristic of Mahayana is the profound view of the emptiness of the ego and of all phenomena, coupled with universal compassion and the desire to deliver all beings from suffering and its causes.

Mahayoga (Skt.; Tib. *rnal 'byor chen po*) The first of the three inner tantras. *Mahayoga* scripture is divided into tantra and sadhana sections. The tantra section consists of the *Eighteen Mahayoga Tantras,* and the sadhana section consists of the *Eight Sadhana Teachings.* It emphasizes the means of the development stage and the view that liberation is attained by growing accustomed to insight into the nature of the indivisibility of the two truths.

Major and minor marks of a Buddha (Tib. *mtshan dang dpe byad*) The thirty-two major physical signs of realization (e.g., the *ushnisha* or crown protuberance) and the eighty minor characteristics (e.g., copper-colored fingernails) that are inherent of all Buddhas.

Mamo (Skt.; Tib. *ma mo*) A class of semidivine beings who sometimes act as protectors of the Dharma.

Mandala (Skt.; Tib. *dkyil 'khor*) Lit., "center and surrounding." A symbolic, graphic representation of a deity's realm of existence.

Mandala offering An offering visualized as the universe; also the offering arrangement in a tantric ritual, which is often placed upon an ornate, circular plate.

Manigenko (Tib. *ma ni dge bkod*) A town in Derge at the junction of different roads leading to Derge, Nangchen, and so forth.

Manjushri (Skt.; Tib. *'jam dpal dyangs*) One of the eight main bodhisattvas who personifies the perfection of transcendent knowledge.

Manjushrimitra (Skt.; Tib. *'jam dpal gshad snyan*) The second human master in the lineage of the Great Perfection, the chief disciple of Garab Dorje. He divided the Dzogchen teachings into the mind class, the space class, and the instruction class.

Mantra (Skt.; Tib. *sngags*) Lit., "mind protection"; thus, syllables or formulas that, when recited with appropriate visualizations, protect the mind of the practitioner from ordinary perceptions. They are invocations and manifestations of the *yidam* deity in the form of sound. It is often a verbal formula that a meditator recites to connect with the energy embodied in the meditation deity.

Mantrika *See* Ngakpa.

Mara *See* Demon.

Maratika (Tib. *ma ra ti ka*) A sacred cave in Nepal where Padmasambhava and his consort Mandarava attained the accomplishment of immortality.

Matrul Rinpoche Taklung Matrul Rinpoche, the head of the Taklung Kagyu school.

Meditate (Tib. *sgom pa*) To let the mind rest on an object of contemplation or to maintain the flow of the view.

Middle Way *See* Madhyamaka.

Milarepa (1040–1123) Lit., "Mila the Cotton-Clad." One of the most famous yogis and poets in Tibetan religious history. Most of the teachings of the Kagyu school passed through him.

Mind class (Tib. *sems sde*) The first of the three divisions of *atiyoga.*

Mind essence (Tib. *sems ngo*) The nature of one's mind, which is taught to be identical to the essence of all enlightened beings. It should be distinguished from "mind" (Tib. *sems*), which refers to ordinary discursive thinking based on ignorance of the nature of thought.

Mind teachings (Tib. *sem khrid*) Instructions on the nature of mind.

Mind treasure (Tib. *dgongs gter*) The revelation in the mind of a treasure revealer of a teaching received in a past life as a disciple of Padmasambhava; such treasures arise spontaneously, without the need of a material treasure.

Mindroling Jetsun Migyur Paldron (1699–1769) The daughter of the founder of Mindroling Monastery, Terdak Lingpa, who became his lineage holder.

Mindroling Monastery (Tib. *o rgyan smin grol gling*) Orgyen Mindroling; the main Nyingma monastery in Central Tibet, founded by Terdak Lingpa in the seventeenth century. It is usually called Mindroling.

Minling Terchen *See* Terdak Lingpa.

Minling Trichen (1931–2008) The eleventh throne holder of Mindroling Monastery and head of the Nyingma school. He is a descendent of Terdak Lingpa, the founder of Mindroling Monastery and was the son of the Tenth Minling Trichen.

Mipham Rinpoche (1846–1912) Lama Mipham, Mipham Gyurmey Mikyod Dorje, was a great Nyingma master and writer of the last century, who was a close student of Jamyang Khyentse Wangpo. He was regarded as a direct emanation of Manjushri and became one of the greatest scholars of his time. His collected works fill more than thirty volumes, and his chief disciple was Shechen Gyaltsap Pema Namgyal.

Mount Kailash (Tib. *ti se*) A sacred mountain in Western Tibet.

Mount Meru (Skt.; Tib. *ri rab*) The mythological mountain at the center of our world-system, surrounded by the four continents and on whose slopes the two lowest classes of gods of the world of desire live. It is encircled by chains of lesser mountains, lakes, continents, and oceans and is said to raise eighty-four thousand leagues above sea level.

Mudra (Skt.; Tib. *phyagrgya*) (1) Secret Mantra gestures. (2) A spiritual consort. (3) The bodily form of a deity.

Naga (Skt.; Tib. *klu*) Powerful, long-lived serpent-like beings dwelling in bodies of water and often guarding great treasures. Nagas belong half to the animal realm and half to the god realm. They generally live in the form of snakes, but many can change into human form.

Nagarjuna (Skt.; Tib. *klu grub*) A great Indian master of philosophy and a tantric siddha. He received the *Lotus Speech* tantras, which he accomplished and transmitted to Padmasambhava. He recovered the *Prajnaparamita* sutras from the land of the nagas and was the founder of the *madyamaka* philosophy. He is said to be a disciple of Dagnyima and the teacher of Kukkuraja.

Nalanda (Skt.; Tib. *na lan dra*) The famous monastic university built at the birthplace of Shariputra some distance north of Bodh Gaya. Nalanda had a long and illustrious history and many of the greatest masters of the Mahayana lived, studied, and taught there. It was destroyed in the thirteenth century.

Namkai Nyingpo A reincarnation of Nub Namkhai Nyingpo, who lives at his monastery in Bumthang, Bhutan. He was a close student of Dilgo Khyentse.

Nangchen (Tib. *nang chen*) A major province in Eastern Tibet.

Nectar (Tib. *bdud rtsi,* Skt. *amrita*) The ambrosia of the gods which confers immortality or other powers.

Nenang Pawo Rinpoche Karma Kagyu master from Nenang Monastery in Central Tibet.

Ngakpa (Tib. *sngags pa*) A Vajrayana practitioner who usually wears white robes and long hair, and can be married.

Ngapo Ngapo Ngawang Jigmey, an influential minister in Lhasa during the fifties who was very devoted to Dilgo Khyentse Rinpoche and helped him while he was in Lhasa.

Ngok Zhedang Dorje One of the main disciples of Drikung Kyobpa, who was a student of Pagmo Drupa.

Ngor Evam Chode (Tib. *ngor e wam chos sde*) The second most important monastery of the Sakya school, founded in 1429 by Ngorchen Kunga Zangpo (1382–1444). It became famous for being the seat of the *Path and Result* teachings, and sheltered a rich library which included a large collection of Sanskrit manuscripts.

Nine vehicles (Tib. *theg pa dgu*) The traditional classification of the Dharma according to the Nyingma school. The first three vehicles are known as the three causal vehicles of the *shravakas, pratyekabuddhas,* and bodhisattvas. Following these are the three vehicles of the outer tantras, namely *kriya-, upa-,* and *yogatantra.* Finally there are the three vehicles of the inner tantras: *maha-, anu-,* and *atiyoga.*

Nirmanakaya (Skt.; Tib. *sprul sku*) Manifested body. The aspect of enlightenment that can be perceived by ordinary beings.

Nirvana (Skt.; Tib. *myang ngan 'das*) Lit., "the state beyond suffering." This term indicates the various levels of enlightenment attainable in both the Hinayana and Mahayana. *See also* Enlightenment.

Nonarising (Tib. *skye ba med pa*) Referring to the state of all phenomena being, according to ultimate truth, devoid of an independent, concrete identity and therefore ultimately free from coming into being, abiding in time and place, or ceasing to exist.

Nonconceptual (Tib. *mi dmigs*) Lit., "thought-free," not held in mind, free of all discursive activity.

Norbu Lingka The summer residence of the Dalai Lama near Lhasa.

Nub Namkhai Nyingpo One of Padmasambhava's twenty-five disciples who was one of the translators sent to India by King Trisong Detsen in order to search for the teachings. Along with his companions he studied the *Yangdag Heruka* doctrine with master Humkara.

Nyak Jnana Kumara An expert translator and disciple of Padmasambhava, Vimalamitra, Vairotsana, and Yudra Nyingpo. He worked closely with Vimalamitra in translating the *mahayoga* and *atiyoga* tantras.

Nyenpa Rinpoche *See* Sangye Nyenpa.

Nyingma (Tib. *rnying ma*) The teachings that were brought to Tibet and translated by Shantarakshita, Padmasambhava, Vimalamitra, and Vairotsana, mainly during the reign of King Trisong Detsen and up until the translator Rinchen Zangpo in the ninth century.

Nyingtik (Tib. *snying thig*) Heart essence; it usually refers to the instruction class of the Dzogchen teachings.

Obscurations (Tib. *sgrib pa,* Skt. *avarana*) Mental factors which veil the true nature of the mind. In the general Buddhist teachings several types are mentioned: the obscuration of karma preventing one from entering the path of enlightenment, the obscuration of disturbing emotions preventing progress along the path, the obscuration of habitual tendencies preventing the vanishing of confusion, and the final obscuration of dualistic knowledge preventing the full attainment of Buddhahood.

Onpo Tenga—Urgyen Tenzin Norbu; a nephew of Gyalsey Shenpen Thaye. He was a disciple of Patrul Rinpoche, the root teacher of Khenpo Shenga and of Dilgo Khyentse's father. People from Onpo Tenga's monastery still believe that Dilgo Khyentse is the reincarnation of Onpo Tenga and that he was taken by force to Shechen Monastery because he had the Khyentse name.

Orgyen Topgyal (1952–) The eldest son of the Third Neten Chokling Pema Drimey. He lives in Bir, India, where he has completed the construction of the Chokling Monastery begun by his father.

Outer tantras (Tib. *phyi rgyud*) The tantras belonging to the three vehicles of *kriya-*, *upa-*, and *yogatantra*.

Padampa Sangye (died 1117) A great Indian siddha who lived around the 11th century and visited Tibet five times, the last time in 1098, where he taught the pacifying system (*shije*), one of the eight practice lineages. His chief Tibetan disciple was the *yogini* Machik Labdrön.

Padmasambhava Lit., "Lotus-Born." Padmasambhava was predicted by the Buddha Shakyamuni as the one who would propagate the teachings of the Vajrayana. Invited to Tibet by King Trisong Detsen in the ninth century, he subjugated the evil forces hostile to the propagation of the Buddhist doctrine there, spread the Secret Mantra teachings, and hid innumerable spiritual treasures for the sake of future generations.

Palpung Monastery (Tib. *dpal spung thub bstan chos 'khor gling*) A monastery in Derge, the monastic seat of the Situ lineage, founded in 1717 by Situ Chökyi Jungney. The retreat center there was started by Jamgön Kongtrül.

Palpung Situ *See* Situ Pema Wangchok Gyalpo.

Panchen Lama The incarnation line of the abbots of Tashi Lhunpo Monastery in Shigatse, which was founded at the time of the Fifth Dalai Lama. The Panchen Lama mentioned in Khandro's story is the ninth Panchen Lama Thupten Chokyi Nyima (1883–1937). The Panchen Lama that Dilgo Khyentse Rinpoche meets upon his return to Kham is the Tenth Panchen Lama, Chokyi Gyaltsen (1938–1989).

Pandita (Skt.; Tib. *pan di ta*) A learned master, scholar, or professor of Buddhist philosophy.

Paramita (Skt.; Tib. *pha rol tu phyin pa*) A transcendent perfection or virtue, the practice of which leads to Buddhahood and therefore forms the practice of bodhisattvas. There are six paramitas: generosity, ethical discipline, patience, diligence, concentration, and wisdom.

Paro Kyechu (Tib. *spa gro skye chu*) A pilgrimage site in Bhutan where King Songtsen Gampo built one of the four district-controlling temples. The temple is still completely intact and is one of the most sacred places in Bhutan. Right next to it is the Guru Temple built by the Queen Mother Kesang Chödrön.

Path (Tib. *lam*, Skt. *marga*) Progress toward enlightenment is described, in both the Mahayana and Hinayana, in terms of the five paths of accumulation, joining, seeing, meditation, and no-more-learning. The first four constitute the path of learning, whereas the path of no-more-learning is Buddhahood.

Patrul Rinpoche (1808–87)   Patrul Urgyen Jigmey Chökyi Wangpo, also known as Dzogchen Palgey. A great nonsectarian master of the nineteenth century who was regarded as the speech emanation of Jigmey Lingpa. He was one of the foremost scholars of his time and was not only known for his scholarship but also for his example of renunciation and compassion. His most famous works include *The Words of My Perfect Teacher* and his commentary on the *Three Lines That Strike the Vital Point,* the epitome of the Dzogchen teachings.

Pema Ösel Dongnak Lingpa   Jamyang Khyentse Wangpo's tertön title given by Padmasambhava.

Pemako (Tib. *pad ma bkod*)   A region in southern Tibet famous for its hidden sacred places; one-third of Pemako is in Tibet and two-thirds is now in the Indian province of Arunachal Pradesh.

Perceptions (Tib. *snang ba*)   That which appears in the eyes of each individual according to his or her tendencies or spiritual development. There are three types of perception: (1) the deluded perceptions that arise in the consciousness of beings of the six realms due to misunderstanding are called the impure, deluded perceptions of the universe and beings; (2) the perceptions of interdependence, magical illusions, corresponding to the eight similes of illusion that one does not apprehend as real; these are the perceptions of the bodhisattvas of the ten levels in their postmeditation state; and (3) the authentic, perfect, perceptions of wisdom; when one has realized the natural state of everything, the beings and the universe appear as the display of the kayas and wisdoms.

Pewar Tulku (born 1933)   A Sakya lama who is now the main lama in Derge Gonchen. He was a close student of Khyentse Chökyi Lodro and received the *Treasury of Precious Termas* from him in Dzongsar at the age of thirteen, together with Dilgo Khyentse, who was then thirty-five.

Peyul Monastery (Tib. *dpal yul*)   One of the four main Nyingma monasteries in Kham.

Pith instructions (Tib. *man ngag,* Skt. *upadesha*)   Instructions explaining the most profound points of practice in a condensed and direct way.

Pointing-out instruction (Tib. *ngo sprod*)   The direct introduction to the nature of mind that is given by the root guru, leading to the recognition of mind's nature.

Prabhahasti   One of the eight Indian vidyadharas who received the *Eight Sadhana Teachings.*

Prajnaparamita (Skt.; Tib. *shes rab kyi pha rol tu phyin pa*)   (1) The *paramita* of transcendent wisdom. (2) The knowledge of emptiness. (3) The collection of sutras belonging to the second turning of the Dharma wheel and expounding the doctrine of emptiness.

Pratimoksha (Tib. *so thar*)   Individual liberation. There are eight sets of individual liberation vows: (1) the eight fasting vows, taken for one day only; the five vows of (2) laymen and (3) laywomen; the vows of (4) male and (5) female novices; (6) additional vows taken by probationer nuns as a step toward becoming full nuns; (7) the discipline of the full nun, *bhikshuni;* and (8) that of the full monk, *bhikshu.*

Pratyekabuddha (Skt.; Tib. *rang sangs rgyas*)   Lit., "solitary buddha"; one who, without relying on a teacher, attains the cessation of suffering by meditating on the twelve links of dependent arising. Though realizing the emptiness of perceived phenomena, *pratyekabuddhas* lack the complete realization of a Buddha and so cannot benefit limitless beings.

Preliminary practices (Tib. *sngon 'gro*)   Comprised of the general outer and the special inner preliminaries. The general outer preliminaries are the four mind changings: reflections on precious human body, impermanence and death, the cause and effect of karma, and the shortcomings of samsaric existence. The special inner preliminaries are the one hundred thousand recitations each of the practices of refuge and *bodhicitta, Vajrasattva,* mandala offering, and guru yoga.

Preta (Skt.; Tib. *yi dvags*)   Famished spirits or hungry ghosts, one of the six classes of beings in samsara.

Primordial purity (Tib. *ka dag*)   The basic nature of sentient beings which is originally untainted by defilement, and beyond confusion and liberation. Sentient beings are by nature primordially pure.

Prince Murub   The second son of King Trisong Detsen who was a close disciple of Padmasambhava and vowed to keep returning to reveal the hidden treasures of Padmasambhava. He reached perfection in learning and at the end of his life attained the rainbow body. He incarnated as a tertön thirteen times, the last time as Chokgyur Lingpa.

Protector   *See* Dharma protector.

Puntsök Chödrön, Queen Mother   The late Royal Grandmother, who was the mother of the previous King of Bhutan. She was the first to invite Dilgo Khyentse to come to Bhutan.

Pure land   *See* Buddhafield.

Pure perception (Tib. *dag snang*)   The perception of the world and its contents as a pure buddhafield or as the display of kayas and wisdoms.

Rabsel Dawa (Tib. *rab-gsal-zla-ba*)   One of Dilgo Khyentse's names, which means "Brilliant Moon."

Rainbow body (Tib. *'ja' lus*)   The death of a practitioner who has reached the exhaustion of all grasping and fixation through the Dzogchen practice of *togal.* For such a practitioner, the five gross elements which compose the physical body dissolve back into their essences, five-colored light. Sometimes only the hair and the nails are left behind.

Raksha Thotreng   One of the twelve manifestations of Guru Rinpoche.

Rakshasa (Skt.; Tib. *srin po*)   (1) One of the eight classes of gods and demons. (2) The cannibal savages inhabiting the southeastern continent of Chamara. (3) The unruly and untamed expression of ignorance and disturbing emotions.

Ratna Lingpa (1403–78)   A treasure revealer who revealed twenty-five profound termas. He was a reincarnation of Langdro Lotsawa and was also called Ratna Lingpa Rinchen Palzangpo.

Rediscovered treasure (Tib. *yang gter*)   A terma that is brought forth again after already having been revealed in the past but not having become widespread before.

Rekong (Tib. *reb gong*)   A place in Amdo which has a large gathering of mantrikas, where Dilgo Khyentse gave the *Treasury of Precious Termas.* Dilgo Khyentse stayed there one year.

Relative truth   *See* Two truths.

Ri-me (Tib. *ris med*)   Nonsectarianism. The Ri-me or nonsectarian movement is a syncretic movement started in nineteenth-century Tibet, intended to minimize sectarian rivalry and revitalize spiritual practice by making use of the texts, commentaries, and procedures from many different Tibetan traditions.

Rinpoche (Tib. *rin po che*)   Lit., "precious." Used as an honorific title to address one's guru, abbot, or any Buddhist teacher.

Roldor Rinpoche (Tib. *rol rdor*)   Roldor Chöktrul Karma Drimey Özer; the reincarnation of Rolpai Dorje, a treasure revealer from Zurmang Monastery. Roldor Chöktrul was one of Dilgo Khyentse's teachers as well as students.

Rumtek   The main seat of the Karma Kagyu lineage in Sikkim, established by the Sixteenth Karmapa.

Sacred commitment   *See Samaya.*

Sadhana (Skt.; Tib. *sgrub thabs*)   Method of accomplishment. A tantric meditative practice involving visualization of deities and the recitation of mantra.

Sakar Monastery (Tib. *sa dkar bsam sgrub gling*)   Sakar Samdrupling, a Sakya monastery at Dilgo Khyentse's village.

Sakya Gongma of Drolma Palace (Tib. *sa skya bdag chen sgrol ma pho brang bdag chen; born 1945*)   The head lama of the Sakya school from the Drolma Palace family. The Puntsök Palace and Drolma Palace families alternate in heading the Sakya school. The present Sakya Trizin is from Drolma Palace, and is the forty-first Sakya Trizin.

Sakya Gongma of Puntsök Palace (Tib. *sa skya bdag chen phun tshogs pho brang;* born 1929)   The head lama of the Sakya school from the Puntsök Palace family. *See also* Sakya Gongma of Drolma Palace.

Sakya Pandita (1182–1251)   Kunga Gyaltsen. One of the founders of the Sakya lineage, who was a renowned scholar and politician.

Samadhi (Skt.; Tib. *bsam gtan*)   Meditative absorption of different degrees.

Samantabhadra (Skt.; Tib. *kun tu bzang po*)   Lit., "Ever-Excellent One." (1) The bodhisattva Samantabhadra, one of the eight close sons of the Buddha, renowned for his offerings emanated through the power of his concentration. (2) The primordial Buddha who has never fallen into delusion, the symbol of awareness, the ever-present pure and luminous nature of the mind.

Samantabhadri (Skt.; Tib. *kun tu bzang mo*)   The consort of the primordial Buddha Samantabhadra. Their union symbolizes the inseparability of the phenomenal world and emptiness.

Samaya (Skt.; Tib. *dam tshig*)   The commitment established between the master and disciples on whom empowerment is conferred.

Sambhogakaya (Skt.; Tib. *longs spyod rdzogs pa'i sku*)   Body of enjoyment. *See* Three kayas.

Samsara (Skt.; Tib. *'khor ba*)   The wheel or round of existence; the state of being unenlightened in which the mind, enslaved by the three poisons of desire, anger, and ignorance, evolves uncontrolled from one state to another, passing through an endless stream of psychophysical experiences, all of which are characterized by suffering.

Samye Monastery (Tib. *bsam yas*)   Lit., "inconceivable." The first monastery in Tibet, located in the Yarlung Valley southeast of Lhasa. It was built by King Trisong Detsen and consecrated by Padmasambhava.

Sangha (Skt.; Tib. *dge 'dun*)   The community of Buddhist practitioners, whether monastic or lay. The term "noble sangha" refers to those members of the Buddhist community who have attained the path of seeing and beyond.

Sangye Nyenpa Sangye Nyenpa Karma Shedrup Tenpai Nyima, the head lama of Benchen Monastery, who was Dilgo Khyentse's elder brother. The present reincarnation lives at Benchen Monastery in Nepal.

Sarasvati (Skt.; Tib. *dbyangs can ma*) Lit., "endowed with melody." A beautiful, muselike goddess of learning.

Secret Mantra (Tib. *gsang sngags*) A branch of the Mahayana, which uses the special techniques of the tantras to traverse the path of enlightenment for all beings more rapidly.

Self-existing wisdom (Tib. *rang byung ye shes*) Basic wakefulness that is independent of intellectual constructs.

Sengtrak Rinpoche A Drukpa Kagyu tulku and student of Ladakh Pema Chogyal, Abo Rinpoche, and Dilgo Khyentse Rinpoche, who lived as a hermit at his retreat place at the Nepalese-Tibetan border, where he had a few hundred monks and nuns in retreat. Dilgo Khyentse often said that he was his most realized disciple. He was Rinpoche's favorite student. Unfortunately he passed away due to a sudden illness in 2005 at the age of 58.

Sentient being (Tib. *sems can*) Any living being in the six realms that has not attained liberation.

Shabkar Tsogdruk Rangdrol (1781–1851) A great master and bodhisattva from Amdo. He lived at Rekong, the place where Dilgo Khyentse first gave the *Treasury of Precious Termas*.

Shakya Shri, Drugu Tokden One of the most famous Drukpa Kagyu yogis, a student of the Sixth Khamtrul Tenpai Nyima, as well as Khyentse Wangpo.

Shamatha (Skt.; Tib. *zhi gnas*) Essentially a concentration in which the mind remains focused on an object of concentration. It is a state of calm abiding, which, though of great importance, is unto itself incapable of overcoming ignorance and the conception of a self.

Shambhala (Tib. *sham bha la*) As taught in the *Kalachakra* tantra, the northern country of Shambhala, a buddhafield with Kalapa as its capital.

Shantarakshita (Skt.; Tib. *zhi ba mtsho*) Also known as Khenpo Bodhisattva. An emanation of the bodhisattva Vajrapani, he was the abbot of Vikramashila and Samye. He ordained the first monks in Tibet and was the founder of a philosophical school combining *madhyamaka* and *yogachara*.

Shantideva (Skt.; Tib. *zhi ba lha*) One of the eighty-four Indian *mahasiddhas*. He composed the famous *The Way of the Bodhisattva* and the *Collected Precepts,* two major texts describing the ideal and practice of a bodhisattva.

Shastra (Skt.; Tib. *bstan bcos*) A commentary on the words of the Buddha.

Shechen Gyaltsap (1871–1926) Shechen Gyaltsap Gyurmey Pema Namgyal, the main disciple of Lama Mipham, and Dilgo Khyentse Rinpoche's root teacher.

Shechen Kongtrül (1901– circa 1960) Shechen Kongtrül Pema Drimey Lekpei Lodro, one of the main lamas at Shechen Monastery in Kham. The present Shechen Kongtrül is Gesar, one of Zurmang Trungpa Rinpoche's sons.

Shechen Rabjam (d. circa 1960) Shechen Rabjam Gyurmey Kunzang Tenpai Nyima, one of the main lamas at Shechen who was one of Dilgo Khyentse's teachers. The present reincarnation is the Seventh Rabjam and is Dilgo Khyentse's grandson, who is abbot of the Shechen Monasteries. He was born in 1966.

Shechen Tennyi Dargyeling (Tib. *zhe chen bstan gnyis dar gyas gling*) The monastery of Shechen Rabjam, Shechen Kongtrül, and Shechen Gyaltsap in Derge. It is one of the four main Nyingma monasteries in Kham. The second Shechen Monastery was built in Bodhnath, Nepal, by Dilgo Khyentse.

Shravaka (Skt.; Tib. *nyan thos*)   A follower of Hinayana, whose goal is to be free of the sufferings of samsara. Unlike the followers of the Mahayana, *shravakas* do not aspire to full enlightenment for the sake of all beings.

Shri Singha   The chief disciple and successor of Manjushrimitra in the lineage of the Dzogchen teachings. He extracted the tantras that had been concealed in Bodh Gaya and went to China, where he classified the *atiyoga* instruction class into four cycles: outer, inner, secret, and innermost secret. His main disciples were Jnana-sutra, Vimalamitra, Padmasambhava, and Vairotsana.

Shri Singha Monastic College   The monastic college belonging to Dzogchen Monastery, where Patrul Rinpoche and many other great masters studied and taught.

Siddha (Skt.; Tib. *grub thob*)   One who has gained accomplishment through the practice of the Vajrayana.

Siddhi   *See* Accomplishment.

Sikkim   An independent kingdom in the Himalayas between Bhutan and Nepal until 1975, when it was annexed by India.

Single sphere (Tib. *thig le nyag gcig*)   A symbolic description of *dharmakaya* as a single sphere, because it is devoid of duality and limitation and defies all conceptual constructs that could be formed about it.

Sitavana (Skt.; Tib. *sil ba'i tshal*)   Cool Grove, a sacred charnel ground to the northeast of Bodh Gaya, which is inhabited by many dakinis and savage beings. It had a great stupa, which contained many special tantras in caskets hidden by the dakinis. Padmasambhava practiced ascetics there for many years. Garab Dorje also spent many years there teaching the dakinis, and it was there that Manjushrimitra met him.

Situ Pema Wangchok Gyalpo (1886–1953)   The Eleventh Situpa from Palpung Monastery. He was enthroned by the Fifteenth Karmapa and studied with Jamgön Kongtrül and Khenpo Shenga. He offered all the Kagyu lineage transmissions to the Sixteenth Karmapa. In this book he is also referred to as Palpung Situ, as opposed to Katok Situ, one of the main lamas from Katok Monastery.

Six doctrines of Naropa   *See* Six yogas.

Six ornaments (Tib. *rgyan drug*)   The six great Indian masters Nagarjuna, Asanga, Dignaga, Aryadeva, Vasubandhu, and Dharmakirti.

Six realms (Tib. *rigs drug*)   Six modes of existence caused and dominated by a particular mental poison: the realms of hells (anger), *pretas* (miserliness), animals (ignorance), humans (desire), demigods (jealousy), and gods (pride). They correspond to deluded perceptions produced by karma and apprehended as real.

Six yogas (Tib. *na ro chos drug*)   The six doctrines of Naropa: *tummo* (mystic heat), illusory body, dream, luminosity, bardo, and *phowa* (consciousness transference).

Skillful means (Tib. *thabs*, Skt. *upaya*)   Refers to compassion, the counterpart of the wisdom of emptiness. By extension, it refers to all kinds of action and training performed with the attitude of *bodhichitta*.

Small hand drum (Skt.; Tib. *da ma ru*)   A small hand drum used in tantric rituals, often made from human skulls.

Smritijana   A great translator. His work marks the boundary of the Nyingma school, the main teachings of which were translated in Tibet before the time of Smritijnana. He came to Tibet early in the eleventh century.

Sogyal Rinpoche (born 1946)   The reincarnation of Tertön Sogyal, also called Lerab Lingpa. The son of Khandro Tsering Chödrön's sister Tselu and Jamga, one of Dilgo Khyentse's nephews. He spent his entire childhood with Khyentse Chökyi Lodro and later moved to England where he studied in Cambridge. He is the director of the worldwide Rigpa centers and the author of the famous book *The Tibetan Book of Living and Dying.*

Songtsen Gampo, King (609–49)   An emanation of Avalokiteshvara, who was the second Dharma king of Tibet. He started to rule the kingdom at thirteen, and at the age of fifteen he ordered his religious minister Gar, an emanation of Vajrapani, to invite the Nepalese princess Bhrikuti and the Chinese princess Wencheng to be his consorts. As dowries these princesses brought images of the Buddha Shakyamuni, as an eight-year-old and a twelve-year-old, respectively.

While the Jokhang temple was being constructed, the building work was disrupted by nonhuman beings. The king and his two consorts then went into retreat in the Maru palace in the Kyechu valley and attained accomplishment by practicing their meditative deity, on whose advice the king built the Border Taming, Further Taming, and District Controlling temples. By doing so, he subdued the malignant earth spirits and was able to successfully erect the Jokhang and the Ramoche temples where the Shakyamuni images were housed. He established a code of laws based on Dharma principles, developed the Tibetan script with the help of his minister Thonmi Sambhota, and began the translation of Buddhist texts into Tibetan.

Space class (Tib. *klong sde*)   The second division of the mind class, which emphasizes emptiness.

Spontaneous presence (Tib. *lhun grub*)   One of the two main aspects of the Dzogchen teaching, the other being primordial purity.

Stupa (Skt.; Tib. *mchod rten*)   Lit., "support of offering"; monuments often containing relics of Buddhist saints. Stupas are built according to universal principles of harmony and order. Often quite large, they are thought to focus and radiate healing energy throughout the six realms of existence.

Suchness (Tib. *de bzhin nyid*, Skt. *tathata*)   A synonym for emptiness or the nature of things, *dharmata.* It is also used to describe the unity of dependent origination and emptiness. *See also Dharmata.*

Sugata (Skt.; Tib. *bde bar gshegs pa*)   Lit., "one who has gone to, and proceeds in, bliss"; an epithet of the buddhas.

Sukhavati (Skt.; Tib. *bde ba can*)   Lit., "the blissful"; the name of the western paradise, the pure land of Buddha Amitabha.

Supreme Heruka (Tib. *dpal chen*)   The main *yidam* of the *Heart Essence of the Great Expanse.*

Sutra (Skt.; Tib. *mdo*)   A discourse or teaching by the Buddha. Also refers to all the causal teachings that regard the path as the cause of enlightenment.

Svabhavikakaya (Skt.; Tib. *ngo bo nyid kyi sku*)   Essence body, the unity of the three kayas. Jamgön Kongtrül defines it as the aspect of *dharmakaya* that is "the nature of all phenomena, emptiness devoid of all constructs and endowed with the characteristic of natural purity." *See also* Four kayas and Three kayas.

Symbol lineage (Tib. *rig 'dzin brda rgyud*) This lineage is transmitted through the awareness holders by means of symbols or gestures, from Manjushrimitra up to and including Vimalamitra.

Taklung (Tib. *stag lung*) A district situated northeast of Lhasa. The Taklung is one of the subsects of the Kagyu school and was founded by Taklung Tangpa about eight hundred years ago.

Taksham Nuden Dorje (born 1655) A treasure revealer also known as Samten Lingpa.

Tantra (Skt.; Tib. *rgyud*) Lit., "continuity." The Vajrayana teachings given by the Buddha in his *sambhogakaya* form. Tantra can also refer to all the resultant teachings of Vajrayana as a whole.

Tantra section (Tib. *rgyud sde*) One of the two divisions of *mahayoga*.

Tantras, scriptures, and instructions (Tib. *rgyud lung man ngag*) Refers to the teachings of *mahayoga, anuyoga,* and *atigyoga,* respectively. Can also refer to the three categories of the fundamental scriptures of Dzogchen.

Tarthang Tulku (born 1934) A Nyingma master who lives in California and has published a large number of sacred texts. He founded the Nyingma Institute in Berkeley, California.

Tashi Namgyal One of Khyentse Chökyi Lodro's closest attendants at Dzongsar. He served the present Dzongsar Khyentse as general secretary, and passed away in 2007.

Tashi Paljor The name given to Dilgo Khyentse by Lama Mipham.

Tashi Tsepel Dilgo Khyentse's grandfather, the governor of Derge.

Tashi Tsering Dilgo Khyentse's father.

Tathagata (Skt.; Tib. *de bzhin gshegs pa*) Lit., "one who has gone thus," a synonym for fully enlightened buddhas.

Tathagatagarbha (Skt.; Tib. *de gshegs snying po*) Buddha nature, the essence of enlightenment present in all sentient beings.

Ten directions (Tib. *phyogs bcu*) The four cardinal and four intermediary directions, together with the zenith and nadir.

Ten levels *See Bhumi.*

Ten principles of a vajra master The ten qualifications of a vajra master: (1) having received the Secret Mantra empowerments and properly keeping the samayas; (2) being very peaceful and teaching ground, path, and result; (3) having studied the tantras and understood their meaning; (4) having completed the recitation practices; and (5) having perfected their outer, inner, and secret signs; (6) having liberated one's being through the wisdom of realizing egolessness; (7) exclusively benefitting others through infinite activities; (8) having given up the eight worldly concerns and only being concerned with the Dharma; (9) having strong revulsion to the sufferings of existence and encouraging others to just that; (10) possessing the blessings of an authentic lineage of masters.

Ten topics of learnedness (Tib. *mkhas bya'i gnas bcu*) The ten topics of learnedness, mentioned in *Gateway to Knowledge.*

Tenga Rinpoche (born 1932) One of the head lamas from Benchen Monastery who now lives at Benchen Monastery in Swayambhunath in the Kathmandu Valley. He was a very close student of Dilgo Khyentse and escaped from Tibet with the Dilgo party. He is the second Tenga Tulku.

Tennyi Lingpa (1480–1535) Tennyi Lingpa Pema Tsewang Gyalpo, a tertön.

Tenzin Dorje A learned master from Benchen Monastery who was Dilgo Khyentse's philosophy teacher.

Terdak Lingpa (1646–1714) A tertön and founder of Mindroling Monastery in Central Tibet, he was the speech emanation of the great translator Vairotsana, and was the brother of Lochen Dharmashri (1654–1717), who was an emanation of Yudra Nyingpo.

Terma (Tib. *gter ma*) Lit., "treasure." The transmission through concealed treasures hidden by Guru Padmasambhava and Yeshe Tsogyal, to be revealed at the proper time by a treasure revealer for the benefit of future disciples. One of the two chief traditions of the Nyingma school, the other being the kahma, or oral lineage. It is said this tradition will continue even long after the *Vinaya* of the Buddha has disappeared. *See also* Kahma and terma.

Tersey Tulku (1887–1955) One of the sons of Chokling Tertön's daughter Konchok Paldron. He was the reincarnation of Wangchok Dorje, Chokling Tertön's son. He was Tulku Urgyen's uncle and teacher.

Tertön (Tib. *gter ston*) A revealer of hidden treasures, who is a reincarnation of one of Padmasambhava's close disciples that made the aspiration to benefit beings in the future.

Tertön Sogyal *See* Lerab Lingpa.

Thangka (Tib. *thang-ka*) A sacred painting on cloth which can be rolled up as a scroll.

Three classes of the Great Perfection (Tib. *rdzogs chen sde gsum*) After Garab Dorje established the 6.4 million Dzogchen tantras in the human world, Manjushrimitra divided them into three categories: the mind class emphasizing luminosity; the space class emphasizing emptiness; and the instruction class emphasizing their inseparability. Also a treasure text revealed by Chokgyur Lingpa.

Three inner tantras (Tib. *nang rgyud gsum*) Mahayoga, anuyoga, and atiyoga. These three tantra classes are the special characteristics of the Nyingma school. They are also known as "development, completion, and Great Perfection," or as "tantras, scriptures, and instructions."

Three Jewels (Tib. *dkon mchog gsum*) The precious Buddha, the precious Dharma, and the precious Sangha.

Three kayas (Tib. *sku gsum*) Dharmakaya, sambhogakaya, and nirmanakaya. The three kayas as ground are "essence, nature, and expression"; as path they are "bliss, clarity, and non-thought"; and as fruition they are the "three kayas of Buddhahood." *See also* four kayas.

Three kinds of discipline (Tib. *tshul khrims gsum*) According to the bodhisattva vehicle, gathering virtues, benefiting sentient beings, and refraining from misdeeds.

Three kinds of wisdom (Tib. *shes rab gsum*) The discriminating wisdoms resulting from hearing, from contemplating, and from practicing the teachings.

Three knowledges (Tib. *mkhyen pa gsum*)   Knowledge of the ground, knowledge of the path, and omniscience.

Three poisons (Tib. *dug gsum*)   The three main afflictions of attachment, hatred, and ignorance.

Three provinces (Tib. *chol kha gsum*)   Central Tibet and Tsang, the province of Dharma; Kham, the province of people; and Amdo, the province of horses.

Three Roots (Tib. *rtsa ba gsum*)   The master, *yidam*, and dakini.

Three *samadhis* (Tib. *ting nge 'dzin gsum*)   In *mahayoga*, the samadhi of suchness, the all-illuminating samadhi, and the samadhi of the seed syllable.

Three services (Tib. *zhabs tog gsum*)   The three ways to serve one's guru: Best is the offering of one's practice; mediocre is to serve him with body and speech; and inferior service is the offering of material things.

Three spheres of reading and abandoning (Tib. *spang klog 'khor lo gsum*)   The three are (1) the study wheel of learning (Tib. *slog pa thos bsam kyi 'khor lo*), (2) the renunciation wheel of contemplation (*spong ba bsam gtan gyi 'khor lo*), and (3) the action wheel of Dharma activity (*bya ba nan tan gyi 'khor lo*).

Three sweets (Tib. *mngar gsum*)   Sugar, honey, and molasses.

Three trainings (Tib. *bslabs pa gsum*, Skt. *trishika*)   Trainings in ethical discipline, concentration, and discriminating knowledge. The three trainings form the basis of the Buddhist path.

Three types of generosity (Tib. *sbyin pa gsum*)   Generosity of material things, of protection from fear, and of the Dharma teachings.

Three whites (Tib. *dkar gsum*)   Yogurt, milk, and butter.

Three worlds (Tib. *khams gsum*)   The world of desire, the world of form, and the world of formlessness.

Tradruk (Tib. *khra 'brug*)   A temple built by King Songtsen Gampo in the Yarlung Valley near Lhasa.

Trangu Rinpoche (born 1933)   The head lama of Trangu Monastery, a Kagyu monastery in Nangchen. At present he lives in the newly established Trangu Monastery in Bodhnath, Nepal. He is the ninth Trangu Tulku.

Transmission (Tib. *lung*)   The direct imparting from master to student in an unbroken line of succession.

Treasure   *See* Terma.

Treasure revealer   *See* Tertön.

Trinley Norbu Rinpoche   A highly realized master who is one of the late Dudjom Rinpoche's sons and the holder of the *New Treasures of Dudjom* lineage. He lives in the United States and has published some amazing books on Buddhism written in English.

Trisong Detsen (790–844)   The third Dharma king of Tibet and an emanation of Manjushri. He appeared in the fifth reign after Songtsen Gampo and was thirteen years old when he started ruling the kingdom. He invited many masters to Tibet to propagate the Dharma, built Samye, and established Buddhism as the state religion of Tibet.

Trulshik Rinpoche (1924–)   The chief disciple of Dudjom Rinpoche and Dilgo Khyentse. His previous incarnation was the Tertön Trulshik Kunzang Thongdrol, who revealed the *Yangti Nagpo* cycle. Trulshik Rinpoche's monastery is in Solukhumbu in

Nepal, where he has four hundred nuns and a hundred monks. He is presently building a second monastery on a hill near Swayambunath in the Kathmandu Valley.

Trungpa Rinpoche Head of the Zurmang Monastery in Nangchen. Trungpa Chökyi Nyinche was one of Dilgo Khyentse's teachers. His reincarnation, the most recent Trungpa, Chökyi Gyamtso (1939–1987), was a student of Dilgo Khyentse who went to the West in the 1960s where he established the Shambhala centers. In the West, he is widely known as Chögyam Trungpa.

Tsadra Rinchen Trak (Tib. *tsa 'dra rin chen brag*) The retreat place of Jamgön Kongtrül above Palpung Monastery in Derge.

Tsampa (Tib. *tsam pa*) Roasted barley four, which is the staple Tibetan food.

Tsar tradition (Tib. *tshar lugs*) The Tsar branch of the Sakya school, founded by Tsarchen Losel Gyamtso (1502–56), a master of extraordinary realization who had pure visions of Padmasambhava, Vajrayogini, Chakrasamvara, and so forth. He transmitted and elaborated on the uncommon oral instructions of the *Path and Result,* as well as the uncommon Vajrayogini practice of *Naro Kechari.*

Tsawarong (Tib. *rgyal mo tsha ba rong*) Gyalmo Tsawarong, a district between Eastern Tibet and China, which is the southeastern part of Kham at the Chinese border, where the translator Vairotsana was banished to.

Tsele Natsok Rangdrol (born 1608) An important master of the Kagyu and Nyingma schools and a disciple of Jatson Nyingpo. He is the author of *Mirror of Mindfulness, Lamp of Mahamudra,* and *Empowerment.*

Tseringma Tashi Tseringma, lit., "Auspicious Lady of Long Life"; the chief of the five sister goddesses of long life, who are protectors of Tibet and the Dharma. Their residence is the five-peaked Jomo Gangkar mountain on the border of Tibet and Nepal.

Tsewang Paljor (1909–1999) General secretary to Khentse Chökyi Lodro at Dzongsar Monastery. Later he married Khandro Tsering Chödrön's sister Tselu, who had previously been married to Dilgo Khyentse's nephew Jamga.

Tsikey Chokling (born 1953) The reincarnation of Chokgyur Lingpa from Tsikey Monastery. The present Tsikey Chokling is a son of Tulku Urgyen and is the father of Dilgo Khyentse's reincarnation. He lives at Ka-Nying Shedrup Ling in Nepal and is the fourth incarnation of Chokgyur Lingpa.

Tsikey Monastery One of the three seats of Chokgyur Lingpa, located at the confluence of the Tsichu and Kela rivers, in Nangchen, ten minutes from the border of the Tibet Autonomous Region (TAR). Above the monastery is Norbu Punsum, the site where Chokgyur Lingpa revealed the *Heart Practice Spontaneously Fulfilling All Wishes* (Thugdrub Sampa Lhundrup).

Tso Pema (Tib. *mtsho pad ma*) Lotus Lake. An Indian town called Rewalsar in the Mandi district of Himachal Pradesh, Northern India, where Guru Padmasambhava is said to have been burned on a pyre with his consort Mandarava. Padmasambhava transformed the fire into a lake.

Tsongkhapa (1357–1419) The founder of the Geluk school, which was a reformation of the Kadam tradition of Atisha.

Tsultrim Rinchen (1697–1774) A Sakya translator from Sakar Monastery.

Tsurphu Monastery (Tib. *mtshur phu*) The seat of the Karmapa in Central Tibet.

Tulku Urgyen (1920–96) A great-grandson of Chokgyur Lingpa who was recognized by the Fifteenth Karmapa as the reincarnation of Guru Chowang. He was a great Dzogchen master and holder of the teachings of Chokgyur Lingpa, Khyentse Wangpo, and Jamgön Kongtrül. He founded the Ka-Nying Shedrup Ling Monastery in Bodhnath, Nepal, as well as a retreat center at the Asura Cave and another at Swayambunath, both in the Kathmandu Valley.

Tushita (Skt.; Tib. *dga' ldan*) Lit., "Joyous," the name of the pure land of the thousand buddhas of this aeon, inhabited only by bodhisattvas and buddhas. The heavenly realm in which Lord Maitreya currently resides awaiting his appearance in this world as the next buddha.

Twelve links of dependent origination (Tib. *rteu 'brel yan lag bcu gnyis*) Namely, ignorance; habitual tendencies; consciousness; name and form; the six activity fields of eye, ear, nose, tongue, body, and intellect; contact; feeling; craving; aggregates; birth; old age; and death.

Twelve manifestations of Guru Rinpoche (Tib. *rnam 'phrul bcu gnyis*) According to the Heart Practice Dispelling All Obstacles, there are twelve manifestations instead of the usual eight. These are all called Vidyadharas, and are Raksha Thotreng, Lion of Speech, Victorious Lineageholder, Eminent Person, Slayer of Demons, Great Magician, Supreme Ornament of Jampudvipa, Lotus-Born, Especially Noble, Vajra Wrath, Guide to the Fortunate, and Great Bliss King.

Two accumulations (Tib. *tshogs gnyis*, Skt. *sambharadvaya*) The accumulations of merit and wisdom.

Two doctrines (Tib. *bstan gnyis*) The Hinayana and Mahayana doctrines.

Two truths (Tib. *bden gnyis*) Relative truth and absolute truth. Relative truth describes the seeming, superficial, and apparent mode of all things. Absolute truth describes the real, true, and unmistaken mode.

Uddiyana (Skt.; Tib. *o rgyan*) Also called Orgyen or Urgyen, a region in ancient India corresponding, according to some authorities, to the valley of Swat between Afghanistan and Kashmir. Uddiyana was the birthplace of Padmasambhava and Garab Dorje.

Vairochana (Skt.; Tib. *rnam par snang mdzad*) The main buddha of the *tathagata* family corresponding to the aggregate of form.

Vairotsana The great Tibetan translator during the reign of King Trisong Detsen. He was sent to India at the age of fifteen to search for the Dzogchen teachings and returned to Tibet when he was in his fifties, after having studied with Shri Singha and other Dzogchen masters in India. Along with Padmasambhava and Vimalamitra, he was one of the three main teachers to bring the Dzogchen teachings to Tibet.

Vajra (Skt.; Tib. *rdo rje*) Diamond or vajra weapon, a symbol of indestructibility; also used to represent skillful means or compassion. The vajra is frequently employed in tantric rituals in conjunction with a bell, which in turn symbolizes the wisdom of emptiness.

Vajradhara (Skt.; Tib. *rdo rje 'dzin pa*) Lit., "Vajra Holder." An emanation of Samantabhadra. The *dharmakaya* buddha of the New schools. Can also refer to one's personal teacher of Vajrayana or to the all-embracing buddha nature.

Vajrakilaya *See* Kilaya.

Vajrapani (Skt.; Tib. *phyag na rdo rje*) A great bodhisattva and one of the eight close sons. He personifies the power and mind of all buddhas.

Vajrasattva (Skt.; Tib. *rdo rje sems dpa'*)   The buddha who embodies the hundred families. The practice of Vajrasattva and recitation of his hundred-syllable mantra are the most effective methods for purifying negative actions. In the *atiyoga* lineage, he is the *sambhogakaya* buddha.

Vajrayana (Skt.; Tib. *rdo rje theg pa*)   The corpus of teachings and practices based on the tantras, which are scriptures that discourse upon the primordial purity of the mind. *See* Secret Mantra.

Vajrayogini (Tib. *rdo-rje phag-mo*)   A tantric Buddhist yidam, which originated in India between the tenth and the twelfth centuries. She is visualized as a sixteen-year-old female, translucent, deep red, holding a skull-cup filled with blood, and a curved vajra knife. Her consort is Chakrasamvara.

Varanasi   A city in northern India located on the Ganges River that is a main place of pilgrimage for Hindus. At nearby Sarnath, the Buddha Shakyamuni turned the first wheel of the Dharma with his teachings on the Four Noble Truths.

Vehicle (Tib. *thegpa*, Skt. *yana*)   The means for traveling the path to enlightenment.

Vidyadhara (Skt.; Tib. *rig 'dzin*)   Lit., "awareness-holder," someone of high attainment in the Vajrayana. According to the Nyingma tradition, there are four levels of vidyadharas corresponding to the ten (sometimes eleven) levels of realization of the Sutrayana. They are (1) the vidyadhara with corporeal residue, (2) the vidyadhara with power over life, (3) the *mahamudra* vidyadhara, and (4) the vidyadhara of spontaneous presence.

View (Tib. *lta ba*, Skt. *dristi*)   In the context of Mahamudra, it refers to the authentic point of view, the actual knowledge and experience of the natural state. It can also be a particular understanding based on the philosophical study.

Vimalamitra (Skt.; Tib. *dri med bshes gnyen;* eighth century)   One of the greatest masters and scholars of Indian Buddhism. He went to Tibet in the ninth century where he taught and translated numerous Sanskrit texts. He was one of the principal sources, together with Guru Padmasambhava, of the Dzogchen teachings in Tibet.

Vishuddha (Skt.; Tib. *yang dag*)   The heruka of the vajra family, or the tantric teachings connected to that wrathful deity; one of the *Eight Sadhana Teachings* of the Nyingma school.

Vow-holder (Tib. *dam can*)   Oath-bound guardians and dharmapalas. *See also* Dharma protector.

Vulture Peak (Tib. *bya rgod phung po'i ri*)   Place near Rajgir in Bihar, central India, where the Buddha taught the *Prajnaparamita* sutras (i.e., the Second Turning of the Dharma Wheel).

Wisdom   (1) (Tib. *shes rab*, Skt. *prajna*) The ability to discern correctly; the understanding of emptiness. (2) (Tib. *ye shes*, Skt. *jnana*) The primordial and non-dual knowing aspect of the nature of the mind.

Wish-fulfilling gem (Tib. *yid bzhin nor bu*, Skt. *chintamani*)   A fabulous jewel found in the realms of the gods or nagas that fulfills all wishes. The Buddha, one's master, and the nature of mind are often referred to as wish-fulfilling gems.

Wish-fulfilling tree (Tib. *dpag bsam gyi shing*)   A magical tree that has its roots in the demigod realm, but bears its fruit in the divine sphere of the Thirty-three.

Wutai Shan (Tib. *ri bo rtse lnga*)   Lit., "Five-Peaked Mountain," a mountain in northeast China that is sacred to Manjushri and where Vimalamitra is said to reside.

Yakchar   The name of a treasure revealer.

Yamantaka (Skt.; Tib. *gshin rje gshed*)   A wrathful form of Manjushri and a *yidam* who is one of the *Eight Sadhana Teachings* of *mahayoga*.

Yamantaka Cave (Tib. *gshin rje'i sgrub phug*)   The cave above Dzogchen Monastery where Patrul Rinpoche stayed in retreat and wrote *The Words of My Perfect Teacher*.

Yanglesho   A cave in the southern part of the Kathmandu Valley in Nepal, where Padmasambhava attained accomplishment of Mahamudra through the practice of Vishuddha and Kilaya.

Yarlha Shampo   (1) A deity who rides a white yak and was bound under oath by Padmasambhava. (2) A mountain in the Yarlung Valley of Central Tibet, where the first king of Tibet is said to have descended from the sky.

Yidam (Tib. *yid-dam*)   A tantric deity representing different aspects of enlightenment. *Yidams* may be peaceful or wrathful, male or female, and are meditated upon according to the nature and needs of the individual practitioner.

Yoga (Skt.; Tib. *rnal 'byor*)   Lit., "joining" or "union" with the natural state of the mind. A term commonly used to refer to spiritual practice.

Yogatantra (Skt.; Tib. *rnal 'byor rgyud*)   The third of the three outer tantras, which relates to the view, rather than the conduct, and regards the deity as being the same level as oneself.

Yogi (Skt.; Tib. *rnal 'byor pa*)   A tantric practitioner. Someone who has already attained stability in the natural state of mind.

Yogini (Skt.; Tib. *rnal 'byor ma*)   A female yogi.

Yudra Nyingpo   The main disciple and lineage holder of Vairotsana. He was the reincarnation of Tsang Lekdrub, and was born in Tsawarong, where he met Vairotsana during his exile.

Yumka (Tib. *yum bka' bde chen rgyal mo*)   Queen of Great Bliss. A female *yidam*; the practice of this *dakini* is part of the *Heart Essence of the Great Expanse* cycle revealed by Jigmey Lingpa.

Zhabdrung (Tib. *zhabs drung*)   A vajra master in charge of tantric ceremonies, whose religious rank is just two steps down from the highest hierarch of the Sakya lineage.

Zurmang Monastery   Zurmang Dutsitil, the monastic seat of the Trungpa Rinpoches in Nangchen, Eastern Tibet.

Selected Bibliography

Abhidharma (Skt.; Tib. *mngon pa*)   The third section of the *Tripitaka* (the other two are the *Vinaya* and *Sutras*). Contains systematic teachings on metaphysics, focused on the training of discriminating knowledge by analyzing elements of experience and investigating the nature of existing things.

Abhirati Vajrasattva (Tib. *rdor sems mngon dga'*)   *Manifest Joy of Vajrasattva,* a Vajrasattva sadhana from the Mindroling tradition.

Adornment of Realization of the Lord of Secrets (Tib. *gsang bdag dgongs rgyan*)   *Sangdag Gongyen,* Minling Lochen Dharmashri's exegesis of the *Guhyagarbha Tantra.*

Amitayus Sutra (Tib. *tshe mdo*).

Chagmey Retreat Manual (Tib. *chags med ri chos*)   A famous retreat manual popular in both the Nyingma and Kagyu traditions, composed by Karma Chagmey.

Chanting the Names of Manjushri (Tib. *'phags pa 'jams dpal gyi mtshan yang dag par brjod pa,* Skt. *manjushri-nama-sangirti*)   The litany of the names of Manjushri.

Clearing the Obstacles of the Path supplication (Tib. *gsol 'debs bar chad lam sel*)   *Barchey Lamsel,* a prayer of the *New Treasures of Chokgyur Lingpa.* This prayer was also discovered by other treasure revealers, but it was Chokgyur Lingpa who discovered the sadhana cycle that goes along with the prayer. The sadhana cycle is called the *Heart Practice Dispelling All Obstacles.*

Combined Sadhana of the Three Roots (Tib. *rtsa gsum dril sgrub*)   *Tsasum Drildrub,* the first terma in Tibet, revealed by Tertön Drodul Sangye Lama (1000–1080). It appeared again as a rediscovered treasure to Jamyang Khyentse Wangpo and as a mind treasure of the Third Karmapa Rangjung Dorje.

Commentary on Valid Cognition (Tib. *tshad ma rnam grel,* Skt. *pramana-vartika*)   The greatest work of Indian Buddhist epistemology and logic, an inquiry into the valid means of knowing, one of the seven treatises on logic by Dharmakirti (seventh century).

Crystal Cave Chronicles (Tib. *pad ma bka' thang shel brag ma*)   A biography of Guru Padmasambhava that was revealed by Urgyen Lingpa (1323–74), so called because it was revealed at the Crystal Cave of Yarlung. Translated and published in two volumes as *The Life and Liberation of Padmasambhava* (Berkeley, Calif.: Dharma Publishing, 1970).

Dispelling the Darkness of the Ten Directions (Tib. *phyogs bcu mun sel*)   A commentary on the *Guhyagarbha Tantra* by Longchenpa.

Eight Commands: Union of the Sugatas (Tib. *bka' brgyad bde 'dus*)   *Kabgye Deshek Dupa,* a terma in nine or thirteen volumes revealed by Nyang Ral Nyima Özer.

Eighteen major scriptures of the mind class (Tib. *sems sde bco brgyad*) The eighteen major scriptures of the mind class. A set of Dzogchen tantras taught by Shri Singha to Vairochana and Tsang Lebdrub, of which the first five were translated by Vairotsana before his exile to Tsawarong, and the remaining thirteen were later translated by Vimalamitra and Yudra Nyingpo.

Eighteen root tantras of *mahayoga* (Tib. *ma ha yo ga'i rgyud sde bco brgyad*) The five root tantras of body, speech, mind, quality, and activity: *Sarvabuddha Samayoga, Secret Moon Essence, Gathering of Secrets, Glorious Supreme Primal Tantra,* and *Activity Garland.* Five display tantras related to sadhana practice: *Heruka Display Tantra, Supreme Steed Display Tantra, Compassion Display Tantra, Nectar Display Tantra,* and *Twelvefold Kilaya Tantra.* Five tantras related to conduct: *Mountain Pile, Awesome Wisdom Lightning, Arrangement of Precepts, One-Pointed Samadhi,* and *Rampant Elephant Tantra.* Two subsequent tantras for amending incompleteness: *Magical Net of Vairotsana* and *Skillful Lasso.* The one outstanding tantra that epitomizes them all is the *Secret Essence,* the tantra of the *Magical Net of Vajrasattva,* known as the *Guhyagarbha Tantra.*

Embodiment of Realization (Tib. *dgongs 'dus*) An abbreviation of the *Embodiment of Realization of All Buddhas;* the most important *anuyoga* scripture.

Embodiment of Realization of the Three Roots (Tib. *rtsa gsum dgongs 'dus*) *Tsasum Gongdu,* a terma by Jamgön Kongtrül Lodro Thaye.

Embodiment of the Three Roots (Tib. *rtsa gsum spyi 'dus snying thig*) *Tsasum Chidu Nyingtik,* an abbreviation of *Heart Essence of the Embodiment of the Three Roots,* an earth treasure revealed by Jamyang Khyentse Wangpo.

Entering the Middle Way (Tib. *dbu ma la 'jug pa,* Skt. *madhyamakavatara*) Philosophical text on the Middle Way by the Indian master Chandrakirti. Translated by the Padmakara Translation Group with the commentary by Mipham Rinpoche and published as *Introduction to the Middle Way* (Boston: Shambhala Publications, 2005).

Excellent Path of Bliss (Tib. *bde-chen lam bzang*) A commentary on the *Heart Essence of Vima Unifying Mother and Son* by Mindroling Jetsun Migyur Paldron.

Extensive Treasury of Instructions (Tib. *rgya chen bka' mdzod*) *Gyachen Kadzo,* one of the *Five Treasuries* of Jamgön Kongtrül, which contains his collected writings.

Finding Rest from Illusion (Tib. *sgyu ma ngal gso*) Part of the *Trilogy of Natural Ease.*

Finely Woven (Tib. *zhib mo rnam 'thag,* Skt. *vaidalya-sutra*). One of the six works on the logic of the Madhyamaka by Nagarjuna.

Five Chronicles (Tib. *bka' thang sde lnga*) The five chronicles revealed by Urgyen Lingpa, dealing respectively with kings, queens, ministers, scholars and translators, and gods and demons.

Five Treasuries (1) *The Treasury of Precious Termas* (Tib. *rin chen gter mdzod*), (2) *The Treasury of Spiritual Instructions* (Tib. *gdam ngag mdzod*), (3) *The Secret Mantra Treasury of the Kagyu Lineage* (Tib. *bka' 'brgyud snags mdzod*), (4) *The Extensive Treasury of Instructions* (Tib. *rgya chen bga' mdzod*), (5) *The Treasury of All-Pervading Knowledge* (Tib. *shes bya kun khyab mdzod*).

Five Treatises of Lord Maitreya (Tib. *byams chos sde lnga*) The five texts taught to Asanga by Maitreya: (1) *Ornament of the Sutras* (Tib. *mdo sde rgyan*), (2) *Analysis of the Middle and Extremes* (Tib. *dbus mtha rnam 'byed*), (3) *Analysis of Phenomena* *and Dharmata* (Tib. *chos dang chos-nyid rnam 'byed*), (4) *Unexcelled Continuity* (Tib. *rgyud bla-ma*), and (5) *Ornament of Realization* (Tib. *mngon rtogs rgyan*).

Four Hundred Stanzas on Madhyamaka (Tib. *dbu ma bzhi brgya pa*, Skt. *madhyamaka-catuhshataka*) A classic text by Aryadeva, a student of Nagarjuna, extensively elucidating the intention of Nagarjuna.

Four Parts of the Heart Essence (Tib. *snying thig ya bzhi*) *Nyingtik Yabzhi,* one of the most famous collections of Dzogchen scriptures. Vimalamitra united the two aspects of the innermost unexcelled cycle—the explanatory lineage with scriptures and the hearing lineage without scriptures—and concealed them to be revealed as the *Heart Essence of Vima.* Longchenpa clarified them in his fifty-one sections of the *Guru's Innermost Essence.* Padmasambhava concealed his teachings on the innermost unexcelled cycle to be revealed in the future as the *Heart Essence of the Dakinis.* Longchenpa also clarified these teachings in his *Quintessence of the Dakinis.* These four exceptional sets of Dzogchen instructions are, together with Longchenpa's additional teachings, *Profound Quintessence,* contained in this collection.

Fundamental Treatise on the Middle Way (Tib. *dbu ma rtsa ba shes rab*, Skt. *madhyamaka-karika*) A classic *madhyamaka* text by Nagarjuna. Numerous translations and commentaries exist. A current edition is *The Fundamental Wisdom of the Middle Way* (New York: Oxford University Press, 1995).

Gangloma (Tib. *gang blo ma*) A famous praise to Manjushri.

Gateway to Knowledge (Tib. *mkhas pa'i tshul la 'jug pa'i sgo*) A text by Mipham Rinpoche, a presentation of the principles and categories of Buddhist scholasticism, translated into English and published in three volumes under the name *Gateway to Knowledge* (Hong Kong: Rangjung Yeshe Publications, 1997).

Gathering of the Vidyadharas (Tib. *rig 'dzin 'dus pa*) The guru yoga practice of the *Heart Essence of the Great Expanse* cycle revealed by Jigmey Lingpa.

General Meaning of the Secret Essence: Core of Luminosity (Tib. *spyi don 'od gsal snying po*) *Chidon Ösel Nyingpo,* a commentary on the *Guhyagarbha Tantra* by Mipham Rinpoche.

Great Chetsun's Profound Essence of Vimala (Tib. *lche btsun chen po bi ma la'i zab thig*) One of the texts belonging to the *Heart Essence of Chetsun* cycle, a mind treasure of Khyentse Wangpo that was directly transmitted to him by Chetsun Senge Wangchuk, who was an emanation of Vimalamitra. He was also one of Khyentse Wangpo's previous incarnations.

Guhyagarbha (Skt.; Tib. *gsang ba'i snying po*) *Secret Essence,* the chief *mahayoga* tantra of the Nyingma school.

Guide to the Words of My Perfect Teacher (Tib. *kun bzang bla ma'i zhal lung gi zin bris*) A commentary by Khenpo Ngakchung on *The Words of My Perfect Teacher.* Its translation by the Padmakara Translation Group was published by Shambhala Publications in 2004.

Guru's Innermost Essence (Tib. *bla ma yang thig yid bzhin nor bu*) *Lama Yangtik,* an abbreviation of the title *Wish-Fulfilling Gem of the Guru's Innermost Essence,* part of Longchenpa's *Four Parts of the Heart Essence;* Longchenpa's commentary on both the *Heart Essence of the Dakinis* and the *Heart Essence of Vima.*

Heart Essence (Tib. *snying thig*) Usually the abbreviation of *Heart Essence of the Great Expanse.*

Heart Essence of Chetsun (Tib. *lce btsun snying thig*)   A rediscovered treasure revealed by Jamyang Khyentse Wangpo, which is one of the most important Dzogchen instructions of recent times.

Heart Essence of Mother and Son (Tib. *snying thig ma bu'i khrid yig*)   A text by Jamgön Kongtrül that comes in the *Treasury of Spiritual Instructions.*

Heart Essence of the Great Expanse (Tib. *klong chen snying thig*)   *Longchen Nyingtik*, a cycle of teachings revealed to Jigmey Lingpa over the course of three visions of Longchenpa.

Heart Essence of the Immortal Arya (Tib. *'chi med 'phags ma'i snying thig*)   *Phagmai Nyingtik*, a long-life sadhana of White Tara in union with the red Avalokiteshvara, which is one of the mind treasures of Khyentse Wangpo. It includes the three longevity divinities, White Tara, Amitayus, and Ushnisha Vijaya.

Heart Essence of the Immortal Lake-Born (Tib. *'chi med mtsho skyes snying thig*)   *Chimey Tsokye Nyingtik*, a terma of Jamyang Khyentse Wangpo.

Heart Essence of Vima (Tib. *bi ma snying thig*)   *Vima Nyingthik*, the collected writings of Vimalamitra. Part of the *Four Parts of the Heart Essence.*

Heart Essence of Yuthok (Tib. *g.yu thog snying thig*)   A practice on Yuthok Yonten Gonpo (708–833), a famous master and physician, written by Dharma Senge.

Heart Practice Dispelling All Obstacles (Tib. *thugs sgrub bar chad kun sel*)   *Tukdrub Barchey Kunsel*, a cycle of teachings revealed by Chokgyur Lingpa together with Jamyang Khyentse Wangpo, consisting of about ten volumes of texts.

Hundred Thousand Nyingma Tantras (Tib. *rnying ma rgyud 'bum*)   *Nyingma Gyubum*, a collection of scriptures belonging to the three inner tantras—the *mahayoga, anuyoga*, and *atigyoga* tantras—gathered by Ratna Lingpa and reedited by Jigmey Lingpa. Dilgo Khyentse Rinpoche published one edition in New Delhi in 1974 which consists of 36 volumes: 10 volumes of *atiyoga*, 3 volumes of *anuyoga*, 6 volumes of the tantra section of *mahayoga*, 13 volumes of the sadhana section of *mahayoga*, 1 volume of protector tantras, and 3 volumes of catalogues and historical background.

Innermost Sealed Essence Guru Sadhana (Tib. *yang gsang bla sgrub thig le rgya can*)   *Tigle Gyachen*, the guru sadhana of Longchen Rabjam that belongs to the *Heart Essence of the Great Expanse.*

Jewel Ornament of Liberation (Tib. *dvags po'i thar rgyan*)   A famous text on the stages of the path by Gampopa, Milarepa's chief disciple and lineage holder. Numerous translations exist, including one by Herbert V. Guenther (Boston: Shambhala Publications, 1986).

Kangyur (Tib. *bka' 'gyur*)   The translated words of the Buddha Shakyamuni in 104 volumes. With the *Tengyur*, it forms the Tibetan Buddhist canon.

Lamp of Speech Grammar (Tib. *dag yig ngag sgron*)   An orthographical dictionary in verse by Palkhang Lotsawa, including a detailed analysis of the final letters.

Letter to a Friend (Tib. *bshes pa'i spring yig*, Skt. *suhrllekha*)   Nagarjuna's letter to his friend, King Surabhibhadra, written in the first or second century. Various translations exist in English, including Kangyur Rinpoche's *Nagarjuna's Letter to a Friend* (Ithaca, N.Y.: Snow Lion Publications, 2006).

Magical Display of the Peaceful and Wrathful Ones (Tib. *sgyu 'phrul zhi khro*, Skt. *shanti-krodha-mayajala*)   *Gyutrul Zhitro*, the *mahayoga* style of the mandala of the hundred peaceful and wrathful deities.

Magical Net (Tib. *sgyu 'phru 'drwa ba*)   An abbreviation of the *Magical Net of Vajrasattva.*

Magical Net of Vajrasattva (Tib. *rdor je sems dpa' sgyu 'phrul 'drwa ba*)   Another name for the *Guhyagarbha Tantra.*

Mindroling Vajrasattva (Tib. *smin gling rdor sems*)   A treasure revealed by Terdak Lingpa.

Northern Treasures (Tib. *byang gter*)   *Jangter,* a cycle of treasures revealed by Rigzin Gödem (1337–1408).

Novice Aphorisms (Tib. *dge tshul ka ri ka*)   *Getsul Karika,* verses explaining the details of the novice vows.

Nyingma Kahma (Tib. *snga 'gyur ma bka' ma*)   The collection of teachings from the oral lineage, as opposed to the treasure lineage, of the Nyingma school, which consists of fifty-six volumes in the expanded version published by Dudjom Rinpoche in Delhi in 1982.

Ocean of Accomplishment (Tib. *dngos grub rol mtsho*)   A liturgy to the protectors.

Ocean of Dharma That Embodies All Teachings (Tib. *bka' 'dus chos kyi rgya mtsho*)   A treasure revealed by Urgyen Lingpa.

Openness of Realization Tantra (Tib. *dgongs pa zang thal gyi rgyud*)   *Gongpa Zang-tal,* a tantric scripture concealed by Guru Rinpoche and revealed by Rigzin Gödem, the master who revealed the *Northern Treasures.* It contains the renowned "Aspirations of Samantabhadra."

Oral Advice (Tib. *gsang bdag zhal lung*)   *Sangdag Zhalung,* Minling Lochen Dharmashri's exegesis of the *Guhyagarbha Tantra.*

Oral Instructions in the Gradual Path of the Wisdom Essence (Tib. *zhal gdams lam rim ye shes snying po*)   *Lamrim Yeshe Nyingpo,* a most precious, concise, and profound teaching by Guru Rinpoche, which condenses the entire path. Praised by Jamyang Khyentse Wangpo as being more valuable than thirty yak-loads of scriptures, it comprises, together with a commentary by Jamgon Kongtrul, the last volume in both the *Treasury of Precious Termas* and the *New Treasures of Chokgyur Lingpa.* It was translated as *The Light of Wisdom* (Boston: Shambhala Publications, 1995).

Ornament of the Middle Way (Tib. *dbu ma rgyan,* Skt. *madhyamakalamkara-karika*)   A treatise on the Middle Way by Shantarakshita, eighth century. It has been translated as *The Adornment of the Middle Way* by the Padmakara Translation Group (Boston: Shambhala Publications, 2005).

Praise to the Vinaya (Tib. *'dul bstod*)   A text by Patrul Rinpoche.

Prajnaparamita Ornament of Realization (Tib. *sher phyin mngon par rtogs pa'i rgyan gyi tshig don rnam par bshad pa ma pham zhal lung*)   A commentary on the monumental systematization of *Prajnaparamita* philosophy, Maitreya's *Ornament of Realization,* by Böpa Tulku Dongak Tenpai Nyima (1907–59).

Primordial Wisdom Guru (Tib. *ye shes bla ma*)   *Yeshe Lama,* a detailed guide to Dzogchen practice by Jigmey Lingpa, which is part of the *Heart Essence of the Great Expanse* cycle.

Profound Inner Topics (Tib. *zab mo nang don*)   Philosophical text written by Karmapa Rangjung Dorje.

Pure Gold Great Perfection cycle (Tib. *rdzogs chen gser zhun*)   Mipham Rinpoche's commentary on Manjushrimitra's *Writing in Gold on Stone* (Tib. *rdo la gser zhun*).

Quintessential Kilaya of the Hearing Lineage (Tib. *bsnyan brgyud gnad thig phur ba*)   A *Vajrakilaya* mind treasure revealed by Khyentse Wangpo.

Radiance of the Moon   *See* Refulgence of the Sun.

Refulgence of the Sun and Radiance of the Moon (Tib. *nyi zla'i snang ba*)   Two texts by Khenpo Yonga (Khenpo Yonten Gyamtso) in three volumes, which are the most elaborate commentaries on the *Treasury of Precious Qualities* and were often taught by Dilgo Khyentse Rinpoche.

Refutation of Criticism (Tib. *rtsod zlog*, Skt. *vigraha-vyavartani*)   A text by Nagarjuna that belongs to his six logical works on *madhyamaka*.

Resting in the Nature of Mind (Tib. *sems nyid ngal gso*)   Part of the *Trilogy of Natural Ease.*

Secret Assembly Longevity Practice (Tib. *tshe sgrub gsang ba 'dus pa*)   *Sangwa Dupa,* a terma revealed by Ratna Lingpa.

Secret Gathering of the Dakinis (Tib. *mkha 'gro gsang 'dus*)   A treasure of the black Vajravarahi revealed by Jamyang Khyentse Wangpo.

Self-Liberation of Suffering Avalokiteshvara (Tib. *thugs rje chen po ngan song sdug bsngal rang grol*)   A cycle of teachings revealed by Jatson Nyingpo, concerned with the propitiation of a form of Avalokiteshvara through reciting the six-syllable mantra: OM MA NI PAD ME HUNG.

Seven Treasuries (Tib. *mdzod bdun*)   Seven volumes written by Longchen Rabjam, comprising (1) the *Treasury of Philosophy* (Tib. *grub mtha' mdzod*), (2) the *Treasury of the Supreme Vehicle* (Tib. *theg mchog mdzod*), (3) the *Wish-Fulfilling Treasury* (Tib. *yid bzhin mdzod*), (4) the *Treasury of Oral Instructions* (Tib. *man ngag mdzod*), (5) the *Treasury of Dharmadhatu* (Tib. *chos dbyings mdzod*), (6) the *Treasury of the Natural State* (Tib. *gnas lugs mdzod*), and (7) the *Treasury on Words and Meaning* (Tib. *tshig don mdzod*).

Seven-Chapter Supplication (Tib. *gsol sdebs le'u bdun ma*)   A supplication to Guru Rinpoche in seven chapters, which is a famous prayer belonging to the *Northern Treasures* revealed by Rigzin Gödem.

Seven-Line Prayer (Tib. *tshig bdun gsol 'debs*)   A famous supplication to Padmasambhava, beginning with "On the northwest border of the country of Uddiyana . . ."

Seventy Verses on Emptiness (Tib. *stong nyid bdun cu pa*, Skt. *shunyatasaptati-karika*)   A treatise by Nagarjuna, written in the first or second century.

Shakyamuni Liturgy (Tib. *thub chog byin rlabs gter mdzod*)   A liturgical method for invoking the blessings of Shakyamuni Buddha composed by Mipham Rinpoche.

Six Scriptures on Reasoning (Tib. *rigs tshogs drug*)   Six works on the logic of *madhyamaka* by Nagarjuna: (1) *Fundamental Treatise on the Middle Way* (Madhyamaka Prajna), (2) *Sixty Stanzas on Reasoning* (Yuki-sastika-karika), (3) *Seventy Verses on Emptiness* (Shunyata-saptali-karika), (4) *Finely Woven* (Vaidalya Sutra), (5) *Refutation of Criticism* (Vigraha-vyavartani), and (6) *Jewel Garland* (Ratnavali).

Six Volumes of Jatson (Tib. *'ja' mtshon pod drug*)   The collected writings of the treasure revealer Jatson Nyingpo in six volumes.

Sixty Stanzas on Reasoning (Tib. *rigs pa drug cu pa*, Skt. *yuki-sastika-karika*). This text belongs to Nagarjuna's six logical works on *madhyamaka*.

Sky Teaching (Tib. *gnam chos*)   A cycle of termas revealed by Mingyur Dorje (1645–67), the nephew of Karma Chagmey.

Sublime Light of Excellent Discourse (Tib. *legs bshad snang ba dam pa*) A text on grammar and spelling by Karma Lhasum Tenpai Gyaltsen.

Sutra Designed like a Jewel Chest (Tib. *mdo sde za ma tog bkod pa*, Skt. *karandavyuhasutra*) A scripture on Avalokiteshvara that appears in the *Mani Kahbum* of King Songtsen Gampo.

Tantric Overview (Tib. *sngags kyi spyi don tshangs dbyangs 'brug sgra*) Longchen Rabjam's commentary on the general meaning of tantra.

Tengyur (Tib. *bstan 'gyur*) The second part of the Buddhist canon, which consists of 213 volumes of commentaries written by Indian masters on the words of the Buddha Shakyamuni.

Three Jewel Commentary (Tib. *dkon mchog 'grel*) *Konchog Drel*, a commentary on the *Guhyagarbha Tantra* by Rongzom Pandita.

Three Lines That Strike the Vital Point (Tib. *tshig gsum gnad brdegs*) *Tsiksum Nedek*, the final testament of Garab Dorje to Manjushrimitra. Patrul Rinpoche wrote a commentary on the root text, which was translated with Dilgo Khyentse's commentary and published in English as *Primordial Purity* (Halifax: Vajra-Vairochana Translation Committee).

Treasury of All-Pervading Knowledge (Tib. *shes bya kun khyab mdzod*) One of the *Five Treasuries* of Jamgön Kongtrül Rinpoche, which contains an encyclopedia of Buddhism and Buddhist culture in three volumes. It was translated under the guidance of Kalu Rinpoche as *Treasury of Knowledge* (Ithaca, N.Y.: Snow Lion Publications, 2003).

Treasury of *Dharmadhatu* (Tib. *chos dbyings mdzod*) One of Longchenpa's *Seven Treasuries*. Translated by Richard Barron as *Precious Treasury of the Basic Space of Phenomena* (Junction City: Padma Publishing, 2001) and *Treasure Trove of Scriptural Transmission*, (Junction City: Padma Publishing, 2001).

Treasury of Precious Qualities (Tib. *yon tan mdzod*) *Yontendzo*, written by Jigmey Lingpa, who wrote both the root text and the commentary. Khenpo Yonga wrote the most extensive commentaries, *Refulgence of the Sun* and *Radiance of the Moon*, on it.

Treasury of Precious Termas (Tib. *rin chen gter mdzod*) One of the *Five Treasuries*. Jamgön Kongtrül's collection of the most important revealed termas from Padmasambhava, Vimalamitra, Vairotsana, and their closest disciples in sixty-three volumes. It was compiled with the help of Jamyang Khyentse Wangpo.

Treasury of Spiritual Instructions (Tib. *gdams ngag mdzod*) A collection of thirteen volumes containing the essential teachings of the eight practice lineages, compiled, structured, and completed by Jamgön Kongtrül Lodro Thaye.

Treasury of Words and Meaning (Tib. *tshig don mdzod*) One of the *Seven Treasuries* of Longchenpa.

Trilogy of Natural Ease (Tib. *ngal gso skor gsum*) Three works on Dzogchen by Longchen Rabjam: *Resting in the Nature of Mind* (Tib. *sems nyid ngal gso*), *Finding Rest from Illusion* (Tib. *sgyu ma ngal gso*), and *Easing Weariness through Meditation* (Tib. *sam gtan ngal gso*). Translated into English by Herbert Guenther under the title *Kindly Bent to Ease Us* (Berkeley, Calif.: Dharma Publishing, 1975).

Tripitaka (Skt.; Tib. *sde snod gsum*) The three collections of the words of the Buddha (*Vinaya*, *Sutra*, and *Abhidharma*). Their purpose is the development of the three trainings of discipline, concentration, and discriminating knowledge, while their function is to remedy the three poisons of desire, anger, and ignorance. The Kangyur is the Tibetan version of the words of the Buddha. The Tripitaka is the Indian version.

Two Analyses (Tib. *'byed gnyis*)   Two works by Maitreya, both belonging to the *Five Treatises of Lord Maitreya*. They are the *Analysis of the Middle and Extremes* (Tib. *dbus dang mtha' rnam par 'byed pa'i bstan bcos*, Skt. *madhyanta-vibhanga*), a treatise in verse on *yogachara* philosophy; and *Analysis of Phenomena and Dharmata* (Tib. *chos dang chos nyid rnam par 'byed pa'i bstan bcos*, Skt. *dharma-dharmata-vibhanga*), about discerning phenomena and true nature.

Two Ornaments (Tib. *rgyan gnyis*)   Two works by Maitreya, both belonging to the *Five Treatises of Lord Maitreya*: the *Ornament of the Sutras* (Tib. *mdo sde rgyan*, Skt. *sutralamkara*) and the *Ornament of Realization* (Tib. *mngon rtogs rgyan*, Skt. *abhisamayalamkara*).

Two Segments (Tib. *brtag gnyis*, Skt. *hevajra-mulatantra-raja*)   *The Exposition Tantra of the Two Segments*, a condensed version of the *Hevajra Tantra*.

Unexcelled Continuity (Tib. *theg pa chen po'i rgyud bla ma'i bstan bcos*, Skt. *uttaratantra-shastra*)   *The Sublime Continuum of the Mahayana*, by Maitreya; one of the *Five Treatises of Lord Maitreya*, written in the fourth century. It deals with the *tathagathagarbha*. It has been translated and published as *The Changeless Nature* and as *Buddha Nature* (Ithaca, N.Y.: Snow Lion Publications, 2000).

Vajra Sunlight (Tib. *rdo rje nyi ma'i snang ba*)   A commentary on the abridged *Kalachakra Tantra*.

Virtuous in the Beginning, Middle, and End (Tib. *thog mtha' bar gsum*)   A famous text by Patrul Rinpoche, based on the recitation of Avalokiteshvara, which was published in English with a commentary by Dilgo Khyentse as *The Heart Treasure of the Enlightened Ones* (Boston: Shambhala Publications, 1992).

Way of the Bodhisattva (Tib. *byang chub sems dpa' spyod pa la 'jug pa*, Skt. *bodhicaryavatara*)   The Indian *pandita* Shantideva's famous text on how to develop *bodhichitta*. Translated by the Padmakara Translation Group as *The Way of the Bodhisattva* (Shambhala Publications, 1997).

White Lotus Commentary (Tib. *rnam bshad pad ma dkar po*)   Mipham Rinpoche's commentary on the "Seven-Line Prayer."

White Lotus Supportive Teaching (Tib. *rgyab chos pad ma dkar po*)   A commentary on Mipham Rinpoche's *Shakyamuni Liturgy*.

Wish-Fulfilling Gem of the Guru's Innermost Essence   Abbreviated as *Guru's Innermost Heart Essence*. Part of Longchenpa's *Four Parts of the Heart Essence*.

Wish-Fulfilling Treasury (Tib. *yid bzhin mdzod*)   Part of Longchenpa's *Seven Treasuries*.

Words of My Perfect Teacher (Tib. *kun bzang bla ma'i zhal lung*)   A popular commentary on the preliminary practices of the *Heart Essence of the Great Expanse* cycle written by Patrul Rinpoche. It was translated by the Padmakara Translation Group (Boston: Shambhala Publications, 1994).

Vinaya (Tib. *'dul ba*)   The name of the Buddhist ethical teachings in general and of the code of monastic discipline in particular.

Yama Destroying Arrogant Spirits (Tib. *gshin rje dregs 'joms*)   A treasure revealed by Minling Terchen.